CW00322051

VOLUME EIGHTY ONE

THE PSYCHOLOGY OF LEARNING AND MOTIVATION

Series Editor

KARA D. FEDERMEIER

Department of Psychology, Program in Neuroscience, and the Beckman Institute for Advanced Science and Technology, University of Illinois, Champaign, IL, United States

VOLUME EIGHTY ONE

THE PSYCHOLOGY OF LEARNING AND MOTIVATION

Edited by

KARA D. FEDERMEIER

Department of Psychology, Program in Neuroscience, and the Beckman Institute for Advanced Science and Technology, University of Illinois, Champaign, IL, United States

Academic Press is an imprint of Elsevier
125 London Wall, London, EC2Y 5AS, United Kingdom
50 Hampshire Street, 5th Floor, Cambridge, MA 02139, United States
525 B Street, Suite 1650, San Diego, CA 92101, United States

First edition 2024

ISBN: 978-0-443-29434-1
ISSN: 0079-7421

For information on all Academic Press publications
visit our website at https://www.elsevier.com/books-and-journals

Publisher: Zoe Kruze
Acquisitions Editor: Mariana Kuhl
Developmental Editor: Sneha Apar
Production Project Manager: Maria Shalini
Cover Designer: Gopalakrishnan Venkatraman
Typeset by MPS Limited, India

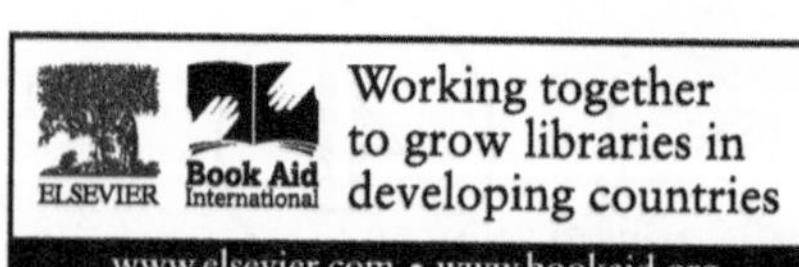

Contents

Contributors

Rebecca E. Bieber
National Military Audiology and Speech Pathology Center, Walter Reed National Military Medical Center; Henry M. Jackson Foundation for the Advancement of Military Medicine Inc, Bethesda, MD, United States

Colt A. Coffman
Department of Kinesiology, Michigan State University, East Lansing, MI, United States

Tracey Covassin
Department of Kinesiology, Michigan State University, East Lansing, MI, United States

Yana Fandakova
Department of Psychology; Institute for Cognitive and Affective Neuroscience, University of Trier, Trier, Germany

Nikole Giovannone
Department of Psychological and Brain Sciences, Villanova University

Stefanie E. Kuchinsky
National Military Audiology and Speech Pathology Center, Walter Reed National Military Medical Center, Bethesda; Department of Hearing and Speech Sciences, University of Maryland, College Park, MD, United States

Eric D. Leshikar
Department of Psychology, University of Illinois Chicago, Chicago, IL, United States

Silvia Murgia
Department of Speech and Hearing Science, University of Illinois Urbana, Champaign, IL, United States

Ian Phillips
National Military Audiology and Speech Pathology Center, Walter Reed National Military Medical Center; Henry M. Jackson Foundation for the Advancement of Military Medicine Inc, Bethesda, MD, United States

Matthew B. Pontifex
Department of Kinesiology, Michigan State University, East Lansing, MI, United States

Julie M. Schneider
Louisiana State University, Baton Rouge, LA, United States

Joseph C. Toscano
Department of Psychological and Brain Sciences, Villanova University

Elisabeth Wenger
Institute for Mind, Brain and Behavior, Department of Psychology, HMU Health and Medical University, Potsdam, Germany

CHAPTER ONE

Skill learning in the developing brain: Interactions of control and representation systems

Yana Fandakova[a,b,*] and Elisabeth Wenger[c,*]
[a]Department of Psychology, University of Trier, Trier, Germany
[b]Institute for Cognitive and Affective Neuroscience, University of Trier, Trier, Germany
[c]Institute for Mind, Brain and Behavior, Department of Psychology, HMU Health and Medical University, Potsdam, Germany
*Corresponding authors. e-mail address: fandakova@uni-trier.de; elisabeth.wenger@hmu-potsdam.de

Contents

Abstract

Human beings possess the remarkable ability to learn new and complex skills. Childhood marks a particularly intensive period for learning when children utilize various forms of learning to comprehend and adapt to their environment. We take a closer look at skill learning during childhood across various domains, including motor and perceptual learning, language acquisition, reading and musical training. Skill learning necessitates structural adaptations in the brain in response to new challenges and demands, a phenomenon known as experience-dependent plasticity. We first discuss research suggesting that a representation and a control system, and their corresponding neural correlates, closely interact to support skill learning in adults. We focus specifically on the time course of skill learning and the notion that control systems are particularly important in the early stages of learning, whereas representation systems dominate later learning stages. Critically, control and representation systems in the brain mature at different timescales. We review evidence that low-level representation systems like motor or

Psychology of Learning and Motivation, Volume 81
ISSN 0079-7421, https://doi.org/10.1016/bs.plm.2024.07.002

auditory cortices mature earlier, while higher-order control systems, including frontal and parietal areas, exhibit protracted maturation well into adolescence. Children often show lower performance in tasks demanding high cognitive control but are generally believed to acquire new skills faster than adults. We explore the potential implications of such misalignment and delve into the possibility that prolonged control system development may reveal benefits for learning, name situations in which such benefits may occur and discuss the corresponding differences in the underlying neural correlates.

1. Introduction

Humans possess the extraordinary ability to learn new and complex skills, such as reading, solving intricate mathematical problems, or mastering complex musical pieces. We can adapt these skills flexibly to confront novel challenges, like reading in a foreign language or playing a new musical instrument. Childhood, in particular, is an intensive learning phase where numerous new skills are acquired. But what enables the developing brain to learn successfully?

In this article, we seek to shed light on the current understanding of the neurocognitive mechanisms that underlie skill learning in childhood. To this end, we first position skill learning among different kinds of learning. Next, we review the mechanisms thought to underlie experience-dependent plasticity and how they change in the course of skill learning. We review theoretical and empirical studies in adults to arrive at a comprehensive understanding of the ways in which control and representation systems closely interact to enable skill learning. On this basis, we then turn to child development and review current knowledge of how control and representation systems develop during childhood and adolescence. We then discuss how maturation is related to skill learning in childhood. Our discussion encompasses studies on motor and perceptual learning, learning to play an instrument, and literacy development. We consider these as representative examples of skill learning, which allow us to identify mechanisms that underpin learning in the developing brain. Our objective is not to provide an exhaustive review of the existing findings but to discuss selected instances that directly illustrate the timeline and mechanisms of learning.

2. Different kinds of learning

Have you ever wondered who learns more in the course of a single day—you or a 4-year-old child? Chances are, it is the preschooler. The world is teeming with new experiences for a young child to absorb and understand. Everyday tasks like doing the laundry or washing dishes can expose a preschooler to a plethora of new concepts: the distinction between animate and inanimate objects, the hidden structure of human language or the collision of different materials, the consequences of gravity when a glass is placed precariously on a counter edge, and much more. Different forms of learning enable children to gain knowledge about their environment and the world. All aspects of human development, from perception to social interaction, rely on these varied learning mechanisms.

Habituation, the simplest and earliest form of learning, involves recognizing previously encountered stimuli. Infants exhibit minimal reaction to familiar stimuli and a stronger response to new ones. This pattern of habituation is a testament to learning: the child has created a memory representation of the recurring, now-familiar stimulus. Habituation plays a vital role in adaptation to diverse environments, allowing children to shift their focus from the old and familiar to the novel, thereby maximizing potential learning opportunities. Children's habituation speed could indicate their overall information processing effectiveness as indicated by positive correlations between habituation speed in childhood and intelligence 18 years later (Colombo, Shaddy, Richman, Maikranz, & Blaga, 2004; Kavšek, 2004; Rose & Feldman, 1997). Already in infancy, individuals are constantly searching for order and regularities in their surroundings, learning a lot by paying close attention to the objects and events they perceive. *Perceptual learning* is characterized by differentiation, that is, the filtering of information about stable and unchanged elements in the environment, and learning about affordances, namely understanding potential actions associated with specific situations or objects. *Statistical learning* denotes a similar form of learning, which involves absorbing information from the environment, particularly forming associations between stimuli that follow a statistically predictable pattern (Aslin, Saffran, & Newport, 1998; Kirkham, Slemmer, & Johnson, 2002; Saffran, Aslin, & Newport, 1996). Our natural environment is filled with regularity and redundancy, with certain events occurring predictably in a specific order and specific objects appearing simultaneously in the same location, among other things. Infants show signs of surprise and pay more attention to stimuli when their predictable order is disrupted. Statistical learning abilities have been observed in various domains, including music, action, and speech (Roseberry, Richie, Hirsh-Pasek, Golinkoff, & Shipley, 2011; Saffran & Griepentrog, 2001; Saffran, Newport, & Aslin, 1996), and are present from birth or even earlier (Bulf, Johnson, & Valenza, 2011; Kudo, Nonaka, Mizuno, Mizuno, & Okanoya, 2011; Teinonen, Fellman, Näätänen, Alku, & Huotilainen, 2009).

Classical conditioning is another form of learning where a previously neutral stimulus is paired with a stimulus that consistently triggers a specific reaction. This form of learning is fundamental in infants' everyday experiences as they begin to understand relationships and associations in their environment. In contrast, *instrumental learning*, also known as operant conditioning, involves learning about the relationships between one's behavior and the ensuing consequences, which could entail different rewards and/or penalties. Memory for these contingencies steadily improves with development, and infants and young children even exhibit anger if a learned action does not yield the expected outcome (Lewis, Alessandri, & Sullivan, 1990; Sullivan, Lewis, & Alessandri, 1992). *Observational learning* is likely the most effective form of learning during infancy and childhood. The ability to imitate others' behavior seems to be present from a very early age, albeit initially in a somewhat limited form (Meltzoff & Moore, 1977, 1983). While children initially mimic others' actions without questioning the reasons (e.g., sticking out the tongue), they gradually begin to analyze why a person exhibits certain behaviors (Buttelmann, Carpenter, Call, & Tomasello, 2008; Gergely, Bekkering, & Király, 2002). The fundamental concept of observational learning is to offer the learner a model of how a skill should be performed, which can then be used as a guide for their actions. This approach saves the learner from the need to build a cognitive representation of the action pattern through gradual trial and error, instead providing a "shortcut". It is believed that observing the action initiates the formation of a cognitive representation in memory, which can then be enacted and refined during overt practice (Bandura, 1986). Infants and children also use their prior knowledge to develop expectations about future events. This process, known as *rational learning*, involves integrating pre-existing beliefs and misconceptions with current environmental observations (Xu & Kushnir, 2013). This phenomenon is further explored in the paradigm of prediction errors. This research method involves presenting young children with an event that contradicts their existing knowledge or beliefs, which should elicit surprise or interest, thereby providing insight into their thought processes. These early forms of learning naturally lead to the acquisition of more complex skills, such as language, reading and writing, or playing an instrument. However, many aspects of learning these more complex skills build upon the foundational learning mechanisms.

Before delving deeper, it is crucial to define the concept of skill learning, which is not trivial. In a narrow sense, a 'skill' can refer to a property of an individual's body, with the body perceived as possessing a set of skills or comprising a network of such skills. This aligns with Piaget (1953), with some authors describing skill learning as the construction and elaboration of a network of sensorimotor schemata incorporated into our bodies (Di Paolo, Buhrmann, & Barandiaran, 2017). Moving beyond this rather restrictive definition, a broader and more flexible definition characterizes learning as changes intended to make an individual adapt to their environment's unique challenges and demands (Gibson & Gibson, 1955; Pacheco, Lafe, & Newell, 2019). This perspective allows for a flexible and more general account of skill learning that can encompass learning in motor tasks as well as perceptual learning (Baggs, Raja, & Anderson, 2020). Recent advancements also suggest that language acquisition and reading development can be considered as forms of skill learning, utilizing similar mechanisms to those used in learning to ride a bicycle, play a musical instrument, or draw a picture (Chater & Christiansen, 2018). This perspective on human skill learning involves re-coding and summarizing complex and time-varying input into increasingly more abstract representations. For instance, low-level visual input is translated into sequences of actions and events, sound streams are decoded into notes and musical phrases, and speech is translated into phonemes, words, morphemes, and multi-word constructions on a moment-by-moment basis. Chater and Christiansen (2018) posit that material at each level is immediately summarized (i.e., chunked) and passed onto a more abstract level of representation; this more abstract representation is then itself again compressed and passed to a higher-level representation, and so forth. Whether or not this "Chunk-and-Pass" processing represents a general mechanism of skill learning remains to be seen in future research. However, the definition of skill learning as encompassing a wide range of complex learning instances has proven valuable for revealing general principles of skill acquisition across various domains.

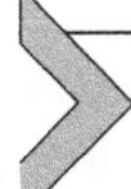

3. Neural plasticity: the brain's potential for adaptation

Clearly, the previously mentioned forms of learning necessitate some level of adaptation in the brain to encode newly acquired skills and information. Structural adaptations in the brain must accompany any behavioral improvements during skill learning, as they code for these newly implemented routines. This adaptive ability of the brain is what we refer to as plasticity—the potential of the brain to change to best meet varying environmental demands (Lövdén et al., 2010). Several cellular processes, particularly those related to synapses, are thought to be crucial for learning. For instance, learning may involve the formation of new synapses (synaptogenesis) and changes in the shape of dendritic spines (spine morphology) (Holtmaat, De Paola, Wilbrecht, & Knott, 2008; Kleim et al., 2002; Trachtenberg et al., 2002; Wilbrecht, Holtmaat, Wright, Fox, & Svoboda, 2010). Likewise, changes in dendritic length, branching, or the actual number of dendritic spines per neuron have also been shown to be relevant for skill learning (Fu & Zuo, 2011; Holtmaat & Svoboda, 2009). Glial processes may also play a significant role, as glial cells maintain ion homeostasis, regulate blood flow in response to neuronal activity, form myelin, and provide support and protection for neurons (Brodal, 2010; Wang, Takano, & Nedergaard, 2009). Myelin, a lipid membrane that encloses axons to enable fast neurotransmission, develops slowly and could potentially play a major role in shaping human behavior and learning, as central myelination appears to be a prerequisite for learning a new motor skill (De Faria et al., 2021; McKenzie et al., 2014). These synaptic, dendritic and glial changes, potentially in concert with other cellular processes like angiogenesis (i.e., the formation of new blood vessels), could serve as the neural substrate for learning processes manifesting on the behavioral level.

Numerous studies using magnetic resonance imaging (MRI) have reported learning-dependent plastic changes in the brain. Both cross-sectional studies comparing subjects with differing expertise (e.g., musicians versus non-musicians (Bengtsson et al., 2005) or taxi drivers versus bus drivers (Maguire, Woollett, & Spiers, 2006)), as well as longitudinal studies examining the effect of training over time (e.g., individuals learning how to juggle (Draganski et al., 2004), taxi drivers during professional training (Woollett & Maguire, 2011), or playing Super Mario (Kühn, Gleich, Lorenz, Lindenberger, & Gallinat, 2014)) have shown structural brain changes. In all these instances, the brain has structurally adapted itself in task-relevant areas to best meet current environmental demands, enabling individuals to play the piano, navigate through London city, master a three-ball juggling cascade, or successfully guide Super Mario through his world. But how exactly does the learning brain implement such changes?

4. The time course of skill learning

The vast network of neural connections in the brain cannot merely be inscribed in the genetic code, as the former significantly outnumbers the latter. Among other tasks, Deoxyribonucleic Acid (DNA) is responsible for encoding various nerve cell forms and different neurotransmitters. However, it cannot specify the precise connections between individual neurons. As such, every brain begins as a relatively structureless but highly flexible network of nerve cells, possessing the intrinsic ability to "wire" itself in a way that best adapts to its unique environment. Over the course of a lifespan, the brain must strike the right balance between achieving flexibility to adapt to varying environmental demands and maintaining stability to avoid wasting precious resources on continuous reconstruction (Kühn & Lindenberger, 2016; Makino, Hwang, Hedrick, & Komiyama, 2016).

Adapting to changing environmental demands cannot involve continuous structural brain growth. Endless expansion is an unlikely solution for lifelong learning, especially considering the fixed size of the human skull. Instead, learning-related neural processes may follow a sequence of Exploration, Selection and Refinement (ESR) of neural circuitry (Lindenberger & Lövdén, 2019; Wenger, Brozzoli, Lindenberger, & Lövdén, 2017b; see Fig. 1). Based on this ESR model, each learning instance triggers a specific plastic response that progresses through three distinct phases.

1. During the initial stages of learning, the *exploration phase*, available neuronal circuits potentially capable of performing the task at hand are widely probed and tested and new circuits are formed (Oby et al., 2019). This exploratory activity could potentially lead to overall tissue growth and expansion. In the context of perceptual and motor skill learning, these circuits would be located in primary and secondary cortices, including the primary and supplementary motor cortices, primary and secondary auditory cortices, and primary visual and associated cortices—hence, *domain-specific representation systems*. In terms of activity, in the initial stages of learning domain-specific representation systems exhibit high trial-to-trial variability in neural activity (Lindenberger & Lövdén, 2019). This is because the individual is in the process of experimenting with diverse ways of executing a novel task.

   Notably, during the initial phase of learning, primary and secondary cortices interact closely with fronto-striatal brain systems to implement

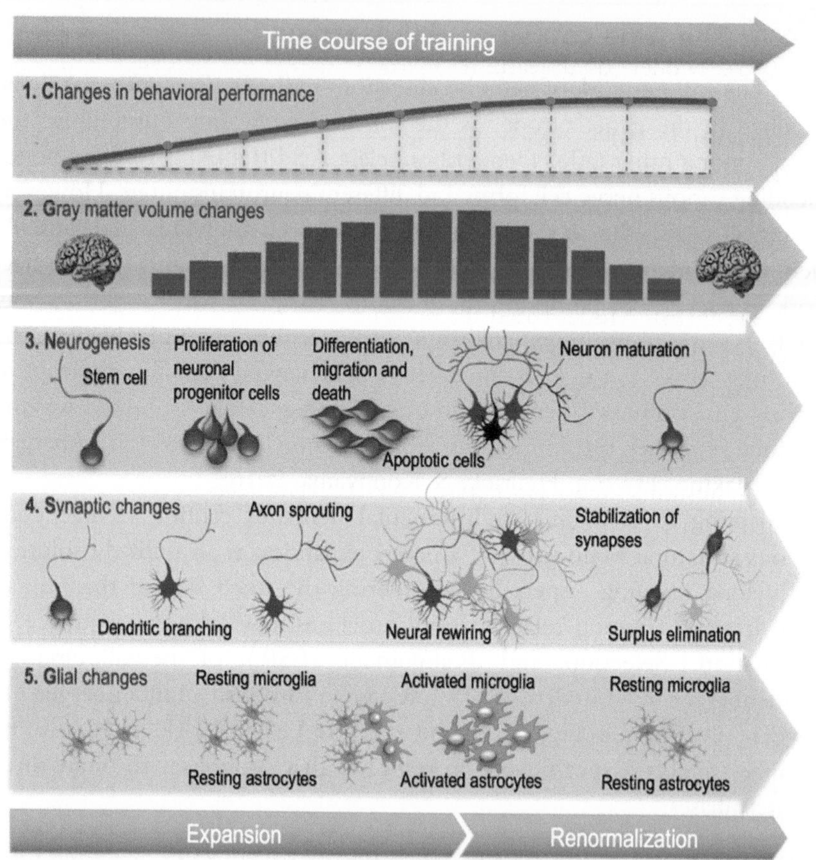

Fig. 1 Summary of potential cellular changes resulting in gray matter volume expansion. (1) During training, behavioral performance increases until it stabilizes. (2) Initial learning phases show an increase in regional gray matter volume estimates, which then either partially or wholly return to baseline levels during later phases when task proficiency is achieved. (3) This learning process may involve adult neurogenesis (limited to specific brain regions), characterized by the proliferation of neuronal progenitor cells, some of which undergo apoptosis. (4) Synaptic changes may mirror this pattern, with an increase in dendritic branching and axonal sprouting during initial learning phases, followed by a return to baseline levels. Pruning—the selective elimination of dendritic branches, axonal projections, and synaptic connections—along with synapse stabilization, enables efficient neural rewiring. 5. Changes in the number and morphology of glial cells may follow a similar pattern. These cells can proliferate and shift from a resting to an activated state, and then return to the resting state once the skill is acquired. These potential cellular processes could contribute to experience-induced alterations and renormalization of gray matter structure, as detectable with MRI. *Reprinted from Wenger, E., Brozzoli, C., Lindenberger, U., & Lövdén, M. (2017). Expansion and renormalization of human brain structure during skill acquisition. Trends in Cognitive Sciences, 21(12), 930–939, Copyright (2017), with permission from Elsevier.*

model-based planning and control (Bassett, Yang, Wymbs, & Grafton, 2015). Model-based learning involves using goal-directed control to guide learning and decision-making by assessing different action options based on a model of their previous outcomes and probability of success (Boureau, Sokol-Hessner, & Daw, 2015). Model-based learning is often contrasted with habitual or model-free learning, which involves decisions based on a cumulative summary of past success without constructing a model of the consequences associated with different actions (Boureau et al., 2015). Model-based learning is thought to engage the prefrontal cortex (PFC) and associated areas, while model-free learning depends primarily on dopaminergic modulation in the dorsal striatum (Daw, Niv, & Dayan, 2005).

Cognitive control processes play a crucial role in scaffolding learning by monitoring and regulating information processing in line with current goals and task demands (Chein & Schneider, 2012; Kelly & Garavan, 2005). Chein and Schneider (2012) proposed three hierarchically organized learning systems. The highest level of the hierarchy is represented by the *metacognitive system* involved in generating new routines, initiating and monitoring different actions and control processes. The anterior PFC is thought to represent a key region of this metacognitive system (Chein & Schneider, 2012), in agreement with the prominent role of this region in metacognition (Fleming & Dolan, 2012) and representing the apex of the PFC hierarchical organization (Badre & Nee, 2018). Next, the *cognitive control system* encompasses frontal, parietal and cingulo-opercular regions, and scaffolds learning by directing attention towards relevant information, inhibiting irrelevant information, and shifting between different actions. Finally, learning depends on the *domain-specific representation systems* that hold the representation of visual, auditory, motor, somatosensory associations. The metacognitive and control systems are thought to be particularly important in the initial stages of learning when new actions have to be configured, processed in a goal-directed manner and closely monitored. Accordingly, in adults, frontal and parietal regions corresponding to these systems typically show enhanced engagement during the early stages of learning (Chein & Schneider, 2012).

2. In the later phases of learning, domain-specific representation systems become more independent from frontal control regions, and there is less interaction with non-domain specific cortices (Bassett et al., 2015). This pattern aligns well with the neural-efficiency hypothesis, which posits that cognitive resources used early in learning are no longer

required in later phases. Instead, the system aims to economize resources (Petersen, Van Mier, Fiez, & Raichle, 1998), limit unnecessary transmission, and favor sparse coding and automaticity (Kuzawa et al., 2014; Makino et al., 2016). Later phases of learning are therefore characterized by reduced communication with control regions and less neural variability in domain-specific representation regions (Dhawale, Smith, & Ölveczky, 2017), as the most efficient neural circuitry is selected during *the selection phase.*

3. In the hypothesized final stage of learning in adults, *the refinement phase,* processing in the selected circuitry is stabilized as surplus neurons that are not activated are eliminated. Of note, even during the later phases of learning, we can expect that representation systems remain connected with control regions to enable flexible changes in established routines if circumstances change (Chein & Schneider, 2012).

Focusing on the timing of changes in the representation systems with learning, we investigated right-handed adult participants who were trained to write and draw with their left, non-dominant hand (Wenger et al., 2017a). This motor training resulted in an increase in gray matter in both the left and right motor cortex. Notably, in the right motor cortex, an inverted U-shaped progression was observed: brain volume initially increased and peaked after 4 weeks of training. Even though participants' proficiency in writing and drawing with the left hand either remained constant or improved even further, gray matter in the right motor cortex started to decrease again and nearly returned to its initial level after the entire 7-week practice period (Wenger et al., 2017a). This observed structural expansion followed by renormalization in the human motor cortex aligns well with the sequence of learning-related expansion, selection, and renormalization of brain activity and structure (Wenger et al., 2017b). In another study exploring a similar phenomenon, young musicians preparing for a professional career at a conservatory were examined in up to 5 sessions over the course of a year. During the final period of preparation for an exam the planum polare, a region in the left auditory cortex, displayed a reduction in gray matter compared to a control group of amateur musicians. Simultaneously, the planum polare exhibited stronger functional connectivity with other brain regions previously related to musical expertise, like auditory cortices, pre- and postcentral gyri, and the cingulate cortex (Wenger, Papadaki, Werner, Kühn, & Lindenberger, 2021). This pattern of results is consistent with the second part of an expansion-renormalization cycle, in which aspiring professional musicians were honing their skills further.

With regard to empirical evidence demonstrating decreasing involvement of control systems with learning, a meta-analysis of 29 functional MRI studies of practice-related change along with an empirical investigation revealed a broadly distributed network of lateral PFC, dorsal anterior cingulate cortex (dACC), posterior parietal and occipito-temporal cortical areas showing decreased activation with practice. Of note, this pattern converged across studies in spite of training different domains, lending support for a domain-general control system (Chein & Schneider, 2005). While multiple sources might underlie the decreasing activation in control regions, including more specific task representations (Garner & Dux, 2015) or more efficient strategies (Poldrack, 2000), these results support the idea of increased demand on control systems during the initial phases of skill learning.

The initial phases of learning in the domain of motor skill learning have also been associated with increased activation in the lateral PFC along with enhanced connectivity between the PFC and the premotor cortex (Dayan & Cohen, 2011). The involvement of these regions decreases during later phases of learning when areas in the primary motor cortex and the supplementary motor area (SMA) show increased engagement during skilled execution of motor actions (Dayan & Cohen, 2011; see Fig. 2). In fact, numerous studies focusing on motor learning have shown that initial activity increases in sensory areas (Kami et al., 1995; Kelly & Garavan, 2005) are followed by activity decreases (Ma et al., 2010; Pascual-Leone, Grafman, & Hallett, 1994; Wymbs & Grafton, 2015; Yotsumoto, Watanabe, & Sasaki, 2008). Intriguingly, there are several demonstrations of motor-learning-related decreases of activity outside primary, i.e., sensory regions (Bassett et al., 2015; Berlot, Popp, & Diedrichsen, 2020; Kami et al., 1995). This suggests a general migration of activity during administration from cortical regions to striatal regions. This shift potentially indicates a move towards more automatic and less controlled task execution (Choi, Shin, & Kim, 2020; Kawai et al., 2015).

In summary, both representation and control systems play their intricate parts during skill learning and show differential involvement across the initial and later stages of learning in adults. With respect to child development, brain maturation exhibits unique variations across brain systems. This is particularly true for control systems, including frontal and parietal areas, and representation systems, including sensorimotor, visual and auditory regions. We delve deeper into these developmental trajectories in the subsequent section and then turn to the ensuing implications for skill learning during childhood.

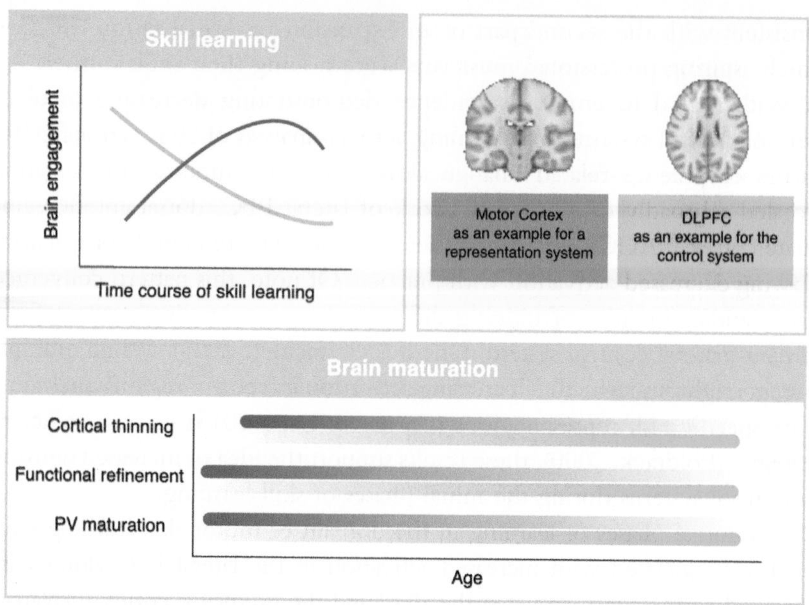

Fig. 2 Illustration of the misalignment of maturation and recruitment during learning. The upper left graph schematically represents the progression of neural activity during the course of skill acquisition. In adults, the initial stages of skill learning are characterized by pronounced frontoparietal activity, which gradually diminishes as the skill becomes automated. This is exemplified by the engagement of the dorsolateral prefrontal cortex (DLPFC), depicted in yellow. As learning progresses towards automatic execution, activity in the representation system, such as the motor cortex (shown in blue), becomes more prominent. The lower graph provides a schematic representation of the distinct maturational trajectories of the control and representation systems. Early development sees the maturation of the motor cortex and other sensorimotor areas, while cognitive control regions, which are critical for initial learning, undergo extended development. *Lower graph reprinted with modification from Sydnor, V. J., Larsen, B., Bassett, D. S., Alexander-Bloch, A., Fair, D. A., Liston, C., Mackey, A. P., Milham, M. P., Pines, A., Roalf, D. R., Seidlitz, J., Xu, T., Raznahan, A., & Satterthwaite, T. D. (2021). Neurodevelopment of the association cortices: Patterns, mechanisms, and implications for psychopathology. Neuron, 109(18). Copyright (2021), with permission from Elsevier.*

5. Development of control and representation systems in childhood

No time in life rivals childhood when it comes to learning new skills. Children learn to ride bikes or play instruments, acquire language and learn to read. Despite the diversity of these skills, they share a common evolution over time. The time course typically involves significant initial improvements—children can perform the skill faster and with fewer errors—followed by periods of slower and less pronounced enhancements. Indeed, the abundance of learning opportunities and requirements has led to the widespread belief that children learn better than adults. But how do the control and representation systems afford the acquisition of these varied skills? To begin addressing this question, we will first take a closer look at the developmental trajectories of the control and representation systems and their neural correlates.

On the neural level, the control and representation systems undergo distinct developmental trajectories across childhood and adolescence. *In vivo* MRI studies have demonstrated that brain maturation is marked by initial increases in brain volume, followed by subsequent decreases. While the exact mechanisms underpinning the changes in gray matter volume are still unclear (Natu et al., 2016; Sydnor et al., 2021), they are generally believed to reflect the initial proliferation of synapses followed by pruning. Pruning is the process of removing inefficient neurons, synapses, and dendrites, leading to the optimization of brain circuits. Alternatively, or additionally, changes in gray matter volume observed in MRI may be indicative of myelination. Myelination denotes the increase in the myelin sheath of axons, facilitating faster and more reliable information transmission across brain regions. Lastly, the patterns of cortical folding and the brain's surface area also change during child development, thereby contributing to the structural changes documented in MRI.

Although the general trajectory of initial increases followed by decreases in gray matter volume is present across brain regions, it is notably heterochronous (Huttenlocher & Dabholkar, 1997). During development, sensorimotor regions display relatively early peaks in gray matter volume, whereas a number of higher-order association regions only reach their volumetric peaks in middle or late childhood (Brain Development Cooperative Group, 2012; Ducharme et al., 2016; Gilmore, Knickmeyer, & Gao, 2018; Mills et al., 2016; Shaw et al., 2008). More specifically, sensorimotor regions undergo various changes during infancy and early childhood. These include significant cortical thinning, increases in intracortical myelination, and white matter tracts, along with functional refinement (Sydnor et al., 2021). Conversely, these structural and functional changes are observed only in late childhood and adolescence in association areas (Sydnor et al., 2021). Particularly, PFC regions, a key hub in the control system (Chein & Schneider, 2012), exhibit accelerated cortical thinning and increased myelination well into early adulthood (Keller et al., 2023). Based on these observations, which align closely with the evolutionary and functional hierarchy of the human brain, a recent framework suggested a hierarchical progression of cortical maturation (Sydnor et al., 2021). The progression is thought to follow a sensorimotor-to-association axis of cortical organization.

The sensorimotor-to-association axis is believed to extend beyond the structural organization of the brain, representing an organizational principle for functional connections among different brain regions. Somatosensory and motor regions primarily exhibit functional connections to local cortical areas. In contrast, areas at the highest level of the association hierarchy, like the PFC, mainly display long-distance functional connections. But how do these connections change during development? Studies examining age differences in resting-state connectivity, i.e., when participants are resting in the MRI machine without any task to attend to, have shown that networks of brain regions become more segregated with age (Grayson & Fair, 2017; Keller et al., 2023). Here, segregation refers to a pattern in which connections among the nodes within a brain network become stronger, while connections with nodes from different brain networks weaken (Power et al., 2011). Of note, somatosensory and motor networks undergo segregation during infancy and early childhood, while networks involving higher-order areas show segregation later in development (Betzel et al., 2014; Gu et al., 2015). Additionally, networks involving higher-order areas display increased patterns of integration with age (Pines et al., 2022). Integration refers to the strengthening of connections with other networks, primarily towards the association pole of the axis. Thus, brain network development strikes a fine balance between the segregation and integration of different systems. This balance ensures efficient information transmission across domain-specific representation systems, coupled with improved communication across different systems, especially those involved in control, enabled by integration (Keller et al., 2023). Balancing efficient local processing with global goal coordination is central for enabling adaptive behavior when faced with novel environmental challenges, such as learning a new skill.

In summary, evidence from both cross-sectional and longitudinal studies suggests that control and representation systems develop at different rates during childhood and adolescence (Fig. 2). While representation systems undergo significant maturational changes and reorganization during infancy and early childhood, brain regions in the frontal and parietal lobes—constituting the control system—display more protracted development extending to late childhood and adolescence.

GABAergic projections to various brain regions, particularly the PFC, also continue to develop across childhood and adolescence. GABA (γ-aminobutyric acid) modulates the brain's inhibitory-excitatory balance, triggers synaptic pruning around puberty, and influences the myelination process by controlling oligodendrocyte precursor cell activity. Parvalbumin positive (PV) GABAergic interneurons regulate the opening and closing of critical periods for experience-dependent plasticity (Fagiolini & Hensch, 2000; Hensch, 2005; Reh et al., 2020). Interestingly, PV interneurons are higher in expression in primary motor and sensory areas relative to trans-modal association areas. In vivo magnetic resonance spectroscopy (MRS) measurements have revealed lower GABA levels in children and adolescents compared to adults (Perica et al., 2022). These age differences reflect the maturation of PV interneurons (Fung et al., 2010) and the strengthening of PV inputs onto pyramidal neurons (Caballero, Flores-Barrera, Cass, & Tseng, 2014; Hensch, 2005). Age-related increases in GABA during child development are associated with the maturation of inhibitory mechanisms in the brain, leading to decreases in the excitation:inhibition (E:I) ratio. A lower E:I ratio corresponds to an enhanced signal-to-noise ratio of local circuits in visual, auditory and sensorimotor areas. This enables more efficient processing of incoming information by suppressing the spontaneous neuronal activity in these circuits (Toyoizumi et al., 2013). Intriguingly, a recent study used pharmacological manipulation of GABA levels in adults to model how GABA variability affected resting-state connectivity patterns (Larsen et al., 2022). The authors then tested for evidence of connectivity differences consistent with the GABA manipulation in a large sample of adolescents. The results supported the hypothesis that GABA changes in adolescence induce changes consistent with a model of reduced E:I ratio. Older adolescents showed a connectivity pattern that more closely resembled the connectivity of adults with drug-enhanced GABA. Furthermore, the study's results suggested that the evidence for increases in inhibitory circuitry, leading to developmental reductions in the E:I ratio, were especially pronounced in transmodal areas in the association cortex (Larsen et al., 2022). Collectively, these results provide (albeit indirect) evidence for a potential critical period of heightened plasticity in association areas during adolescence. They also lend support to the observation that PV interneurons reach adult levels later in association areas compared to the earlier maturing sensorimotor areas (Sydnor et al., 2021). Together, these findings suggest that plasticity is enhanced in representation systems during early childhood, including auditory, visual, and sensorimotor areas (Hensch, 2005), whereas control systems may display an enhanced potential for change during late childhood and early adolescence (Larsen & Luna, 2018), with downstream implications for acquiring new skills.

The maturation of PV interneurons is believed to be experience-dependent, suggesting that the differences in timing between representation and control systems may reflect the specific experiences children are exposed to at different ages. Sensory experiences typically dominate infancy and early childhood, while higher-order cognitive experiences take precedence later in the course of child development (Reh et al., 2020; Takesian & Hensch, 2013). The notion of heightened plasticity in sensorimotor systems during early childhood aligns well with the timeframe of sensitive periods in these regions (Hensch, 2005), and the acquisition of several key abilities during this period, including language (Werker & Hensch, 2015), walking (Adolph & Robinson, 2015), or vision (Gerhardstein, Shroff, Dickerson, & Adler, 2009). In contrast, the notion of enhanced plasticity in control systems has not yet received robust empirical support (Laube, Van Den Bos, & Fandakova, 2020).

The reviewed developmental changes in the neural correlates of representation and control systems raise several critical, yet unaddressed, questions pertaining to the acquisition of new skills in children and adolescents: (1) Do children and adolescents differ in the extent and nature of control system involvement during the acquisition of a new skill? (2) To what extent do such differences, if present, depend on the maturational status of the corresponding functional and structural connections within and between control and domain-specific representation systems supporting the skill? (3) Can skill acquisition scaffold or induce (plastic) changes in control systems during adolescence (more so than earlier in childhood)? These questions gain further relevance when we consider the way adults typically approach learning and decision-making.

Adults typically rely on mental models to guide their decisions and actions towards a desired goal, especially in highly structured environments (Collins, 2018; Daw, Gershman, Seymour, Dayan, & Dolan, 2011). While even infants are capable of acquiring abstract hierarchical rules (Schonberg, Marcus, & Johnson, 2018; Werchan, Collins, Frank, & Amso, 2016), this ability continues to improve during childhood (Unger, Ackerman, Chatham, Amso, & Badre, 2016). As a result, children become better at acquiring and utilizing more complex rule structures (Hartley, Nussenbaum, & Cohen, 2021). Younger children, compared to adolescents and adults, rely less heavily on model-based learning (Decker, Otto,

Daw, & Hartley, 2016) and external advice or instructions (Rodriguez Buritica, Heekeren, & van den Bos, 2019). The protracted development of the ability to form mental models of the task at hand may influence how individuals approach learning a new skill. Additionally, children show difficulties flexibly engaging sustained and transient control processes when handling multiple tasks in close temporal succession (Schwarze, Fandakova, & Lindenberger, 2024). At the same time, complex skills often require rule shifting depending on dynamic environmental changes. Indeed, children, especially younger ones, rely more heavily on reactive rather than proactive control of behavior (Braver, 2012). In other words, when provided the opportunity to prepare for an upcoming task, younger children are less likely to do so proactively. Instead, they evoke and use the relevant information only when it becomes necessary (Munakata, Snyder, & Chatham, 2012). Children also have difficulties inhibiting irrelevant information (e.g., Luna, Garver, Urban, Lazar, & Sweeney, 2004), making them more susceptible to distraction in the presence of irrelevant information. Finally, working memory continues to develop during child development (e.g., Cowan, 2016), particularly with respect to selecting information to enter working memory and influence actions (Unger et al., 2016). Thus, children may face greater difficulty maintaining skill-relevant rules and dynamically using this information to execute the necessary actions during the initial stages of skill acquisition.

What learning mechanisms may support skill acquisition in childhood? As mentioned earlier, statistical learning is evident from early infancy and serves as a crucial mechanism for learning across various domains, including language acquisition (Saffran & Kirkham, 2018) or the development of category and cause-effect representations (Kushnir & Gopnik, 2005; Schlichting, Guarino, Schapiro, Turk-Browne, & Preston, 2017). On the neural level, statistical learning in infants engages the hippocampus, similarly to adults (Ellis et al., 2021; Schapiro, Gregory, Landau, McCloskey, & Turk-Browne, 2014). The hippocampus continues to develop throughout childhood (Ghetti & Fandakova, 2020), suggesting potential developmental changes in statistical learning as well (Schlichting et al., 2017). The possibility of a stronger reliance on statistical learning for acquiring new skills in childhood raises the intriguing question of whether the hippocampus may play a more prominent, or different, role in skill acquisition in childhood compared to adolescence and adulthood. Although not typically discussed in the context of skill acquisition, a recent study (Jacobacci et al., 2020) noted rapid structural changes in the hippocampus during motor skill learning.

These changes were suggested to reflect plasticity mechanisms occurring during the rest periods between practicing the skill, when the hippocampus also demonstrated enhanced activation. Similarly, during the training of an oculomotor sequence learning task, Albouy et al. (2008) found that overnight improvements in learning were positively correlated with activation in the hippocampus and the strength of hippocampal-striatal functional connectivity during initial practice. Interestingly, one study showed attenuated overnight sleep-dependent consolidation of procedural memory (finger sequence tapping) in children between 6 and 8 years of age compared to adults (Wilhelm, Diekelmann, & Born, 2008). These findings lend indirect support for the idea that the involvement of the hippocampus in skill acquisition may differ between childhood and adulthood. However, whether and how the hippocampus supports skill learning in children remains an open question for future research.

In summary, converging evidence suggests that control and representation systems develop at different timescales throughout child development. More specifically, domain-specific representation systems mature earlier in development, whereas higher-order control systems exhibit protracted maturation extending well into adolescence. The neural evidence of prolonged frontal development, coupled with the behavioral findings of age differences in the ability to construct mental models and adaptively control behavior, collectively suggest that control systems may play a less prominent role in the scaffolding skill learning during childhood. What are the implications of these developmental trends for skill learning in childhood? To answer this question, we will next turn to examples of empirical studies investigating skill learning and the corresponding neural changes in children.

6. The time course of skill acquisition in childhood: empirical examples

Even though many studies have explored the effects of developing expertise on performance and the underlying neural correlates in adults (e.g., Draganski et al., 2004; Kühn et al., 2014; Woollett & Maguire, 2011; for review see e.g., Wenger & Kühn, 2021), studies investigating skill acquisition within a developmental context are relatively scarce. Below we provide examples from studies conducted in children's natural settings (e.g., learning to read or play an instrument) and laboratory studies (e.g., motor sequence learning, perceptual learning). The former studies typically occur over extended periods (i.e., days to months) and are well-integrated in participants' daily routines. In contrast, the latter studies often comprise several sessions executed under high experimental control.

6.1 Language and reading

Developing reading abilities have shown positive correlation with gray matter volume in the left superior temporal gyrus (STG) at approximately 7.5 years of age, a known peak in gray matter maturation in this area (Linkersdörfer et al., 2015). Intriguingly, a year later, improved reading skills were linked to more pronounced GM volume decreases in the left inferior parietal lobule and the pre- and postcentral gyri (Linkersdörfer et al., 2015). This finding aligns broadly with the ESR model outlined above. Similarly, in a broader age group ranging from 5 to 15 years, gray matter decreases in parietal and inferior frontal regions over two years were associated with better reading performance, particularly better word decoding, reading fluency, and rapid automatized naming (Houston et al., 2014). Thus, the maturation of the frontoparietal network may contribute to reading development. However, the causal relationship remains unclear, as faster maturation could be the result of successful reading learning rather than its cause (Chyl, Fraga-González, Brem, & Jednoróg, 2021).

The acquisition of reading skills requires substantial restructuring of both sensory and associative cortices involved in language processing (Horowitz-Kraus, Vannest, Gozdas, & Holland, 2014; Martin, Schurz, Kronbichler, & Richlan, 2015; Turkeltaub, Eden, Jones, & Zeffiro, 2002). Specifically, successful reading development appears to depend on the specialization of the ventral visual systems to print. In a longitudinal study of reading acquisition, Dehaene-Lambertz, Monzalvo, and Dehaene (2018) scanned 6-year-old children every two months before and during the first year of school. Before school began, the visual word form area (VWFA), an area in the left fusiform gyrus involved in letter and word recognition (Dehaene & Cohen, 2011), was not activated when words were presented. After the first four months of schooling, word presentation activated the VWFA in most children, and its location was comparable to VWFA activation in adults. Notably, VWFA and parietal lobe activation showed an inverted U-shape, with a steep increase at the beginning of schooling followed by later decreases. These results align with the ESR model and illustrate the dynamic emergence of reading-related representations over time in childhood. In another study, successful reading acquisition was linked to decreasing functional connectivity between a ventral visual area and the left inferior frontal gyrus during a reading task (Morken, Helland, Hugdahl, & Specht, 2017). Connections between representation areas and frontal regions seem vital for establishing reading skill, but are down-regulated when a higher proficiency level, i.e., automaticity is reached.

A laboratory study by Berger and Batterink (2024) examining age differences in learning a new hidden linguistic rule showed that 8–10-year-olds learned the hidden linguistic rule faster than adults. Specifically, children exhibited longer response times and reduced accuracy on an unrelated task when the hidden rule was violated. This pattern became apparent in children during the initial day of training, while adults only demonstrated sensitivity to the hidden rule in a following session after sleep. Moreover, children outperformed adults in generalizing the hidden linguistic rule. They eventually performed above chance in classifying nonword examples based on their hidden animacy dimension, while adults did not show evidence of such generalization. A similar pattern emerged in a study on the acquisition of phonotactic constraints (Smalle, Muylle, Szmalec, & Duyck, 2017). Here, 9- to 10-year-olds reliably learned second-order phonotactic constraints, while adults only exhibited this effect in a subsequent session following a night of sleep. Although these findings relate to the timeline of learning only indirectly, they represent instances in the language domain where children learned quicker than adults. Notably, both studies indicated that adult learning is closely tied to sleep-based consolidation, echoing the earlier discussion on the potentially greater role of consolidation mechanisms for skill acquisition in adulthood.

6.2 Musical training

The ability to play a musical instrument is mostly positively related to age, yet relatively few studies have attempted to disentangle the effects of expertise from those of development. Among these, one study investigated individuals aged between 5 and 33 years during music processing in the MRI scanner, incorporating tasks of melodic and rhythmic discrimination (Ellis, Bruijn, Norton, Winner, & Schlaug, 2013). The study found positive behavioral effects of both expertise and age. Both factors were associated with enhanced abilities to discriminate between different melodies and rhythms. However, there was no interaction between age and expertise. Age was positively correlated with increased activation during musical processing in the temporofrontal junction (TFJ), the ventral premotor cortex (vPMC), and the intraparietal sulcus (IPS). The authors of the study suggested that age differences in activation might reflect age-related increases in the effects of attention in the TFJ (i.e., improved attention to the unfolding of music in pitch space and time) and improved working memory in the IPS. Concurrently, the number of training hours, or level of expertise, positively correlated with activity in posterior STG/planum polare, an area typically activated in response to auditory stimuli. Together, the results of this study indicated that the effects of age and expertise on musical processing differ, with expertise closely tied to changes in the auditory systems.

Focusing on the time course of musical training, one study used magnetoencephalography (MEG) to examine children aged 4–6 years (Fujioka, Ross, Kakigi, Pantev, & Trainor, 2006). Children were presented with violin tones and noise bursts at four different measurement occasions spread across a year. Critically, half of the children participated in musical training during this period. Over the course of the year, the training children not only demonstrated enhanced musical discrimination but also exhibited morphological changes in the Auditory Evoked Magnetic Field (AEF), a component which provides information about when and where sounds are processed. This change was specifically observed for the violin tone, but not for the noise burst. Another MEG-component, the N250m in response to violin tones, also exhibited more rapid changes in children who underwent musical training compared to those in the control group. Together, these findings indicate that musical training influences the development of neuronal networks involved in auditory processing. More specifically, the networks evolved differently over the course of a year with the increasing demands of auditory processing due to musical training. A comparative study was conducted among children in the same age group (4–6 years) over a period of 20 days, where they underwent either computerized musical training or visual art training (Moreno, Friesen, & Bialystok, 2011). The children who received musical training displayed improvements in verbal and executive functioning abilities. An electroencephalography (EEG) component known as the P2, which is associated with high-order perceptual processing modulated by attention in parieto-occipital regions (Luck & Hillyard, 1994), also exhibited enhancements with musical training. These broader impacts of musical training on higher cognitive processes could be attributed to the increased demands on sensory-motor integration and coordination akin to musical training (Zatorre, Chen, & Penhune, 2007). Thus, skills that put higher demands on scaffolding through the control system may lead to changes in those systems as well.

An intriguing avenue for future research is to explore the extent to which such effects are more likely to occur during childhood and adolescence (Kühn & Lindenberger, 2016; Laube et al., 2020) as opposed to adulthood, and to assess their durability.

With respect to structural change, Hyde and colleagues (2009) conducted a study in children aged 5–7 years, who either underwent instrumental music training (i.e., keyboard lessons) over 15 months, or were part of a control group who did not receive any form of training. The authors used deformation-based morphometry, a method that utilizes deformation fields to identify differences in the relative positions of brain structures (Gaser, 2016). Their findings revealed differences in structural change between the children who underwent musical training and the control group. More specifically, the children who received training displayed a significant increase in relative voxel size in the motor cortex, which includes the precentral gyrus (motor hand area), corpus callosum, and primary auditory cortex (lateral aspect of Heschl's gyrus). These changes were positively correlated with behavioral improvements in motor and auditory musical tests. Interestingly, the researchers also observed structural differences between the training and control groups in several frontal areas, including the middle and superior frontal gyrus. Although these changes did not correlate with improved musical skills, they lend support to the idea that alongside plastic changes associated with the primary functions or aspects of a skill (in this case, playing an instrument), changes can also occur in domain-general areas involved in sensorimotor integration (Hyde et al., 2009) and cognitive control. Along the same lines, there is growing evidence that adult musicians tend to engage additional sensory and associative cortices, which support cognitive aspects such as attention and memory, more heavily during auditory task performance compared to non-musicians (Baumann, Meyer, & Jäncke, 2008; Gaab & Schlaug, 2003; Haslinger et al., 2005; Pallesen et al., 2010; Stewart et al., 2003). The frequent activation of these higher-order brain regions during sensory processing while playing music might trigger synaptic plasticity. This could in turn promote an enhanced top-down control over basic auditory processes such as frequency tuning, response timing, or neuronal recruitment (Strait & Kraus, 2014). This reinforced cognitive-sensory connectivity could then potentially alter any passive or active sound processing. It could thereby also affect other everyday non-musical functions such as language and cognitive skills. For instance, beat synchronization and rhythm perception have been linked to auditory attention and reading abilities (Tierney & Kraus, 2013).

6.3 Motor learning

In the domain of motor learning, Thomas and colleagues (2004) compared children aged 7–11 years with adults. The researchers utilized a serial reaction time task combined with functional MRI, which enabled them to compare the neural correlates of early versus late learning. Their findings revealed that learning (defined as savings in reaction time for the practiced sequence compared to a random novel sequence) was enhanced in adults relative to children. However, it is worth noting that adults in this study had overall higher accuracy and quicker responses than children. Thus, potential differences in the difficulty of the learning task might contribute to the observed age differences in speed and efficiency of learning. On the neural level, children exhibited higher activation than adults in subcortical structures associated with motor performance, including the putamen. In contrast, adults displayed enhanced activation in the premotor cortex (BA4/6) and the parahippocampal cortex. It is worth noting that these age differences were not modulated by learning, suggesting that they may reflect differences in overall task-related factors such as task difficulty or strategy. Interestingly, activation in several brain regions—including the extrastriate cortex, superior temporal/insular cortex, basal ganglia, middle frontal gyrus, and dACC—decreased with repetition to a similar degree in children and adults. Given that most of these regions are part of networks underlying control during initial stages of learning (Chein & Schneider, 2012), these results suggest a potentially comparable involvement of control systems during motor sequence learning in children and adults.

In line with the age differences in the time course for language learning highlighted above, another study on motor sequence learning (Adi-Japha, Badir, Dorfberger, & Karni, 2014) demonstrated a partial stabilization of a learned motor sequence within 15 min of learning in 9-year-olds. In contrast, adults did not show any evidence of performance stabilization even after a longer time interval. These two examples reveal opposite patterns of age differences in learning between children and adults. The mixed findings in the literature may be related to a number of factors, including differences in procedure, children's age, utilized outcome measures or task difficulty. Meta-analyses could be particularly helpful for identifying the specific factors that influence patterns of age differences in motor sequence learning.

6.4 Perceptual learning

Research focusing on age differences in perceptual learning (Frank et al., 2021) or perceptual discrimination (Blanco & Sloutsky, 2019) has highlighted fundamental differences between children and adults. Adults tend to modulate attention in a goal-directed manner, suppressing irrelevant features and focusing on task-relevant information. Conversely, children typically pay greater attention to and acquire more task-irrelevant information. These differences in learning might reflect differences in the extent to which children and adults engage in model-based learning (Hartley et al., 2021). On the neural level, the ongoing segregation of brain networks that support control processes, coupled with coordinated changes in the gray matter of local brain structures, are likely to contribute to the less specific response observed during perceptual learning in children. Recently, Frank and colleagues (2022) employed functional MRS to compare changes in GABA concentrations during visual perceptual learning in early visual areas between children (aged 8–11 years) and adults. During the training task, participants were shown two images in succession—one containing a Gabor patch overlaid with a noise pattern, and the other comprising only a noise pattern. The participants' task was to indicate which of the two images contained the Gabor patch. Children exhibited increased GABA levels from pre- to post-training, whereas GABA levels in adults remained unchanged. These changes occurred during training and were maintained during the post-training period, in line with improvements in perceptual learning. The researchers hypothesized that the swift increase in GABA during training could have led to earlier stabilization of learning in children compared to adults, echoing the motor results discussed above (Adi-Japha et al., 2014). In line with this interpretation, an independent behavioral sample showed that children were less susceptible to interference than adults in the same paradigm. These results suggest that GABA might play a crucial role in stabilizing learning during childhood, resulting in more efficient perceptual learning in children.

When considering the development of auditory perceptual skills, two key phenomena emerge: perceptual maturation extends through adolescence, and the age at which children reach adult-like behavior varies greatly across skills (Sanes & Woolley, 2011). For instance, while frequency resolution (tone detection in the presence of a second nearby tone) reaches adult-like levels by about 6 months, frequency discrimination (i.e., discerning a difference between two sequentially presented tones) does not fully mature until around 10 years of age (Abdala & Keefe, 2012). Just as perception of frequency and intensity exhibits considerable variability in maturation, the perception of temporal cues also varies across development (Sanes & Woolley, 2011). Generally, children exhibit shallower psychometric functions than adults, such as in intensity discrimination or measurements of tone thresholds in the presence of noise (Allen & Wightman, 1994; Buss, Hall, & Grose, 2006; Buss, Hall, & Grose, 2009). Thus, while adults display a typical pattern of a sudden change in behavior from near-chance detection to excellent detection at a certain "break point", children's behavior improves more gradually over time. A major question in the study of perceptual maturation is whether the underlying mechanisms operate at the level of encoding (i.e., constitute sensory factors), or at the cognitive level (i.e., non-sensory but higher-order factors such as attention, memory, or motivation). Children often display more variable performance than adults, leading to the conclusion that they cannot focus attention as effectively as older ones (Moore, Cowan, Riley, Edmondson-Jones, & Ferguson, 2011). However, the maturation rates for different auditory tasks are not correlated, which would be expected if indeed a higher-order factor like attention was the primary determining factor (Banai, Sabin, & Wright, 2011; Hartley et al., 2021; Moore et al., 2011). Thus, while developing attention may play a role, it seems unlikely to be the sole explanation of perceptual maturation. Children may also employ different strategies than adults. Adults are typically better at detecting an expected stimulus (i.e., a sound frequency, duration, or presentation time), a phenomenon known as selective listening (Greenberg & Larkin, 1968; Wright & Fitzgerald, 2004). Their listening experience is thus governed more strongly by top-down processes. With this strategy, adults excel at detecting a tone that is presented with the highest probability (i.e., a tone at 1000 Hz), but struggle when low probability tones are delivered. Infants, on the other hand, appear to listen more broadly across the entire frequency spectrum, without predefined expectations, and perform quite well with unexpected stimuli (Bargones & Werner, 1994). This could be considered a prime example of a learning advantage for systems with immature control systems that, as a result, favor bottom-up over top-down processing.

In summary, the examples from various learning domains highlight several overarching themes regarding the time course and mechanisms of skill acquisition in childhood. First, skill learning and the development of expertise in childhood is related to changes in the corresponding domain-specific representation systems. Additionally, some studies suggest that there are differences in task-related activation (Thomas et al., 2004) and in GABA concentration levels (Frank et al., 2022) between children and adults. These aspects warrant exploration in future research. Second, there are instances where skills are acquired and/or stabilized faster in children than in adults. However, our understanding of this learning advantage is still limited with respect to boundary conditions and the ages at which it occurs. It is also unclear whether such a learning advantage varies across skills due to differences in the maturation of the different representation systems and their connections to the rest of the brain. Third, the evidence above suggests potential differences between children and adults with respect to the role of consolidation processes in skill maintenance and stabilization. This area requires future investigation. Finally, the one study that focused on whole-brain activation changes during motor skill acquisition (Thomas et al., 2004) reported comparable practice-related decreases in frontal activation between children and adults. This finding appears to contradict the generally accepted notion of protracted development of these brain areas. Future studies examining the time course of both representation and control systems are necessary to reveal the dynamic interactions between these systems during childhood.

But might there be an actual advantage of protracted control system development for skill learning? In the next section, we delve into this question, discussing its impact on skill learning during childhood.

7. Potential advantage of protracted control development?

Children frequently show lower performance on tasks that place high demands on cognitive control, including working memory, inhibition or task switching (Crone & Steinbeis, 2017; Schwarze et al., 2023). At the same time, children are generally believed to acquire new skills faster than adults do. As evidenced by some of the examples above, there is support for this notion from studies on motor and perceptual learning as well as language acquisition (Kuhl, 2004). This co-occurrence has led to the proposition that the children's superior learning in some situations is due to the protracted development of cognitive control. In particular, one proposal posits that in circumstances where learning does not benefit from individuals' predictions of the environment, but can instead rely on associative learning mechanisms, children are more likely to demonstrate superior learning compared to adults (Thompson-Schill, Ramscar, & Chrysikou, 2009). Accordingly, in the context of language acquisition, associative learning models, which reinforce the most frequently experienced input, are highly capable of modeling specific aspects of children's language learning. For instance, they can effectively model the acquisition of irregular plural forms (e.g., mouse—mice) in children (Ramscar & Yarlett, 2007), which adults generally find more challenging to acquire. Furthermore, (younger) children may be less affected by additional control demands during learning. This could make newly formed memory traces less susceptible to interference from environmental changes. In contrast, older children and adults might have a greater ability to generalize acquired skills when faced with similar learning situations. This pattern would align well with the notion of a developing system that prioritizes learning over flexibility in performance. Expanding on this framework, Chrysikou, Weber, and Thompson-Schill (2014) propose that the control system contributes to learning in situations where the task or skill is based on rules, top-down, and directed towards a goal. This is especially the case when an abstract understanding of task-related concepts or rules is required, and the task depends on maintaining and manipulating explicit representations. In contrast, reduced control system involvement might benefit learning when the task is bottom-up or stimulus-driven, not amenable to abstraction, or exceeding working memory capacity. In such situations, children would be expected to learn new skills more efficiently than adults due to protracted control development.

Consistent with these ideas, it has recently been suggested that childhood may represent an evolutionary solution to the well-known explore-exploit dilemma (Gopnik, 2020). In this dilemma, an agent must choose between exploring an unknown environment to uncover potential unknown rewards or exploiting known rewarding options, thereby potentially missing out on higher rewards. Similarly, during learning, an individual may opt for a narrow search of viable strategies to solve a task or embark on a broader exploratory search. While the latter is more time-consuming and costly, it can reveal more options. Children, even by middle and late childhood, exhibit a learning pattern that is more strongly characterized by exploration (Nussenbaum & Hartley, 2019; Schulz, Wu, Ruggeri, & Meder, 2019; Sumner et al., 2019). Children's exploration is not random—they systematically avoid repeating the choice that was made on the previous trial (Blanco & Sloutsky, 2024) and direct exploration in line with the value of information (Schulz et al., 2019). Enhanced exploration in younger children occurs alongside less selective modulation of attention. For instance, preschoolers tend to distribute their attention more broadly than older children and adults (Blanco & Sloutsky, 2019) and demonstrate better memory for task-irrelevant information (Deng & Sloutsky, 2016; Plebanek & Sloutsky, 2017). Collectively, these findings have been hypothesized to reflect immature cognitive control and protracted PFC maturation. To date, however, direct evidence linking higher exploration to more distributed attention and observable frontal differences is lacking. Furthermore, individual differences across various learning domains, to the best of our knowledge, have yet to be addressed.

Considering skill acquisition in childhood, these frameworks and related findings suggest that the protracted development of the control system might provide an advantage for explorative behavior during the initial stages of learning. Together with findings suggesting that children have a broader attentional focus and learn more irrelevant information, children may be expected to show an advantage in skill acquisition situations that require the exploration of different strategies, or the initial exploration phases in the representation areas of the ESR-model. This concept aligns with the previously discussed advantage children have in learning linguistic rules. However, distributing attention during learning and information processing can have a downside. It can lead to slower and less efficient performance on the task at hand due to the concurrent processing of irrelevant information (Chein & Schneider, 2012; Desimone & Duncan, 1995). Conversely, the optimization of our limited attentional resources can obscure a potential risk (Blanco, Turner, & Sloutsky, 2023): If currently irrelevant information becomes relevant later on, we may continue to ignore it (Hoffman & Rehder, 2010; Rich & Gureckis, 2018) or have difficulty learning it once it becomes relevant for behavior (Kruschke & Blair, 2000). With development, children accumulate increasingly more knowledge and experience, allowing them to identify patterns in their surroundings, construct mental models, and deftly manipulate cognitive control to strike a balance between stability and flexibility in less predictable environments (Egner, 2023). With limited experience and knowledge in childhood, ignoring potentially critical information may incur higher costs for learning and action (Gopnik, 2020), hence favoring increased exploration and distributed attention. However, it should be noted that these phenomena do not apply to all learning situations. For instance, Pelz and Kidd (2020) examined children aged between one and 12 years in a complex environment, and demonstrated that younger children do not explore universally, but instead exploration becomes more elaborate with age.

In conclusion, while the characteristics of childhood learning provide opportunities for unique advantages, they also come with their own set of challenges. The interplay between distributed attention, exploration, and the development of a control system presents a complex landscape that requires further investigation, particularly to understand the nuances of learning across different ages and situations, and the ensuing consequences for experience-dependent plasticity in domain-specific representation systems.

8. Conclusions

Childhood is recognized as a pivotal period for acquiring skills, with diverse learning methods contributing to the mastery of complex abilities like language proficiency, literacy, and musical aptitude. Central to this process is the concept of brain plasticity, which refers to the brain's adaptive ability to master new skills.

Empirical evidence suggests that children can outpace adults in learning in situations that favor bottom-up over top-down processing. The favoring of bottom-up processing presumably results from the protracted development of cognitive control regions in the brain, though direct evidence linking these phenomena is missing. In conclusion, the dynamics and complexity of skill acquisition during childhood underscore the need for continued research in this area. Future investigations should aim to further understand the developmental changes and interactions between control and representations systems in the brain. More specifically, researchers should focus on how these changes and interactions influence skill acquisition not only during childhood but also during adolescence, a period of significant cognitive and emotional growth. This deeper understanding could potentially inform and improve educational strategies and practices, ultimately fostering individual learners at various points in their development.

References

Abdala, C., & Keefe, D. H. (2012). Morphological and functional ear development. In L. Werner, R. R. Fay, & A. N. Popper (Eds.). *(Hrsg.), Human auditory development* (pp. 19–59). Springer New York. https://doi.org/10.1007/978-1-4614-1421-6_2.

Adi-Japha, E., Badir, R., Dorfberger, S., & Karni, A. (2014). A matter of time: Rapid motor memory stabilization in childhood. *Developmental Science, 17*(3), https://doi.org/10.1111/desc.12132.

Adolph, K. E., & Robinson, S. R. (2015). *Motor development.* 7. Aufl., S*Handbook of child psychology and developmental science.* John Wiley & Sons, Inc1–45 7. Aufl., S.

Albouy, G., Sterpenich, V., Balteau, E., Vandewalle, G., Desseilles, M., Dang-Vu, T., ... Degueldre, C. (2008). Both the hippocampus and striatum are involved in consolidation of motor sequence memory. *Neuron, 58*(2).

Allen, P., & Wightman, F. (1994). Psychometric functions for children's detection of tones in noise. *Journal of Speech, Language, and Hearing Research, 37*(1), https://doi.org/10.1044/jshr.3701.205.

Aslin, R. N., Saffran, J. R., & Newport, E. L. (1998). Computation of conditional probability statistics by 8-month-old infants. *Psychological Science, 9*(4), https://doi.org/10.1111/1467-9280.00063.

Badre, D., & Nee, D. E. (2018). Frontal cortex and the hierarchical control of behavior. *Trends in Cognitive Sciences, 22*(2), https://doi.org/10.1016/j.tics.2017.11.005.

Baggs, E., Raja, V., & Anderson, M. L. (2020). Extended skill learning. *Frontiers in Psychology, 11*. https://doi.org/10.3389/fpsyg.2020.01956.

Banai, K., Sabin, A. T., & Wright, B. A. (2011). Separable developmental trajectories for the abilities to detect auditory amplitude and frequency modulation. *Hearing Research, 280*(1–2), https://doi.org/10.1016/j.heares.2011.05.019.

Bandura, A. (1986). *Social Foundations of Thought and Action: A Social Cognitive Theory*. Englewood Cliffs, NJ: Prentice-Hall.

Bargones, J. Y., & Werner, L. A. (1994). Adults listen selectively; infants do not. *Psychological Science, 5*(3), https://doi.org/10.1111/j.1467-9280.1994.tb00655.x.

Bassett, D. S., Yang, M., Wymbs, N. F., & Grafton, S. T. (2015). Learning-induced autonomy of sensorimotor systems. *Nature Neuroscience, 18*(5), https://doi.org/10.1038/nn.3993.

Baumann, S., Meyer, M., & Jäncke, L. (2008). Enhancement of auditory-evoked potentials in musicians reflects an influence of expertise but not selective attention. *Journal of Cognitive Neuroscience, 20*(12), https://doi.org/10.1162/jocn.2008.20157.

Bengtsson, S. L., Nagy, Z., Skare, S., Forsman, L., Forssberg, H., & Ullén, F. (2005). Extensive piano practicing has regionally specific effects on white matter development. *Nature Neuroscience, 8*(9), https://doi.org/10.1038/nn1516.

Berger, S., & Batterink, L. J. (2024). Children extract a new linguistic rule more quickly than adults. *Developmental Science*, e13498. https://doi.org/10.1111/desc.13498.

Berlot, E., Popp, N. J., & Diedrichsen, J. (2020). A critical re-evaluation of fMRI signatures of motor sequence learning. *eLife, 9*, e55241. https://doi.org/10.7554/eLife.55241.

Betzel, R. F., Byrge, L., He, Y., Goñi, J., Zuo, X.-N., & Sporns, O. (2014). Changes in structural and functional connectivity among resting-state networks across the human lifespan. *Neuroimage, 102*, 345–357. https://doi.org/10.1016/j.neuroimage.2014.07.067.

Blanco, N. J., & Sloutsky, V. M. (2019). Adaptive flexibility in category learning? Young children exhibit smaller costs of selective attention than adults. *Developmental Psychology, 55*(10), https://doi.org/10.1037/dev0000777.

Blanco, N. J., & Sloutsky, V. M. (2024). Exploration, exploitation, and development: Developmental shifts in decision-making. *Child Development*, cdev.14070. https://doi.org/10.1111/cdev.14070.

Blanco, N. J., Turner, B. M., & Sloutsky, V. M. (2023). The benefits of immature cognitive control: How distributed attention guards against learning traps. *Journal of Experimental Child Psychology, 226*, 105548. https://doi.org/10.1016/j.jecp.2022.105548.

Boureau, Y.-L., Sokol-Hessner, P., & Daw, N. D. (2015). Deciding how to decide: Self-control and meta-decision making. *Trends in Cognitive Sciences, 19*(11), https://doi.org/10.1016/j.tics.2015.08.013.

Brain Development Cooperative Group. (2012). Total and regional brain volumes in a population-based normative sample from 4 to 18 years: The NIH MRI study of normal brain development. *Cerebral Cortex, 22*(1), https://doi.org/10.1093/cercor/bhr018.

Braver, T. S. (2012). The variable nature of cognitive control: A dual mechanisms framework. *Trends in Cognitive Sciences, 16*(2), https://doi.org/10.1016/j.tics.2011.12.010.

Brodal, P. (2010). *Glia* (S.) *The central nervous system: Structure and function.* Oxford University Press,19–27 (S.).

Bulf, H., Johnson, S. P., & Valenza, E. (2011). Visual statistical learning in the newborn infant. *Cognition, 121*(1) Article 1.

Buss, E., Hall, J. W., III, & Grose, J. H. (2006). Development and the role of internal noise in detection and discrimination thresholds with narrow band stimuli. *The Journal of the Acoustical Society of America, 120*(5), https://doi.org/10.1121/1.2354024.

Buss, E., Hall, J. W., III, & Grose, J. H. (2009). Psychometric functions for pure tone intensity discrimination: Slope differences in school-aged children and adults. *The Journal of the Acoustical Society of America, 125*(2), https://doi.org/10.1121/1.3050273.

Buttelmann, D., Carpenter, M., Call, J., & Tomasello, M. (2008). Rational tool use and tool choice in human infants and great apes. *Child Development, 79*(3), https://doi.org/10.1111/j.1467-8624.2008.01146.x.

Caballero, A., Flores-Barrera, E., Cass, D. K., & Tseng, K. Y. (2014). Differential regulation of parvalbumin and calretinin interneurons in the prefrontal cortex during adolescence. *Brain Structure and Function, 219*(1), https://doi.org/10.1007/s00429-013-0508-8.

Chater, N., & Christiansen, M. H. (2018). Language acquisition as skill learning. *The Evolution of Language, 21*, 205–208. https://doi.org/10.1016/j.cobeha.2018.04.001.

Chein, J. M., & Schneider, W. (2005). Neuroimaging studies of practice-related change: fMRI and meta-analytic evidence of a domain-general control network for learning. *Cognitive Brain Research, 25*(3), https://doi.org/10.1016/j.cogbrainres.2005.08.013.

Chein, J. M., & Schneider, W. (2012). The brain's learning and control architecture. *Current Directions in Psychological Science, 21*(2), https://doi.org/10.1177/0963721411434977.

Choi, Y., Shin, E. Y., & Kim, S. (2020). Spatiotemporal dissociation of fMRI activity in the caudate nucleus underlies human de novo motor skill learning. *Proceedings of the National Academy of Sciences, 117*(38), https://doi.org/10.1073/pnas.2003963117.

Chrysikou, E. G., Weber, M. J., & Thompson-Schill, S. L. (2014). A matched filter hypothesis for cognitive control. *Neuropsychologia, 62*, 341–355. https://doi.org/10.1016/j.neuropsychologia.2013.10.021.

Chyl, K., Fraga-González, G., Brem, S., & Jednoróg, K. (2021). Brain dynamics of (a) typical reading development—A review of longitudinal studies. *npj Science of Learning, 6*(1), https://doi.org/10.1038/s41539-020-00081-5.

Collins, A. G. E. (2018). The tortoise and the hare: Interactions between reinforcement learning and working memory. *Journal of Cognitive Neuroscience, 30*(10), https://doi.org/10.1162/jocn_a_01238.

Colombo, J., Shaddy, D. J., Richman, W. A., Maikranz, J. M., & Blaga, O. M. (2004). The developmental course of habituation in infancy and preschool outcome. *Infancy: The Official Journal of the International Society on Infant Studies, 5*(1), https://doi.org/10.1207/s15327078in0501_1.

Cowan, N. (2016). Working memory maturation: Can we get at the essence of cognitive growth? *Perspectives on Psychological Science, 11*(2), https://doi.org/10.1177/1745691615621279.

Crone, E. A., & Steinbeis, N. (2017). Neural perspectives on cognitive control development during childhood and adolescence. *Trends in Cognitive Sciences, 21*(3), https://doi.org/10.1016/j.tics.2017.01.003.

Daw, N. D., Gershman, S. J., Seymour, B., Dayan, P., & Dolan, R. J. (2011). Model-based influences on humans' choices and striatal prediction errors. *Neuron, 69*(6), https://doi.org/10.1016/j.neuron.2011.02.027.

Daw, N. D., Niv, Y., & Dayan, P. (2005). Uncertainty-based competition between prefrontal and dorsolateral striatal systems for behavioral control. *Nature Neuroscience, 8*(12), https://doi.org/10.1038/nn1560.

Dayan, E., & Cohen, L. G. (2011). Neuroplasticity subserving motor skill learning. *Neuron, 72*(3), https://doi.org/10.1016/j.neuron.2011.10.008.

De Faria, O., Pivonkova, H., Varga, B., Timmler, S., Evans, K. A., & Káradóttir, R. T. (2021). Periods of synchronized myelin changes shape brain function and plasticity. *Nature Neuroscience, 24*(11), https://doi.org/10.1038/s41593-021-00917-2.

Decker, J. H., Otto, A. R., Daw, N. D., & Hartley, C. A. (2016). From creatures of habit to goal-directed learners: Tracking the developmental emergence of model-based reinforcement learning. *Psychological Science, 27*(6), https://doi.org/10.1177/0956797616639301.

Dehaene, S., & Cohen, L. (2011). The unique role of the visual word form area in reading. *Trends in Cognitive Sciences, 15*(6), https://doi.org/10.1016/j.tics.2011.04.003.

Dehaene-Lambertz, G., Monzalvo, K., & Dehaene, S. (2018). The emergence of the visual word form: Longitudinal evolution of category-specific ventral visual areas during reading acquisition. *PLoS Biology, 16*(3), https://doi.org/10.1371/journal.pbio.2004103.

Deng, W. S., & Sloutsky, V. M. (2016). Selective attention, diffused attention, and the development of categorization. *Cognitive Psychology, 91*, 24–62. https://doi.org/10.1016/j.cogpsych.2016.09.002.

Desimone, R., & Duncan, J. (1995). Neural mechanisms of selective visual attention. *Annual Review of Neuroscience, 18*, 193–222. https://doi.org/10.1146/annurev.ne.18.030195.001205.

Dhawale, A. K., Smith, M. A., & Ölveczky, B. P. (2017). The role of variability in motor learning. *Annual Review of Neuroscience, 40*(1), https://doi.org/10.1146/annurev-neuro-072116-031548.

Di Paolo, E., Buhrmann, T., & Barandiaran, X. (2017). *Sensorimotor life: An enactive proposal.* Oxford University Press. https://doi.org/10.1093/acprof:oso/9780198786849.001.0001.

Draganski, B., Gaser, C., Busch, V., Schuierer, G., Bogdahn, U., & May, A. (2004). Changes in grey matter induced by training. *Nature, 427*(6972), https://doi.org/10.1038/427311a.

Ducharme, S., Albaugh, M. D., Nguyen, T.-V., Hudziak, J. J., Mateos-Pérez, J. M., Labbe, A., ... Karama, S. (2016). Trajectories of cortical thickness maturation in normal brain development—The importance of quality control procedures. *Neuroimage, 125*, 267–279. https://doi.org/10.1016/j.neuroimage.2015.10.010.

Egner, T. (2023). Principles of cognitive control over task focus and task switching. Article 11 *Nature Reviews Psychology, 2*(11), https://doi.org/10.1038/s44159-023-00234-4.

Ellis, R. J., Bruijn, B., Norton, A. C., Winner, E., & Schlaug, G. (2013). Training-mediated leftward asymmetries during music processing: A cross-sectional and longitudinal fMRI analysis. *Neuroimage, 75*, 97–107. https://doi.org/10.1016/j.neuroimage.2013.02.045.

Ellis, C. T., Skalaban, L. J., Yates, T. S., Bejjanki, V. R., Córdova, N. I., & Turk-Browne, N. B. (2021). Evidence of hippocampal learning in human infants. *Current Biology, 31*(15), https://doi.org/10.1016/j.cub.2021.04.072.

Fagiolini, M., & Hensch, T. K. (2000). Inhibitory threshold for critical-period activation in primary visual cortex. *Nature, 404*(6774), https://doi.org/10.1038/35004582.

Fleming, S. M., & Dolan, R. J. (2012). The neural basis of metacognitive ability. *Philosophical Transactions of the Royal Society B: Biological Sciences, 367*(1594), https://doi.org/10.1098/rstb.2011.0417.

Frank, S. M., Becker, M., Qi, A., Geiger, P., Frank, U. I., Rosedahl, L. A., ... Watanabe, T. (2022). Efficient learning in children with rapid GABA boosting during and after training. *Current Biology, 32*(23), https://doi.org/10.1016/j.cub.2022.10.021.

Frank, S. M., Bründl, S., Frank, U. I., Sasaki, Y., Greenlee, M. W., & Watanabe, T. (2021). Fundamental differences in visual perceptual learning between children and adults. *Current Biology, 31*(2), https://doi.org/10.1016/j.cub.2020.10.047.

Fu, M., & Zuo, Y. (2011). Experience-dependent structural plasticity in the cortex. *Trends in Neurosciences, 34*(4), https://doi.org/10.1016/j.tins.2011.02.001.

Fujioka, T., Ross, B., Kakigi, R., Pantev, C., & Trainor, L. J. (2006). One year of musical training affects development of auditory cortical-evoked fields in young children. *Brain, 129*(10), https://doi.org/10.1093/brain/awl247.

Fung, S. J., Webster, M. J., Sivagnanasundaram, S., Duncan, C., Elashoff, M., & Weickert, C. S. (2010). Expression of interneuron markers in the dorsolateral prefrontal cortex of the developing human and in schizophrenia. *American Journal of Psychiatry, 167*(12), https://doi.org/10.1176/appi.ajp.2010.09060784.

Gaab, N., & Schlaug, G. (2003). The effect of musicianship on pitch memory in performance matched groups. *Neuroreport, 14*(8), 8. https://doi.org/10.1097/01.wnr.0000093587.33576.f7.

Garner, K. G., & Dux, P. E. (2015). Training conquers multitasking costs by dividing task representations in the frontoparietal-subcortical system. *Proceedings of the National Academy of Sciences, 112*(46), https://doi.org/10.1073/pnas.1511423112.

Gaser, C. (2016). Structural MRI: Morphometry (S.). In M. Reuter, & C. Montag (Eds.). *(Hrsg.), Neuroeconomics* (pp. 399–409). Springer Berlin Heidelberg. (S.). https://doi.org/10.1007/978-3-642-35923-1_21 (S.).

Gergely, G., Bekkering, H., & Király, I. (2002). Rational imitation in preverbal infants. *Nature, 415*(6873), Article 6873.

Gerhardstein, P., Shroff, G., Dickerson, K., & Adler, S. (2009). *The developement of object recognition through infancy. New directions in developmental psychobiology*. Nova Science Publishers Inc. S. 79–115.

Ghetti, S., & Fandakova, Y. (2020). Neural development of memory and metamemory in childhood and adolescence: Toward an integrative model of the development of episodic recollection. *Annual Review of Developmental Psychology, 2*(1), https://doi.org/10.1146/annurev-devpsych-060320-085634.

Gibson, J. J., & Gibson, E. J. (1955). Perceptual learning: Differentiation or enrichment? *Psychological Review, 62*(1), Article 1.

Gilmore, J. H., Knickmeyer, R. C., & Gao, W. (2018). Imaging structural and functional brain development in early childhood. *Nature Reviews. Neuroscience, 19*(3), https://doi.org/10.1038/nrn.2018.1.

Gopnik, A. (2020). Childhood as a solution to explore–exploit tensions. *Philosophical Transactions of the Royal Society B: Biological Sciences, 375*(1803), https://doi.org/10.1098/rstb.2019.0502.

Grayson, D. S., & Fair, D. A. (2017). Development of large-scale functional networks from birth to adulthood: A guide to the neuroimaging literature. *Functional Architecture of the Brain, 160*, 15–31. https://doi.org/10.1016/j.neuroimage.2017.01.079.

Greenberg, G. Z., & Larkin, W. D. (1968). Frequency-response characteristic of auditory observers detecting signals of a single frequency in noise: The probe-signal method. *The Journal of the Acoustical Society of America, 44*(6), https://doi.org/10.1121/1.1911290.

Gu, S., Satterthwaite, T. D., Medaglia, J. D., Yang, M., Gur, R. E., Gur, R. C., & Bassett, D. S. (2015). Emergence of system roles in normative neurodevelopment. *Proceedings of the National Academy of Sciences, 112*(44), https://doi.org/10.1073/pnas.1502829112.

Hartley, C. A., Nussenbaum, K., & Cohen, A. O. (2021). Interactive development of adaptive learning and memory. *Annual Review of Developmental Psychology, 3*(1), https://doi.org/10.1146/annurev-devpsych-050620-030227.

Haslinger, B., Erhard, P., Altenmüller, E., Schroeder, U., Boecker, H., & Ceballos-Baumann, A. O. (2005). Transmodal sensorimotor networks during action observation in professional pianists. *Journal of Cognitive Neuroscience, 17*(2), https://doi.org/10.1162/0898929053124893.

Hensch, T. K. (2005). Critical period plasticity in local cortical circuits. *Nature Reviews. Neuroscience, 6*(11), https://doi.org/10.1038/nrn1787.

Hoffman, A. B., & Rehder, B. (2010). The costs of supervised classification: The effect of learning task on conceptual flexibility. *Journal of Experimental Psychology: General, 139*(2), https://doi.org/10.1037/a0019042.

Holtmaat, A., De Paola, V., Wilbrecht, L., & Knott, G. W. (2008). Imaging of experience-dependent structural plasticity in the mouse neocortex in vivo. *Behavioural Brain Research, 192*(1), https://doi.org/10.1016/j.bbr.2008.04.005.

Holtmaat, A., & Svoboda, K. (2009). Experience-dependent structural synaptic plasticity in the mammalian brain. *Nature Reviews. Neuroscience, 10*(9), https://doi.org/10.1038/nrn2699.

Horowitz-Kraus, T., Vannest, J. J., Gozdas, E., & Holland, S. K. (2014). Greater utilization of neural-circuits related to executive functions is associated with better reading: A longitudinal fMRI study using the verb generation task. *Frontiers in Human Neuroscience, 8.* https://doi.org/10.3389/fnhum.2014.00447.

Houston, S. M., Lebel, C., Katzir, T., Manis, F. R., Kan, E., Rodriguez, G. G., & Sowell, E. R. (2014). Reading skill and structural brain development. *Neuroreport, 25*(5), https://doi.org/10.1097/WNR.0000000000000121.

Huttenlocher, P. R., & Dabholkar, A. S. (1997). Regional differences in synaptogenesis in human cerebral cortex. *The Journal of Comparative Neurology, 387*(2), 2. https://doi.org/10.1002/(SICI)1096-9861(19971020)387:2%3C167::AID-CNE1%3E3.0.CO;2-Z.

Hyde, K. L., Lerch, J., Norton, A., Forgeard, M., Winner, E., Evans, A. C., & Schlaug, G. (2009). Musical training shapes structural brain development. *The Journal of Neuroscience, 29*(10), https://doi.org/10.1523/JNEUROSCI.5118-08.2009.

Jacobacci, F., Armony, J. L., Yeffal, A., Lerner, G., Amaro, E., Jovicich, J., ... Della-Maggiore, V. (2020). Rapid hippocampal plasticity supports motor sequence learning. *Proceedings of the National Academy of Sciences, 117*(38), https://doi.org/10.1073/pnas.2009576117.

Kami, A., Meyer, G., Jezzard, P., Adams, M. M., Turner, R., & Ungerleider, L. G. (1995). Functional MRI evidence for adult motor cortex plasticity during motor skill learning. *Nature, 377*(6545), https://doi.org/10.1038/377155a0.

Kavšek, M. (2004). Predicting later IQ from infant visual habituation and dishabituation: A meta-analysis. *Journal of Applied Developmental Psychology, 25*(3), Article 3.

Kawai, R., Markman, T., Poddar, R., Ko, R., Fantana, A. L., Dhawale, A. K., ... Ölveczky, B. P. (2015). Motor cortex is required for learning but not for executing a motor skill. *Neuron, 86*(3), https://doi.org/10.1016/j.neuron.2015.03.024.

Keller, A. S., Sydnor, V. J., Pines, A., Fair, D. A., Bassett, D. S., & Satterthwaite, T. D. (2023). Hierarchical functional system development supports executive function. *Trends in Cognitive Sciences, 27*(2), https://doi.org/10.1016/j.tics.2022.11.005.

Kelly, A. M. C., & Garavan, H. (2005). Human functional neuroimaging of brain changes associated with practice. *Cerebral Cortex, 15*(8), https://doi.org/10.1093/cercor/bhi005.

Kirkham, N. Z., Slemmer, J. A., & Johnson, S. P. (2002). Visual statistical learning in infancy: Evidence for a domain general learning mechanism. *Cognition, 83*(2), Article 2.

Kleim, J. A., Barbay, S., Cooper, N. R., Hogg, T. M., Reidel, C. N., Remple, M. S., & Nudo, R. J. (2002). Motor learning-dependent synaptogenesis is localized to functionally reorganized motor cortex. *Neurobiology of Learning and Memory, 77*(1), https://doi.org/10.1006/nlme.2000.4004.

Kruschke, J. K., & Blair, N. J. (2000). Blocking and backward blocking involve learned inattention. *Psychonomic Bulletin & Review, 7*(4), https://doi.org/10.3758/bf03213001.

Kudo, N., Nonaka, Y., Mizuno, N., Mizuno, K., & Okanoya, K. (2011). On-line statistical segmentation of a non-speech auditory stream in neonates as demonstrated by event-related brain potentials: Segmentation of non-speech auditory stream. *Developmental Science, 14*(5), https://doi.org/10.1111/j.1467-7687.2011.01056.x.

Kuhl, P. K. (2004). Early language acquisition: Cracking the speech code. *Nature Reviews. Neuroscience, 5*(11), https://doi.org/10.1038/nrn1533.

Kühn, S., Gleich, T., Lorenz, R. C., Lindenberger, U., & Gallinat, J. (2014). Playing Super Mario induces structural brain plasticity: Gray matter changes resulting from training with a commercial video game. *Molecular Psychiatry, 19*(2), https://doi.org/10.1038/mp.2013.120.

Kühn, S., & Lindenberger, U. (2016). Research on human plasticity in adulthood: A lifespan agenda (S.) . In K. W. Schaie, & S. L. Willis (Eds.). *(Hrsg.), Handbook of the psychology of aging* (pp. 105–123)(8th ed.). Academic Press. https://doi.org/10.1016/B978-0-12-411469-2.00006-6 (S.).

Kushnir, T., & Gopnik, A. (2005). Young Children infer causal strength from probabilities and interventions. *Psychological Science, 16*(9), https://doi.org/10.1111/j.1467-9280.2005.01595.x.

Kuzawa, C. W., Chugani, H. T., Grossman, L. I., Lipovich, L., Muzik, O., Hof, P. R., ... Lange, N. (2014). Metabolic costs and evolutionary implications of human brain development. *Proceedings of the National Academy of Sciences, 111*(36), https://doi.org/10.1073/pnas.1323099111.

Larsen, B., Cui, Z., Adebimpe, A., Pines, A., Alexander-Bloch, A., Bertolero, M., ... Satterthwaite, T. D. (2022). A developmental reduction of the excitation:inhibition ratio in association cortex during adolescence. *Science Advances, 8*(5), https://doi.org/10.1126/sciadv.abj8750.

Larsen, B., & Luna, B. (2018). Adolescence as a neurobiological critical period for the development of higher-order cognition. *Neuroscience & Biobehavioral Reviews, 94*, 179–195. https://doi.org/10.1016/j.neubiorev.2018.09.005.

Laube, C., Van Den Bos, W., & Fandakova, Y. (2020). The relationship between pubertal hormones and brain plasticity: Implications for cognitive training in adolescence. *Developmental Cognitive Neuroscience, 42*, 100753. https://doi.org/10.1016/j.dcn.2020.100753.

Lewis, M., Alessandri, S. M., & Sullivan, M. W. (1990). Violation of expectancy, loss of control, and anger expressions in young infants. *Developmental Psychology, 26*(5), https://doi.org/10.1037/0012-1649.26.5.745.

Lindenberger, U., & Lövdén, M. (2019). Brain plasticity in human lifespan development: The exploration–selection–refinement model. *Annual Review of Developmental Psychology, 1*(1), https://doi.org/10.1146/annurev-devpsych-121318-085229.

Linkersdörfer, J., Jurcoane, A., Lindberg, S., Kaiser, J., Hasselhorn, M., Fiebach, C. J., & Lonnemann, J. (2015). The association between gray matter volume and reading proficiency: A longitudinal study of beginning readers. *Journal of Cognitive Neuroscience, 27*(2), https://doi.org/10.1162/jocn_a_00710.

Lövdén, M., Bodammer, N. C., Kühn, S., Kaufmann, J., Schütze, H., Tempelmann, C., ... Lindenberger, U. (2010). Experience-dependent plasticity of white-matter microstructure extends into old age. *Neuropsychologia, 48*(13), Article 13. https://doi.org/10.1016/j.neuropsychologia.2010.08.026.

Luck, S. J., & Hillyard, S. A. (1994). Electrophysiological correlates of feature analysis during visual search. *Psychophysiology, 31*(3), 291–308. https://doi.org/10.1111/j.1469-8986.1994.tb02218.x PMID: 8008793.

Luna, B., Garver, K. E., Urban, T. A., Lazar, N. A., & Sweeney, J. A. (2004). Maturation of cognitive processes from late childhood to adulthood. *Child Development, 75*(5), https://doi.org/10.1111/j.1467-8624.2004.00745.x.

Ma, L., Wang, B., Narayana, S., Hazeltine, E., Chen, X., Robin, D. A., ... Xiong, J. (2010). Changes in regional activity are accompanied with changes in inter-regional connectivity during 4 weeks motor learning. *Brain Research, 1318*, 64–76. https://doi.org/10.1016/j.brainres.2009.12.073.

Maguire, E. A., Woollett, K., & Spiers, H. J. (2006). London taxi drivers and bus drivers: A structural MRI and neuropsychological analysis. *Hippocampus, 16*(12), https://doi.org/10.1002/hipo.20233.

Makino, H., Hwang, E. J., Hedrick, N. G., & Komiyama, T. (2016). Circuit mechanisms of sensorimotor learning. *Neuron, 92*(4), https://doi.org/10.1016/j.neuron.2016.10.029.

Martin, A., Schurz, M., Kronbichler, M., & Richlan, F. (2015). Reading in the brain of children and adults: A meta-analysis of 40 functional magnetic resonance imaging studies. *Human Brain Mapping, 36*(5), https://doi.org/10.1002/hbm.22749.

McKenzie, I. A., Ohayon, D., Li, H., Paes De Faria, J., Emery, B., Tohyama, K., & Richardson, W. D. (2014). Motor skill learning requires active central myelination. *Science (New York, N. Y.), 346*(6207), https://doi.org/10.1126/science.1254960.

Meltzoff, A. N., & Moore, M. K. (1977). Imitation of facial and manual gestures by human neonates. *Science (New York, N. Y.), 198*(4312), https://doi.org/10.1126/science.198.4312.75.

Meltzoff, A. N., & Moore, M. K. (1983). Newborn infants imitate adult facial gestures. *Child Development*, 702–709.

Mills, K. L., Goddings, A.-L., Herting, M. M., Meuwese, R., Blakemore, S.-J., Crone, E. A., ... Tamnes, C. K. (2016). Structural brain development between childhood and adulthood: Convergence across four longitudinal samples. *Neuroimage, 141*, 273–281. https://doi.org/10.1016/j.neuroimage.2016.07.044.

Moore, D. R., Cowan, J. A., Riley, A., Edmondson-Jones, A. M., & Ferguson, M. A. (2011). Development of auditory processing in 6- to 11-yr-old children. *Ear and Hearing, 32*(3), https://doi.org/10.1097/AUD.0b013e318201c468.

Moreno, S., Friesen, D., & Bialystok, E. (2011). Effect of music training on promoting preliteracy skills: Preliminary causal evidence. *Music Perception, 29*(2), https://doi.org/10.1525/mp.2011.29.2.165.

Morken, F., Helland, T., Hugdahl, K., & Specht, K. (2017). Reading in dyslexia across literacy development: A longitudinal study of effective connectivity. *Neuroimage, 144*, 92–100. https://doi.org/10.1016/j.neuroimage.2016.09.060.

Munakata, Y., Snyder, H. R., & Chatham, C. H. (2012). Developing cognitive control: Three key transitions. *Current Directions in Psychological Science, 21*(2), https://doi.org/10.1177/0963721412436807.

Natu, V. S., Barnett, M. A., Hartley, J., Gomez, J., Stigliani, A., & Grill-Spector, K. (2016). Development of neural sensitivity to face identity correlates with perceptual discriminability. *The Journal of Neuroscience, 36*(42), https://doi.org/10.1523/JNEUROSCI.1886-16.2016.

Nussenbaum, K., & Hartley, C. A. (2019). Reinforcement learning across development: What insights can we draw from a decade of research? *Developmental Cognitive Neuroscience, 40*, 100733. https://doi.org/10.1016/j.dcn.2019.100733.

Oby, E. R., Golub, M. D., Hennig, J. A., Degenhart, A. D., Tyler-Kabara, E. C., Yu, B. M., ... Batista, A. P. (2019). New neural activity patterns emerge with long-term learning. *Proceedings of the National Academy of Sciences, 116*(30), https://doi.org/10.1073/pnas.1820296116.

Pacheco, M. M., Lafe, C. W., & Newell, K. M. (2019). Search strategies in the perceptual-motor workspace and the acquisition of coordination, control, and skill. *Frontiers in Psychology, 10*, 468672. https://doi.org/10.3389/fpsyg.2019.01874.

Pallesen, K. J., Brattico, E., Bailey, C. J., Korvenoja, A., Koivisto, J., Gjedde, A., & Carlson, S. (2010). Cognitive control in auditory working memory is enhanced in musicians. *PLoS One, 5*(6), https://doi.org/10.1371/journal.pone.0011120.

Pascual-Leone, A., Grafman, J., & Hallett, M. (1994). Modulation of cortical motor output maps during development of implicit and explicit knowledge. *Science (New York, N. Y.), 263*(5151), https://doi.org/10.1126/science.8122113.

Pelz, M., & Kidd, C. (2020). The elaboration of exploratory play. *Philosophical Transactions of the Royal Society B: Biological Sciences, 375*(1803), https://doi.org/10.1098/rstb.2019.0503.

Perica, M. I., Calabro, F. J., Larsen, B., Foran, W., Yushmanov, V. E., Hetherington, H., ... Luna, B. (2022). Development of frontal GABA and glutamate supports excitation/inhibition balance from adolescence into adulthood. *Progress in Neurobiology, 219*, 102370. https://doi.org/10.1016/j.pneurobio.2022.102370.

Petersen, S. E., Van Mier, H., Fiez, J. A., & Raichle, M. E. (1998). The effects of practice on the functional anatomy of task performance. *Proceedings of the National Academy of Sciences, 95*(3), https://doi.org/10.1073/pnas.95.3.853.

Piaget, J. (1953). *The origin of intelligence in the child.* London: Routledge.

Pines, A. R., Larsen, B., Cui, Z., Sydnor, V. J., Bertolero, M. A., Adebimpe, A., ... Satterthwaite, T. D. (2022). Dissociable multi-scale patterns of development in personalized brain networks. *Nature Communications, 13*(1), https://doi.org/10.1038/s41467-022-30244-4.

Plebanek, D. J., & Sloutsky, V. M. (2017). Costs of selective attention: When children notice what adults miss. *Psychological Science, 28*(6), https://doi.org/10.1177/0956797617693005.

Poldrack, R. A. (2000). Imaging brain plasticity: Conceptual and methodological issues—A theoretical review. *Neuroimage, 12*(1), https://doi.org/10.1006/nimg.2000.0596.

Power, J. D., Cohen, A. L., Nelson, S. M., Wig, G. S., Barnes, K. A., Church, J. A., ... Petersen, S. E. (2011). Functional network organization of the human brain. *Neuron, 72*(4), https://doi.org/10.1016/j.neuron.2011.09.006.

Ramscar, M., & Yarlett, D. (2007). Linguistic self-correction in the absence of feedback: A new approach to the logical problem of language acquisition. *Cognitive Science, 31*(6), https://doi.org/10.1080/03640210701703576.

Reh, R. K., Dias, B. G., Nelson, C. A., Kaufer, D., Werker, J. F., Kolb, B., ... Hensch, T. K. (2020). Critical period regulation across multiple timescales. *Proceedings of the National Academy of Sciences, 117*(38), https://doi.org/10.1073/pnas.1820836117.

Rich, A. S., & Gureckis, T. M. (2018). Exploratory choice reflects the future value of information. *Decision, 5*(3), https://doi.org/10.1037/dec0000074.

Rodriguez Buritica, J. M., Heekeren, H. R., & van den Bos, W. (2019). The computational basis of following advice in adolescents. *Journal of Experimental Child Psychology, 180*, 39–54. https://doi.org/10.1016/j.jecp.2018.11.019.

Rose, S. A., & Feldman, J. F. (1997). Memory and speed: Their role in the relation of infant information processing to later IQ. *Child Development,* 630–641.

Roseberry, S., Richie, R., Hirsh-Pasek, K., Golinkoff, R. M., & Shipley, T. F. (2011). Babies catch a break: 7- to 9-month-olds track statistical probabilities in continuous dynamic events. *Psychological Science, 22*(11), https://doi.org/10.1177/0956797611422074.

Saffran, J. R., Aslin, R. N., & Newport, E. L. (1996). Statistical learning by 8-month-old infants. *Science (New York, N. Y.), 274*(5294), https://doi.org/10.1126/science.274.5294.1926.

Saffran, J. R., & Griepentrog, G. J. (2001). Absolute pitch in infant auditory learning: Evidence for developmental reorganization. *Developmental Psychology, 37*(1) Article 1.

Saffran, J. R., & Kirkham, N. Z. (2018). Infant statistical learning. *Annual Review of Psychology, 69*(1), https://doi.org/10.1146/annurev-psych-122216-011805.

Saffran, J. R., Newport, E. L., & Aslin, R. N. (1996). Word segmentation: The role of distributional cues. *Journal of Memory and Language, 35*(4) Article 4.

Sanes, D. H., & Woolley, S. M. N. (2011). A behavioral framework to guide research on central auditory development and plasticity. *Neuron, 72*(6), https://doi.org/10.1016/j.neuron.2011.12.005.

Schapiro, A. C., Gregory, E., Landau, B., McCloskey, M., & Turk-Browne, N. B. (2014). The necessity of the medial temporal lobe for statistical learning. *Journal of Cognitive Neuroscience, 26*(8), https://doi.org/10.1162/jocn_a_00578.

Schlichting, M. L., Guarino, K. F., Schapiro, A. C., Turk-Browne, N. B., & Preston, A. R. (2017). Hippocampal structure predicts statistical learning and associative inference abilities during development. *Journal of Cognitive Neuroscience, 29*(1), https://doi.org/10.1162/jocn_a_01028.

Schonberg, C., Marcus, G. F., & Johnson, S. P. (2018). The roles of item repetition and position in infants' abstract rule learning. *Infant Behavior and Development, 53*, 64–80. https://doi.org/10.1016/j.infbeh.2018.08.003.

Schulz, E., Wu, C. M., Ruggeri, A., & Meder, B. (2019). Searching for rewards like a child means less generalization and more directed exploration. *Psychological Science, 30*(11), https://doi.org/10.1177/0956797619863663.

Schwarze, S. A., Fandakova, Y., & Lindenberger, U. (2024). Cognitive flexibility across the lifespan: developmental differences in the neural basis of sustained and transient control processes during task switching. *Current Opinion in Behavioral Sciences, 58*, 101395.

Schwarze, S. A., Laube, C., Khosravani, N., Lindenberger, U., Bunge, S. A., & Fandakova, Y. (2023). Does prefrontal connectivity during task switching help or hinder children's performance? *Developmental Cognitive Neuroscience, 60*, 101217.

Shaw, P., Kabani, N., Lerch, J., Eckstrand, K., Lenroot, R., Gogtay, N., ... Wise, S. (2008). Neurodevelopmental trajectories of the human cerebral cortex. *The Journal of Neuroscience: The Official Journal of the Society for Neuroscience, 28*, 3586–3594. https://doi.org/10.1523/JNEUROSCI.5309-07.2008.

Smalle, E. H. M., Muylle, M., Szmalec, A., & Duyck, W. (2017). The different time course of phonotactic constraint learning in children and adults: Evidence from speech errors. *Journal of Experimental Psychology: Learning, Memory, and Cognition, 43*(11), https://doi.org/10.1037/xlm0000405.

Stewart, L., Henson, R., Kampe, K., Walsh, V., Turner, R., & Frith, U. (2003). Brain changes after learning to read and play music. *Neuroimage, 20*(1), https://doi.org/10.1016/S1053-8119(03)00248-9.

Strait, D. L., & Kraus, N. (2014). Biological impact of auditory expertise across the life span: Musicians as a model of auditory learning. *Music: A Window into the Hearing Brain, 308*, 109–121. https://doi.org/10.1016/j.heares.2013.08.004.

Sullivan, M. W., Lewis, M., & Alessandri, S. M. (1992). Cross-age stability in emotional expressions during learning and extinction. *Developmental Psychology, 28*(1), https://doi.org/10.1037/0012-1649.28.1.58.

Sumner, E., Li, A. X., Perfors, A., Hayes, B., Navarro, D., & Sarnecka, B. W. (2019). The Exploration Advantage: Children's instinct to explore allows them to find information that adults miss. *PsyArXiv*. https://doi.org/10.31234/osf.io/h437v.

Sydnor, V. J., Larsen, B., Bassett, D. S., Alexander-Bloch, A., Fair, D. A., Liston, C., ... Satterthwaite, T. D. (2021). Neurodevelopment of the association cortices: Patterns, mechanisms, and implications for psychopathology. *Neuron, 109*(18), https://doi.org/10.1016/j.neuron.2021.06.016.

Takesian, A. E., & Hensch, T. K. (2013). Chapter 1—Balancing plasticity/stability across brain development. Bd. 207, S. In M. M. Merzenich, M. Nahum, & T. M. Van Vleet (Eds.). *(Hrsg.), Progress in brain research* (pp. 3–34). Elsevier. Bd. 207, S. https://doi.org/10.1016/B978-0-444-63327-9.00001-1 Bd. 207, S .

Teinonen, T., Fellman, V., Näätänen, R., Alku, P., & Huotilainen, M. (2009). Statistical language learning in neonates revealed by event-related brain potentials. *BMC Neuroscience, 10*(1), https://doi.org/10.1186/1471-2202-10-21.

Thomas, K. M., Hunt, R. H., Vizueta, N., Sommer, T., Durston, S., Yang, Y., & Worden, M. S. (2004). Evidence of developmental differences in implicit sequence learning: An fMRI study of children and adults. *Journal of Cognitive Neuroscience, 16*(8), https://doi.org/10.1162/0898929042304688.

Thompson-Schill, S. L., Ramscar, M., & Chrysikou, E. G. (2009). Cognition without control: When a little frontal lobe goes a long way. *Current Directions in Psychological Science, 18*(5), https://doi.org/10.1111/j.1467-8721.2009.01648.x.

Tierney, A. T., & Kraus, N. (2013). The ability to tap to a beat relates to cognitive, linguistic, and perceptual skills. *Brain and Language, 124*(3), https://doi.org/10.1016/j.bandl.2012.12.014.

Toyoizumi, T., Miyamoto, H., Yazaki-Sugiyama, Y., Atapour, N., Hensch, T. K., & Miller, K. D. (2013). A theory of the transition to critical period plasticity: Inhibition selectively suppresses spontaneous activity. *Neuron, 80*(1), https://doi.org/10.1016/j.neuron.2013.07.022.

Trachtenberg, J. T., Chen, B. E., Knott, G. W., Feng, G., Sanes, J. R., Welker, E., & Svoboda, K. (2002). Long-term in vivo imaging of experience-dependent synaptic plasticity in adult cortex. *Nature, 420*(6917), https://doi.org/10.1038/nature01273.

Turkeltaub, P. E., Eden, G. F., Jones, K. M., & Zeffiro, T. A. (2002). Meta-analysis of the functional neuroanatomy of single-word reading: Method and validation. *Neuroimage, 16*(3 Part A), https://doi.org/10.1006/nimg.2002.1131.

Unger, K., Ackerman, L., Chatham, C. H., Amso, D., & Badre, D. (2016). Working memory gating mechanisms explain developmental change in rule-guided behavior. *Cognition, 155*, 8–22.

Wang, X., Takano, T., & Nedergaard, M. (2009). Astrocytic calcium signaling: Mechanism and implications for functional brain imaging. Bd. 489, S. In F. Hyder (Ed.). *(Hrsg.), Dynamic brain imaging* (pp. 93–109). Humana Press. Bd. 489, S. http://link.springer.com/10.1007/978-1-59745-543-5_5 Bd. 489, S.

Wenger, E., Brozzoli, C., Lindenberger, U., & Lövdén, M. (2017b). Expansion and renormalization of human brain structure during skill acquisition. *Trends in Cognitive Sciences, 21*(12), https://doi.org/10.1016/j.tics.2017.09.008.

Wenger, E., & Kühn, S. (2021). Cognitive training: An overview of features and applications. In T. Strobach, & J. Karbach (Eds.). *Neuroplasticity* (pp. 69–83)(2). Springer. https://doi.org/10.1007/978-3-030-39292-5_6.

Wenger, E., Kühn, S., Verrel, J., Mårtensson, J., Bodammer, N. C., Lindenberger, U., & Lövdén, M. (2017a). Repeated structural imaging reveals nonlinear progression of experience-dependent volume changes in human motor cortex. *Cerebral Cortex, 27*(5), https://doi.org/10.1093/cercor/bhw141.

Wenger, E., Papadaki, E., Werner, A., Kühn, S., & Lindenberger, U. (2021). Observing plasticity of the auditory system: Volumetric decreases along with increased functional connectivity in aspiring professional musicians. *Cerebral Cortex Communications, 2*(2), https://doi.org/10.1093/texcom/tgab008.

Werchan, D. M., Collins, A. G., Frank, M. J., & Amso, D. (2016). Role of prefrontal cortex in learning and generalizing hierarchical rules in 8-month-old infants. *Journal of Neuroscience, 36*(40).

Werker, J. F., & Hensch, T. K. (2015). Critical periods in speech perception: New directions. *Annual Review of Psychology, 66*, 173–196. https://doi.org/10.1146/annurev-psych-010814-015104.

Wilbrecht, L., Holtmaat, A., Wright, N., Fox, K., & Svoboda, K. (2010). Structural plasticity underlies experience-dependent functional plasticity of cortical circuits. *The Journal of Neuroscience, 30*(14), https://doi.org/10.1523/JNEUROSCI.6403-09.2010.

Wilhelm, I., Diekelmann, S., & Born, J. (2008). Sleep in children improves memory performance on declarative but not procedural tasks. *Learning & Memory, 15*(5), https://doi.org/10.1101/lm.803708.

Woollett, K., & Maguire, E. A. (2011). Acquiring "the knowledge" of London's layout drives structural brain changes. *Current Biology, 21*(24), https://doi.org/10.1016/j.cub.2011.11.018.

Wright, B. A., & Fitzgerald, M. B. (2004). The time course of attention in a simple auditory detection task. *Perception & Psychophysics, 66*(3), https://doi.org/10.3758/BF03194897.

Wymbs, N. F., & Grafton, S. T. (2015). The human motor system supports sequence-specific representations over multiple training-dependent timescales. *Cerebral Cortex, 25*(11), https://doi.org/10.1093/cercor/bhu144.

Xu, F., & Kushnir, T. (2013). Infants are rational constructivist learners. *Current Directions in Psychological Science, 22*(1), https://doi.org/10.1177/0963721412469396.

Yotsumoto, Y., Watanabe, T., & Sasaki, Y. (2008). Different dynamics of performance and brain activation in the time course of perceptual learning. *Neuron, 57*(6), https://doi.org/10.1016/j.neuron.2008.02.034.

Zatorre, R. J., Chen, J. L., & Penhune, V. B. (2007). When the brain plays music: Auditory–motor interactions in music perception and production. *Nature Reviews. Neuroscience, 8*(7), https://doi.org/10.1038/nrn2152.

CHAPTER TWO

Further steps towards a mechanistic functionalist framework for understanding individual differences in language and cognition

Nikole Giovannone* **and Joseph C. Toscano**
Department of Psychological and Brain Sciences, Villanova University
*Corresponding author. e-mail address: nikole.giovannone@villanova.edu

Contents

Abstract

Despite a growing focus on individual differences in cognitive psychology, research in this area is complicated by several issues related to how such differences are defined and measured. These challenges create a significant roadblock for the field. To combat this issue,

Psychology of Learning and Motivation, Volume 81
ISSN 0079-7421, https://doi.org/10.1016/bs.plm.2024.07.003

we argue that the next critical step for language and cognitive science is careful and thorough investigation of the specific mechanisms that drive individual differences. In this chapter, our goal is to extend the process-based mechanistic functional normativist framework and to provide a test case for how researchers can leverage computational modeling to investigate individual differences in cognitive mechanisms (using pattern learning in the serial reaction time task as an example). By shifting our focus to characterizing the mechanisms that drive individual differences in language and cognition, the field stands to advance both theoretical frameworks and methodological approaches for studying these processes.

Human behavior is simultaneously stable enough to lend itself to scientific investigation, yet variable enough that individual differences provide meaningful insights into the functioning of the mind and opportunities to address real-world challenges. As a field, cognitive psychology has tended to focus on group-level differences and factors that researchers can easily manipulate, establishing causal relationships between variables that presumably underlie cognitive processes. This has led to a framework for research that focuses primarily on highly-controlled laboratory experiments that readily lend themselves to such causal inferences.

At the same time, there is a long tradition in cognitive psychology, and in other subfields of psychology, of studying individual differences. Indeed, some of this work dates to the origins of psychology as a science, such as work on intelligence testing (e.g., Spearman, 1904). More recently, there has been renewed interest in characterizing individual differences in order to better understand differences in cognition that may be clinically informative (e.g., McMurray et al., 2023), and to better understand the factors that influence human cognition more broadly across different environmental and cultural contexts (Barrett, 2020; Gutchess & Rajaram, 2023).

Despite this interest in studying individual differences in cognition, the approaches commonly used to study cognitive processes are still centered around paradigms designed to assess group-level effects and factors that can be experimentally manipulated. While there are clear advantages to such experimental approaches, they may not be well-suited to research questions that aim to fully assess the nature of individual differences and the underlying cognitive processes that lead to them.

Moreover, theoretical frameworks for understanding cognition may need to be adjusted to better accommodate research focused on individual differences. Specifically, mechanistic models that give rise to individual differences are needed, along with corresponding tasks or paradigms that can capture variability in those mechanisms. Research in cognitive psychology, and in other areas, tends to seek construct validity by demonstrating that tasks or other instruments designed to measure the same underlying construct are highly correlated with each other. Yet, construct validity alone does not tell us whether the underlying construct is a *mechanistic* aspect of cognition. For example, there may be reliable measures of working memory (e.g., Hockey & Geffen, 2004; Klein & Fiss, 1999; Lo et al., 2012; Unsworth et al., 2005; though see Scharfen et al., 2018), but it is not clear that differences in working memory represent the underlying mechanistic processes that give rise to individual differences in cognition.

Thus, advances in both theoretical frameworks and methodological approaches for studying cognition are needed to fully characterize individual differences and center the field on these meaningful sources of variability. Such advances are critical for understanding cognition generally and for developing better tools to be used in clinical and other applied settings.

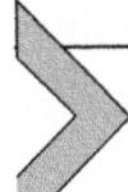

1. Computational modeling as a framework for studying cognitive mechanisms

What would a framework centered on explaining individual differences in cognition look like? As noted above, some of the constructs developed for studying group-level effects and experimentally-manipulated variables may not provide clear links to underlying mechanisms, or may not be well-suited to characterizing individual differences in cognition. On the other hand, some factors lend themselves well to a mechanistic framework. Learning rate, for example, is a promising candidate for a meaningful mechanistic variable that may account for individual differences in cognition across various contexts. It applies to a wide range of cognitive processes and corresponding tasks, and it is potentially variable between but stable within individuals. Moreover, it can be instantiated in process-based models of cognition.

Indeed, *computational models* of cognition provide a rich toolkit and set of theoretical concepts for investigating the mechanisms underlying cognition from an individual differences standpoint. Computational models are advantageous because they require the modeler to make their predictions specific and quantifiable, they can be used to study a wide range of processes, and they offer a link between theoretical concepts and data from human subjects. Different computational frameworks have different advantages and disadvantages (see McClelland, 2009 for an overview). Here, we focus on connectionist (neural network) modeling, which has a rich history in cognitive psychology, and, as a result, provides a well-developed theoretical framework and approach for studying different aspects of cognition. These include distinctions between different types of representations (localist vs. distributed), types of learning (unsupervised vs. self-supervised vs. supervised), and information flow (bottom-up vs. top-down connections in models).

Moreover, connectionist models instantiate, as model parameters, variables that may be of interest in developing theories focused on mechanisms. Using the example above, learning rate is a parameter in most connectionist models that implement some form of learning. Learning rate corresponds to the rate at which connection weights in the network change as a consequence of experience with different inputs and outputs. Thus, learning rate may represent both a model parameter that is well described by connectionist theory and a variable that could describe stable individual differences in cognition. By developing tasks and paradigms that can be simulated using a connectionist network and assessing whether variability in those tasks can be explained by varying this parameter, we can begin to establish learning rate (or other variables) as meaningful mechanistic factors describing individual differences in cognition.

1.1 More steps "towards a functionalist psycholinguistics of individual differences, development, and disorders"

In a recent paper, McMurray et al. (2023) outlined a mechanistic functional normativist perspective on language processing that highlights many of these issues. That framework is described in detail below. Our goal in this piece is to advance the framework developed by McMurray et al. in order to move toward a model for research in cognitive psychology that is centered on individual differences, which are defined as stable, meaningful, and value-neutral differences in cognitive processes that are linked to specific mechanisms that underlie cognition. We hope that this change in the paradigms we use to study cognition will allow us to better understand individual differences, and, as a result, advance theories about cognition more broadly.

As McMurray et al. did, we focus primarily on studies of individual differences in speech and language processing, though the arguments presented here can apply to other aspects of cognition as well (indeed, in the test case we present, we focus on sequence learning). Our claim is that the next critical step for language science, and for cognitive science more broadly, is careful and thorough investigation of the specific mechanisms that drive individual differences in cognition and behavior. We will illustrate this with a specific example: pattern learning in the serial reaction time (SRT) task (Nissen & Bullemer, 1987), which we link to specific mechanisms instantiated in a computational model (a simple recurrent network [SRN]; Elman, 1990). While we do not make any claims that the SRT task or the SRN are special, we argue that they demonstrate the potential of focusing on tasks that can be linked to specific mechanisms, defined and quantified using computational models that capture the types of general processes that are characteristic of cognition.

We will begin with a review of extant approaches to assessing individual differences in language and cognitive science. Then, we propose a framework for the study of basic mechanisms used for language and cognition within a mechanistic functional normativist perspective (cf. McMurray et al., 2023). Lastly, we present data assessing individual variability in the SRT task and preliminary results from a model designed to measure the mechanisms that lead to variability in performance on the task. We conclude with suggestions for the field to move forward with the development of theoretical frameworks and methodological approaches for studying individual differences in cognitive processes.

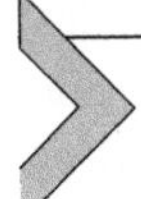

2. Group differences and individual variation in psychological research

Historically, psychological research has fallen into two camps: experimental psychology and correlational psychology (Cronbach, 1957). Experimental psychology is generally associated with the manipulation of some number of independent variables, such as experimental condition or group assignment, and the subsequent measurement of the effects of those manipulations on some number of dependent variables. This approach has tended to emphasize internal validity at the expense of external validity, and is common in areas such as cognitive psychology.

One perceived benefit of the experimental approach is that averaging data from multiple research subjects who have received the same experimental treatment should, in theory, reduce noise in the data to achieve a more stable estimate of the differences between groups. In this context, "noise" includes individual variability in behavior or performance, whereas the "signals" of interest are underlying mechanisms that are common across individuals. Efforts to mitigate variability between groups (or experimental conditions within groups) are also often taken, including strategies like careful selection of research subjects and tight control of the research environment, both of which can help to boost the ability of the researcher to draw statistically valid conclusions.

On the other hand, the correlational approach focuses on examining the relationships between variables that are not manipulated, either because it is infeasible to manipulate the variables of interest or because the research questions do not require it. Rather, correlational work tends to explore more naturally occurring relationships. In contrast to experimental methods, correlational methods often center the individual differences that might be seen as "noise" from an experimentalist perspective. As a result, they tend to be higher in external validity than experimental approaches. By uncovering the relationships between certain variables, such as specific traits and behaviors, correlational research (especially research related to human cognition) often seeks to describe the patterns in the natural variability that is present in the data. The correlational approach therefore not only explicitly acknowledges the variation between individuals, but seeks to quantify it as well.

While psychology has, in general, been more focused on quantifying group-level effects—for both experimental and correlational approaches—large bodies of work that instead center individual differences have emerged in parallel. Some of the first forays into quantifying individual differences in cognition came as early as the late 19th and early 20th centuries from the field of intelligence testing. The primary goal of early measures of intelligence, like the Binet-Simon Scale and the Stanford-Binet Intelligence Scale, was to quantify individuals' cognitive abilities on a scale that offered straightforward comparisons between individuals (Boake, 2002). Many of these early measures were aligned with ideas from Spearman's theory of general intelligence, a factor that was proposed to predict an individual's performance across a range of cognitive tasks (Spearman, 1904).

The idea of a centralized general intelligence, often referred to as "g", suggests a singular mechanism that leads to individual differences in cognition (i.e., a single dimension along which individuals can differ that has high explanatory power for their behavior). In contrast, Gardner's theory of multiple intelligences (1983) questioned that idea, instead proposing that intelligence is multifaceted and that individuals' cognitive abilities can vary along multiple dimensions. Gardner's theory has grown over time to include nine types of independently operating intelligences (Gardner, 1999), including a specific linguistic intelligence. However, empirical support for the theory is lacking (Waterhouse, 2006, 2023), perhaps in part due to difficulty in isolating measures of each proposed intelligence (Allix, 2000; Chen, 2004). Furthermore, many of the different types of intelligences have been found to be intercorrelated (Castejon et al., 2010; Visser et al., 2006), suggesting that they are not tapping distinct processes. Thus, while it seems likely that multiple mechanisms underlie cognitive processing, the specific aspects suggested by Gardner's theory may not map onto those mechanisms.

2.1 Cognitive and linguistic testing in clinical populations

The approach taken by most intelligence scales, like those described above, is essentially mass testing. In order to derive a more generalized measure of intelligence, multiple tasks are administered, and their results are averaged together to form a composite score. Binet and Simon went so far as to say that "a particular test isolated from the rest is of little value," and that "one test signifies nothing" (Binet & Simon, 1916, p. 329).

This approach has been carried over to subfields that have more direct clinical applications, such as neuropsychology and communication disorders. The overall approach of using a series of tasks informing a composite score is still a hallmark of many standardized test batteries used in these subfields. However, the goal of clinical testing is focused on assessment and treatment of the individual, not assessing population-level distributions of individual variation.

At its core, a clinical evaluation is a case study in individual differences. Standardized assessments used in clinical fields like neuropsychology and speech-language pathology are designed to quantify an individual's relative strengths and weaknesses compared to the test's normative sample. Neuropsychologists and speech-language pathologists alike use batteries of standardized tests to assess a variety of cognitive skills, including language, memory, attention, motor skills, emotional and social functioning, and more. The results of these batteries serve a variety of purposes, including making diagnoses, tracking progression of various conditions, and planning treatment for individuals.

Given the clinical applications of these tests, the full range of performance is often not given as much attention compared to the lower range of performance. Historically, standardized assessments were often used to determine an individual's eligibility for services in a binary way (for examples in speech-language pathology, see Betz et al., 2013; Spaulding et al., 2006), meaning that individuals might only qualify for services if they score below a certain threshold (usually 1–2 standard deviations below the mean; see Selin et al., 2019 for discussion of ranges). While the relative score below this threshold might have offered clinical utility for planning treatment, the full range of variability in performance was typically only relevant in that it allowed for the mean and standard deviation of the normative sample to be calculated. This strict dichotomy (i.e., that only individuals scoring below threshold receive services) is not often maintained in today's clinical landscape, but rather multiple sources of information (including case history, teacher and parent reports, criterion-based testing, and more) are considered for clinical decision-making (American Speech-Language-Hearing Association, 2004). However, it is still the case that both clinical and research resources tend to be focused on the lower end of the range, rather than the full range of performance.

2.2 Contemporary approaches to individual differences in language and cognition

The classic work and clinical practices described above contrast with many approaches used in current work focused on individual differences. Rather than attempting to identify a singular factor that describes cognition, for example, current research often branches out to quantify multiple, potentially more specific, trait-like constructs, including constructs such as working memory, vocabulary, attention switching, decision making, problem solving, error monitoring, and more. These constructs, which are often assumed to reflect something stable and trait-like about an individual, may then be assessed for potential relationships with other trait-like measures, or to performance on a task thought to tap some process of interest (for example, aspects of perception, learning, or language processing). This approach is reminiscent of similar approaches that have been successful in personality psychology for identifying stable personality traits (e.g., the five-factor model; see Soto & Jackson, 2013, for review).

For example, work in the language sciences has leveraged this approach to explore the relationships between potentially more trait-like measures like overall language ability and lexical processes during speech perception (e.g., Colby et al., 2018; Giovannone & Theodore 2021a, 2021b), as well as relationships between executive functioning capabilities like attention switching (e.g., Colby et al., 2018; Scharenborg et al., 2015) or inhibitory control (e.g., Kim et al., 2020) and perceptual adaptation processes, to name a few. Individual differences research in domains other than language has sought to explore the connections between potential trait-like measures like working memory capacity and intelligence (e.g., Colom et al., 2005;

Engle et al., 1999; Hockey & Geffen, 2004; Just & Carpenter, 1992; Kane et al., 2004), arithmetic ability (e.g., Hitch et al., 2001; Siegel & Ryan, 1989), and reading comprehension (e.g., Daneman & Carpenter, 1980), for example.

3. Current challenges in individual differences research

Despite its growing presence in the literature, individual differences research faces several challenges. In the domain of working memory, for example, debates regarding how working memory is defined contribute to challenges in quantifying stable differences across individuals. While some researchers equate the concepts of working memory and short-term memory, using the terms interchangeably to refer to the capacity to hold information for later use while engaging in other cognitive processes, others draw a distinction between the two, stipulating that these terms refer to separate processes that operate at different time scales (e.g., Jarrold & Towse, 2006). This variability in the definition of working memory makes it difficult to use it as a stable, trait-like construct to study variability between individuals.

Another challenge is that there are multiple ways to operationalize working memory in the context of an experimental task or assessment. Tasks like n-back, various span tasks (e.g., digit span, reading span, operation span, etc.), non-word repetition, free recall, and others have all been used to quantify individual differences in working memory, either independently or as contributors to a composite-type score. These tasks could tap into the same underlying construct(s) or they might measure different (but overlapping) constructs. These differences in construct definition and task use have the potential to yield conflicting results based on the measure of working memory used (e.g., Jaeggi et al., 2010; Kane et al., 2007; Sánchez-Cubillo et al., 2009). In turn, this makes it difficult to assess the range of individual differences in aspects of cognition like working memory.

These challenges are reflective of an overall theme in individual differences research, which is that we often have a poor understanding of what the tasks used in research on language and cognition are actually measuring. At minimum, a task used for individual differences research should (1) measure the construct it is intended to measure, (2) not measure other constructs (i.e., have discriminant validity), (3) vary among individuals in the population, and (4) measure something that is stable about the individual completing the task. However, assuming these conditions to be true is often premature, or even unfounded, creating a significant roadblock for developing theories centered around individual differences in language and cognition.

Continuing with our example of working memory, the degree to which a single task is a "good" measure of working memory is often unknown. Efforts to correlate individuals' performance across multiple tasks purported to measure working memory has yielded mixed results (e.g., Jaeggi et al., 2010; Kane et al., 2007; Sánchez-Cubillo et al., 2009; Unsworth et al., 2005). Some measures of working memory are thought to be moderately stable measures of an individual's performance (e.g., Hockey & Geffen, 2004; Klein & Fiss, 1999; Lo et al., 2012; Unsworth et al., 2005), though their stability can be difficult to assess due to strong practice effects in many tasks (Scharfen et al., 2018). As a result, it is unclear whether working memory provides a theoretically useful construct for studying individual differences in cognition.

A substantial portion of working memory research attempts to mitigate some of these issues by taking to heart Binet and Simon's opinion that "one test signifies nothing" (1916, p. 329), utilizing multiple and/or composite measures of working memory. However, the practice of using multiple tasks to quantify a single construct is not always a given in other domains. For example, much of today's individual differences research in language can depend on singular tasks to represent a construct, many of which are not psychometrically validated. Although standardized tests of many linguistic processes exist, not all are well-suited for use in the context of individual differences research. Many standardized tests of linguistic functioning are validated for specific populations. For example, the Clinical Evaluations of Language Fundamentals (CELF; Wiig, Semel, & Secord, 2013) and the Test of Word Reading Efficiency (TOWRE; Torgesen, Wagner, & Rashotte, 2012) are often used in individual differences research (e.g., Fischer-Baum et al., 2018; Giovannone & Theodore, 2021a, 2021b; McMurray et al., 2014; Theodore et al., 2020), but are only validated up to ages 21 and 24, respectively.

Other commonly used standardized language measures like the Peabody Picture Vocabulary Test (PPVT; Dunn & Dunn, 1997) and the Woodcock-Johnson Oral Language Battery (WJ OL; Woodcock, McGrew, Schrank, & Mather, 2007) are validated through age 90. While this much wider age range certainly makes these test batteries more broadly applicable for individual differences research, paywalls and other regulations can create additional challenges for their implementation. Many standardized tests are licensed by for-profit companies, which can create both financial barriers to access and barriers to using these tasks in online settings (see Drown et al., 2023, for discussion). For many of these reasons, individual differences researchers might seek to use alternative measures with fewer barriers for implementation, often at the cost of using a task that is not psychometrically validated.

3.1 Psychometric validation

Two assumptions are implicit in the work outlined above: (1) the assumption that tasks measure a specific and known construct, and (2) that they reflect something truly stable and trait-like about a person's performance. The first assumption relates to a task's *construct validity*, which reflects the extent to which the task is measuring what it is proposed to measure. One way to assess construct validity is by comparing whether individuals' performance on one task correlates with their performance on a different task that is proposed to measure the same construct (a subtype of construct validity known as *convergent validity*). If individuals perform similarly on both tasks, convergent validity is high, and it can be more readily assumed that the tasks are, at the very least, measuring similar constructs. Similarly, the task should not correlate with measures of other constructs (*discriminant validity*).

The second assumption relates to the reliability of the task. A task might be considered reliable if an individual's performance on it is consistent over time (*test-retest reliability*) and across items (*split-half reliability*). High test-retest reliability is particularly relevant for measuring stable individual differences: if individuals perform similarly on a task at multiple time points, it is then more likely that the task is measuring something stable about that individual rather than something about their state during each test session.

While construct validity and test-retest reliability are relatively straightforward to assess, there is a relative dearth of research regarding these properties for many of the tasks that are commonly used in individual differences research (with the exception of standardized tests, which are necessarily psychometrically validated but often inappropriate in the context of individual differences work). Fortunately, a growing body of work (Basu Mallick et al., 2015; Clayards, 2018; Cristia et al., 2016; Farris-Trimble & McMurray, 2013; Giovannone et al., 2023; Hedge et al., 2018; Heffner et al., 2022; Idemaru et al., 2012; Ishida et al., 2016; Strand et al., 2018; Wilbiks et al., 2022) has acknowledged this fundamental challenge in linguistic and cognitive research, and has begun to provide psychometric evaluation of tasks commonly used to measure individual differences.

As might be expected, results related to validity and reliability are quite varied. For example, a number of studies have recently assessed construct validity for measures of speech and language processing. Ishida et al. (2016) found moderate convergent validity for two tasks assessing lexical contributions to speech perception (phonemic restoration and locally time-reversed speech tasks). However, Giovannone and Theodore (2023) found no evidence of convergence across three similar tasks (shortened versions of the same phonemic restoration and locally time-reversed speech tasks, plus a Ganong, 1980, task). Similarly, Strand et al. (2018) found low convergent validity across seven tasks tapping listening effort, including subjective self-ratings, speech recognition and recall measures, and pupillometry-based measures of listening effort. Wilbiks et al. (2022) measured convergent validity across four tasks purported to measure audiovisual integration, using both linguistic (McGurk, audiovisual benefit) and non-linguistic (sound-induced flash illusion, audiovisual integration capacity task) measures. However, they found no evidence of convergence between any of these tasks, regardless of whether they were both linguistic tasks or both non-linguistic tasks.

Other studies have found more evidence for convergent validity for some tasks. Heffner et al. (2022) found variable construct validity across five tasks designed to tap perceptual flexibility in native and non-native speech sound learning contexts. Rather than assessing convergent validity as in the above-described studies, Heffner et al. took the approach of comparing individuals' performance across two different stimulus sets within the same task, finding moderate to high correlations for performance across stimulus sets for three of the five tasks. Similarly, Clayards (2018) found moderate convergent validity in individuals' relative cue-weighting during speech perception, finding that degree of reliance on primary cues to phoneme identity (for example, voice onset time for a /d/-/t/ contrast and frication noise for a /s/-/ʃ / contrast) was correlated across multiple types of contrasts.

Results with respect to test-retest reliability are similarly mixed, though seemingly more promising than results related to construct validity. Strong test-retest reliability has been observed for a number of psycholinguistic tasks, including tasks assessing lexical contributions to speech perception (Giovannone & Theodore, 2023), eye gaze fixations in the visual world paradigm (Farris-Trimble & McMurray, 2013), relative cue weighting during stop consonant perception (Idemaru et al., 2012), and the McGurk effect (Basu Mallick et al., 2015). In all of these cases, participants completed the same task using the same stimuli twice, separated in time by anywhere from one week (Farris-Trimble & McMurray, 2013) to a year (Basu Mallick et al., 2015).

Individuals' performance on these tasks was moderately to strongly correlated. Giovannone and Theodore (2023) observed correlations of r = 0.37, 0.72, and 0.74 for each of their lexical effect tasks (phonemic restoration, Ganong, and locally time-reversed speech, respectively). Farris-Trimble and McMurray (2013) compared multiple aspects of eye gaze fixations to the different stimulus types in the visual world paradigm, finding moderate to strong correlations for aspects of the visual response including, for example, slope of target fixations (r = 0.75). Idemaru et al. (2012) found that individuals' weighting of duration-based cues to stop consonants in Japanese was consistent (r = 0.69), and Basu Mallick et al. (2015) found a strikingly high correlation (r = 0.92) for individuals' performance on a McGurk task with a full year between sessions.

In contrast, other studies have found weaker evidence for test-retest reliability. Hedge et al. (2018) assessed the test-retest reliability of seven tasks commonly used in cognitive psychology (such as the Flanker, Posner, and Stroop tasks) using intraclass correlation (ICC), and found highly variable ICC values for the primary measures that researchers typically extract from these tasks (ranging from 0 to 0.82). Further, Cristia et al. (2016) analyzed thirteen samples of infants, each of which completed a task commonly used in infant speech perception research (for example, habituation to speech sounds), and found overall poor test-retest reliability: only three of the samples showed a significant correlation in performance between sessions (two having done habituation tasks, and the last having done a wordform recognition task). Still, these three correlations were highly variable, with r values of 0.32 and 0.87 for the habituation tasks, and 0.46 for the wordform recognition task.

The overall variability in convergent validity and test-retest reliability described above demonstrates that it may not always be the case that our tasks measure the constructs we think they are measuring or measure something stable about the individual, though we often assume that they do both. Low validity and reliability limit overall generalizability, making it possible that results can only be interpreted within the scope of that specific instance of that specific task, and not the broader construct or individual trait. However, even if we do ensure that a task is indeed measuring some stable construct for an individual, individual differences researchers might still face a potentially more problematic issue—is the proposed task measuring a construct, or is it measuring a mechanism?

3.2 Constructs versus mechanisms

Perhaps the largest theoretical challenge that individual differences research must contend with is what constitutes an individual difference in the first place. A key terminological distinction must be considered here: what is a *construct*, and what is a *mechanism?*

Constructs are measurement-based tools that can help us quantify and understand cognitive processes. For example, working memory is a construct; as outlined above, the phrase "working memory" can invoke different operational definitions and can be measured with several different tasks. Performance on an n-back task and performance on a digit span task can both be described as reflecting working memory capacity despite the differences between these tasks.

But is working memory a *mechanism?* A mechanism is a specific, often low-level process from which differences in behavior can stem. In this chapter, we are specifically considering mechanisms of cognitive processes (i.e., those occurring at the computational and algorithmic levels in Marr's [1982] framework) rather than neural mechanisms (i.e., those occurring at the implementational level). Cognitive mechanisms of working memory, for example, might include processes like encoding. Information encoding is a general process that is characteristic of many cognitive processes, not just those related to memory—for example, auditory information must be encoded for successful speech perception to occur (Toscano, McMurray, et al., 2010). Although we do not focus on specific *neural* mechanisms here, there are cases in which individual differences in such mechanisms may be of interest (e.g., differences in neurotransmitters that give rise to inhibitory processes that may be relevant for evaluating the efficacy of a drug in a clinical trial). The relationship between individual differences in neural mechanisms and the types of cognitive processes we focus on here is likely to be complex and is an important issue for future research under this framework.

Given this, we argue that a construct itself is not necessarily a source of individual differences. Rather, observable differences in constructs, such as working memory, may be the cumulative result of individual differences in a set of more basic mechanisms, including (but not limited to) encoding, inhibition, representational capacity, and more. The same can be said of any construct. Using an example from language science, individual differences in perceptual adaptation to input like an unfamiliar accent, while measurable, might not be most accurately described as an individual difference in adapting to accents. Instead, it may be better described as the cumulative result of variation in low-level cognitive processes like encoding, inhibitory control, and representational capacity, but also initial state (i.e., how much an individual must adjust their representations to be considered "adapted"), relative weighting of bottom-up input versus top-down context, prediction, error evaluation, learning rate, and more.

As mentioned above, a process like encoding, which might vary in its sensitivity on an individual level, might feed into multiple constructs, including working memory and auditory processing, giving rise to measurable individual differences. What is unknown, however, is the extent to which mechanisms like encoding (or learning rate, or prediction, etc.) are stable both within an individual and in the degree to which they contribute similarly to different types of processes.

This idea is not new—in fact, this sort of multi-determinism is one of the cornerstones of McMurray et al.'s (2023) *mechanistic functional normativist* framework of language disorders, and mechanistic functionalism more generally (e.g., Bechtel & Abrahamsen, 2005; Glennan, 1996). The mechanistic functional normativist framework laid out by McMurray et al. describes how, at its core, language is the result of multiple interacting mechanisms (which may include processes like prediction, activation, inhibition, etc.; see McMurray et al., 2023, Fig. 1), which contribute in various combinations to language functions like speech production, speech perception, reading, and more. Individual differences in mechanisms can then feed into observable individual differences on a functional level. For example, a lower learning rate (a potential cognitive mechanism) might lead to differences in speed or accuracy with which an individual adapts to an unfamiliar accent (a function of language). Critically, that same learning rate mechanism might also contribute to functions like first or second language acquisition.

Critically, McMurray et al. (2023) argue that we must move away from the measurement-based framework of individual differences, and instead shift our focus to more sophisticated paradigms that can tap actual underlying processing in order to quantify the range of individual differences in various cognitive mechanisms. They illustrate this point through numerous examples. We review one here: how cochlear implant (CI) users navigate spoken word recognition given reduced access to the bottom-up speech signal.

In general, spoken word recognition is thought to be incremental (Marslen-Wilson, 1987), with potential candidate words in a listener's lexicon

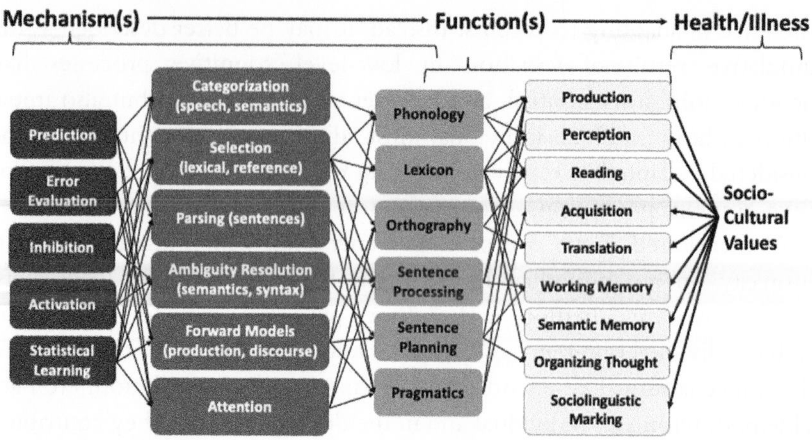

Fig. 1 Same as Fig. 1 from McMurray et al. (2023), showing a visual model representation of McMurray et al.'s mechanistic functional normativist framework as applied to a language disorder. We reiterate their note that the specific mechanisms and functions in this figure are simply meant as examples and not as a complete list. *Figure reproduced with permission.*

changing in relative activation as the spoken word unfolds. Using the visual world paradigm (VWP; Allopenna et al., 1998), researchers can track these changes in activation in real time through an individual's eye movements. In general, listeners without CIs activate a host of potential candidate words during the early stages of spoken word recognition, narrowing in on the target word through inhibition of competitors as the signal unfolds. Using the VWP, Farris-Trimble et al. (2014) found that CI users who became deaf later in life (and so were implanted post-lingually) initially activate a wide range of candidate words during early spoken word recognition, but do not inhibit competitors to the same degree as non-CI users, instead keeping candidates active over a longer timecourse. On the other hand, pre-lingually implanted CI users seem to refrain from initially activating potential candidates, instead taking a "wait and see" approach, allowing more of the speech signal to become available before the activation of a narrower range of potential candidates occurs (McMurray et al., 2017).

Using the VWP allowed McMurray and colleagues (Farris-Trimble et al., 2014; McMurray et al., 2017) to explore differences in terms of the more basic mechanisms of activation and inhibition across these different types of listeners. But despite the observed differences in activation profiles, pre-lingually implanted CI users, post-lingually implanted CI users, and non-CI users can, in general, recognize spoken words. Though they might do so with different levels of accuracy or at different paces (as was the case in Farris-Trimble et al., 2014, and McMurray et al., 2017), measurements like speed and accuracy do not accurately convey the different patterns of activation and inhibition that drive spoken word recognition in these variable groups of listeners. In other words, the measures (i.e., speed/accuracy) don't always speak to the potential driving mechanisms (i.e., patterns of activation).

Another example drawn from some of our own work relates to how listeners with weaker receptive language ability resolve ambiguities in the speech signal (Giovannone & Theodore, 2021a, 2021b). When listeners hear a potentially ambiguous speech sound (like a sound midway between the phonemes /g/ and /k/), lexical context can aid in resolving the ambiguity. For example, when this ambiguous sound is followed by the lexical context *-ift,* listeners are more likely to perceive the word as "gift," in line with lexical context. However, when the same ambiguous sound is instead followed by the lexical context *-iss,* listeners are instead more likely to perceive the word as "kiss" (Ganong, 1980).

We have found that listeners with relatively lower receptive language ability (which is characteristic of diagnoses like developmental language disorder [DLD]) exhibit a larger effect of lexical context on the categorization of an ambiguous phoneme than listeners with relatively higher receptive language ability. This result may be indicative of greater reliance on top-down lexical information versus bottom-up acoustic-phonetic information during speech perception in listeners with relatively lower receptive language ability (Giovannone & Theodore, 2021a, 2021b). However, this result tells us very little about what is mechanistically happening to drive increased lexical reliance. While we initially hypothesized that increased lexical reliance may be a compensatory mechanism for reduced access to acoustic-phonetic detail, a recent experiment revealed no differences in phonemic encoding sensitivity as a function of language ability (Giovannone et al., in prep).

An alternative account might be that listeners with lower receptive language ability experience increased competition during spoken word recognition, perhaps as a result of mechanisms like decreased inhibition of competitors or higher activation decay (McMurray et al., 2010, 2014). The resultant overall higher lexical activation could result in a higher weighting of lexical information during speech perception.

A third potential mechanism for increased lexical reliance in listeners with lower receptive language ability could even be related to a learning mechanism. In this task, listeners have been observed to start off more reliant on lexical information, but shift the relative weights of these cues as they learn from exposure that the acoustic-phonetic cues are likely more informative than lexical cues (Bushong & Jaeger, 2019). A difference in this learning mechanism could theoretically lead to apparent greater reliance on lexical information if listeners with lower receptive language ability do not adapt to the task, but listeners with relatively higher receptive language ability do.

Again, the measure (lexical reliance) doesn't necessarily speak to the mechanism. This is especially true when we consider that the finding of increased lexical reliance in individuals with lower receptive language ability was found using a singular task (a Ganong task). Recall that, as mentioned earlier, there is limited evidence of convergence across tasks designed to assess lexical reliance (Giovannone & Theodore, 2023; Ishida et al., 2016); had we used a different measure of lexical recruitment, the pattern of results may have been different. We may not have identified this apparent difference in lexical recruitment at all, or might be considering different potential mechanisms of individual differences depending on the demands of the specific task.

4. A potential path forward

Given the challenges inherent in current approaches for assessing individual differences, we agree with the call to action put forth by McMurray et al. (2023) for a transition from a measurement-based approach to a process-based approach for individual differences research in both language and cognition more broadly. McMurray et al. specifically call for a shift towards "leveraging more sophisticated paradigms [...] not as measures, but in the context of the theoretical mechanisms that they were originally designed for" (2023, p. 587). In the remainder of this chapter, we will expand upon the mechanistic functional normativist framework proposed by McMurray et al. by providing a potential paradigm and model that may allow for deeper insight into specific mechanisms that drive individual differences in cognition and behavior, specifically investigating individual differences in pattern learning using the SRT task (Nissen & Bullemer, 1987).

4.1 The serial reaction time task as a test case

The SRT task (Nissen & Bullemer, 1987) was designed as a measure of implicit sequence learning. In an SRT experiment, a target stimulus appears on a visual display. The participants' task is to press a button corresponding to the location of that stimulus (for example, which quadrant of a screen the stimulus appeared in) as quickly and accurately as possible. In a typical experiment, stimuli initially appear in a random location on each trial. After some number of random trials, the sequence of stimulus locations becomes fixed without explicitly informing the participant about this change. As the sequence repeats over multiple blocks, participants' reaction time (RT) decreases if they have successfully learned the pattern (i.e., if they can anticipate the next item in the sequence). This decrease is reflective of more than simple practice effects, as disruption of the sequence (i.e., another block of random trials) leads to a subsequent increase in RT, and reintroduction of the sequence after a block of random trials results in a decrease in RT, reflective of implicit sequence learning occurring over the course of the task (Fig. 2).

The SRT task has been used extensively to assess sequential and procedural learning since its introduction (see Schwarb & Schumacher, 2012 for review), including use in individual differences work. Individual variability in SRT task performance has been observed both in terms of magnitude of learning (Misyak, Christiansen, & Tomblin, 2010; Unsworth & Engle, 2005) and learning rate (Unsworth & Engle, 2005). Perhaps unsurprisingly, performance on the SRT task has been found to correlate with aspects of working memory, including visuospatial working memory (Bo et al., 2011) and overall working memory capacity (Frensch & Miner, 1994). While the SRT task has recently been under some scrutiny due to questionable reliability (see meta-analysis by Oliveira et al., 2023), variations of SRT tasks that follow specific characteristics (like specific task format and length) and correction procedures have been found to be acceptably reliable (test-retest $r > 0.50$; Farkas et al., 2024), especially considering the overall lower test-retest reliability often observed in tasks that involve learning.

4.2 Using the SRT task to test the mechanistic functional normativist approach

To assess whether participants' performance on the SRT task can be mapped to a specific mechanism, we simulated the SRT task using a simple recurrent network (SRN; Elman, 1990) and varied the model's learning rate parameter to account for variability among individuals in the size of their SRT effect. An SRN is a recurrent network with a single hidden layer and an additional set of context units that contains a copy of the hidden unit activation from the previous time step. Activation from the context units feeds into the hidden layer on the current time step, providing a short-term memory store for the model (Fig. 3).

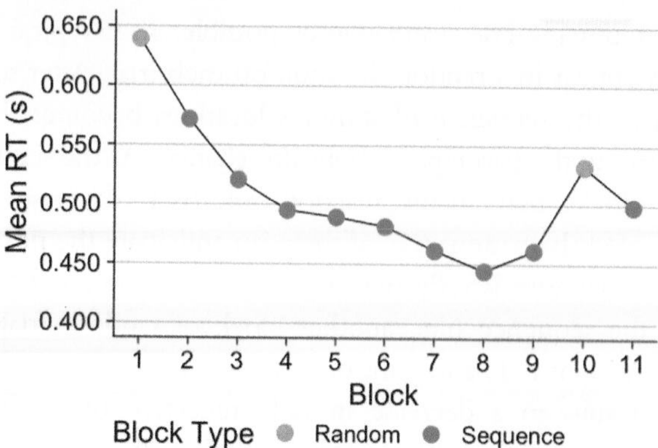

Fig. 2 Data from the SRT experiment described in Section 4.3, showing a typical pattern of results observed over the course of an SRT task. Color represents block type (random sequence versus fixed pattern). Initially, RTs are relatively high. Over time, reaction times decrease, indicative of learning. When the pattern is disrupted, as depicted above by the sequence becoming random in Block 10, reaction times increase, but subsequently decrease again when the pattern is reinstated in Block 11.

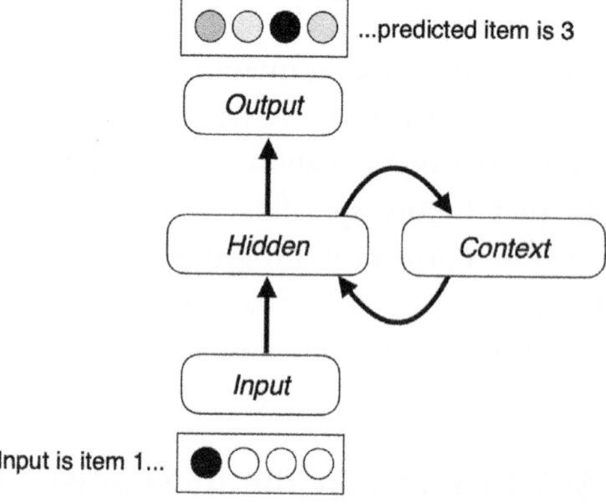

Fig. 3 Schematic representation of the SRN used to model the SRT task. On each trial, one input unit is activated, corresponding to a specific element in the sequence. The target output is the unit corresponding to the next element in the sequence.

SRNs are typically trained using a self-supervised approach in which the target output activation corresponds to the input at the next time step. The structure of the network and the self-supervised learning approach makes the SRN well suited to a variety of sequence processing tasks. For example, Elman (1990) demonstrated that the SRN can learn representations that provide information about word boundaries by predicting sequences of letters, without any explicit information about the locations of those boundaries. Similarly, he demonstrated that the network can learn grammatical classes of words (Elman, 1990) and meaning (Elman, 2004) when given sequences of words as input.

SRNs have also been used to model sequence learning tasks similar to the SRT task described above. Cleeremans and McClelland (1991) demonstrated that an SRN can capture the ability of human participants to learn a finite state grammar that required tracking long-distance dependencies over four time steps. Similarly, Misyak, Christiansen, and Tomblin, 2009 demonstrated that an SRN can learn a grammar with non-adjacent dependencies of the form *aXc*, where *a* and *c* are non-words that co-occur in a sequence and *X* varies. Data from human participants demonstrated larger differences in RT between the first string (e.g., *a*) and the final string (*c*) over the course of exposure to the grammar, indicating that participants learned the non-adjacent dependencies between the strings. An SRN was trained on the same task and demonstrated a similar pattern of results.

SRNs have also been used to study individual differences in performance on the SRT task. Toscano et al. investigated this, specifically looking at differences related to DLD and genetic variation in FOXP2 (Toscano, Mueller, McMurray, & Tomblin, 2010). Data from children with and without DLD suggest that children with DLD take longer to learn the sequence in an SRT task, resulting in a different learning trajectory than children without DLD. Similar patterns are observed for individuals with allelic variations in the FOXP2 gene, which has been linked to language disorders (Lai et al., 2001). Toscano et al. varied a number of SRN parameters (learning rate, number of hidden units, activation strength, etc.) and measured learning over the course of the pattern blocks in the SRT task, providing a comparison of the model's performance with the human data. They then identified the constellation of parameter values that reproduced the learning trajectories observed for each group. Overall, they found that several parameters accounted for differences between children with and without DLD, as well as differences between groups with different FOXP2 alleles. This demonstrates that an SRN can be used to model individual performance in the SRT task and that behavioral measures (i.e., changes in RT in the SRT task) can be linked to specific model parameters using this approach.

In the current set of simulations, we specifically assessed whether one model parameter, learning rate, can account for differences in a single behavioral measure, SRT effect size. Learning rate is one of several parameters that can be varied in the model and might provide insights into basic mechanisms driving individual differences. Others include the number of hidden units (corresponding to representational capacity) and parameters related to the activation functions at each layer (e.g., the temperature parameter in a logistic activation function). While one-to-one mappings between mechanism and behavioral outcomes, like the one we test here, may be uncommon for many of the cognitive processes we are interested in, the current example nonetheless provides an illustration of the approach we propose.

4.3 Data

SRT data were collected from 64 participants, and the SRT effect size for each participant (described below) was used as the target for optimizing the model's learning rate. Participants were recruited from the Villanova University community and were compensated with general psychology course credit. All participants were over the age of 18 years and provided informed consent following Villanova IRB protocols. Ten participants were excluded from analysis on the basis of having a negative SRT effect. All participants reported normal or corrected-to-normal vision. The experiment was completed in a single session and took approximately five minutes.

Participants were seated at a computer in a quiet testing room. The SRT task consisted of a set of four white circle outlines arrayed horizontally on a black background. On each trial, one circle became filled in with white, indicating the target stimulus for that trial. Participants were instructed to press the corresponding key on the keyboard's number bar (one through four, corresponding to the circles' positions from left to right) to indicate which circle was filled. Once the participant gave their response, the fill of the target stimulus disappeared, rendering all circles as outlines. The process then repeated itself for the next trial.

After receiving verbal task instructions from the experimenter and reading written task instructions on the screen, participants were given a set of five randomized warm-up trials to demonstrate their understanding of the task. After the warm-up trials, the main task began with a block of 12 random trials. The random trials were different for each participant. After the initial random block, participants received eight blocks of a 12-trial sequence. This sequence (1, 4, 1, 3, 2, 4, 3, 2, 1, 3, 4, 2) was held constant across all participants. Then, participants received a subsequent random block (which was again fully randomized between participants), followed by a final sequence block. Thus, each participant's data consists of 132 trials (11 blocks $\times$ 12 trials/block).

To calculate each participant's SRT effect, we first calculated the mean RT for correct trials on blocks 9 (pattern block), 10 (random block), and 11 (pattern block), and subtracted the mean RT across blocks 9 and 11 from the mean RT on block 10. Overall, participants SRT effect sizes ranged from less than 1 ms to 309 ms, with a mean effect size of 82 ms and standard deviation of 68 ms, demonstrating a range of SRT effects across the group of participants (Fig. 4).

4.4 Model architecture and training

We then trained SRNs on the same task in order to identify whether differences in learning rate could account for differences in the SRT effect size observed in the human data. The model is a standard SRN consisting of 4 input units, 4 output units, and 15 hidden units (Fig. 2), implemented in MATLAB (Mathworks, Natick, MA). Layers are fully connected via feedforward weights, and the vector of hidden unit activation is copied back to a set of context units via non-tunable connections. A logistic activation function with a temperature of 0.013 is used at both the hidden and output units. Weights are updated via backpropagation (Rumelhart et al., 1986).

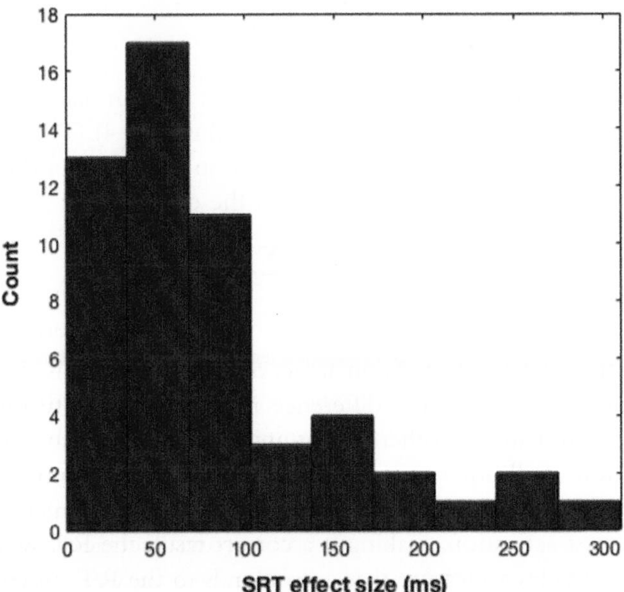

Fig. 4 Histogram of SRT effect sizes (ms).

Before training, the model is initialized with a random set of weights, scaled to $\pm$ 0.3. On each trial, the network is presented with one of the four elements in the sequence by activating the corresponding input node. Its task (i.e., the target output) is to predict the element for the next item in the sequence. The model is trained on the same task as the human participants described above (omitting the warm-up trials): one block (12 trials) with a random sequence, eight blocks (12 trials each) with the fixed sequence pattern, a subsequent random block, and a final sequence block. Thus, as with the data from the human participants, each run of the model consists of 132 trials (11 blocks × 12 trials/block).

To convert model outputs to RT, we followed a procedure similar to previous studies (Cleeremans & McClelland, 1991; Toscano, Mueller, McMurray, & Tomblin, 2010; Misyak, Christiansen, & Tomblin, 2009). We first determined whether the model made a correct response based on which output unit had the greatest activation. If this was the target output, the model was considered to have made a correct response on that trial. For correct trials, we then calculated a Luce choice ratio for the output units by dividing the activation of each output unit by the summed activation across all output units:

$$\hat{o}_j = \frac{o_j}{\sum_{i=1}^{n} o_i} \tag{1}$$

where o is the output activation of a unit, $\hat{o}$ is the normalized activation, and n is the total number of output units (in this case, 4). These values are then converted to RTs by subtracting the mean activation of the incorrect units from the inverse of the activation of the correct unit:

$$RT = \frac{1}{\hat{o}_c} - \frac{\sum_{i=1}^{n} \hat{o}_i}{n} \tag{2}$$

where n is the total number of non-target output units (in this case, 3). This gives a value that reflects the difference in the relative activation of the target output unit and the other output units. If the target activation is high and activation of all other output units is low, the RT will be low. If the activation values are more similar to each other (but the target output still has the highest activation, making it a correct trial), the RT will be high. Thus, this provides a measure that corresponds to the RT values obtained from human participants. SRT effect sizes were computed using the same approach used for human participants.

4.5 Parameter fitting

In order to identify the learning rate parameter that produces a model SRT effect corresponding to an individual participant's SRT effect, a non-linear optimization method was used (fmincon function in MATLAB), which minimized the difference between the SRN effect size and the participant effect size by varying the learning rate parameter. The initial learning rate was set to 0.1 (as in Misyak, Christiansen, & Tomblin, 2009) and was constrained to values between 0 and 100. Because both the initial weights and the particular random sequences in the SRT task introduce stochasticity into the model, the fitting process was repeated 10,000 times for each participant's data, initializing MATLAB's random number generator with different seeds for each simulation run (using the same 10,000 seeds for each participant).

4.6 Results

Before assessing how well learning rate can account for differences in participants' responses, we first discarded model runs that did not yield a valid estimate of the learning rate. On a small proportion of these runs, the optimizer returned an invalid value ("not a number"; 5.93% of runs). More frequently, however, the optimizer returned a value that was close to the lower bound for the learning rate parameter (a learning rate less than 0.001; 46.04% of runs). Because such a low learning rate corresponds to an SRN in which the weights change very little from their initial random values, this did not seem to necessarily represent an accurate estimate of the participant's learning rate, and therefore, these runs were excluded from further analysis.

For the remaining runs, we calculated the average learning rate value for each participant. Fig. 5A shows these values as a function of each participant's SRT effect size. As SRT effect size increases, the estimated learning rate increases. The pattern of results is explained very well by a four-parameter logistic function fit to the average learning rate estimates for each participant, which is shown in the figure as well (RMSE=0.0084).[1] Conceptually, they also align with intuitions about the expected

[1] Note that there is no a priori reason to predict that the relationship between estimated learning rates and SRT effect sizes should follow a logistic function; this function was simply chosen because it illustrates the relationship well for these data. As a result, it is not clear that the extremely good fit of that function to the subject averages is meaningful or would generalize to other mappings between mechanisms and participants' responses.

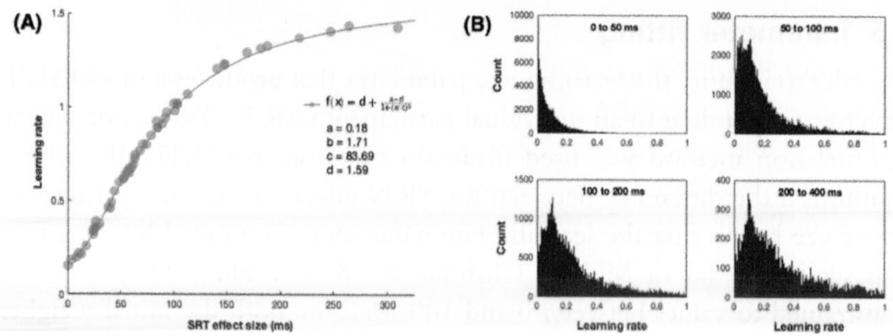

Fig. 5 Average learning rate value per participant. Learning rate calculation is described in Section 4.5. Panel (A) Learning rate values as a function of SRT effect size. Each point represents one participant. Points are jittered to promote visualization. Panel (B) Distribution of learning rate parameter estimates across the analyzed runs, binned by SRT effect sizes.

relationship between learning rate and SRT effect size: participants with faster learning rates should learn the pattern more readily, and therefore, should show larger SRT effects.

Fig. 5B shows the distribution of learning rate parameter estimates across the analyzed runs, binned by SRT effect size (0–50 ms; 50–100 ms; 100–200 ms; 200–400 ms). As expected, the distribution shifts to the right as SRT effect size increases. Overall, these results demonstrate that the learning rate parameter in the SRN corresponds well to individual differences in the size of the learning effect in the SRT task.

4.7 A framework for thinking about basic mechanisms

The experiment and model simulations presented here provide an example of how we can implement the mechanistic functional normativist perspective. The SRT task provides a useful paradigm for studying sequence learning, and it introduces sufficient variability between participants for assessing differences in performance. Note that one factor not considered in the current experiment is the reliability of the SRT effect within an individual participant; additional data demonstrating good test-retest reliability would be needed to establish this as a measure of an individual difference using the criteria proposed here.

The simulations with the SRN model show that the network can learn the sequence in the SRT task similarly to human participants, and further, they demonstrate that the variation in subject performance can be accounted by varying the model's learning rate. This illustrates the key ideas behind the mechanistic functional normativist perspective: a specific task is linked with an underlying mechanism, implemented in a model of the processes involved with the task.

These results can be extended in several ways that may provide further insights. For example, are there other sequence processing tasks that the SRN is well suited to that also produce variation among individuals that can be explained by the model's learning rate? Are there other parameters in the model that can explain differences in performance in the task? Are there other aspects of the SRT task that can be explained by one or more parameters in the model? Does the estimated learning rate for an individual in the SRT task generalize to their learning rate for other tasks described by different neural network models? Many complex aspects of behavior are also likely to depend on multiple mechanisms. Thus, it will be important to extend this approach by identifying how multiple model parameters may give rise to a set of different behavioral variables.

5. Conclusions

Despite a growing focus on individual differences in cognitive psychology, research in this area is complicated by several issues related to how such differences are defined and measured. These challenges culminate in a significant roadblock for the field, which is that the tasks we use are often not suitable for assessing individual differences. In this chapter, our goal has been to provide a framework for mitigating these challenges related to measurement-based approaches by extending the process-based mechanistic functional normativist framework outlined by McMurray et al. (2023).

Specifically, we act on their call for a shift towards the use of paradigms that can provide specific insight into potential mechanisms by providing an example of how we can investigate mechanistic individual differences in cognition using a computational framework. Using the SRT task (Nissen & Bullemer, 1987) as an example, we simulated how individual differences in a potential domain-general mechanism like learning rate relate to differences in subjects' performance in the task. This example is incomplete, however. As described above, there are many ways that our model can be extended to better understand individual differences in sequence learning. Further, there are a multitude of other potential tasks and paradigms that can be leveraged and compared to promote understanding of individual differences in domain-general cognitive processes.

We must also emphasize that, for the purposes of the framework developed here, there is nothing necessarily special about the SRT task and its relationship to cognition. In theory, any task that would allow for analysis of individual differences that are linked to process-based models (like the SRN for the SRT task) would serve just as well. In fact, what is needed to build fully-specified theories based on individual differences in cognition via a mechanistic functional normativist framework is multiple tasks across multiple modalities that all allow for the assessment of similar underlying mechanisms. In developing this framework further, the field can move closer to the goal of uncovering the mechanisms that explain individual differences in language and cognition, and, in turn, advance our understanding of these processes more broadly.

Acknowledgments

We would like to thank Kimberly Halvorson, John Kurtz, Bob McMurray, and Rachel Theodore for valuable discussions of these issues. We would also like to thank the members of the Word Recognition and Auditory Perception Lab at Villanova for their assistance with data collection. This material is based upon work supported by the National Science Foundation under Grant No. 1945069. NG is supported by a Mendel Science Experience Postdoctoral Fellowship from Villanova University.

References

Allix, N. M. (2000). The theory of multiple intelligences: A case of missing cognitive matter. *Australian Journal of Education, 44*(3), 272–288. https://doi.org/10.1177/000494410004400306.

Allopenna, P. D., Magnuson, J. S., & Tanenhaus, M. K. (1998). Tracking the time course of spoken word recognition using eye movements: Evidence for continuous mapping models. Article 4 *Journal of Memory and Language, 38*(4), https://doi.org/10.1006/jmla.1997.2558.

American Speech-Language-Hearing Association. (2004). *Preferred practice patterns for the profession of speech-language pathology* [Preferred Practice Patterns]. Available from www.asha.org/policy/.

Barrett, H. C. (2020). Deciding what to observe: Thoughts for a post-WEIRD generation. *Evolution and Human Behavior, 41*(5), 445–453. https://doi.org/10.1016/j.evolhumbehav.2020.05.006.

Bechtel, W., & Abrahamsen, A. (2005). Explanation: A mechanist alternative. *Studies in History and Philosophy of Science Part C: Studies in History and Philosophy of Biological and Biomedical Sciences, 36*(2), 421–441. https://doi.org/10.1016/j.shpsc.2005.03.010.

Betz, S. K., Eickhoff, J. R., & Sullivan, S. F. (2013). Factors influencing the selection of standardized tests for the diagnosis of specific language impairment. *Language, Speech, and Hearing Services in Schools, 44*(2), 133–146. https://doi.org/10.1044/0161-1461(2012/12-0093).

Binet, A., & Simon, T. (1916). New investigation upon the measure of the intellectual level among school children. (L'Année Psych., 1911, pp. 145-201) (Trans.). In E. S. Kite (Ed.). *The development of intelligence in children (The Binet-Simon Scale)* (pp. 274–329). Williams & Wilkins Co. (Trans.). https://doi.org/10.1037/11069-005 (Trans.).

Bo, J., Jennett, S., & Seidler, R. D. (2011). Working memory capacity correlates with implicit serial reaction time task performance. *Experimental Brain Research, 214*(1), 73–81. https://doi.org/10.1007/s00221-011-2807-8.

Boake, C. (2002). From the Binet–Simon to the Wechsler–Bellevue: Tracing the history of intelligence testing. *Journal of Clinical and Experimental Neuropsychology, 24*(3), 383–405. https://doi.org/10.1076/jcen.24.3.383.981.

Bushong, W., & Jaeger, T. F. (2019). Dynamic re-weighting of acoustic and contextual cues in spoken word recognition. *The Journal of the Acoustical Society of America, 146*(2), https://doi.org/10.1121/1.5119271.

Castejon, J. L., Perez, A. M., & Gilar, R. (2010). Confirmatory factor analysis of Project Spectrum activities. A second-order *g* factor or multiple intelligences? *Intelligence, 38*(5), 481–496. https://doi.org/10.1016/j.intell.2010.07.002.

Chen, J. Q. (2004). Theory of multiple intelligences: Is it a scientific theory? *Teachers College Record, 106*(1), 17–23.

Clayards, M. (2018). Differences in cue weights for speech perception are correlated for individuals within and across contrasts. *The Journal of the Acoustical Society of America, 144*(3), EL172–EL177. https://doi.org/10.1121/1.5052025.

Cleeremans, A., & McClelland, J. L. (1991). Learning the structure of event sequences. *Journal of Experimental Psychology: General, 120*(3), 235–253. https://doi.org/10.1037/0096-3445.120.3.235.

Colby, S., Clayards, M., & Baum, S. (2018). The role of lexical status and individual differences for perceptual learning in younger and older adults. Article 8 *Journal of Speech, Language, and Hearing Research, 61*(8), https://doi.org/10.1044/2018_JSLHR-S-17-0392.

Colom, R., Flores-Mendoza, C., Quiroga, M. Á., & Privado, J. (2005). Working memory and general intelligence: The role of short-term storage. *Personality and Individual Differences, 39*(5), 1005–1014. https://doi.org/10.1016/j.paid.2005.03.020.

Cristia, A., Seidl, A., Singh, L., & Houston, D. (2016). Test–retest reliability in infant speech perception tasks. *Infancy: The Official Journal of the International Society on Infant Studies, 21*(5), https://doi.org/10.1111/infa.12127.

Cronbach, L. J. (1957). The two disciplines of scientific psychology. *American Psychologist, 12*(11), 671–684. https://doi.org/10.1037/h0043943.

Daneman, M., & Carpenter, P. A. (1980). Individual differences in working memory and reading. *Journal of Verbal Learning and Verbal Behavior, 19*(4), 450–466. https://doi.org/10.1016/S0022-5371(80)90312-6.

Drown, L., Giovannone, N., Pisoni, D. B., & Theodore, R. M. (2023). Validation of two measures for assessing English vocabulary knowledge on web-based testing platforms: Long-form assessments. *Linguistics Vanguard, 9*(1), 113–124. https://doi.org/10.1515/lingvan-2022-0115.

Dunn, L. M., & Dunn, L. M. (1997). *PPVT-III: Peabody picture vocabulary test* (3rd ed.). MN: AGS: Circle Pines.

Elman, J. L. (1990). Finding structure in time. *Cognitive Science, 14*(2), 179–211. https://doi.org/10.1207/s15516709cog1402_1.

Elman, J. L. (2004). An alternative view of the mental lexicon. *Trends in Cognitive Sciences, 8*(7), 301–306. https://doi.org/10.1016/j.tics.2004.05.003.

Engle, R. W., Laughlin, J. E., Tuholski, S. W., & Conway, A. R. A. (1999). Working memory, short-term memory, and general fluid intelligence: A latent-variable approach. *Journal of Experimental Psychology: General, 128*(3), 309–331. https://doi.org/10.1037/0096-3445.128.3.309 Scopus.

Farkas, B. C., Krajcsi, A., Janacsek, K., & Nemeth, D. (2024). The complexity of measuring reliability in learning tasks: An illustration using the Alternating Serial Reaction Time Task. *Behavior Research Methods, 56*(1), 301–317. https://doi.org/10.3758/s13428-022-02038-5.

Farris-Trimble, A., McMurray, B., Cigrand, N., & Tomblin, J. B. (2014). The process of spoken word recognition in the face of signal degradation. *Journal of Experimental Psychology: Human Perception and Performance, 40*(1), 308–327. https://doi.org/10.1037/a0034353.

Farris-Trimble, A., & McMurray, B. (2013). Test-retest reliability of eye tracking in the visual world paradigm for the study of real-time spoken word recognition. *Journal of Speech, Language, and Hearing Research: JSLHR, 56*(4). https://doi.org/10.1044/1092-4388(2012/12-0145).

Fischer-Baum, S., Kook, J. H., Lee, Y., Ramos-Nuñez, A., & Vannucci, M. (2018). Individual differences in the neural and cognitive mechanisms of single word reading. *Frontiers in Human Neuroscience, 12*. https://doi.org/10.3389/fnhum.2018.00271.

Frensch, P. A., & Miner, C. S. (1994). Effects of presentation rate and individual differences in short-term memory capacity on an indirect measure of serial learning. *Memory & Cognition, 22*(1), 95–110. https://doi.org/10.3758/BF03202765.

Ganong, W. F. (1980). Phonetic categorization in auditory word perception. *Journal of Experimental Psychology: Human Perception and Performance, 6*(1), https://doi.org/10.1037/0096-1523.6.1.110.

Gardner, H. (1983). *Frames of mind: The theory of multiple intelligences*. Basic Books.

Gardner, H. (1999). *Intelligence reframed: Multiple intelligences for the 21st century*. Basic Books.

Giovannone, N., Cummings, S. N., García-Sierra, A., Magnuson, J. S., & Theodore, R. M. (In preparation.) Early neural encoding of acoustic-phonetic information is consistent across language ability.

Giovannone, N., & Theodore, R. M. (2021a). Individual differences in lexical contributions to speech perception. *Journal of Speech, Language, and Hearing Research, 64*(3), https://doi.org/10.1044/2020_JSLHR-20-00283.

Giovannone, N., & Theodore, R. M. (2021b). Individual differences in the use of acoustic-phonetic versus lexical cues for speech perception. *Frontiers in Communication, 6*, 120. https://doi.org/10.3389/fcomm.2021.691225.

Giovannone, N., & Theodore, R. M. (2023). Do individual differences in lexical reliance reflect states or traits? *The Journal of the Acoustical Society of America, 151*(4), https://doi.org/10.1121/10.0011280.

Glennan, S. (1996). Mechanisms and the nature of causation. *Erkenntnis, 44*(1), https://doi.org/10.1007/BF00172853.

Gutchess, A., & Rajaram, S. (2023). Consideration of culture in cognition: How we can enrich methodology and theory. *Psychonomic Bulletin & Review, 30*(3), 914–931. https://doi.org/10.3758/s13423-022-02227-5.

Hedge, C., Powell, G., & Sumner, P. (2018). The reliability paradox: Why robust cognitive tasks do not produce reliable individual differences. *Behavior Research Methods, 50*(3), 1166–1186. https://doi.org/10.3758/s13428-017-0935-1.

Heffner, C. C., Fuhrmeister, P., Luthra, S., Mechtenberg, H., Saltzman, D., & Myers, E. B. (2022). Reliability and validity for perceptual flexibility in speech. *Brain and Language, 226*, 105070. https://doi.org/10.1016/j.bandl.2021.105070.

Hitch, G. J., Towse, J. N., & Hutton, U. (2001). What limits children's working memory span? Theoretical accounts and applications for scholastic development. *Journal of Experimental Psychology: General, 130*(2), 184–198. https://doi.org/10.1037/0096-3445.130.2.184.

Hockey, A., & Geffen, G. (2004). The concurrent validity and test-retest reliability of a visuospatial working memory task. *Intelligence, 32*(6), 591–605. https://doi.org/10.1016/j.intell.2004.07.009.

Idemaru, K., Holt, L. L., & Seltman, H. (2012). Individual differences in cue weights are stable across time: The case of Japanese stop lengths. *The Journal of the Acoustical Society of America, 132*(6), 3950–3964. https://doi.org/10.1121/1.4765076.

Ishida, M., Samuel, A. G., & Arai, T. (2016). Some people are "more lexical" than others. *Cognition, 151*, 68–75. https://doi.org/10.1016/j.cognition.2016.03.008.

Jaeggi, S. M., Buschkuehl, M., Perrig, W. J., & Meier, B. (2010). The concurrent validity of the *N*-back task as a working memory measure. *Memory, 18*(4), 394–412. https://doi.org/10.1080/09658211003702171.

Jarrold, C., & Towse, J. N. (2006). Individual differences in working memory. *Neuroscience, 139*(1), 39–50. https://doi.org/10.1016/j.neuroscience.2005.07.002.

Just, M. A., & Carpenter, P. A. (1992). A capacity theory of comprehension: Individual differences in working memory. *Psychological Review, 99*(1), 122–149.

Kane, M. J., Conway, A. R. A., Miura, T. K., & Colflesh, G. J. H. (2007). Working memory, attention control, and the n-back task: A question of construct validity. *Journal of Experimental Psychology: Learning, Memory, and Cognition, 33*(3), 615–622. https://doi.org/10.1037/0278-7393.33.3.615.

Kane, M. J., Hambrick, D. Z., Tuholski, S. W., Wilhelm, O., Payne, T. W., & Engle, R. W. (2004). The generality of working memory capacity: A latent-variable approach to verbal and visuospatial memory span and reasoning. *Journal of Experimental Psychology: General, 133*(2), 189–217. https://doi.org/10.1037/0096-3445.133.2.189.

Kim, D., Clayards, M., & Kong, E. J. (2020). Individual differences in perceptual adaptation to unfamiliar phonetic categories. *Journal of Phonetics, 81*, 100984. https://doi.org/10.1016/j.wocn.2020.100984.

Klein, K., & Fiss, W. H. (1999). The reliability and stability of the turner and Engle working memory task. *Behavior Research Methods, Instruments, & Computers, 31*(3), 429–432. https://doi.org/10.3758/BF03200722.

Lai, C. S. L., Fisher, S. E., Hurst, J. A., Vargha-Khadem, F., & Monaco, A. P. (2001). A forkhead-domain gene is mutated in a severe speech and language disorder. *Nature, 413*(6855), 519–523. https://doi.org/10.1038/35097076.

Lo, A. H. Y., Humphreys, M., Byrne, G. J., & Pachana, N. A. (2012). Test–retest reliability and practice effects of the Wechsler Memory Scale-III. *Journal of Neuropsychology, 6*(2), 212–231. https://doi.org/10.1111/j.1748-6653.2011.02023.x.

Mallick, D. B., Magnotti, J. F., & Beauchamp, M. S. (2015). Variability and stability in the McGurk effect: Contributions of participants, stimuli, time, and response type. *Psychonomic Bulletin & Review, 22*(5), 1299–1307. https://doi.org/10.3758/s13423-015-0817-4.

Marr, D. (1982). *Vision: A Computational Investigation into the Human Representation and Processing of Visual Information*. San Francisco, CA: W. H. Freeman.

Marslen-Wilson, W. D. (1987). Functional parallelism in spoken word-recognition. *Cognition, 25*(1), https://doi.org/10.1016/0010-0277(87)90005-9.

McClelland, J. L. (2009). The place of modeling in cognitive science. *Topics in Cognitive Science, 1*(1), 11–38. https://doi.org/10.1111/j.1756-8765.2008.01003.x.

McMurray, B., Baxelbaum, K. S., Colby, S., & Bruce Tomblin, J. (2023). Understanding language processing in variable populations on their own terms: Towards a functionalist psycholinguistics of individual differences, development, and disorders. *Applied Psycholinguistics, 44*(4), https://doi.org/10.1017/S0142716423000255.

McMurray, B., Farris-Trimble, A., & Rigler, H. (2017). Waiting for lexical access: Cochlear implants or severely degraded input lead listeners to process speech less incrementally. *Cognition, 169*, 147–164. https://doi.org/10.1016/j.cognition.2017.08.013.

McMurray, B., Munson, C., & Tomblin, J. B. (2014). Individual differences in language ability are related to variation in word recognition, not speech perception: Evidence from eye movements. *Journal of Speech, Language, and Hearing Research: JSLHR, 57*(4), https://doi.org/10.1044/2014_JSLHR-L-13-0196.

McMurray, B., Samelson, V. M., Lee, S. H., & Bruce Tomblin, J. (2010). Individual differences in online spoken word recognition: Implications for SLI. *Cognitive Psychology, 60*(1), https://doi.org/10.1016/j.cogpsych.2009.06.003.

Misyak, J. B., Christiansen, M. H., & Tomblin, J. B. (2009). Statistical Learning of Nonadjacencies Predicts On-line Processing of Long-Distance Dependencies in Natural Language. *Proceedings of the Annual Meeting of the Cognitive Science Society, 31.*

Misyak, J. B., Christiansen, M. H., & Tomblin, J. B. (2010). On-line individual differences in statistical learning predict language processing. *Frontiers in Psychology, 1.* https://doi.org/10.3389/fpsyg.2010.00031.

Nissen, M. J., & Bullemer, P. (1987). Attentional requirements of learning: Evidence from performance measures. *Cognitive Psychology, 19*(1), https://doi.org/10.1016/0010-0285(87)90002-8.

Oliveira, C. M., Hayiou-Thomas, M. E., & Henderson, L. M. (2023). The reliability of the serial reaction time task: Meta-analysis of test–retest correlations. *Royal Society Open Science, 10*(7), 221542. https://doi.org/10.1098/rsos.221542.

Rumelhart, D. E., Hinton, G. E., & Williams, R. J. (1986). Learning representations by back-propagating errors. *Nature, 323*(6088), 533–536. https://doi.org/10.1038/323533a0.

Sánchez-Cubillo, I., Periáñez, J. A., Adrover-Roig, D., Rodríguez-Sánchez, J. M., Ríos-Lago, M., Tirapu, J., & Barceló, F. (2009). Construct validity of the Trail Making Test: Role of task-switching, working memory, inhibition/interference control, and visuomotor abilities. *Journal of the International Neuropsychological Society, 15*(3), 438–450. https://doi.org/10.1017/S1355617709090626.

Scharenborg, O., Weber, A., & Janse, E. (2015). The role of attentional abilities in lexically guided perceptual learning by older listeners. *Attention, Perception, & Psychophysics,* 77(2), https://doi.org/10.3758/s13414-014-0792-2.

Scharfen, J., Jansen, K., & Holling, H. (2018). Retest effects in working memory capacity tests: A meta-analysis. *Psychonomic Bulletin & Review, 25*(6), 2175–2199. https://doi.org/10.3758/s13423-018-1461-6.

Schwarb, H., & Schumacher, E. H. (2012). Generalized lessons about sequence learning from the study of the serial reaction time task. *Advances in Cognitive Psychology, 8*(2), 165–178. https://doi.org/10.2478/v10053-008-0113-1.

Selin, C. M., Rice, M. L., Girolamo, T., & Wang, C. J. (2019). Speech-language pathologists' clinical decision making for children with specific language impairment. *Language, Speech, and Hearing Services in Schools, 50*(2), 283–307. https://doi.org/10.1044/2018_LSHSS-18-0017.

Siegel, L. S., & Ryan, E. B. (1989). The development of working memory in normally achieving and subtypes of learning disabled children. *Child Development, 60*(4), 973. https://doi.org/10.2307/1131037.

Soto, C. J., & Jackson, J. J. (2013). Five-factor model of personality. In C. J. Soto, & J. J. Jackson (Eds.). *Psychology* Oxford University Press. https://doi.org/10.1093/obo/9780199828340-0120.

Spaulding, T. J., Plante, E., & Farinella, K. A. (2006). Eligibility criteria for language impairment. *Language, Speech, and Hearing Services in Schools, 37*(1), 61–72. https://doi.org/10.1044/0161-1461(2006/007).

Spearman, C. (1904). "General intelligence," objectively determined and measured. *The American Journal of Psychology, 15*(2), 201. https://doi.org/10.2307/1412107.

Strand, J. F., Brown, V. A., Merchant, M. B., Brown, H. E., & Smith, J. (2018). Measuring listening effort: Convergent validity, sensitivity, and links with cognitive and personality measures. *Journal of Speech, Language, and Hearing Research, 61*(6), 1463–1486. https://doi.org/10.1044/2018_JSLHR-H-17-0257.

Theodore, R. M., Monto, N. R., & Graham, S. (2020). Individual differences in distributional learning for speech: What's ideal for ideal observers? *Journal of Speech, Language, and Hearing Research, 63*(1), https://doi.org/10.1044/2019_JSLHR-S-19-0152.

Torgesen, J. K., Wagner, R. K., & Rashotte, C. A. (2012). Test of Word Reading Efficiency (2nd ed.). Austin, TX: Pro-Ed.

Toscano, J. C., McMurray, B., Dennhardt, J., & Luck, S. J. (2010). Continuous perception and graded categorization: Electrophysiological evidence for a linear relationship between the acoustic signal and perceptual encoding of speech. *Psychological Science, 21*(10), https://doi.org/10.1177/0956797610384142.

Toscano, J. C., Mueller, K. L., McMurray, B., & Tomblin, J. B. (2010). Simulating individual differences in language ability and genetic differences in FOXP2 using a neural network model of the SRT task. *Proceedings of the Annual Meeting of the Cognitive Science Society, 32.*

Unsworth, N., & Engle, R. W. (2005). Individual differences in working memory capacity and learning: Evidence from the serial reaction time task. *Memory & Cognition, 33*(2), 213–220. https://doi.org/10.3758/BF03195310.

Unsworth, N., Heitz, R. P., Schrock, J. C., & Engle, R. W. (2005). An automated version of the operation span task. *Behavior Research Methods, 37*(3), 498–505. https://doi.org/10.3758/BF03192720.

Visser, B. A., Ashton, M. C., & Vernon, P. A. (2006). Beyond *g*: Putting multiple intelligences theory to the test. *Intelligence, 34*(5), 487–502. https://doi.org/10.1016/j.intell.2006.02.004.

Waterhouse, L. (2006). Multiple intelligences, the Mozart effect, and emotional intelligence: A critical review. *Educational Psychologist, 41*(4), 207–225. https://doi.org/10.1207/s15326985ep4104_1.

Waterhouse, L. (2023). Why multiple intelligences theory is a neuromyth. *Frontiers in Psychology, 14.* https://doi.org/10.3389/fpsyg.2023.1217288.

Wiig, E. H., Semel, E., & Secord, W. (2013). *Clinical Evaluation of Language Fundamentals* (5th ed.). Bloomington, MN: Pearson.

Wilbiks, J. M. P., Brown, V. A., & Strand, J. F. (2022). Speech and non-speech measures of audiovisual integration are not correlated. *Attention, Perception, & Psychophysics, 84*(6), 1809–1819. https://doi.org/10.3758/s13414-022-02517-z.

Woodcock, R. W., McGrew, K. S., Schrank, F. A., & Mather, N. (2007). *Woodcock-Johnson III Normative Update.*. IL: Riverside: Rolling Meadows.

CHAPTER THREE

Listening difficulty: From hearing to language

Stefanie E. Kuchinsky[a,b,*], Ian Phillips[a,c], and Rebecca E. Bieber[a,c]
[a]National Military Audiology and Speech Pathology Center, Walter Reed National Military Medical Center, Bethesda, MD, United States
[b]Department of Hearing and Speech Sciences, University of Maryland, College Park, MD, United States
[c]Henry M. Jackson Foundation for the Advancement of Military Medicine Inc, Bethesda, MD, United States
*Corresponding author. e-mail address: stefanie.e.kuchinsky.civ@health.mil

Contents

Abstract

Under the ideal conditions of a clinical audiology booth or a well-controlled laboratory environment, speech understanding can feel like a relatively automatic and effortless task. However, with increasing demands on hearing and language processing (such as those that occur in the complex environments of the real world) or with individual differences in processing (as occurs in heterogeneous populations), listening can quickly become a difficult endeavor. Traditionally, the fields of cognitive hearing science and psycholinguistics have investigated listening difficulty from different perspectives, with different methodologies, and with different applied goals. However, cross-disciplinary research suggests that greater integration across the fields may enhance outcomes in both. In this chapter, we start by providing brief overviews of the historical development of each field to contextualize their respective

Psychology of Learning and Motivation, Volume 81
ISSN 0079-7421, https://doi.org/10.1016/bs.plm.2024.07.001

approaches to the study of listening. We then highlight research that has contributed to our basic understanding of the mechanisms that support listening and to applications that could benefit the many millions of people who experience listening difficulties, even in the absence of audiometric hearing loss. We describe work that has already forged a path for studying interactions among auditory, linguistic, and cognitive processes and conclude with near- and long-term recommendations for expanding this interdisciplinary approach.

"To listen is an effort and just to hear is no merit. A duck hears also."

–Igor Stravinsky (1956 interview; Stravinsky & Craft, 2002)

1. Introduction

The relative ease with which people are generally able to translate acoustic signals into meaning belies the hierarchical and interactive processes that drive language understanding. However, with damage to, differences in, or increased demands on these processes, comprehension can be error-prone and/or effortful. As Stravinsky notes, successful listening involves mental processes beyond hearing alone. Indeed, challenges can arise at many levels of processing across peripheral to central systems.

While it has long been known that hearing, language, and cognition jointly contribute to aural communication, the fields of psycholinguistics and cognitive hearing science have investigated speech comprehension from traditionally distinct perspectives: one broadly focused on elucidating the mental architecture that supports language processing, and the other on assessing and improving individuals' listening abilities to meet their communication goals. However, an increasing number of interdisciplinary studies have noted interactive effects of auditory and linguistic processing on listening difficulty, which includes poorer speech recognition scores, subjective perceptions of listening challenges, and increases in listening-related mental effort.

This chapter overviews research on the factors that contribute to listening difficulty from the perspectives of cognitive hearing science and psycholinguistics, as an example of a language-related research area that is ripe for increased cross-collaboration. We provide brief histories of each field as context for understanding their differing priorities and approaches to studying speech recognition. We then describe research that has investigated one or more of the myriad factors that impact the ease of listening, noting how research in both fields complements, contradicts, or extends one another. We focus on the factors related to (1) the quality of the auditory signal, (2) the content of the auditory signal, and (3) individual differences in the factors that support listening, rather than detailing all possible factors thought to drive listening difficulty (e.g., Gagné et al., 2017; Van Engen & McLaughlin, 2018; Zekveld et al., 2018).

The aim of this chapter is to highlight a subset of auditory and linguistic factors that have historically been investigated in separate literatures. Throughout, we point readers to scoping reviews and representative studies for further, more detailed, discussions of these and other factors. Here, we highlight the importance of considering each factor's impact on listening—why it matters and in what ways research might benefit from greater cross-disciplinary connection. We conclude with near-term and long-term recommendations related to fostering greater interdisciplinary collaboration that would benefit both fields moving forward.

2. Historical perspectives

Our summary of the historical development of cognitive hearing science and psycholinguistics focuses on their perspectives on difficult speech processing. Their basic research origins—broadly physics/psychoacoustics vs. philosophy/linguistics—and their applied goals have followed different trajectories. However, both fields were spurred on by the cognitive revolution of the 1950s, indicative of their recognition of the importance of the mind in explaining human performance. This overlap may serve as an important foundation for fostering expanded interdisciplinary collaborations that will lead to critical insights into the sources of listening difficulty.

2.1 Cognitive hearing science

In-depth histories of hearing science and its subfield cognitive hearing science can be found in works by Carterette and Friedman (1978, especially Part I) and Arlinger et al. (2009), respectively, as well as many others. Interests within hearing science have encompassed acoustics (emphasizing the physics of sound), audition (emphasizing the perception of sound) and, relatively more recently, the recognition and comprehension of speech in varying listening conditions. Along with the development of physics centuries ago, early Eastern and Western civilizations sought to measure and define laws describing the features of sound—including its speed, frequency, and wavelength. The subfield of psychoacoustics highlighted that hearing is influenced not only by signal properties, but also by sensory and perceptual processes. For example, sound pressure level (SPL) is a physical measure of intensity that does not have a one-to-one relationship with perceived loudness.

Following World War II, there was a recognized need to apply the principles of psychoacoustics to assess and treat the communication challenges of service members experiencing noise-induced hearing loss. Clinical audiology emerged as its own discipline, with military hospitals establishing programs that included assessments of hearing problems as well as hearing device fittings and other aural rehabilitation strategies. Advances in methods such as electrophysiology and electroacoustics allowed scientists to further probe the nature of the peripheral and central auditory systems, and advancements in electronics spurred on new strategies for treatment and improved health outcomes.

The cognitive revolution of the 1950s emphasized the consideration of higher-order mental systems in the processing of sensory input. As Arlinger et al. (2009) note, cognitive psychology and hearing science research were relatively isolated from each other for several decades. While hearing science originated with the study of sensory systems, *cognitive* hearing science emerged as it became clear that peripheral and central auditory mechanisms alone could not fully explain individuals' experiences of listening in complex environments. The move towards cross-disciplinary research, especially in the late 1990s, was driven in part by a recognition of the importance of listening in ecologically valid settings (e.g., McAdams & Bigand, 1993), the impact of aging, which yields changes in sensory and cognitive functioning (e.g., Pichora-Fuller et al., 1995), as well as efforts to optimize hearing devices (Edwards, 2007) and enhance counseling and aural rehabilitation (e.g., Kraus et al., 1995).

Thus, cognitive hearing science has generally focused on three domains: "(1) language processing in challenging listening conditions; (2) the use of auditory communication technologies or the visual modality to boost performance; (3) changes in performance with development, aging, and rehabilitative training." (Arlinger et al., 2009, p. 371). While basic research aims to elucidate the mechanisms that support speech recognition in challenging conditions, these goals are tightly linked to application. There is a particular emphasis on translating basic research findings to clinical practice, for example by understanding the role of individual differences on speech recognition outcomes (e.g., Akeroyd, 2008) and by developing clinically feasible outcome measures that align with patients' reported communication difficulties.

2.2 Psycholinguistics

Psycholinguistics is a multidisciplinary field concerned with the mental processes that support human language acquisition, production, and comprehension. Its rich history has been chronicled by Blumenthal (1987), Altmann (2006), Levelt (2013), and others. As Levelt (2013) details, psycholinguistics has roots in eighteenth and nineteenth century study of the origin of language and empirical research on language in the brain, child language acquisition, and language perception and production. The emergence of psycholinguistics as a discipline occurred in the 1950s through efforts to integrate the fields of linguistics and psychology to better understand processes involved in communication.

In the following decade, the Chomskyan revolution shifted the focus in linguistics (at least in the United States) from describing the grammatical properties of languages to characterizing a mental faculty capable of acquiring and generating language. This shift ushered in the modern era of psycholinguistics with a focus on discovering universal properties of language processing and acquisition (Altmann, 2006). The breadth of topics that modern psycholinguistic inquiry has since grown to include are detailed in several edited volumes, including Traxler and Gernsbacher (2006) and Fernández and Cairns (2017).

Early efforts to identify universal processes involved in language comprehension gave little recognition to potential variation across speakers of different languages (Bates et al., 2001; Cutler, 2009). However, during the 1980s researchers began to recognize the importance of crosslinguistic differences in language comprehension processes and to leverage them to advance psycholinguistic theory (see Norcliffe et al., 2015). Studies that identified crosslinguistic differences in the suprasegmental features used by listeners to segment words from the speech stream (e.g., syllable versus stress based; Cutler et al., 1983) and in the assignment of different syntactic structures to ambiguous sentences (e.g., in attachment preferences for relative clauses; Cuetos & Mitchell, 1988) had profound impacts on the field.

Along with the recognition that crosslinguistic differences in language processing may hold the key to discovering universal processing mechanisms (Bates et al., 2001), language processing in bilinguals—individuals who use two or more languages in their everyday lives (Grosjean, 1989, 2010)—has become a prominent topic in psycholinguistics (e.g., Schwartz & Kroll, 2006). Research in this area has led to development of models that can account for phonological, lexical, and sentence processing in bilinguals (Desmet & Duyck, 2007) and has highlighted the malleability of language processing mechanisms to changes in language exposure and use (e.g., Dussias & Sagarra, 2007).

Although the questions that dominated psycholinguistic inquiry 60 years ago continue to drive the field today, new approaches that embrace individual differences in linguistic and other cognitive systems long-recognized for their role in language comprehension (e.g., working memory; Pickering & Van Gompel, 2006) are beginning to shed new light on old questions (Kidd et al., 2018; McMurray et al., 2023; Yu & Zellou, 2019). As the recognition of crosslinguistic differences opened new avenues for discovering language processing universals, growing research on individual differences in linguistic and cognitive systems and their potential interactions may prove critical to advancing our understanding of linguistic processes that drive language understanding (Kidd et al., 2018).

2.3 Difficulty in cognitive models of listening

Two of the most highly cited models of listening difficulty in cognitive hearing science are the Ease of Language Understanding model (ELU; Rönnberg et al., 2008, 2013) and the Framework for Understanding Effortful Listening (FUEL; Pichora-Fuller et al., 2016) among other relevant models in cognitive hearing science (Herrmann & Johnsrude, 2020; Strauss & Francis, 2017) and in psycholinguistics (for a historical overview see Altmann, 1990). The ELU model emphasizes the role of cognition in speech processing both in the early and later stages of speech understanding (Rönnberg et al., 2008, 2013). Working memory and other attentional processes are engaged to resolve mismatches between a degraded acoustic input and its phonological representation in long-term semantic memory. When inputs and representations match to a sufficient level, lexical access can proceed automatically, without effort. Similarities between input and representation that do not surpass such a threshold may lead to the more effortful retrieval of the word along with its phonological neighbors (Luce & Pisoni, 1998).

An extension of Kahneman's capacity-limited model of attention (Kahneman, 1973), FUEL describes factors that influence the allocation of a single set of domain-general mental resources to listening (Pichora-Fuller et al., 2016). Listening effort arises as resources are engaged to meet the demands of a listening task. As more are devoted to listening, fewer resources remain to allocate to other simultaneous tasks. Importantly, effort is dissociable from recognition accuracy (Winn & Teece, 2021): two individuals may work differentially hard to achieve a given level of performance. Effort allocation is impacted by factors including input-related demands associated with variation in the source of the acoustic signal (e.g., talker characteristics), transmission quality of the signal (e.g., background noise), listener-related abilities (e.g., sensory or cognitive capacity), linguistic properties of the message (e.g., familiar vocabulary/melody, semantic context), and the context in which listening occurs (e.g., visual scene). Other influences on effortful listening include variation in a listener's alertness or motivation (Herrmann & Johnsrude, 2020; Strauss & Francis, 2017).

ELU and FUEL have been impactful in cognitive hearing science, in part, because of their explicit recognition of the interactive role of cognition and audition in driving listening difficulty. However, relatively less consideration has been given to the range of linguistic processes (particularly beyond phonemes or words)—and their interactions with auditory and cognitive processes—that may be required during effortful listening. Psycholinguistic models of speech recognition may help to fill in some of these gaps.

Cognitive models of lexical segmentation developed in the psycholinguistic tradition have generally sought to explain how people derive words and meaning from a continuous acoustic input. One noted difference between models of speech recognition in cognitive hearing science and psycholinguistics is the extent to which early perceptual processes are defined as active versus passive (Heald & Nusbaum, 2014). Active mechanisms allow for top-down, context- or goal-driven changes in the processing of auditory inputs unlike passive mechanisms for which there is a fixed mapping between input and higher-order representations (e.g., pattern matching). While word and phoneme recognition have generally been modeled as active processes, early acoustic-to-phonetic mapping has not been (NAM: Luce & Pisoni, 1998; Cohort Model: Marslen-Wilson & Welsh, 1978; TRACE: McClelland & Elman, 1986; Shortlist: Norris, 1994). For example, in the Cohort model of lexical retrieval, the onset of speech sounds automatically activates lexical candidates (i.e., cohorts) with subsequent sounds deactivating now-irrelevant candidates (e.g., "can-" activates both "candy" and "candle" until the final phoneme unfolds). In the original version of the Cohort model, active processing could occur at the lexical, but not phoneme, level. Though some model versions have included active components below the phoneme level (e.g., McClelland et al., 2006), they have been met with debate over the existence of evidence of lexical influences on sublexical processing (McQueen et al., 2006; cf. Mirman et al., 2006).

Reminiscent of Stravinsky, Heald and Nusbaum (2014) argue that listening to speech is a cognitive process, with aspects of even early auditory encoding impacted by top-down attention. Cognition is required to constrain the possible interpretations of an acoustic input, especially with variations in the quality of the talker, the quality of the listening environment, and in the linguistic context. In line with cognitive hearing models, Heald and Nusbaum (2014) describe critical roles for working memory and shifting states of attention to relevant cues. Cognitive hearing science has revealed the consequences of such early auditory-cognitive interactions; hearing loss has been associated with an upregulation of additional cognitive mechanisms to compensate for peripheral and central auditory deficits (for a review see Peelle & Wingfield, 2016). Even when words are accurately perceived, the extra cognitive effort it takes to listen comes at the cost of poorer performance on later memory for those items (McCoy et al., 2005). Furthermore, auditory rehabilitation, such as speech-perception training, is thought to be enhanced when auditory and cognitive systems are jointly engaged (Ferguson & Henshaw, 2015).

In summary, the relative emphasis on auditory-cognitive versus linguistic-cognitive interactions has differed across models of listening in the fields of cognitive hearing science and psycholinguistics. Greater connections through interdisciplinary work are likely to have benefits for a richer understanding of the myriad interactive factors that contribute to listening difficulties.

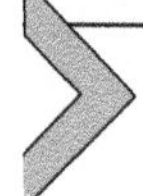

3. Factors that influence listening difficulty: insights from cognitive hearing science and psycholinguistics

In this section, we highlight key findings from cognitive hearing science and psycholinguistics regarding the factors that influence listening difficulty, noting where the results of each field support and extend the results of the other. We discuss sources of difficulty that may be internal or external to the listener (Strauss & Francis, 2017), including variations in the quality of the auditory input and the nature of the linguistic information being processed as well as the role of individual differences in speech processing. Critically, we note increasing evidence of interactions between auditory and linguistic factors that underscore the need for continued interdisciplinary research.

3.1 Quality of the auditory input

Acoustic demands that impact listening difficulty include the features of the speech signal and the acoustic environment. In FUEL, these are referred to as source and transmission factors, respectively (Pichora-Fuller et al., 2016). Despite differences in the goals and methods used to investigate these factors, research from cognitive hearing science and psycholinguistic perspectives point to important interactions between acoustic and linguistic processes that impact listening difficulty.

3.1.1 The speech signal

Speech is variable across and within talkers. In daily life, most individuals engage in spoken communications with a variety of conversation partners, including talkers who are familiar and/or unfamiliar to them, talkers who do or do not share the native language of the listener/environment, talkers with different emotional states, talkers of different ages, etc. Successful communication depends on the listener's ability to account for these factors in processing and recognition of speech. While this lack of invariance in speech for the most part does not prevent successful communication, there is evidence that these factors can contribute to the relative ease of listening (e.g., Van Engen & Peelle, 2014).

Early psycholinguistic models of speech recognition assumed that listeners performed some sort of normalization to variable and/or challenging stimuli such that variability would not impede recognition, but the current understanding is that listeners do not recognize speech in this exemplar fashion, but rather make use of the information inherent to the variability to aid recognition (Pisoni, 1997). For example, while a non-native accent alters the acoustic characteristics of a speech signal relative to the typical characteristics of native-accented speech, the presence of a non-native accent is also a type of indexical feature that may serve as a cue to the speaker's identity. Indexical features include information about the talker, including their gender, age, language background, affective state, etc. Work by Pisoni and colleagues (e.g., Nygaard & Pisoni, 1998; Pisoni, 1997) has documented that listeners retain not only the lexical aspects of target speech, but also the indexical properties of the speakers they have heard, and they can use this information to improve speech recognition. These findings have informed our understanding of the speech recognition process, with acoustic, lexical, and indexical properties of speech all contributing to the mapping of incoming signals to flexible mental representations. Similarly, Cai et al. (2017) proposed that listeners use a "speaker-model" of speech recognition, in which information about the talker (i.e., indexical information) is used to help predict speech and interpret meaning to facilitate recognition.

The impact of talker-related factors on predictive processing for speech understanding, and the resulting effort associated with successful speech recognition, has been well explored in the psycholinguistic literature. Factors such as talker dialect/accent, familiarity to the listener, and their interactions with characteristics of the listener have all been shown to impact speech processing and listening effort (Bent et al., 2016; Bieber et al., 2022; Brown et al., 2020; Magnuson et al., 2021; Van Engen & Peelle, 2014).

From the hearing science perspective, consideration of talker-related factors was historically situated in the context of explaining (and minimizing) potential sources for variability in speech-based audiometric tests. In other words, variation in speech recognition outcomes due to differences in talker intelligibility was historically identified and discussed as a factor to be controlled for in order to make an accurate reliable measurement of speech recognition ability. Due in part to the field's specific focus on clinical assessments of auditory abilities, talker factors were mostly considered in the construction of word lists that could be used in clinical audiology assessments which contributed, for example, to recommendations for using recorded word lists rather than using the clinician's monitored live voice (Hood & Poole, 1980; Kreul et al., 1968; Penrod, 1979). It was not until relatively recently that talker factors were considered as strongly for their potential influence on a patient's perceived communication abilities and challenges.

Throughout the development of clinical speech testing materials, it was acknowledged that diagnostic tests did not necessarily align with patient report, and/or the type of communication situations that individuals experience outside of the lab or clinic (Giolas & Epstein, 1963; Kirk, Pisoni, & Miyamoto, 1997). These acknowledgments eventually lead to the development of clinical speech recognition tests which include multiple talkers and/or multiple dialect varieties (Gilbert et al. 2013; Spahr et al., 2012). However, at present, a single-talker phonemically balanced test of monosyllabic word recognition in quiet remains the most common test of speech recognition administered with regularity in audiological clinical practice, despite common patient reports of difficulty understanding speech from particular talker groups, particularly in the presence of background noise, and calls to shift testing to more closely align with patients' real-world listening demands (Fitzgerald et al., 2023; Keidser et al., 2020; Parmar et al., 2022).

3.1.2 The auditory environment

Transmission-related demands arising from the auditory environment can include background noise, reverberation, or signal alterations associated with hearing devices, like hearing aids or cochlear implants (Pichora-Fuller et al., 2016). Communication in the real world involves listening in complex environments that are not often examined in laboratory settings. While gaps in the ecological validity of research have been noted in the fields of hearing science (e.g., Keidser et al., 2020) and psycholinguistics (e.g., Speed, Wnuk, & Majid, 2017), cognitive hearing science has generally emphasized the role of transmission factors in understanding real-world listening.

One well-studied transmission factor in cognitive hearing science is the presence, nature, and degree of background noise. Understanding speech in noise represents a common yet challenging real-world listening situation (Burke & Naylor, 2020), even for younger adults (Zekveld et al., 2010). Listening in noise drives many hearing complaints, even in individuals with normal hearing sensitivity (Beck et al., 2018). The need to quantify speech recognition challenges in the clinic has driven the development of standardized speech-in-noise tests (for an overview of tests see Taylor, 2003). Factors that impact test outcomes include the properties of the speech signal, the noise or competing speech interferer, and the abilities of the listeners themselves (e.g., Festen & Plomp, 1990; French & Steinberg, 1947; Peters et al., 1998).

However, accuracy scores alone may insufficiently characterize the challenges of real-world listening (Keidser et al., 2020). Individuals may achieve the same recognition score but work differentially hard to do so (Winn & Teece, 2021). To maintain a given level of performance, increasing cognitive effort typically must be engaged in the presence of increasing background noise (Kuchinsky et al., 2013; Zekveld et al., 2010), especially for noise that comprises intelligible speech (Koelewijn et al., 2014) or a same-gender irrelevant talker (Zekveld et al., 2014).

Basic research in psycholinguistics has examined the impact of noise on listening from a differing perspective. The phoneme restoration effect is the phenomenon of a speech sound in a sentence being perceived as intact when it has in fact been replaced by a noise (e.g., a cough or white noise) but not when replaced by silence (for a summary see Samuel, 1996). Although noise is used to induce an illusory effect to probe the mechanisms that underlie language processing, the phoneme restoration literature does have implications for understanding the role of contextual support in noisy environments. For example, psychoacoustic factors, such as the acoustic similarity of the missing phoneme and its replacement noise impact the phoneme restoration effect (Warren & Obusek, 1971), pointing to critical roles for bottom-up and top-down influences on phoneme perception.

In summary, the impact of noise on speech processing has been investigated in cognitive hearing science and psycholinguistic traditions from different perspectives and with different methodologies. These results together with those reviewed in the next sections point to the importance of considering interactions between auditory and linguistic processes that can impact the ease of listening.

3.2 Content and situational context of the auditory input

Though a focus of the cognitive hearing perspective has been on understanding the impact of the quality of the speech and auditory environment on listening difficulty, FUEL recognizes that variation in message content and situational context can also impact listening-related effort. These factors have historically been more of the focus of psycholinguistic research but are gaining attention in cognitive hearing science as potential sources of variability in everyday listening demands.

3.2.1 Message

Standardized speech recognition tests have generally aimed to limit variability across test items to enhance reliability while minimizing test time. Items are often subset into lists that yield similar average recognition accuracy across listening conditions (e.g., Nilsson et al., 1994; Wilson, 2003). While item selection for word stimuli has often included phonemic or phonetic balancing (e.g., aligning the distribution of speech sounds in the test to that of English), little consideration has been given to alignment of the lexical, syntactic, semantic, and other linguistic properties of clinical test items to the distribution of these in the language as whole.

Beyond the clinic, experiments in cognitive hearing science have commonly utilized these standard test stimuli, thus potentially limiting the generalizability of research to only these materials. Though models such as the Neighborhood Activation Model (NAM) emphasize that neighborhood density, phonetic similarity, and word frequency influence spoken word recognition (Luce & Pisoni, 1998), gaps remain in our understanding of how higher-order linguistic factors interact with acoustic demands in impacting listening difficulty.

With increasing linguistic demands, greater mental effort has been observed when listening to foreign-accented speech (Schmidtke, 2014), words with larger neighborhood densities (especially for younger adults, McLaughlin et al., 2022); syntactically complex versus simple sentences (Ayasse & Wingfield, 2018), or sentences with low-supportive semantic context (Winn, 2016). The presence of noise appears to modulate these effects. Increases in effort with poorer signal-to-noise ratios (SNRs) have been shown to be exacerbated when listening to words that occur less frequently in English (Kuchinsky et al., 2023). Evidence for benefits of supportive sentence context have also been observed especially in background noise (e.g., Fitzgerald et al., 2024).

While such results highlight the importance of considering interactions between acoustic and linguistic demands on speech recognition accuracy and effort, they represent a limited range of the phonological, lexical, syntactic, semantic, and pragmatic variation that occurs in real-world communication. Key insights in psycholinguistic research have emerged through the use of the visual world paradigm (VWP) to study how and when listeners integrate varied sources of linguistic and contextual information (for a review see Huettig et al., 2011).

In the VWP, participants listen to a sentence while their eye movements are recorded as they view a display of items that are relevant or irrelevant to the interpretation of that sentence. Targets and distractors may be designed to compete for attention in varying ways, allowing for the examination of the extent to which lexical, syntactic, and semantic information interactively impact comprehension across time. In a classic VWP study (Allopenna et al., 1998), listeners heard instructions like "pick up the beaker" while their eye movements were tracked as they viewed four on-screen response options. Compared to an unrelated image (e.g., carriage), fixation patterns indicated that listeners initially considered both the target item (beaker) and an onset competitor (beetle), but importantly, as the end of the word unfolded, also considered a rhyme competitor (speaker). Such evidence supports interactive-activation models of speech recognition in which lexical access is a continuous (e.g., TRACE, Shortlist) rather than a sequential (e.g., Cohort) process.

More recent work has observed that VWP effects can be altered by the presence of background noise. These include evidence of interactions between variation in SNR and lexical competition effects (Kuchinsky et al., 2013), and differential changes in onset versus rhyme competition with noise, particularly among older adults (Ben-David et al., 2011). Thus, the VWP represents a psycholinguistic paradigm that could be leveraged to understand the time course of interactions between acoustic and linguistic demands.

3.2.2 Situational context

Listening difficulty can also be influenced by the broader situational context in which communication occurs. As FUEL notes, the visual scene as well as schematic and real-world knowledge can support speech recognition (Pichora-Fuller et al., 2016). Speech perception rarely takes place in the absence of visual or other supportive contextual information. Yet that is how speech perception is typically measured in the clinic, with single words and or sentences that generally minimize the ability to use contextual knowledge.

Studies of situational context in cognitive hearing science have predominantly focused on understanding the roles of multisensory integration (e.g., alignment of an auditory signal with mouth movements) and multitasking demands on listening difficulty. For example, while multisensory integration appears to occur in an automatic, effortless fashion, attentional resources appear to be engaged particularly during later stages of integration and especially when stimuli are presented near one's perceptual threshold (for a review, Koelewijn et al., 2010). Dual-task studies have revealed interactive effects between acoustic, linguistic, and multitasking demands (e.g., performing a visual identification task while listening to speech in noise) on the effort it takes to recognize speech (Kuchinsky et al., 2023).

Another cognitive hearing science approach for assessing speech recognition in situationally relevant contexts comes from tests conducted in real-world environments, such as in a library, cafeteria, restaurant, or bar, that naturally include auditory and visual distractors to varying degrees (Barrett et al., 2021; Brungart et al., 2020). Advances in virtual and augmented reality technology have provided an additional way forward for probing changes in speech recognition and effort when listening in complex scenarios (Hohmann et al., 2020; Stecker, 2019). Such methods allow for systematic investigations of contextually relevant factors, such as the impact of audiovisual (vs. audio only) speech, spatially separated sounds, as well as multitasking demands on listening (Devesse et al., 2020).

In psycholinguistics, the VWP has been used to examine the impact of schematic knowledge on spoken language comprehension. In a classic study, participants listened to sentences like "The boy will eat the cake" or "The boy will move the cake" with onscreen images of a boy, a cake, and toys (Altmann & Kamide, 1999). Eye movement patterns revealed earlier looks to the cake following hearing the verb "eat" compared to "move" indicating that verb information can be quickly used to constrain the set of possible upcoming referents. Other VWP studies have revealed similar effects for other lexical, syntactic, and semantic information (for a review, see Huettig et al., 2011). VWP studies have also provided key evidence for visual constraints (Tanenhaus et al., 1995) as well as pragmatic information (Huang & Snedeker, 2009) impacting the time course of sentence interpretation. However, the extent to which these effects may be impacted by changes in speaker quality or the auditory environment, for example, is generally unknown, thus representing an open area for collaboration.

3.3 Individual differences in the factors that support listening

In addition to demands imposed by the listening task (both in quality and content), individuals vary across the cognitive, linguistic, and sensory systems that support listening. The effects of individual differences in factors that support listening is one area in which hearing sciences and psycholinguistics have focused considerable attention, albeit for different reasons. In hearing science, the focus on individual differences is driven by the goal of caring for the individual patient. In psycholinguistics, individual differences are of interest for their potential to illuminate universal language processing mechanisms. Here, we discuss hearing loss and language history, two individual factors which have received much attention from the fields of cognitive hearing science and psycholinguistics, respectively, but which are worth greater consideration by researchers in both disciplines.

3.3.1 Hearing loss

Individual differences at all levels of the auditory system can impact a listeners' ability to hear and understand speech and the difficulty associated with listening. Hearing loss can result from any number of temporary and/ or permanent etiologies, including (but not limited to) cerumen (earwax) impaction, middle ear disease, noise exposures, neurologic disease, and aging. As a result of its origins in the clinical and psychoacoustic realms, the field of (cognitive) hearing science has traditionally had a central focus on the impacts of hearing status and hearing loss on various auditory outcomes. Intuitively, changes in hearing sensitivity can impact speech recognition accuracy (e.g., Ching & Dillon, 2013; Humes & Roberts, 1990), with the impacts of sensorineural (i.e., inner ear) hearing loss relating to both overall attenuation of the signal (i.e., changes in the threshold of sound detection) and distortion of the signal (i.e., altered perception of a signal presented above threshold; Plomp, 1978). The effects of hearing loss on domains including frequency sensitivity, temporal resolution, loudness perception and others have been studied extensively and comprehensively reviewed (e.g., Moore, 2007).

Because differences in pure-tone audiometric thresholds are known to impact speech recognition outcomes, this factor is often controlled for or explicitly manipulated in hearing science studies which seek to investigate the effects of higher-level cognitive factors or other processes such as aging on auditory outcomes, which can impact speech recognition independent of or in interaction with peripheral hearing loss (e.g., Dubno et al., 1984; Pichora-Fuller et al., 1995). Similarly, it is common practice in the field to report details such as stimulus presentation levels and, if appropriate, SNRs, as these stimulus-level factors are known to interact with individual factors such as hearing loss to influence speech recognition outcomes (Eisenberg et al., 1995; Vermiglio et al., 2020; Wilson et al., 2007).

While calculations such as the speech intelligibility and articulation indices have been developed with the goal of predicting an individual's level of speech recognition performance based on their pure-tone thresholds (ANSI, 1969, 1997), there is a clear consensus among hearing scientists that differences in pure-tone hearing sensitivity do not fully explain variability in subjective and objective measures of speech-in-noise performance (Grant & Walden, 2013; Hannula et al., 2011). As noted in Section 2.1, these inconsistencies and the well-known phenomenon of individuals experiencing greater hearing difficulty than predicted by their results on a pure-tone threshold test led to the study of higher-level processes contributing to hearing difficulty, and to the study of outcome measures outside of recognition accuracy to examine the impacts of hearing loss on communication function.

Measures of listening effort are thought to be more sensitive to challenges faced by individuals with hearing loss compared to audiometry and speech recognition accuracy measures alone (for reviews see Brungart et al., 2022; Kuchinsky & DeRoy Milvae, 2024). Currently, the impact of hearing loss on listening effort appears to be complex, with some studies finding a positive association (i.e., more loss, more effort), some finding no association, and some finding a negative association (for a review see Zekveld et al., 2018). Results may critically depend on overall task demands and the mental resource capacities of the listeners (Kuchinsky & DeRoy Milvae, 2024)—as listening becomes extremely challenging, participants begin to "give up" and exert less effort (Ohlenforst et al., 2017). For related issues when examining individual differences in cognitive capacity and personality on listening effort, see Strand et al. (2018). Though a consensus is still emerging, this line of research suggests that equivalent performance among individuals with and without hearing loss should not necessarily be taken as evidence of equivalent mental processing of difficult speech stimuli.

3.3.2 Language history

It goes without saying that knowing a language is a prerequisite for understanding speech in that language. Perhaps for this reason, "knowing the language," particularly beyond the lexical level, is not often discussed in models of listening difficulty in cognitive hearing science. However, psycholinguistic research indicates that language experience and proficiency vary greatly across individuals, along with differences in the representation and processing of linguistic information (e.g., Grosjean, 1998a; Pakulak & Neville, 2010). These differences may affect listening difficulty in some obvious and some not-so-obvious ways and present a challenge to hearing scientists and clinicians who wish to characterize speech recognition in linguistically heterogeneous populations.

The effects of bilingual language experience have been examined extensively in psycholinguistic studies of word recognition and sentence processing. In most current views, word recognition is a probabilistic outcome of activation of multiple lexical forms that is driven by acoustic properties of the speech signal in conjunction with the listener's knowledge of the phonological patterns of the language, lexical items and their frequency of occurrence, and the availability of contextual information (McQueen, 2007). Hearing a word activates lexical items in each of a bilingual's languages (e.g., Canseco-Gonzalez et al., 2010; Marian & Spivey, 2003). Language coactivation in bilinguals cannot be completely suppressed, although it can be modulated by the communicative context (i.e., whether the listener is closer to being in a monolingual or bilingual language mode; Grosjean, 1998b) and the listener's language experience, including the age at which language acquisition began (Canseco-Gonzalez et al., 2010), proficiency at the time of testing (e.g., Titone et al., 2021; for a summary, see Van Hell & Tanner, 2012), and ability to accurately perceive phonological units of the test language (Broersma & Cutler, 2011; Weber & Cutler, 2004). Thus, spoken word recognition requires the bilingual listener to engage additional control processes to achieve the same outcome as a monolingual listener (Friesen et al., 2016).

Word recognition feeds into higher level syntactic and semantic structure building processing. When a listener hears a speech in a language they know, they immediately begin to build grammatical structure based on each incoming word (Pickering & Van Gompel, 2006). This process is influenced by several factors, including lexical features of the words and an individual's language experience (Hernández et al., 2007). For example, languages vary in how structurally ambiguous strings are grammatically interpreted (e.g., Cuetos & Mitchell, 1988). However, these and other aspects of sentence processing are malleable to changes in language exposure (Dussias & Sagarra, 2007) and proficiency (Bice & Kroll, 2021). That said, it is critical to recognize that even though bilingual sentence processing may appear to engage strategies specific to one language, sentence processing in either of a bilingual's languages is unlike monolingual sentence processing due to differences in phonological and lexical representations and processes (Broersma & Cutler, 2011; Schmidtke, 2014; Weber & Cutler, 2004) and crosslinguistic interactions noted above that may have cascading effects at each stage of language processing (Grosjean, 1989).

Differences due to bilingual language experience have also received growing attention in the last two decades in hearing science. Considerable variation in the linguistic profiles of the bilinguals who are tested and in the tasks used across studies has resulted in a complex set of findings (for summaries see: Cowan et al., 2022; Shi, 2018; Von Hapsburg & Peña, 2002). One consistent pattern is that bilingual adults who learn the target language after childhood have more difficulty understanding degraded speech than monolinguals and bilinguals who learn the target language in childhood. Growing evidence also suggests that other, more dynamic aspects of bilingual language experience can impact listening difficulty, including language proficiency (Kilman et al.,

2014; Rimikis et al., 2013), dominance (Cowan et al., 2023; Regalado et al., 2019; Shi & Sánchez, 2010), and use patterns (Bieber et al., 2024; Suite et al., 2023). Further, SNR and type of auditory degradation (noise, reverb, time compression) can affect listening difficulty differently for monolinguals and across bilinguals with varying language backgrounds (Shi, 2018).

Language experience also impacts the level of effort exerted during listening. Greater listening effort has been measured during word and sentence recognition for bilinguals compared to monolinguals (Borghini & Hazan, 2018, 2020; Desjardins et al., 2019; Schmidtke, 2014) and for nonnative compared to native speakers of the test language (Strand et al., 2023). Notably, recognizing degraded speech can be more effortful even for highly proficient bilinguals who acquired English at a young age (Desjardins et al., 2019). Consistent with behavioral findings, differences are not categorical, but rather are mediated by language experience (e.g., proficiency in the test language and the age when learning began) and lexical properties of the stimuli (Schmidtke, 2014; Strand et al., 2023).

The parallels between the influences of bilingual language experience during language processing and during listening tasks, paired with the rather consistent finding of either no difference in non-linguistic auditory ability between monolinguals and bilinguals or an advantage for bilinguals (e.g., Krizman et al., 2017; Onoda et al., 2006; Skoe & Karayanidi, 2019) suggests that increased listening difficulties experienced by bilinguals are linguistic rather than auditory in nature (Phillips et al., 2024; Skoe & Karayanidi, 2019). Crucially, these linguistic and other cognitive systems that support language processing may change with healthy aging, including inhibitory control (Baum & Titone, 2014), sentence processing strategies (Federmeier et al., 2010), and the efficiency of linguistic and domain-general cognitive processes (Colby & McMurray, 2023; Salthouse, 1996). These shifts may drive potentially unique age-related changes in language processing for bilinguals (Rossi & Diaz, 2016) with concomitant effects on listening difficulty. Indeed, recent studies are beginning to uncover steeper age-related declines in masked speech recognition for 1) bilingual adults with normal or near-normal hearing sensitivity compared to monolinguals (Bieber et al., 2024) and s2) for self-identified nonnativecompared to native speakers of English (Phillips et al., 2024). How age-related changes in language processing may interact with individual differences in language experience and other individual factors such as hearing loss and auditory processing as well as different types of auditory demands (e.g., SNR, degradation type) is an important open question (Shi, 2018) that invites cross-disciplinary collaboration.

3.4 Summary

In this section, we presented evidence of factors that have been observed to contribute to listening difficulty from the fields of cognitive hearing science and psycholinguistics. We highlighted examples, with cognitive hearing science research having had a relatively greater focus on the quality of the signal (e.g., talker characteristics) and the auditory environment (e.g., background noise) and psycholinguistic research having relatively greater focus on the content of the auditory signal (e.g., lexical properties) and the situational context (e.g., schematic knowledge constraints). Both fields have provided critical insights into individual-difference factors that impact listening difficulty, particularly hearing loss (cognitive hearing science) and language history (psycholinguistics).

We also highlighted the increasing body of interdisciplinary work that has examined interactions between auditory and linguistics demands as well as between individual differences in auditory and language abilities. Cognitive hearing science and psycholinguistics have thus built strong foundations on which collaborations can continue to be built in support of improved basic understanding and applications to enhance assessments and remediations of listening challenges.

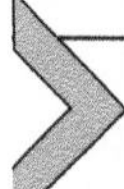

4. Integrating across fields to improve basic understanding and clinical care

Continued integration of cognitive hearing science and psycholinguistics is clearly aligned with the goal of understanding the range of challenges—from acoustic to linguistic and cognitive—that people face in real-world communication. In this section, we present some tangible recommendations for cross-collaboration which can be implemented in the near-term as well as the long-term. Of course, there are many challenges in conducting interdisciplinary research, such as differences in goals, terminology, and methods (Menken et al., 2016). However, as we have outlined, listening is an inherently interactive process, and thus interdisciplinary research may be key to more fully understand how it works under both ideal and suboptimal conditions and how to provide the most effective support to listeners who need it (Drouin & Theodore, 2020).

4.1 Opportunities for increased cross-collaboration: near-term recommendations

Table 1 summarizes recommendations for studies of listening difficulty that bring together insights and best practices from the fields of cognitive hearing science and psycholinguistics.

4.1.1 Quality of the auditory input

In this chapter, we reviewed evidence that source factors such as talker accent/dialect and background noise impact listening difficulty and noted evidence of their potential interactions with other high-order linguistic and cognitive demands. Other critical factors that have been shown to impact listening effort (for a review see Zekveld et al., 2018) include the intensity (i.e., sound pressure level in decibels, dB) of the speech signal and noise, the nature of the noise (e.g., stationary vs. fluctuating), and other types of signal degradation (e.g., signal vocoding), often in the absence of differences in performance. Indeed, listening effort findings highlight that merely ensuring that participants can accurately perceive speech stimuli does not guarantee that they are engaging the same mental processes to do so (Winn & Teece, 2021). Thus, these auditory factors should be carefully considered and controlled for/manipulated when formulating research studies and reported in detail when disseminating findings.

Table 1 Near- and long-term recommendations for fostering cross-disciplinary collaboration between cognitive hearing science and psycholinguistics to enhance our ability to address basic and applied questions related to difficult speech understanding.

Near-term recommendations	Long-term recommendations
• Measure (or at least standardize) and report presentation level of auditory stimuli • Consider linguistic properties of speech materials at the trial level • Screen/measure and report hearing sensitivity of participants • Consider interactions of acoustic and linguistic factors • Query and report meaningful language history of participants	• Build collaborative teams with consideration of basic, translational, and applied research questions • Increase diversity of participants and of linguistic representation in research • Expand recruitment and data collection beyond limitations imposed by traditional practices • Develop collaborations across fields with synergistic research interests • Carefully consider how differences due to language are framed in clinical contexts

In the field of cognitive hearing science, it is standard practice to report the sound presentation level, details of the auditory delivery system, and to measure and report hearing thresholds of the listeners. Presentation level is most accurately measured with a Type 2 sound level meter. However, with advances in technology and efforts in the field to promote feasibility of remote and alternative forms of data collection, many have detailed recommended procedures for ensuring valid and consistent presentation levels across participants (Mok et al., 2024; Peng et al., 2022; Zhao et al., 2022). Reporting specific transducers (e.g., make and model of headphones, loudspeakers, etc.) is highly recommended. If stimuli are to be presented at "a comfortable listening level" with the potential for adjustments above a known minimum intensity, this procedure should be described in detail, including the stimuli used for calibration and how acoustically similar they are to the actual test materials. Researchers should also recognize that equating overall intensity (e.g., scaling stimuli by their average root-mean-square intensity) does not ensure that all speech sounds will be perceived as equally loud, which is particularly important when contrasting the perception of speech sounds with different frequency spectra.

Work in cognitive hearing science thus emphasizes the importance of, at a minimum, standardizing the quality of the auditory input across participants and items (as appropriate), with the procedures for doing so clearly stated and justified. However, integrated cognitive hearing science and psycholinguistic perspectives suggest a need to move beyond consideration of these factors as sources of extraneous noise, but rather to systematically vary them in conjunction with linguistic factors that contribute to listening difficulty.

4.1.2 Content and situational context of the auditory input

This chapter pointed to evidence for phonological, syntactic, semantic, and pragmatic factors impacting how speech recognition unfolds across time. Given clear demonstrations that item variability matters and particularly so in the presence of noise (Brungart et al., 2021; Kuchinsky et al., 2023), the potential generalizability of speech stimuli in a cognitive hearing science experiment should be clearly stated, and the potential impact of item variance either modeled as a source of noise (e.g., random effects; Baayen et al., 2008) or as a moderating effect of interest (e.g., fixed effects) on speech perception processes.

Furthermore, aligned with the previous section's recommendation, we emphasize the importance of considering interactions among acoustic and linguistic factors, not only to enhance ecological validity but also because linguistic processes that may proceed automatically under easy listening conditions, may require more and/or different mental processes to support them under harder listening conditions. Indeed, in some psycholinguistic theories, speech perception, spoken word recognition, and sentence processing are not construed as distinct stages of language comprehension (McQueen, 2007), indicating that speech perception should not be considered in isolation from higher-level linguistic processes.

4.1.3 Individual differences in the factors supporting listening

The literature examining the impact of listener factors on listening difficulty indicates the importance of considering individual variation in auditory and linguistic abilities in studies of speech processing. We focused on two of the commonly examined individual differences in cognitive hearing science and psycholinguistics—hearing loss and language history. We contend that relatively small modifications related to study recruitment and surveys have the potential to increase the generalizability of findings or to better identify subpopulations of individuals who are differentially impacted by listening difficulties.

With respect to individual differences in hearing status, we recommend that studies that intend to present auditory stimuli to normal-hearing listeners include, at a minimum, an objective screening for normal hearing sensitivity in all participants: if a full audiogram is not possible, then it is important to at least ensure that a minimum level can be heard across the frequencies that are most critical for speech (e.g., ≤ 20 dB HL at 0.5, 1.0, 2.0, and 4.0 kHz). Self-report of hearing difficulty does not necessarily correspond to presence or absence of measurable hearing loss, for example with one estimate as low as 16% of adults with hearing loss correctly identifying their hearing status (Angara et al., 2021). Indeed, adults may report normal hearing while having thresholds (especially mildly elevated ones, Ramkissoon & Cole, 2011) that could impact their recognition of auditory research stimuli, depending on specifics of the stimuli, frequency response of sound delivery devices, and overall sound presentation level.

Recent developments in freely-available online tools for estimating hearing thresholds (De Sousa et al., 2022; Grassi et al., 2024) puts hearing screening or measurement of hearing thresholds within reach for researchers who do not have access to a clinical audiometer. Particularly for studies of aging, researchers should avoid using descriptors such as "age-normal hearing" which is often used to suggest that older adults may be compared to younger adults without concern for audiometric differences. ASHA definition of hearing loss starts at thresholds poorer than 15 dB HL across frequencies (Anastasiadou & Al Khalili, 2023). "Age-normal hearing," which can sometimes mean thresholds as poor as 30 dB HL or more depending on the study, is still hearing loss, and it is critical to acknowledge and/or control for its potential impacts on audibility and distortion.

With respect to individual differences in language history, a straightforward recommendation predominantly for cognitive hearing science research is to ask participants about their language experience. Even when language status is not of primary interest in a study, there are potentially two sets of problems with relying on individuals to self-report as being a "native speaker" for inclusion. One set is that the meaning of "native speaker" varies across individuals (Cheng et al., 2021), which impacts interpretability and replicability of findings, and it ignores other aspects of language experience (e.g., simultaneous bilingualism) that could contribute to listening differences (Grosjean, 1998a). For example, so-called heritage language bilinguals in the United States attend school primarily in English but receive early (often exclusive) exposure to a non-English home language during early childhood. These individuals are native speakers of English but are simultaneous or early sequential bilinguals whose language processing would be expected to differ from that of monolingual native speakers. A second set of problems relates to the fact that excluding linguistic diversity (rather than aiming to generalize across or examining its impact), severely limits the generalizability of a study's results to the world population, and even increasingly so to the U.S. population (Strand et al., 2023).

4.2 Opportunities for increased cross-collaboration: long-term recommendations

Beyond a better understanding of the systems that support speech comprehension, increased cross-disciplinary collaborations between cognitive hearing science and psycholinguistics has the long-term potential to enhance the ecological validity and generalizability of research as well as enhance clinical care.

4.2.1 Enhancing ecological validity

Ecological validity refers to the extent to which study results are predictive of effects in daily life situations and is thought to minimally include consideration of the correspondence between experimental and real-world settings, stimuli, and responses (Schmuckler, 2001). Indeed, there is increasing awareness that ecological validity is severely limited when only conducting speech recognition studies in quiet, visually sparse settings with a restricted range of linguistic stimuli (e.g., Beechey, 2022; Keidser et al., 2020; Mellinger & Hanson, 2022; Sánchez et al., 2022). Advances in technology are making it more feasible to perform testing "in the field" (Barrett et al., 2021; Brungart et al., 2020) or in increasingly well-simulated naturalistic environments (Hohmann et al., 2020; Stecker, 2019). This is true not just for observational or behavioral research, but also for physiological, eye tracking, and even some neural measures (Kaongoen et al., 2023). We encourage researchers to consider now how basic, translational, and applied research can be mutually informative for their particular research questions. One straightforward way to begin this process is to build teams of collaborative researchers that comprise expertise across the basic-to-applied spectrum. Emerging parallel interests particularly in applied cognitive hearing science and psycholinguistics research, such as speech and language processing during interactive dialog that more closely mirrors natural communication (Garnham et al., 2006; Keidser et al., 2020) and the impact of noise during classroom language use and language learning (Bloomfield et al., 2010; Nelson et al., 2005) present opportunities for building cross-disciplinary collaborations.

4.2.2 Enhancing generalizability

Because experiments can typically only sample subsets of the people and speech stimuli from their populations of interest, generalizability of study results is of critical concern. As stated in near-term recommendations, cognitive hearing science studies would benefit from greater consideration and modeling of the relationship between sampled stimuli and the larger set of speech materials that they would like to generalize to (e.g., all consonant-vowel-consonant words spoken by a male talker, all words spoken by any talker, etc.). Longer-term, cognitive hearing science would benefit from including more diverse sets of language materials, particularly for effects that have been predominantly demonstrated using a clinical or highly-normed set of stimuli spoken by a particular voice actor. As the goals of the development of these materials has generally been to reduce variability (e.g., in order to get more reliable measures of speech processing for the clinic), it is unclear how generalizable the results from these studies are to the language that listeners experience in their daily lives.

Participant samples that have traditionally been studied in both fields have disproportionately included individuals from Western, Educated, Industrialized, Rich, and Democratic (WEIRD) populations (Henrich et al., 2010). The commonly used inclusion criterion that participants be monolingual native English speakers is likely to exacerbate this problem (Strand et al., 2023). Suggestions for addressing this issue in psycholinguistics have included recommendations to increase the diversity of languages and participants included in research by expanding the study of psycholinguistic phenomena to a greater variety of languages and conducting studies online or in public spaces to increase participation of individuals not typically recruited for laboratory studies (Speed et al., 2017). Cognitive hearing science could benefit from similar efforts to expand linguistic representation in research and modeling the impact of these factors on listening (e.g., variation in language experience among bilinguals as well as monolinguals).

Likewise, the generalizability of psycholinguistic research stands to benefit by increasing participant diversity with respect to factors that cognitive hearing science has prioritized such as variation in hearing and auditory processing abilities: One should either be clear about the limitations in generalizability by not sampling from the broader population, which includes differences along these dimensions or, when possible, model the impact of these factors on language processing. Indeed, similar calls for greater cross-disciplinary integration have recommended that researchers consider the interplay of sensory, cognitive, and linguistic factors in the context of language comprehension in healthy aging (Vonk et al., 2017) and recognize the potential for individual differences in language ability and cognition to advance psycholinguistic inquiry (e.g., Kidd et al., 2018).

There is some evidence that relaxing restrictive enrollment criteria may have little impact on some well-known speech recognition effects (Strand et al., 2023). Whether this holds across other participant samples and auditory phenomena is an empirical question. Addressing this topic and, further, appropriately modeling the effects of variation in auditory and linguistic abilities will require data sets much larger than those typically collected in a laboratory setting. Although the idea of collecting listening data in the field is not new, newer hardware and software applications, such as the WAHTS headset (WAHTS Hearing LLC) and TabSINT mobile application (Shapiro et al. 2020), permit tighter control of stimulus properties across sites. Combining these technologies with other commercially available devices such as virtual reality head mounted displays with eye-tracking and other physiological measurement capabilities may also permit large-scale measurement of physiological indices of listening effort (Phillips et al., 2023). Advances in computing and statistical approaches (e.g., machine learning, generalized additive mixed modeling) can support this endeavor by permitting analysis of large multidimensional data sets and extracting novel insights (for examples of these approaches in psycholinguistics, see Fromont et al., 2020; Meulman et al., 2015).

4.2.3 Enhancing clinical care

Research in cognitive hearing science has been motivated by patient complaints, such as problems understanding speech in noise despite normal hearing thresholds (Edwards, 2020). However, there remains a disconnect between the field's acknowledgment of these problems and the clinical measures that are available, clinically feasible, and used widely to validate them (Fitzgerald et al., 2023). Although changing standard of care protocols for assessments and interventions can be a challenging endeavor, it is a long-term goal worth striving for.

Several studies of masked speech recognition in bilingual populations have noted that listening difficulties (reflected in accuracy) for some bilinguals with normal hearing thresholds and no history of auditory processing disorder present similarly to difficulties experienced by monolinguals with a mild hearing loss or auditory processing disorder (e.g., Lucks Mendel & Widner, 2016; Phillips et al., 2024; Shi & Zaki, 2014). This raises the possibility that language differences have the potential to be misinterpreted as auditory deficits in a clinical setting, even among highly proficient bilinguals. Insights from psycholinguistics can provide a framework for understanding how linguistic factors may contribute to listening difficulty and can help guide selection and interpretation of performance on speech-based auditory tests (e.g., Shi, 2011, 2014).

Indeed, a growing number of listening studies have appealed to psycholinguistic mechanisms to explain listening differences among bilinguals (e.g., Bieber et al., 2024; Desjardins et al., 2019; Regalado et al., 2019; Schmidtke, 2016; Skoe & Karayanidi, 2019; Suite et al., 2023). These have pointed to differences in lexical representation, crosslinguistic interference, and the well-characterized relationship between the age at which one begins to learn a second language and attainment in that language (Long, 1990). Other insights from psycholinguistics may prove similarly useful in predicting and interpreting listening differences. For example, psycholinguistic evidence that mechanisms involved in spoken word recognition and sentence processing can shift with changes in language exposure (e.g., Dussias & Sagarra, 2007) and proficiency (e.g., Gilbert et al., 2021) can provide a framework for interpreting the impacts of these dynamic aspects of language experience on speech recognition. Similarly, psycholinguistic research on age-related changes in crosslinguistic competition (Baum & Titone, 2014; Titone et al., 2021), processing strategies (Federmeier et al., 2010), and processing efficiency (Colby & McMurray, 2023) may shed light on the mechanisms that drive interactions between age and language experience on difficult listening tasks involving multiword stimuli. The influence of language mode on crosslinguistic activation (e.g., Canseco-Gonzalez et al., 2010) may also predict differences in listening difficulty related to the languages used in the clinical encounter. However, for these insights to ultimately benefit all patients, much more work is needed to identify how various language experience variables affect clinical auditory tests and how these may interact with other individual differences in sensory and cognitive systems to impact listening difficulty and, ultimately, clinical recommendations.

Above all, it is critical that work in this area carefully considers how language-related differences are contextualized. Bilingualism is the norm around the world (Grosjean, 2010) and increasingly in the United States (Dietrich & Hernandez, 2022). The ability to acquire multiple languages is an evolutionary adaptation (Hirschfeld, 2008) and the benefits of bilingualism are many (for a recent review, see Dentella et al., 2024). Framing differences due to language as "deficits" has the potential to further stigmatize the language practices of already marginalized groups and hamper efforts to promote bilingualism in the United States. Researchers should keep this in mind as we seek to understand the impacts of bilingualism on listening difficulty and we should be careful to consider differences not as a departure from a WEIRD norm, but rather in their own terms (see McMurray et al., 2023 for a parallel proposal in psycholinguistics).

5. Conclusion

The fields of cognitive hearing science and psycholinguistics have historically had different approaches to understanding the processes that support listening. Broadly, cognitive hearing science has focused on the acoustic factors that make speech recognition challenging, particularly for individuals with hearing complaints. Psycholinguistics has historically emphasized understanding the basic mechanisms that support language acquisition and language use. This chapter has aimed to highlight that both perspectives are critically important to our understanding of what makes listening difficult. A growing cross-disciplinary literature has provided evidence that speech processing is interactively impacted by acoustic, linguistic, and cognitive demands that are likely to occur in our daily lives and likely to vary across individuals with differing abilities and experiences. By continuing to make concerted efforts to bring together the rich literatures, advanced methods, and diverse populations of these (and other) fields, we stand to gain a better theoretical understanding of the systems that support listening as well as better diagnostic tools and more effective interventions. Long-term, understanding the myriad hierarchical and interactive sources of communication challenges experienced in the real world will allow us to not only be able to hear our patients' complaints, but to truly listen.

Disclaimer

The identification of specific products or scientific instrumentation is considered an integral part of the scientific endeavor and does not constitute endorsement or implied endorsement on the part of the authors, DoD, or any component agency. The views expressed in this article are those of the authors and do not necessarily reflect the official policy of the Department of Defense or the U.S. Government.

References

Akeroyd, M. A. (2008). Are individual differences in speech reception related to individual differences in cognitive ability? A survey of twenty experimental studies with normal and hearing-impaired adults. *International Journal of Audiology, 47*(Suppl. 2), https://doi.org/10.1080/14992020802301142.

Allopenna, P. D., Magnuson, J. S., & Tanenhaus, M. K. (1998). Tracking the time course of spoken word recognition using eye movements: Evidence for continuous mapping models. *Journal of Memory and Language, 38*(4), 419–439. https://doi.org/10.1006/jmla.1997.2558.

Altmann, G. T. M. (1990). *Cognitive models of speech processing: An introduction. Cognitive models of speech processing: Psycholinguistic and computational perspectives.* MIT Press, 1–23.

Altmann, G. T. M. (2006). History of psycholinguistics. *The encyclopedia of language and linguistics.* Elsevier. http://www.psycholinguistics.com/gerry_altmann/research/papers/files/encyclopedia.pdf.

Altmann, G. T. M., & Kamide, Y. (1999). Incremental interpretation at verbs: Restricting the domain of subsequent reference. *Cognition, 73*(3), 247–264. https://doi.org/10.1016/S0010-0277(99)00059-1.

Anastasiadou, S., & Al Khalili, Y. (2023, March 23). *Hearing loss.* StatPearls. https://www.ncbi.nlm.nih.gov/books/NBK542323/.

Angara, P., Tsang, D. C., Hoffer, M. E., & Snapp, H. A. (2021). Self-perceived hearing status creates an unrealized barrier to hearing healthcare utilization. *The Laryngoscope, 131*(1), E289–E295. https://doi.org/10.1002/lary.28604.

ANSI. (1969). *ANSI S3.5–1969.* American National Standard Methods for the Calculation of the Articulation Index. ANSI.

ANSI. (1997). ANSI S3.5–1997. American National Standard Methods for the Calculation of the Speech Intelligibility Index. ANSI.

Arlinger, S., Lunner, T., Lyxell, B., & Pichora-Fuller, K. M. (2009). The emergence of cognitive hearing science. *Scandinavian Journal of Psychology, 50*(5), 371–384. https://doi.org/10.1111/j.1467-9450.2009.00753.x.

Ayasse, N. D., & Wingfield, A. (2018). A tipping point in listening effort: Effects of linguistic complexity and age-related hearing loss on sentence comprehension. *Trends in Hearing, 22*. https://doi.org/10.1177/2331216518790907.

Baayen, R. H. H., Davidson, D. J. J., & Bates, D. M. M. (2008). Mixed-effects modeling with crossed random effects for subjects and items. *Journal of Memory and Language, 59*(4), 390–412. https://doi.org/10.1016/j.jml.2007.12.005.

Barrett, M. E., Gordon-Salant, S., & Brungart, D. S. (2021). The cafeteria study: Effects of facial masks, hearing protection, and real-world noise on speech recognition. *The Journal of the Acoustical Society of America, 150*(6), 4244–4255. https://doi.org/10.1121/10.0008898.

Bates, E., Devescovi, A., & Wulfeck, B. (2001). Psycholinguistics: A cross-language perspective. *Annual Review of Psychology, 52*(1), 369–396. https://doi.org/10.1146/annurev.psych.52.1.369.

Baum, S., & Titone, D. (2014). Moving toward a neuroplasticity view of bilingualism, executive control, and aging. *Applied Psycholinguistics, 35*(5), 857–894. https://doi.org/10.1017/S0142716414000174.

Beck, D. L., Danhauer, J. L., Abrams, H. B., Atcherson, S. R., Brown, D. K., Chasin, M., ... Wolfe, J. (2018). Audiologic considerations for people with normal hearing sensitivity yet hearing difficulty and/or speech-in-noise problems. *Hearing Review, 25*(10), 28–38.

Beechey, T. (2022). Ecological validity, external validity, and mundane realism in hearing science. *Ear & Hearing, 43*(5), 1395–1401. https://doi.org/10.1097/AUD.0000000000001202.

Ben-David, B. M., Chambers, C. G., Daneman, M., Pichora-Fuller, M. K., Reingold, E. M., & Schneider, B. A. (2011). Effects of aging and noise on real-time spoken word recognition: Evidence from eye Movements. *Journal of Speech Language and Hearing Research, 54*(1), 243. https://doi.org/10.1044/1092-4388(2010/09-0233).

Bent, T., Baese-Berk, M., Borrie, S. A., & McKee, M. (2016). Individual differences in the perception of regional, nonnative, and disordered speech varieties. *The Journal of the Acoustical Society of America, 140*(5), 3775–3786. https://doi.org/10.1121/1.4966677.

Bice, K., & Kroll, J. F. (2021). Grammatical processing in two languages: How individual differences in language experience and cognitive abilities shape comprehension in heritage bilinguals. *Journal of Neurolinguistics, 58*, 100963. https://doi.org/10.1016/j.jneuroling.2020.100963.

Bieber, R. E., Brodbeck, C., & Anderson, S. (2022). Examining the context benefit in older adults: A combined behavioral-electrophysiologic word identification study. *Neuropsychologia, 170*, 108224. https://doi.org/10.1016/j.neuropsychologia.2022.108224.

Bieber, R. E., Phillips, I., Ellis, G. M., & Brungart, D. S. (2024). *Current age and language use impact speech-in-noise differently for monolingual and bilingual adults*. OSF. https://doi.org/10.31234/osf.io/7jxvc.

Bloomfield, A., Wayland, S. C., Rhoades, E., Blodgett, A., Linck, J., & Ross, S. (2010). *What makes listening difficult? Factors affecting second language listening comprehension*. Defense Technical Information Center. https://doi.org/10.21236/ADA550176.

Blumenthal, A. L. (1987). The emergence of psycholinguistics. *Synthese*, 313–323.

Borghini, G., & Hazan, V. (2018). Listening effort during sentence processing is increased for non-native listeners: A pupillometry study. *Frontiers in Neuroscience, 12*. https://doi.org/10.3389/fnins.2018.00152.

Borghini, G., & Hazan, V. (2020). Effects of acoustic and semantic cues on listening effort during native and non-native speech perception. *The Journal of the Acoustical Society of America, 147*(6), 3783–3794. https://doi.org/10.1121/10.0001126.

Broersma, M., & Cutler, A. (2011). Competition dynamics of second-language listening. *Quarterly Journal of Experimental Psychology, 64*(1), 74–95.

Brown, V. A., McLaughlin, D. J., Strand, J. F., & Van Engen, K. J. (2020). Rapid adaptation to fully intelligible nonnative-accented speech reduces listening effort. *Quarterly Journal of Experimental Psychology*, 174702182091672. https://doi.org/10.1177/1747021820916726.

Brungart, D. S., Barrett, M. E., Cohen, J. I., Fodor, C., Yancey, C. M., & Gordon-Salant, S. (2020). Objective assessment of speech intelligibility in crowded public spaces. *Ear and Hearing, 41*, 68S. https://doi.org/10.1097/AUD.0000000000000943.

Brungart, D. S., Makashay, M. J., & Sheffield, B. M. (2021). Development of an 80-word clinical version of the modified rhyme test (MRT 80). *The Journal of the Acoustical Society of America, 149*(5), 3311–3327. https://doi.org/10.1121/10.0003563.

Brungart, D. S., Sherlock, L. P., Kuchinsky, S. E., Perry, T. T., Bieber, R. E., Grant, K. W., & Bernstein, J. G. W. (2022). Assessment methods for determining small changes in hearing performance over time. *The Journal of the Acoustical Society of America, 151*(6), 3866–3885. https://doi.org/10.1121/10.0011509.

Burke, L. A., & Naylor, G. (2020). Daily-life fatigue in mild to moderate hearing impairment: An ecological momentary assessment study. *Ear and Hearing, 0*, 1518–1532. https://doi.org/10.1097/AUD.0000000000000888.

Cai, Z. G., Gilbert, R. A., Davis, M. H., Gaskell, M. G., Farrar, L., Adler, S., & Rodd, J. M. (2017). Accent modulates access to word meaning: Evidence for a speaker-model account of spoken word recognition. *Cognitive Psychology, 98*, 73–101. https://doi.org/10.1016/j.cogpsych.2017.08.003.

Canseco-Gonzalez, E., Brehm, L., Brick, C. A., Brown-Schmidt, S., Fischer, K., & Wagner, K. (2010). Carpet or Cárcel: The effect of age of acquisition and language mode on bilingual lexical access. *Language and Cognitive Processes, 25*(5), 669–705.

Carterette, E. C., & Friedman, M. P. (1978). *Handbook of perception, Vol. IV*. Elsevier.

Cheng, L. S. P., Burgess, D., Vernooij, N., Solís-Barroso, C., McDermott, A., & Namboodiripad, S. (2021). The problematic concept of native speaker in psycholinguistics: Replacing vague and harmful terminology with inclusive and accurate measures. *Frontiers in Psychology, 12*. https://www.frontiersin.org/articles/10.3389/fpsyg.2021.715843.

Ching, T. Y. C., & Dillon, H. (2013). A brief overview of factors affecting speech intelligibility of people with hearing loss: Implications for amplification. *American Journal of Audiology, 22*(2), 306–309. https://doi.org/10.1044/1059-0889(2013/12-0075).

Colby, S. E., & McMurray, B. (2023). Efficiency of spoken word recognition slows across the adult lifespan. *Cognition, 240*, 105588. https://doi.org/10.1016/j.cognition.2023.105588.

Cowan, T., Calandruccio, L., Buss, E., Rodriguez, B., & Leibold, L. J. (2023). Predicting language dominance in Spanish/English bilingual adults based on relative speech-in-speech recognition scores. *International Journal of Bilingualism*, 13670069231195394. https://doi.org/10.1177/13670069231195394.

Cowan, T., Paroby, C., Leibold, L. J., Buss, E., Rodriguez, B., & Calandruccio, L. (2022). Masked-speech recognition for linguistically diverse populations: A focused review and suggestions for the future. *Journal of Speech, Language, and Hearing Research, 65*(8), 3195–3216. https://doi.org/10.1044/2022_JSLHR-22-00011.

Cuetos, F., & Mitchell, D. C. (1988). Cross-linguistic differences in parsing: Restrictions on the use of the Late Closure strategy in Spanish. *Cognition, 30*(1), 73–105. https://doi.org/10.1016/0010-0277(88)90004-2.

Cutler, A. (2009). Psycholinguistics in our time. In P. Rabbitt (Ed.). *Inside psychology: A science over 50 years* (pp. 91–101). Oxford University Press.

Cutler, A., Mehler, J., Norris, D., & Segui, J. (1983). A language-specific comprehension strategy. *Nature, 304*(5922), 159–160.

De Sousa, K. C., Smits, C., Moore, D. R., Chada, S., Myburgh, H., & Swanepoel, D. W. (2022). Global use and outcomes of the hearWHO mHealth hearing test. 20552076221113204 *Digital Health, 8*, 20552076221113204. https://doi.org/10.1177/20552076221113204.

Dentella, V., Masullo, C., & Leivada, E. (2024). Bilingual disadvantages are systematically compensated by bilingual advantages across tasks and populations. *Scientific Reports, 14*(1), https://doi.org/10.1038/s41598-024-52417-5.

Desjardins, J. L., Barraza, E. G., & Orozco, J. A. (2019). Age-related changes in speech recognition performance in Spanish–English bilinguals' first and second languages. *Journal of Speech, Language, and Hearing Research, 62*(7), 2553–2563. https://doi.org/10.1044/2019_JSLHR-H-18-0435.

Desmet, T., & Duyck, W. (2007). Bilingual language processing. *Language and Linguistics Compass, 1*(3), 168–194.

Devesse, A., van Wieringen, A., & Wouters, J. (2020). AVATAR assesses speech understanding and multitask costs in ecologically relevant listening situations. *Ear and Hearing, 41*(3), 521. https://doi.org/10.1097/AUD.0000000000000778.

Dietrich, S., & Hernandez, E. (2022). *Language Use in the United States: 2019* (American Community Survey Reports). U.S. Census Bureau. https://www.census.gov/library/publications/2022/acs/acs-50.html.

Drouin, J. R., & Theodore, R. M. (2020). Leveraging interdisciplinary perspectives to optimize auditory training for cochlear implant users. *Language and Linguistics Compass, 14*(9), e12394. https://doi.org/10.1111/lnc3.12394.

Dubno, J. R., Dirks, D. D., & Morgan, D. E. (1984). Effects of age and mild hearing loss on speech recognition in noise. *Journal of the Acoustical Society of America, 76*, 87–96.

Dussias, P. E., & Sagarra, N. (2007). The effect of exposure on syntactic parsing in Spanish-English bilinguals. *Bilingualism: Language and Cognition, 10*(01), 101–116.

Edwards, B. (2007). The future of hearing aid technology. *Trends in Amplification, 11*(1), 31–45. https://doi.org/10.1177/1084713806298004.

Edwards, B. (2020). Emerging technologies, market segments, and MarkeTrak 10 insights in hearing health technology. *Seminars in Hearing, 41*(1), 37–54. https://doi.org/10.1055/s-0040-1701244.

Eisenberg, L. S., Dirks, D. D., & Bell, T. S. (1995). Speech recognition in amplitude-modulated noise of listeners with normal and listeners with impaired hearing. *Journal of Speech, Language, and Hearing Research, 38*(1), 222–233. https://doi.org/10.1044/jshr.3801.222.

Federmeier, K. D., Kutas, M., & Schul, R. (2010). Age-related and individual differences in the use of prediction during language comprehension. *Brain and Language, 115*(3), 149–161. https://doi.org/10.1016/j.bandl.2010.07.006.

Ferguson, M. A., & Henshaw, H. (2015). How does auditory training work? Joined-up thinking and listening. *Seminars in Hearing, 36*(4), 237–249. https://doi.org/10.1055/s-0035-1564456.

Fernández, E. M., & Cairns, H. S. (Eds.). (2017). *The handbook of psycholinguistics*(1st ed.). Wiley.

Festen, J. M., & Plomp, R. (1990). Effects of fluctuating noise and interfering speech on the speech-reception threshold for impaired and normal hearing. *The Journal of the Acoustical Society of America, 88*, 1725–1736. https://doi.org/10.1121/1.400247.

Fitzgerald, L. P., DeDe, G., & Shen, J. (2024). Effects of linguistic context and noise type on speech comprehension. *Frontiers in Psychology, 15*. https://doi.org/10.3389/fpsyg.2024.1345619.

Fitzgerald, M. B., Gianakas, S. P., Qian, Z. J., Losorelli, S., & Swanson, A. C. (2023). Preliminary guidelines for replacing word-recognition in quiet with speech in noise assessment in the routine audiologic test battery. *Ear and Hearing, 44*(6), 1548. https://doi.org/10.1097/AUD.0000000000001409.

French, N. R., & Steinberg, J. C. (1947). Factors governing the intelligibility of speech sounds. *The Journal of the Acoustical Society of America, 19*(1), 90–119. https://doi.org/10.1121/1.1916407.

Friesen, D. C., Chung-Fat-Yim, A., & Bialystok, E. (2016). Lexical selection differences between monolingual and bilingual listeners. *Brain and Language, 152*, 1–13. https://doi.org/10.1016/j.bandl.2015.11.001.

Fromont, L. A., Royle, P., & Steinhauer, K. (2020). Growing Random Forests reveals that exposure and proficiency best account for individual variability in L2 (and L1) brain potentials for syntax and semantics. *Brain and Language, 204*, 104770. https://doi.org/10.1016/j.bandl.2020.104770.

Gagné, J.-P., Besser, J., & Lemke, U. (2017). Behavioral assessment of listening effort using a dual-task paradigm. *Trends in Hearing, 21*, 1–25. https://doi.org/10.1177/2331216516687287.

Garnham, A., Garrod, S., & Sanford, A. (2006). Observations on the past and future of psycholinguistics. In M. J. Traxler, & M. A. Gernsbacher (Eds.). *Handbook of psycholinguistics* (pp. 1–18)(2nd ed.). Elsevier/Academic Press.

Gilbert, A. C., Lee, J. G., Coulter, K., Wolpert, M. A., Kousaie, S., Gracco, V. L., ... Baum, S. R. (2021). Spoken word segmentation in first and second language: When ERP and behavioral measures diverge. *Frontiers in Psychology, 12*. https://doi.org/10.3389/fpsyg.2021.705668.

Gilbert, J. L., Tamati, T. N., & Pisoni, D. B. (2013). Development, reliability, and validity of PRESTO: A new high-variability sentence recognition test. *Journal of the American Academy of Audiology, 24*(1), 26–36. https://doi.org/10.3766/jaaa.24.1.4.

Giolas, T. G., & Epstein, A. (1963). Comparative intelligibility of word lists and continuous discourse. *Journal of Speech and Hearing Research, 6*(4), 349–358. https://doi.org/10.1044/jshr.0604.349.

Grant, K. W., & Walden, T. C. (2013). Understanding excessive SNR loss in hearing-impaired listeners. *Journal of the American Academy of Audiology, 24*(04), 258–273. https://doi.org/10.3766/jaaa.24.4.3.

Grassi, M., Felline, A., Orlandi, N., Toffanin, M., Goli, G. P., Senyuva, H. A., ... Contemori, G. (2024). PSYCHOACOUSTICS-WEB: A free online tool for the estimation of auditory thresholds. *Behavior Research Methods*. https://doi.org/10.3758/s13428-024-02430-3.

Grosjean, F. (1989). Neurolinguists, beware! The bilingual is not two monolinguals in one person. *Brain and Language, 36*(1), 3–15. https://doi.org/10.1016/0093-934X(89)90048-5.

Grosjean, F. (1998a). Studying bilinguals: Methodological and conceptual issues. *Bilingualism: Language and Cognition, 1*(2), 131–149. https://doi.org/10.1017/S136672899800025X.

Grosjean, F. (1998b). Transfer and language mode. *Bilingualism: Language and Cognition, 1*(3), 175–176.

Grosjean, F. (2010). *Bilingual: Life and reality*. Harvard University Press.

Hannula, S., Bloigu, R., Majamaa, K., Sorri, M., & Mäki-Torkko, E. (2011). Self-reported hearing problems among older adults: Prevalence and comparison to measured hearing impairment. *Journal of the American Academy of Audiology, 22*(8), 550–559. https://doi.org/10.3766/jaaa.22.8.7.

Heald, S., & Nusbaum, H. C. (2014). Speech perception as an active cognitive process. *Frontiers in Systems Neuroscience, 8*. https://doi.org/10.3389/fnsys.2014.00035.

Henrich, J., Heine, S. J., & Norenzayan, A. (2010). The weirdest people in the world? *Behavioral and Brain Sciences, 33*(2–3), 61–83.

Hernández, A. E., Fernández, E. M., & Aznar-Besé, N. (2007). Bilingual sentence processing. In M. G. Gaskell (Ed.). *The Oxford handbook of psycholinguistics* (pp. 371–384). Oxford University Press.

Herrmann, B., & Johnsrude, I. S. (2020). A model of listening engagement (MoLE). *Hearing Research, 397*, 108016. https://doi.org/10.1016/j.heares.2020.108016.

Hirschfeld, L. A. (2008). The bilingual brain revisited: A comment on Hagen (2008). *Evolutionary Psychology, 6*(1), 147470490800600120. https://doi.org/10.1177/147470490800600120.

Hohmann, V., Paluch, R., Krueger, M., Meis, M., & Grimm, G. (2020). The virtual reality lab: Realization and application of virtual sound environments. *Ear and Hearing, 41*, 31S. https://doi.org/10.1097/AUD.0000000000000945.

Hood, J. D., & Poole, J. P. (1980). Influence of the speaker and other factors affecting speech intelligibility. *Audiology: Official Organ of the International Society of Audiology, 19*(5), 434–455. https://doi.org/10.3109/00206098009070077.

Huang, Y. T., & Snedeker, J. (2009). Online interpretation of scalar quantifiers: Insight into the semantics–pragmatics interface. *Cognitive Psychology, 58*(3), 376–415. https://doi.org/10.1016/j.cogpsych.2008.09.001.

Huettig, F., Rommers, J., & Meyer, A. S. (2011). Using the visual world paradigm to study language processing: A review and critical evaluation. *Acta Psychologica, 137*(2), 151–171. https://doi.org/10.1016/j.actpsy.2010.11.003.

Humes, L. E., & Roberts, L. (1990). Speech-recognition difficulties of the hearing-impaired elderly. *Journal of Speech, Language, and Hearing Research, 33*(4), 726–735. https://doi.org/10.1044/jshr.3304.726.

Kahneman, D. (1973). *Attention and effort*. Prentice-Hall, https://doi.org/10.2307/1421603.

Kaongoen, N., Choi, J., Choi, J. W., Kwon, H., Hwang, C., Hwang, G., ... Jo, S. (2023). The future of wearable EEG: A review of ear-EEG technology and its applications. *Journal of Neural Engineering, 20*(5), 051002. https://doi.org/10.1088/1741-2552/acfcda.

Keidser, G., Naylor, G., Brungart, D. S., Caduff, A., Campos, J., Carlile, S., ... Smeds, K. (2020). The quest for ecological validity in hearing science: What it is, why it matters, and how to advance it. *Ear and Hearing, 41*(Suppl. 1), 5S–19S. https://doi.org/10.1097/AUD.0000000000000944.

Kidd, E., Donnelly, S., & Christiansen, M. H. (2018). Individual differences in language acquisition and processing. *Trends in Cognitive Sciences, 22*(2), 154–169. https://doi.org/10.1016/j.tics.2017.11.006.

Kilman, L., Zekveld, A., Hällgren, M., & Rönnberg, J. (2014). The influence of non-native language proficiency on speech perception performance. *Frontiers in Psychology, 5*, 651.

Kirk, K. I., Pisoni, D. B., & Miyamoto, R. C. (1997). Effects of stimulus variability on speech perception in listeners with hearing impairment. *Journal of Speech, Language, and Hearing Research, 40*(6), 1395–1405. https://doi.org/10.1044/jslhr.4006.1395.

Koelewijn, T., Bronkhorst, A., & Theeuwes, J. (2010). Attention and the multiple stages of multisensory integration: A review of audiovisual studies. *Acta Psychologica, 134*(3), 372–384. https://doi.org/10.1016/j.actpsy.2010.03.010.

Koelewijn, T., Zekveld, A. A., Festen, J. M., & Kramer, S. E. (2014). The influence of informational masking on speech perception and pupil response in adults with hearing impairment. *The Journal of the Acoustical Society of America, 135*(3), 1596–1606. https://doi.org/10.1121/1.4863198.

Kraus, N., McGee, T., Carrell, T. D., King, C., Tremblay, K., & Nicol, T. (1995). Central auditory system plasticity associated with speech discrimination training. *Journal of Cognitive Neuroscience*, 7(1), 25–32. https://doi.org/10.1162/jocn.1995.7.1.25.

Kreul, E. J., Nixon, J. C., Kryter, K. D., Bell, D. W., Lang, J. S., & Schubert, E. D. (1968). A proposed clinical test of speech discrimination. *Journal of Speech and Hearing Research, 11*(3), 536–552. https://doi.org/10.1044/jshr.1103.536.

Krizman, J., Bradlow, A. R., Lam, S. S.-Y., & Kraus, N. (2017). How bilinguals listen in noise: Linguistic and non-linguistic factors. *Bilingualism: Language and Cognition, 20*(4), 834–843. https://doi.org/10.1017/S1366728916000444.

Kuchinsky, S. E., Ahlstrom, J. B., Vaden, K. I., Cute, S. L., Humes, L. E., Dubno, J. R., & Eckert, M. A. (2013). Pupil size varies with word listening and response selection difficulty in older adults with hearing loss. *Psychophysiology, 50*(1), 23–34. https://doi.org/10.1111/j.1469-8986.2012.01477.x.

Kuchinsky, S. E., & DeRoy Milvae, K. (2024). Pupillometry in audiology. In M. H. Papesh, & S. D. Goldinger (Eds.). *Modern pupillometry* (pp. 229–258). Springer. https://doi.org/10.1007/978-3-031-54896-3_8.

Kuchinsky, S. E., Razeghi, N., & Pandža, N. B. (2023). Auditory, lexical, and multitasking demands interactively impact listening effort. *Journal of Speech, Language, and Hearing Research,* 1–17. https://doi.org/10.1044/2023_JSLHR-22-00548.

Levelt, W. J. (2013). *A history of psycholinguistics: The pre-Chomskyan era.* Oxford University Press.

Long, M. H. (1990). Maturational constraints on language development. *Studies in Second Language Acquisition, 12*(3), 251–285. https://doi.org/10.1017/S0272263100009165.

Luce, P. A., & Pisoni, D. B. (1998). Recognizing spoken words: The neighborhood activation model. *Ear & Hearing, 19*(1), 1–36. https://doi.org/10.1097/00003446-199802000-00001.

Lucks Mendel, L., & Widner, H. (2016). Speech perception in noise for bilingual listeners with normal hearing. *International Journal of Audiology, 55*(2), 126–134. https://doi.org/10.3109/14992027.2015.1061710.

Magnuson, J. S., Nusbaum, H. C., Akahane-Yamada, R., & Saltzman, D. (2021). Talker familiarity and the accommodation of talker variability. *Attention, Perception, and Psychophysics, 83*(4), 1842–1860. https://doi.org/10.3758/S13414-020-02203-Y/FIGURES/8.

Marian, V., & Spivey, M. (2003). Competing activation in bilingual language processing: Within- and between-language competition. *Bilingualism: Language and Cognition, 6*(2), 97–115. https://doi.org/10.1017/S1366728903001068.

Marslen-Wilson, W. D., & Welsh, A. (1978). Processing interactions and lexical access during word recognition in continuous speech. *Cognitive Psychology, 10*(1), 29–63. https://doi.org/10.1016/0010-0285(78)90018-X.

McAdams, S., & Bigand, E. (Eds.). (1993). *Thinking in sound: The cognitive psychology of human audition*Oxford University Press, https://doi.org/10.1093/acprof:oso/9780198522577.001.0001.

McClelland, J. L., & Elman, J. L. (1986). The TRACE model of speech perception. *Cognitive Psychology, 18*(1), 1–86. https://doi.org/10.1016/0010-0285(86)90015-0.

McClelland, J. L., Mirman, D., & Holt, L. L. (2006). Are there interactive processes in speech perception? *Trends in Cognitive Sciences, 10*(8), 363–369. https://doi.org/10.1016/j.tics.2006.06.007.

McCoy, S. L., Tun, P. A., Cox, L. C., Colangelo, M., Stewart, R. A., & Wingfield, A. (2005). Hearing loss and perceptual effort: Downstream effects on older adults' memory for speech. *The Quarterly Journal of Experimental, 58*(1), 22–33. https://doi.org/10.1080/02724980443000151.

McLaughlin, D. J., Zink, M. E., Gaunt, L., Brent Spehar, Van Engen, K. J., Sommers, M. S., & Peelle, J. E. (2022). Pupillometry reveals cognitive demands of lexical competition during spoken word recognition in young and older adults. *Psychonomic Bulletin and Review, 29*(1), 268–280. https://doi.org/10.3758/s13423-021-01991-0.

McMurray, B., Baxelbaum, K. S., Colby, S., & Tomblin, J. B. (2023). Understanding language processing in variable populations on their own terms: Towards a functionalist psycholinguistics of individual differences, development, and disorders. *Applied Psycholinguistics, 44*(4), 565–592. https://doi.org/10.1017/S0142716423000255.

McQueen, J. M. (2007). Eight questions about spoken word recognition. In M. G. Gaskell, & G. Altmann (Eds.). *The Oxford handbook of psycholinguistics* (pp. 37–53). Oxford University Press.

McQueen, J. M., Norris, D., & Cutler, A. (2006). Are there really interactive processes in speech perception? *Trends in Cognitive Sciences, 10*(12), 533. https://doi.org/10.1016/j.tics.2006.10.004.

Mellinger, C. D., & Hanson, T. A. (2022). Considerations of ecological validity in cognitive translation and interpreting studies. *Translation, Cognition & Behavior, 5*(1), 1–26. https://doi.org/10.1075/tcb.00061.mel.

Menken, S., Keestra, M., Rutting, L., Post, G., Roo, M., De, Blad, S., & Greef, L. D. (Eds.). (2016). *An introduction to interdisciplinary research: Theory and practice*. Amsterdam University Press.

Meulman, N., Wieling, M., Sprenger, S. A., Stowe, L. A., & Schmid, M. S. (2015). Age effects in L2 grammar processing as revealed by ERPs and how (not) to study them. *PLoS One, 10*(12), e0143328. https://doi.org/10.1371/journal.pone.0143328.

Mirman, D., McClelland, J. L., & Holt, L. L. (2006). Response to McQueen et al.: Theoretical and empirical arguments support interactive processing. *Trends in Cognitive Sciences, 10*(12), 534. https://doi.org/10.1016/j.tics.2006.10.003.

Mok, B. A., Viswanathan, V., Borjigin, A., Singh, R., Kafi, H., & Bharadwaj, H. M. (2024). Web-based psychoacoustics: Hearing screening, infrastructure, and validation. *Behavior Research Methods, 56*(3), 1433–1448. https://doi.org/10.3758/s13428-023-02101-9.

Moore, B. C. J. (2007). *Cochlear hearing loss: Physiological, psychological and technical issues*. John Wiley & Sons.

Nelson, P., Kohnert, K., Sabur, S., & Shaw, D. (2005). Classroom noise and children learning through a second language: Double jeopardy? *Language, Speech, and Hearing Services in Schools, 36*, 219–229.

Nilsson, M., Soli, S. D., & Sullivan, J. A. (1994). Development of the Hearing In Noise Test for the measurement of speech reception thresholds in quiet and in noise. *The Journal of the Acoustical Society of America, 95*(2), 1085. https://doi.org/10.1121/1.408469.

Norcliffe, E., Harris, A. C., & Jaeger, T. F. (2015). Cross-linguistic psycholinguistics and its critical role in theory development: Early beginnings and recent advances. *Language, Cognition and Neuroscience, 30*(9), 1009–1032. https://doi.org/10.1080/23273798.2015.1080373.

Norris, D. (1994). Shortlist: A connectionist model of continuous speech recognition. *Cognition, 52*(3), 189–234. https://doi.org/10.1016/0010-0277(94)90043-4.

Nygaard, L. C., & Pisoni, D. B. (1998). Talker-specific learning in speech perception. *Perception & Psychophysics, 60*(3), 355–376. https://doi.org/10.3758/BF03206860.

Ohlenforst, B., Zekveld, A. A., Lunner, T., Wendt, D., Naylor, G., Wang, Y., ... Kramer, S. E. (2017). Impact of stimulus-related factors and hearing impairment on listening effort as indicated by pupil dilation. *Hearing Research, 351*, 68–79. https://doi.org/10.1016/j.heares.2017.05.012.

Onoda, R. M., Pereira, L. D., & Guilherme, A. (2006). Temporal processing and dichotic listening in bilingual and non-bilingual descendants. *Brazilian Journal of Otorhinolaryngology, 72*(6), 737–746. https://doi.org/10.1016/S1808-8694(15)31040-5.

Pakulak, E., & Neville, H. J. (2010). Proficiency differences in syntactic processing of monolingual native speakers indexed by event-related potentials. *Journal of Cognitive Neuroscience, 22*(12), 2728–2744.

Parmar, B. J., Rajasingam, S. L., Bizley, J. K., & Vickers, D. A. (2022). Factors affecting the Use of speech testing in adult audiology. *American Journal of Audiology, 31*(3), 528–540. https://doi.org/10.1044/2022_AJA-21-00233.

Peelle, J. E., & Wingfield, A. (2016). The neural consequences of age-related hearing loss. *Trends in Neurosciences, 39*(7), 486–497. https://doi.org/10.1016/j.tins.2016.05.001.

Peng, Z. E., Waz, S., Buss, E., Shen, Y., Richards, V., Bharadwaj, H., ... Venezia, J. H. (2022). FORUM: Remote testing for psychological and physiological acoustics. *The Journal of the Acoustical Society of America, 151*(5), 3116–3128. https://doi.org/10.1121/10.0010422.

Penrod, J. P. (1979). Talker effects on word-discrimination scores of adults with sensorineural hearing impairment. *Journal of Speech and Hearing Disorders, 44*(3), 340–349. https://doi.org/10.1044/jshd.4403.340.

Peters, R. W., Moore, B. C. J., & Baer, T. (1998). Speech reception thresholds in noise with and without spectral and temporal dips for hearing-impaired and normally hearing people. *The Journal of the Acoustical Society of America, 103*(1), 577–587. https://doi.org/10.1121/1.421128.

Phillips, I., Bieber, R. E., Dirks, C., Grant, K. W., & Brungart, D. S. (2024). Age impacts speech-in-noise recognition differently for nonnative and native listeners. *Journal of Speech, Language, and Hearing Research.* https://doi.org/10.1044/2024_JSLHR-23-00470.

Phillips, I., Ellis, G. M., McNamara, B., Lefler, J., DeRoy Milvae, K., Gordon-Salant, S., & Brungart, D. S. (2023, May 8). *Examining the feasibility of integrating pupillometry measures of listening effort into clinical audiology assessments* [Poster]. 184th Meeting of the Acoustical Society of America, Chicago, Il.

Pichora-Fuller, M. K., Kramer, S. E., Eckert, M. A., Edwards, B., Hornsby, B. W. Y., Humes, L. E., ... Wingfield, A. (2016). Hearing impairment and cognitive energy: The framework for understanding effortful listening (FUEL). *Ear and Hearing, 37*, 5S–27S. https://doi.org/10.1097/AUD.0000000000000312.

Pichora-Fuller, M. K., Schneider, B. A., & Daneman, M. (1995). How young and old adults listen to and remember speech in noise. *The Journal of the Acoustical Society of America, 97*(1), 593–608. https://doi.org/10.1121/1.412282.

Pickering, M. J., & Van Gompel, R. P. G. (2006). Syntactic parsing. In M. J. Traxler, & M. A. Gernsbacher (Eds.). *Handbook of psycholinguistics* (pp. 455–504)(2nd ed.). Elsevier/Academic Press.

Pisoni, D. B. (1997). Some thoughts on "normalization" in speech perception. In J. Mullennix, & K. Johnson (Eds.). *Talker variability in speech processing* (pp. 9–32). Academic Press.

Plomp, R. (1978). Auditory handicap of hearing impairment and the limited benefit of hearing aids. *The Journal of the Acoustical Society of America, 63*, 533–549. https://doi.org/10.1121/1.381753.

Ramkissoon, I., & Cole, M. (2011). Self-reported hearing difficulty versus audiometric screening in younger and older smokers and nonsmokers. *Journal of Clinical Medicine Research, 3*(4), 183–190. https://doi.org/10.4021/jocmr611w.

Regalado, D., Kong, J., Buss, E., & Calandruccio, L. (2019). Effects of language history on sentence recognition in noise or two-talker speech: Monolingual, early bilingual, and late bilingual speakers of English. *American Journal of Audiology, 28*(4), 935–946. https://doi.org/10.1044/2019_AJA-18-0194.

Rimikis, S., Smiljanic, R., & Calandruccio, L. (2013). Nonnative English speaker performance on the Basic English Lexicon (BEL) sentences. *Journal of Speech, Language, and Hearing Research, 56*(3), 792–804. https://doi.org/10.1044/1092-4388(2012/12-0178).

Rönnberg, J., Lunner, T., Zekveld, A., Sörqvist, P., Danielsson, H., Lyxell, B., ... Rudner, M. (2013). The Ease of Language Understanding (ELU) model: Theoretical, empirical, and clinical advances. *Frontiers in Systems Neuroscience, 7*, 1–17. https://doi.org/10.3389/fnsys.2013.00031.

Rönnberg, J., Rudner, M., Foo, C., & Lunner, T. (2008). Cognition counts: A working memory system for ease of language understanding (ELU). *International Journal of Audiology, 47*(*Suppl. 2*), S99–S105. https://doi.org/10.1080/14992020802301167.

Rossi, E., & Diaz, M. (2016). How aging and bilingualism influence language processing. *Linguistic Approaches to Bilingualism, 6*(1/2), 9–42. https://doi.org/10.1075/lab.14029.ros.

Salthouse, T. A. (1996). The processing-speed theory of adult age differences in cognition. *Psychological Review, 103*(3), 403.

Samuel, A. (1996). Phoneme restoration. *Language and Cognitive Processes, 11*(6), 647–654. https://doi.org/10.1080/016909696387051.

Sánchez, L. M., Struys, E., & Declerck, M. (2022). Ecological validity and bilingual language control: Voluntary language switching between sentences. *Language, Cognition and Neuroscience*. https://www.tandfonline.com/doi/full/10.1080/23273798.2021.2016873.

Schmidtke, J. (2014). Second language experience modulates word retrieval effort in bilinguals: Evidence from pupillometry. *Frontiers in Psychology, 5*, 1–16. https://doi.org/10.3389/fpsyg.2014.00137.

Schmidtke, J. (2016). The bilingual disadvantage in speech understanding in noise is likely a frequency effect related to reduced language exposure. *Frontiers in Psychology, 7*. https://www.frontiersin.org/article/10.3389/fpsyg.2016.00678.

Schmuckler, M. A. (2001). What is ecological validity? A dimensional analysis. *Infancy: The Official Journal of the International Society on Infant Studies, 2*(4), 419–436. https://doi.org/10.1207/S15327078IN0204_02.

Schwartz, A. I., & Kroll, J. F. (2006). Language processing in bilingual speakers. In M. J. Traxler, & M. A. Gernsbacher (Eds.). *Handbook of psycholinguistics* (pp. 967–1000)(2nd ed.). Elsevier/Academic Press.

Shapiro, M. L., Norris, J. A., Wilbur, J. C., Brungart, D. S., & Clavier, O. H. (2020). TabSINT: Open-source mobile software for distributed studies of hearing. *International Journal of Audiology, 59*(Suppl. 1), S12–S19. https://doi.org/10.1080/14992027.2019.1698776.

Shi, L.-F. (2011). How "proficient" is proficient? Subjective proficiency as a predictor of bilingual listeners' recognition of English words. *American Journal of Audiology, 20*(1), 19–32. https://doi.org/10.1044/1059-0889(2011/10-0013).

Shi, L.-F. (2014). Validating models of clinical word recognition tests for Spanish/English bilinguals. *Journal of Speech, Language, and Hearing Research, 57*(5), 1896–1907. https://doi.org/10.1044/2014_JSLHR-H-13-0138.

Shi, L.-F. (2018). Assessing perception and comprehension in bilingual adults. In F. Grosjean, & K. Byers-Heinlein (Eds.). *The listening bilingual: Speech perception, comprehension, and bilingualism* (pp. 129–150)(1st ed.). John Wiley & Sons, Inc.

Shi, L.-F., & Sánchez, D. (2010). Spanish/English bilingual listeners on clinical word recognition tests: What to expect and how to predict. *Journal of Speech, Language, and Hearing Research, 53*(5), 1096–1110. https://doi.org/10.1044/1092-4388(2010/09-0199).

Shi, L.-F., & Zaki, N. A. (2014). Psychometric function for NU-6 word recognition in noise: Effects of first language and dominant language. *Ear and Hearing, 35*(2), 236–245. https://doi.org/10.1097/AUD.0b013e3182a698c4.

Skoe, E., & Karayanidi, K. (2019). Bilingualism and speech understanding in noise: Auditory and linguistic factors. *Journal of the American Academy of Audiology, 30*(2), 115–130. https://doi.org/10.3766/jaaa.17082.

Spahr, A. J., Dorman, M. F., Litvak, L. M., Wie, S. V., Gifford, R. H., Loizou, P. C., ... Cook, S. (2012). Development and validation of the AzBio sentence lists. *Ear and Hearing, 33*(1), 112. https://doi.org/10.1097/AUD.0b013e31822c2549.

Speed, L. J., Wnuk, E., & Majid, A. (2017). Studying psycholinguistics out of the Lab. In A. De Groot, & P. Hagoort (Eds.). *Research methods in psycholinguistics and the neurobiology of language* (pp. 190–207)(1st ed.). Wiley. https://doi.org/10.1002/9781394259762.ch10.

Stecker, G. C. (2019). Using virtual reality to assess auditory performance. *The Hearing Journal, 72*(6), 20. https://doi.org/10.1097/01.HJ.0000558464.75151.52.

Strand, J. F., Brown, V. A., Merchant, M. B., Brown, H. E., & Smith, J. (2018). Measuring listening effort: Convergent validity, sensitivity, and links with cognitive and personality measures. *Journal of Speech, Language, and Hearing Research, 61*(6), 1463–1486. https://doi.org/10.1044/2018_JSLHR-H-17-0257.

Strand, J., Brown, V. A., Lin, Y., & Sewell, K. (2023). *Assessing the effects of "native speaker" status on classic findings in speech research.* OSF. https://doi.org/10.31234/osf.io/6ard2.

Strauss, D. J., & Francis, A. L. (2017). Toward a taxonomic model of attention in effortful listening. *Cognitive, Affective & Behavioral Neuroscience, 17*(4), 809–825. https://doi.org/10.3758/s13415-017-0513-0.

Stravinsky, I., & Craft, R. (2002). *Memories and commentaries.* Faber & Faber.

Suite, L., Freiwirth, G., & Babel, M. (2023). Receptive vocabulary predicts multilinguals' recognition skills in adverse listening conditions. *The Journal of the Acoustical Society of America, 154*(6), 3916–3930. https://doi.org/10.1121/10.0023960.

Tanenhaus, M. K., Spivey-Knowlton, M. J., Eberhard, K. M., & Sedivy, J. C. (1995). Integration of Visual and Linguistic Information in Spoken Language Comprehension. *Science (New York, N. Y.), 268*(5217), 1632–1634. https://doi.org/10.1126/science.7777863.

Taylor, B. (2003). Speech-in-noise tests. *The Hearing Journal, 56*(1), 40. https://doi.org/10.1097/01.HJ.0000293000.76300.ff.

Titone, D., Mercier, J., Sudarshan, A., Pivneva, I., Gullifer, J., & Baum, S. (2021). Spoken word processing in bilingual older adults: Assessing within-and cross-language competition using the visual world task. *Linguistic Approaches to Bilingualism, 11*(4), 578–610.

Traxler, M. J., & Gernsbacher, M. A. (Eds.). (2006). *Handbook of psycholinguistics*(2nd ed.). Elsevier/Academic Press.

Van Engen, K. J., & McLaughlin, D. J. (2018). Eyes and ears: Using eye tracking and pupillometry to understand challenges to speech recognition. *Hearing Research, 369*, 56–66. https://doi.org/10.1016/j.heares.2018.04.013.

Van Engen, K. J., & Peelle, J. E. (2014). Listening effort and accented speech. *Frontiers in Human Neuroscience, 8.* https://doi.org/10.3389/fnhum.2014.00577.

Van Hell, J. G., & Tanner, D. (2012). Second language proficiency and cross-language lexical activation. *Language Learning, 62*(s2), 148–171. https://doi.org/10.1111/j.1467-9922.2012.00710.x.

Vermiglio, A. J., Soli, S. D., Freed, D. J., & Fang, X. (2020). The effect of stimulus audibility on the relationship between pure-tone average and speech recognition in noise ability. *Journal of the American Academy of Audiology, 31*(03), 224–232. https://doi.org/10.3766/jaaa.19031.

Von Hapsburg, D., & Peña, E. D. (2002). Understanding bilingualism and its impact on speech audiometry. *Journal of Speech, Language, and Hearing Research, 45*(1), 202–213. https://doi.org/10.1044/1092-4388(2002/015).

Vonk, J. M. J., Higby, E., & Obler, L. K. (2017). Comprehension in older adult populations: Healthy aging, aphasia, and dementia. In E. M. Fernández, & H. S. Cairns (Eds.). *The handbook of psycholinguistics* (pp. 411–437)(1st ed.). Wiley. https://doi.org/10.1002/9781118829516.

Warren, R. M., & Obusek, C. J. (1971). Speech perception and phonemic restorations. *Perception & Psychophysics, 9*(3), 358–362. https://doi.org/10.3758/BF03212667.

Weber, A., & Cutler, A. (2004). Lexical competition in non-native spoken-word recognition. *Journal of Memory and Language, 50*(1), 1–25. https://doi.org/10.1016/S0749-596X(03)00105-0.

Wilson, R. H. (2003). Development of a speech-in-multitalker-babble paradigm to assess word-recognition performance. *Journal of the American Academy of Audiology, 14*(9), 453–470.

Wilson, R. H., McArdle, R. A., & Smith, S. L. (2007). An evaluation of the BKB-SIN, HINT, QuickSIN, and WIN materials on listeners with normal hearing and listeners with hearing loss. *Journal of Speech, Language, and Hearing Research, 50*(4), 844–856. https://doi.org/10.1044/1092-4388(2007/059).

Winn, M. B. (2016). Rapid release from listening effort resulting from semantic context, and effects of spectral degradation and cochlear implants. *Trends in Hearing, 20*, 233121651666972. https://doi.org/10.1177/2331216516669723.

Winn, M. B., & Teece, K. H. (2021). Listening effort is not the same as speech intelligibility score. *Trends in Hearing, 25*, 233121652110276. https://doi.org/10.1177/23312165211027688.

Yu, A. C. L., & Zellou, G. (2019). Individual differences in language processing: Phonology. *Annual Review of Linguistics, 5*, 131–150. https://doi.org/10.1146/annurev-linguistics-011516-033815.

Zekveld, A. A., Koelewijn, T., & Kramer, S. E. (2018). The pupil dilation response to auditory stimuli: Current state of knowledge. *Trends in Hearing, 22*, 2331216518777174. https://doi.org/10.1177/2331216518777174.

Zekveld, A. A., Kramer, S. E., & Festen, J. M. (2010). Pupil response as an indication of effortful listening: The influence of sentence intelligibility. *Ear and Hearing, 31*(4), 480–490. https://doi.org/10.1097/AUD.0b013e3181d4f251.

Zekveld, A. A., Rudner, M., Kramer, S. E., Lyzenga, J., & Rönnberg, J. (2014). Cognitive processing load during listening is reduced more by decreasing voice similarity than by increasing spatial separation between target and masker speech. *Frontiers in Neuroscience, 8*, 1–11. https://doi.org/10.3389/fnins.2014.00088.

Zhao, S., Brown, C. A., Holt, L. L., & Dick, F. (2022). Robust and efficient online auditory psychophysics. *Trends in Hearing, 26*, 233121652211187. https://doi.org/10.1177/23312165221118792.

CHAPTER FOUR

Social episodic memory

Eric D. Leshikar*
Department of Psychology, University of Illinois Chicago, Chicago, IL, United States
*Corresponding author. e-mail address: leshikar@uic.edu

Contents

Abstract

In this paper, I focus on social episodic memory which is the ability to remember specific details associated with specific social targets. In particular, I focus on factors that influence social episodic memory, and how social episodic memory is used in social decisions, especially decisions to approach or avoid social targets (i.e., other people). This paper is organized into four parts. In part one, I review evidence for the self-reference effect, which is the finding that relevance to the self has a strong influence on memory. In part two, I show a self-reference-like effect in social episodic memory that we call the self-similarity effect. The self-similarity effect is a social episodic memory phenomenon where similarity between the self and another social

Psychology of Learning and Motivation, Volume 81
ISSN 0079-7421, https://doi.org/10.1016/bs.plm.2024.06.001

target has a strong effect on memory. In part three, I show that social episodic memory representations, especially memory representations containing affectively positive and negative details, strongly affect subsequent social decisions. In part four, I suggest future directions to better understand how memory for specific social targets might influence a variety of social decisions. Over the course of this paper, I also refer to many domains of knowledge such as aging, schema influence on memory, functional brain activity, effects of political-implying information associated with targets, false memories, and valence effects on memory. Overall, this work examines factors that influence social episodic memory, and further, how social episodic memory representations impact subsequent social decisions, especially decisions to approach or avoid others (i.e., social targets).

1. Opening vignette

Imagine that you (yes you, the reader) are friendly, extraverted, and kind. You value being respectful to all people you interact with, and, further, you value supporting and nurturing others, especially people more junior to you. You go to a social gathering hosted by Terry, and at this event you meet several people. You meet Lauram. Lauram is smiley and extraordinarily warm, genuine, and friendly. You meet Randibi, who is energetic and enthusiastic to talk with you. You meet Nathant. Nathant tells you that he engages respectfully with others, even people he disagrees with. You meet Jennio, who explains that she works with youth in the community, and it is clear she puts substantial effort into building up people around her. Finally, you meet Patwa. Patwa shares his many liberal and progressive beliefs with you, and he tells you his opinions about policy changes that would improve the country. Overall, you form positive impressions of everyone you meet at the gathering. How likely are you to remember details about Lauram, Randibi, Nathant, Jennio, and Patwa, and, further, are there memory-related principles that might account for your memory for these individuals?

Over the next month, you encounter Lauram, Randibi, Nathant, Jennio, and Patwa in your daily life. Will you choose to interact with them? And are there factors, such as what you remember about each person, that will guide how likely you are to approach these individuals? Over the course of the current paper, I will describe evidence yielding insights to these fundamental questions about memory for people, and how memory for people is used in social decisions, especially decisions to approach or avoid other people (i.e., social targets).

2. Introduction

Humans are social. In social contexts, we think about, make inferences of, and remember prior experiences with other people (e.g., social targets) routinely, reflexively, and habitually. Sociality is such a core human experience that work in some branches of science suggests that many of our complex cognitive functions may have arisen to develop and maintain knowledge about complex social structures (Byrne & Bates, 2007). In the present paper, I will focus on one social cognitive function that we call social episodic memory. **Social episodic memory** is the ability to remember specific episodic details associated with specific social targets (e.g., such as remembering that you formed a positive impression of the friendly Lauram). In this paper, I will focus on a factor that has a strong influence over social episodic memory that we call the self-similarity effect (described below), and I will show how social episodic memory representations are used to make social decisions, especially decisions to approach or avoid social targets (such as deciding whether or not to interact with Lauram when you see her in your daily life).

This current paper is organized into four parts. In the first part I talk about a memory phenomenon known as the self-reference effect, which is a memory effect associated with improved episodic memory (e.g., memory for previous events) for studied materials. Although the self-reference effect is not exclusively a phenomenon for social materials (e.g., social targets), the principles laid out in the first part will be highly relevant to the second part that *is* focused on social episodic memory. In the second part I describe a self-reference-like effect in social episodic memory that we call the self-similarity effect. To foreshadow that discussion, I show that similarity to the self (e.g., the extent that a social target is similar to the self) has a strong impact on memory. In the third part I show evidence that people use their social episodic memory representations (i.e., memory for specific episodic details associated with specific social targets) in social decision-making, specifically making the decision to approach or avoid previously encountered targets. In the fourth part I briefly describe future directions to better understand how memory influences social decision making (e.g., expanding on the work I present in part three of the current paper). Importantly, in all four parts I discuss how valence (e.g., positive or negative affective details) influences many of the memory-related phenomena I describe. In addition, I also occasionally cover topics related to aging (i.e., how aging affects some of the memory processes I describe), schemas (i.e., how knowledge structures affects some of the memory effects I mention), brain activity (i.e., regions that support memory processes I describe), false memories (i.e., falsely remembering details about targets not seen before), and political ideology (i.e., how political information affects some aspects of social episodic memory representations). It is worth noting that this paper is not meant to be a thorough review of all relevant work across the many topics I cover. Instead, I will primarily focus on evidence that we have uncovered in our lab. Indeed, there are many highly relevant literatures that I do not describe or cite to keep the narrative of the current paper focused.

3. Part one: Self-reference effect

Although this paper is focused on social episodic memory (i.e., memory for specific episodic details associated with specific social targets), I will begin by describing a memory phenomenon that is not exclusively about memory for social content, and that is the self-reference effect. The self-reference effect is a memory phenomenon where information that is relevant to the self tends to be better remembered compared to information that is less relevant to the self (Burden et al., 2021; Ilenikhena et al., 2021; Rogers, Kuiper, & Kirker, 1977; Symons & Johnson, 1997). The reason I describe the self-reference effect first is because principles associated with this memory phenomenon will lay the foundation for work I describe in the second part of the current paper that *is* focused on social episodic memory. An additional reason I focus on the self-reference effect is because expansive evidence in the social domain suggests that people use knowledge about the self (i.e., information about the self that is contained in one's self-schema) when thinking about, evaluating, and, as I show later, remembering social targets (Alicke, Dunning, & Krueger, 2013; Banaji & Prentice, 1994; Festinger, 1954; Markus, 1977; McElwee, Dunning, Tan, & Hollmann, 2001; Selfhout, Denissen, Branje, & Meeus, 2009). In what follows below, I first offer a highly abbreviated review of the self-reference effect in memory. Then I review work demonstrating an important memory-related principle important for the second part of this paper: *that self-referential processing leads to formation of episodic memory representations that are rich in episodic details (i.e., processing self-relevant materials leads to detail-rich episodic memory representations).*

3.1 Highly abbreviated review of the self-reference effect

People have a sense of self (e.g., self-schema) that is built up from a lifetime of experiences. Decades of memory-related research suggest that people use their knowledge or schemas about the world to help organize incoming information, which, in turn, improves memory (Anderson, 2018; Bartlett, 1932; Van Kesteren, Ruiter, Fernández, & Henson, 2012). The self-schema (i.e., knowledge of the self) is one of the most robust, well-developed, and highly-organized schematic structures a person has, and thus it logically follows that processing self-relevant information can lead to formation of enriched memory representations since self-relevant information should be easier to encode and store in memory. Building off these ideas (e.g., that the self is a schema, and that well-developed schemas can make information more memorable), the self-reference effect was first articulated in a seminal paper in 1977. Evidence from Rogers et al. (1977) showed that information processed in reference to the self (e.g., does this word describe me?) leads to improved memory for studied materials compared to control conditions where information is not processed with respect to the self (e.g., is this word written in upper or lower case?). Almost immediately after the publication of this seminal paper, an era of intense investigation to understand the role of the self-schema in memory began. The resulting research has shown that information processed in reference to the self typically leads to improved memory for studied materials compared to information processed in non-self control conditions (Liu, Wen, Liu, & Hu, 2023; Sui & Humphreys, 2015; Symons & Johnson, 1997). Self-reference effects have been shown for a range of different types of information, such as for words (Bower & Gilligan, 1979; Brown, Keenan, & Potts, 1986; Durbin, Mitchell, & Johnson, 2017; Fossati et al., 2003; Gutchess, Kensinger, & Schacter, 2007; Gutchess, Kensinger, Yoon, & Schacter, 2007; Heatherton et al., 2006; Macrae, Moran, Heatherton, Banfield, & Kelley, 2004; Morel et al., 2014; Mueller, Wonderlich, & Dugan, 1986; Yaoi, Osaka, & Osaka, 2015; Yoshimura et al., 2009), pictures (Cunningham, Brebner, Quinn, & Turk, 2014; Dulas, Newsome, & Duarte, 2011; Durbin et al., 2017; Hou, Grilli, & Glisky, 2019), and faces (Sui & Zhu, 2005; Yamawaki et al., 2017), and these effects occur in many populations such as in older adults (Colton, Leshikar, & Gutchess, 2013; Glisky & Marquine, 2009; Gutchess et al., 2015; Gutchess, Kensinger, Yoon, et al., 2007; Jackson et al., 2019), children (Cunningham, Vergunst, Macrae, & Turk, 2013; Hutchison, Ross, & Cunningham, 2021), and different clinical populations (Grilli & Glisky, 2010; Leblond et al., 2016; Rosa, Deason, Budson, & Gutchess, 2016; Wong et al., 2017). More recently, there is accumulating empirical evidence that processing self-relevant information leads to enriched episodic memory representations (i.e., memories that contain a variety of different types of episodic details). Importantly, this idea will be relevant to part two of the current paper where I describe a self-reference-like memory phenomenon in social episodic memory, which we call the self-similarity effect. In what follows below, I describe experimental evidence that shows self-referencing leads to formation of detail-rich episodic memory representations, using a variety of different approaches to measure memory for a variety of different types of details.

3.2 Self-reference leads to detail-rich episodic memory representations

I will first start with Leshikar and Duarte (2012) who showed that self-referential processing leads to improved source memory relative to a non-self control condition in a functional magnetic resonance imaging (fMRI) investigation. Source memory is the ability to remember the source or context in which information is encountered, such as whether an object was encountered in one condition or another (Johnson & Raye, 1981; Johnson, Hashtroudi, & Lindsay, 1993; Mitchell & Johnson, 2009). Because source memory procedures measure the ability to retrieve specific episodic details associated with encountering materials (e.g., the condition in which a studied item was processed, etc.), this is one experimental approach to measure detail-rich episodic memory representations. In Leshikar and Duarte (2012), participants were shown common objects (e.g. cherry, clock, lion, etc.) that were superimposed on one of three different background scenes (a mountain scene, a beach scene, a desert scene) under two different encoding/study tasks: self-reference and non-self-reference condition. In the self-reference condition, participants decided whether they liked the object paired with the background. We chose this "liking" task as the self-reference condition because prior work suggests that making personal preference judgments is self-referential in nature (Jacobsen, Schubotz, Hofel, & Cramon, 2006; Johnson et al., 2005; Zysset, Huber, Ferstl, & von Cramon, 2002). In the non-self-reference conditions, participants judged whether the color of the object was identical to the color of the background scene. At test, participants made two types of source judgments to measure episodic details: with which background an object was presented (background source memory), and in which encoding condition did the object appear (condition source memory). Memory results showed that memory for both types of source details (i.e., background source memory, condition source memory) was significantly better for materials studied in the self-reference compared to the non-self-reference condition. In addition to the memory results, we also showed that a region of the brain, the dorsal medial prefrontal cortex (dmPFC), supported improved source memory in the self-reference compared to non-self-reference condition. Interestingly, many past investigations have shown that regions of the medial prefrontal cortex, including the dmPFC, support a range of different types of self-focused processes, such as self-referencing (Moran, Heatherton, & Kelley, 2009; Northoff & Bermpohl, 2004; Northoff et al., 2006; Schneider et al., 2008). Overall, Leshikar and Duarte (2012) showed some of the first evidence that self-referencing leads to detail-rich memory representations as measured by source memory procedures, as others have also shown (Hamami, Serbun, & Gutchess, 2011; Serbun, Shih, & Gutchess, 2011).

In a follow-up experiment, Leshikar and Duarte (2014) investigated self-reference source memory effects in an investigation into aging effects that included both younger and older adults in an fMRI experiment. The driving question behind this follow-up investigation was this: would older adults show similar improvement in source memory under self-reference conditions as younger adults? Decades of research suggests that older adults show poorer episodic memory relative to younger adults (Park et al., 2002), especially detailed memory representations such as source memory (Old & Naveh-Benjamin, 2008; Spencer & Raz, 1995). Interestingly, however, there is some evidence that older adults show preserved self-reference effects that are similar in magnitude to younger adults (Gutchess et al., 2007; Gutchess, Kensinger, Yoon, et al., 2007). In Leshikar and Duarte (2014), groups of younger and older adults processed common objects superimposed on background scenes in either a self-reference or a non-self-reference condition at encoding/study (using a design similar to Leshikar & Duarte, 2012). At test, participants judged with which background scene objects were paired (i.e., background source memory). Although older adults showed poorer memory compared to younger adults overall, source memory results revealed that both younger and older adults showed similar increases in source memory in the self-reference compared to the non-self-reference condition (i.e., the magnitude of memory improvement in the self-reference compared to the non-self-reference condition was essentially identical in both younger and older adults). Finding self-reference effects in both age groups is consistent with the idea that self-referencing yields detail-rich memory representations, at least as measured by source memory procedures, and further is consistent with prior work showing preserved self-reference effects in older adults. Turning to the brain imaging findings, in both younger and older adults self-reference source memory effects were supported by brain activity in the dmPFC. It is interesting to note that in addition to supporting self-focused processing, regions of the medial prefrontal cortex, including the dmPFC, are involved in processing information about other people (e.g., social targets; Cassidy, Leshikar, Shih, Aizenman, & Gutchess, 2013; Saxe, Moran, Scholz, & Gabrieli, 2006). The reason why I briefly mention activity in the medial prefrontal cortex here is to foreshadow a result in part two of the current paper, where I will show that activity of the medial prefrontal cortex is involved in social episodic memory processes (involving the self). Overall, source memory results from both Leshikar and Duarte (2012) and Leshikar and Duarte (2014) show that self-referencing yields detail-rich episodic memory representations as measured by source memory procedures.

In the prior two paragraphs, I reviewed evidence that self-referencing improves source memory, but there are additional experimental procedures that can measure the extent episodic memory representations are detail-rich, such as investigating recollection memory effects using recollection/familiarity experimental procedures. In these paradigms, participants study materials and then are asked to make "recollection" or "familiarity" judgments about studied materials (Tulving, 1985; Yonelinas, 2002). Specifically, participants are instructed to report they can "recollect" studied materials if they can retrieve specific episodic details (e.g., such as the font color a word was presented in, whether a word was spoken by a male or female voice, etc.). In this way, "recollection" is another experimental approach to measure the extent participants are retrieving episodic details that underlie enriched episodic memory representations. By contrast, participants are instructed to report that studied materials are "familiar" if they know they have encountered the material before but cannot remember any episodic details. Now that I have described the recollection/familiarity procedure, I will report findings from Leshikar, Dulas, and Duarte (2015) who examined self-reference recollection effects for both positive and negative words (i.e., valenced materials). Participants in Leshikar et al. (2015, Experiment 1) studied words that described personality characteristics (both positive and negative words: kind, happy, sad, angry, etc.) under self-reference (does this word describe you?) or non-self-reference conditions (is this word a commonly used word?) at encoding/study. At test, participants were shown studied words and asked to make recollection/familiarity judgments, and in addition, they were asked to make source memory judgments (in which condition did you encounter this word?). First, results replicated the source memory self-reference effect we have seen before, where memory was better in the self-reference compared to the non-self-reference condition. Second, and more importantly, recollection memory results showed improved recollection for words studied in the self-reference compared to the non-self-reference condition, suggesting that self-referencing induced development of memory representations rich in episodic details. As for valence, recollection effects were of similar magnitude for both the positive and negative stimuli, suggesting that self-referencing enhances recollection memory for both positive and negative stimuli. Interestingly, for the studied materials in the non-self-reference conditions there was evidence for a negativity bias driven by enhanced rates of recollection for the negative relative to the positive words. Such a negativity effect is consistent with work outside of the self-reference literature, which shows that memory is sometimes better for negative emotional stimuli compared to positive (as well as neutral) stimuli (Kensinger & Corkin, 2003; Kensinger, Garoff-Eaton, & Schacter, 2007; Kensinger, 2007). Overall, finding that self-referencing increases recollection for studied materials (both positive and negative stimuli) is additional converging evidence that self-referential processing leads to memory representations rich in episodic details.

Work reviewed so far has shown self-reference effects as measured by both source and recollection memory experimental procedures. These procedures, however, do have some limitations in assessing detail-rich episodic memory representations that are worth describing briefly. Source memory procedures are generally designed to measure one, and only one, episodic detail at a time (e.g., condition in which an object was encountered; font color in which a word was presented; etc.), but such an approach does not capture many other episodic details that a participant may be able to retrieve about studied material, which is a limitation of source memory assessments. By contrast, although recollection judgments do index memory representations that contain episodic detail(s), this approach does not specify what type or quantity of detail(s) a participant may be retrieving in service of making a recollection judgment (e.g., when participants rate studied material as "recollected" it is unclear exactly what specific episodic detail or details they are bringing to mind to make recollection judgments). A more fine-grained approach to measure the contents of episodic memory representation (e.g., what kind of episodic details a participant can bring to mind) is using what is known as a Memory Characteristics Questionnaire (MCQ; Johnson, Foley, Suengas, & Raye, 1988). In MCQ tasks, participants are asked to judge the "amount" of information they can retrieve for a variety of different types of episodic details, such as visual details, auditory details, extraneous thoughts (i.e., such as remembering that studied information reminded you of something else), extraneous feelings (i.e., remembering that an item made you experience some affect), etc. To gain a richer understanding of the extent self-referential processing yields detail-rich memory representations, Leshikar et al. (2015, Experiment 2) used MCQ to assess memory for a variety of episodic details for materials studied under self-reference and non-self-reference conditions. In that investigation, participants studied positive and negative personality descriptive words (kind, happy, sad, angry, etc.) presented visually in two different colors as well as in two different types of fonts. In addition, while each word was visually presented on screen, the word was also spoken in either a male or female voice auditorily. Our rationale for presenting words at encoding/study in this way (varying in visual and auditory detail), was to allow participants to form detail-rich memory representations which could be measured by MCQ. At test, participants were shown studied words, and were asked to rate the amount of details (visual, auditory, extraneous thoughts, extraneous feelings) they could retrieve for each studied word using MCQ procedures. In addition, participants also made recollection/familiarity judgments, as well as source memory judgments for studied words. MCQ results showed a self-reference effect for the visual, auditory, thoughts, and feelings measures, which was driven by higher rates of retrieved details for words studied in the self-reference compared to the non-self-reference conditions. Importantly, this finding suggests that self-referencing leads to episodic memory representations that contain many different types of episodic details. As for valence, MCQ self-reference effects were generally of a similar magnitude for both the positive and negative stimuli, similar to the findings of Experiment 1 reviewed in the paragraph directly above (Leshikar et al., 2015). Such MCQ findings strongly suggest processing self-relevant information yields memory representations that are rich in episodic details. Further, results again showed self-reference effects as measured by source memory and recollection measures that replicated our prior work (Leshikar & Duarte, 2012, 2014; Leshikar et al., 2015, Experiment 1). Overall, the findings of Leshikar et al. (2015) provide additional converging evidence that self-referencing yields detail-rich episodic memory representations.

3.3 Interim summary of part one

In part one, I have shown that encountering information relevant to the self leads to formation of detail-rich memory representations for such self-relevant information. The idea that using the self-schema to form enriched episodic memories is consistent with the long-standing idea that schematic representations (e.g., knowledge structures) play an important role in memory. In all the work I reviewed above, we showed processing information relevant to the self allows for the formation of memory where studied information (e.g., objects, words) is associated with many different types of enriched episodic details (e.g., remembering that *this* studied item is associated with *those* episodic details) across different populations (i.e., in younger adults; in older adults). The idea that processing information relevant to the self leads to memory representations where studied information (e.g., an object) is linked or associated with specific episodic details will play a central role in part two of this paper, where I show a self-reference-like effect for social targets, which we call the self-similarity effect. To foreshadow the central thesis in part two, I will show that when a social target exhibits characteristics that are relevant or true of the self (e.g., you are a friendly person and you encounter a social target who is also friendly), this has a strong influence on memory for that target (e.g., remembering that *this* person is associated with *those* episodic details, such as remembering the impression you formed of the specific social target). Overall, understanding ways that memory can be enhanced is an essential scientific enquiry (Bjork & Bjork, 2011; Frankenstein, Udeogu, McCurdy, Sklenar, & Leshikar, 2022; Giannakopoulos et al., 2021; Giannakopoulos et al., 2024; Gutchess, Hebrank, et al., 2007; Leach, McCurdy, Trumbo, Matzen, & Leshikar, 2019; Leshikar, Gutchess, Hebrank, Sutton, & Park, 2010; Leshikar, Duarte, & Hertzog, 2012; Leshikar et al., 2017; Matzen, Trumbo, Leach, & Leshikar, 2015; McCurdy & Leshikar, 2022; McCurdy, Leach, & Leshikar, 2017, 2019; McCurdy, Frankenstein, Sklenar, Levy, & Leshikar, 2021; McCurdy, Sklenar, Frankenstein, & Leshikar, 2020; McCurdy, Viechtbauer, Sklenar, Frankenstein, & Leshikar, 2020; Meyers, McCurdy, Leach, Thomas, & Leshikar, 2020; Villaseñor et al., 2021), and the results of the work reviewed above suggest a powerful way to enhance memory: the self-reference effect.

4. Part two: Self-similarity effect

Up to this point I have exclusively focused on the self-reference effect, which is a well-known and well-characterized "cognitive" memory phenomenon (Symons & Johnson, 1997). I will now turn our attention to our primary "social cognitive" construct of interest, which is social episodic memory, specifically the self-similarity effect. As I described earlier in the current paper, social episodic memory is the ability to remember that a specific social target is associated with specific episodic details. Borrowing memory principles associated with the self-reference effect and using them in the social domain allows us to ask the following question: what happens to social episodic memory representations when you encounter a person who is similar to the self? To help situate this question, let us return for a moment to the opening vignette. If you remember, you met Lauram who was friendly and you met Randibi who was extraverted. In the opening vignette, you imagined that these characteristics (friendly; extraverted) are also descriptive of your personality (i.e., true of you). How will this similarity in attributes between yourself and these social targets affect how you remember Lauram and Randibi later? We begin to answer that question in this part of the current paper. In what follows below, I first give a highly abbreviated review of theoretical work that describes how memory for people is organized. Then I describe early (and mostly unsuccessful) work investigating the extent self-other similarity affects memory for social targets. After that, I review evidence for self-similarity effects, which suggests that social targets' similarity to the self strongly affects social episodic memory. Then, to close out this section, I review one factor that seems to disrupt the self-similarity effect (and that is learning political-ideological information about social targets).

4.1 Highly abbreviated review of theoretical work on person memory

Theoretical work on person memory[1] (e.g., memory for other people) flourished in the 1970s and 1980s. Much of this theoretical work focused on the nature or organization of information about social targets (Hastie & Kumar, 1979; Srull & Wyer, 1989; Srull, Lichtenstein, & Rothbart, 1985;

[1] My use of the term *social episodic memory* differs from the more overarching term *person memory* from earlier work. Social episodic memory, in our review, is memory for specific episodic details associated with a specific social targets (e.g., being able to retrieve a detail about a target that is specific to a prior encounter, such as remembering that you formed a positive impression of a specific person). The term person memory does not require such episodic specificity (again, remembering a detail associated with a particular target tied to a specific moment in time, or episode). The term person memory is an umbrella term that include social episodic memory representations, but it can also include non-episodic details that are not tied to a specific moment in time.

Srull, 1981; Wyer, Bodenhausen, & Srull, 1984), and in particular, this work focused on understanding the contents of memory about social targets (i.e., what types of details people remember after encountering social targets). These early theoretical and empirical works show that memory for social targets can include specific behaviors a target performs (e.g., that a person smiles), and it can include inferences made about a target's character based on behaviors (e.g., inferring that a person is friendly because they smile, etc.). Further, and perhaps most important for the current paper, this theoretical work also shows that memory for social targets can include an overall generalized positive or negative feeling (e.g., impression) formed about targets (which is the type of memory representations we primarily focus on when describing the self-similarity effect). Although much of this early work investigated many factors that influenced person memory (such as physical appearance of targets, or how information inconsistent with what one knows about a target affects memory, etc.), much less work focused on the extent self-other similarity affects person memory, with a few exceptions which I briefly review next.

4.2 Highly abbreviated review of early work on the extent self-other similarity affects social episodic memory

At about the same time theoretical work on person memory was flourishing, some investigators became interested in the extent that self-other overlap, or similarity, might influence social episodic memory. Perhaps the best example of this is the seminal work done by Hazel Markus (and colleagues) on what they called "schematics" (i.e., a domain of expertise that a person has, such as a person who is high in masculinity and thus would be considered a "masculine schematic"). Specifically, this work on schematics examined the extent that self-other similarity affects different types of social cognitive processes such as person perception (Catrambone & Markus, 1987; Fong & Markus, 1982; Markus, 1977), and more importantly, social episodic memory. In one investigation on social episodic memory, masculine schematics (participants who self-reported high amounts of masculine characteristics) and masculine aschematics (participants who self-reported low amounts of masculine characteristics) watched videos of a social target performing both masculine and non-masculine behaviors in a dorm room setting (Markus, Smith, & Moreland, 1985). While watching the videos, participants were instructed to make a button press to denote meaningful units of action (e.g., lifting weights, eating an apple, etc.). After watching the videos, participants were given a recall test for the behaviors depicted in the video. Results showed that schematics were better at identifying discrete "masculine" behaviors than aschematics; however, the schematics did not show better memory for such masculine behaviors compared to the aschematics. These results hinted that the masculine schematic participants were processing behavioral information that was relevant to the self (i.e., masculine behaviors) differently than aschematics, but this work did not show a memory advantage for such schematic behaviors. Indeed, other work by Markus and colleagues using similar procedures failed to find improved memory for social targets performing schematic behaviors that were aligned with the self (Markus & Smith, 1981). It is worth noting, however, that memory performance in these investigations was close to ceiling, which may have obscured detection of potential self-similarity social episodic memory effects. Interestingly, in later work conducted by a different group, Carpenter (1988) showed that self-other overlap for "career-oriented" schematics did indeed lead to improved memory, when memory performance was not at ceiling, and under conditions where participants were simply told to "form an impression" about social targets they encountered. This Carpenter result was among the first, if not the first, to hint that a self-reference-like effect in social episodic memory exists. In the decades following this Carpenter finding, there have been few investigations that have examined the extent that self-other overlap between the self and a social target affects social episodic memory (until our work which I review next). It is easy to speculate that the prominent Markus findings (Markus & Smith, 1981; Markus et al., 1985), which did not show strong evidence for social episodic memory effects, may have reduced interest in pursuing work on the extent that self-other similarity influences memory.

4.3 Self-similarity effect in social episodic memory

Before I describe evidence for the self-similarity effect, I will first describe the general experimental approach that is relevant for all experiments I review in the remainder of part two of the current paper. I will also walk through an example of how this self-similarity experimental procedure can be used to "bin" social targets as a function of self-similarity. Overall, our self-similarity procedure involves three experimental phases: impression formation/encoding, memory test, and self-relevant rating (as you will see below, we use the self-relevant ratings to bin social targets into high-, medium-, and low-self-similarity). For each phase of the self-similarity procedure (i.e., impression formation/encoding, memory test, self-relevant rating), I also briefly describe background literatures that support key features of our experimental design where relevant. The self-similarity experimental procedure I devised is a variant of the impression memory procedure (Cassidy, Zebrowitz, & Gutchess, 2012; Gilron & Gutchess, 2012). In impression memory procedures, participants are shown a social target (e.g., picture of target, name of target, etc.) and a behavior performed by that target. In the *impression formation/encoding phase* of our self-similarity procedures, participants generate a positive or negative impression of targets based on their face/name and associated behavior. Importantly, the behaviors we use strongly imply a single characteristic about the target (e.g., "enjoys talking to people at parties", implies extraversion). In our self-similarity procedures, we created hundreds of behavioral sentences that each imply a different specific characteristic (e.g., behaviors that imply a target is: kind, sad, helpful, eager, generous, etc.) Using behaviors that imply a specific characteristic or single trait about a target follows work on so-called spontaneous trait inferences (Newman & Uleman, 1989; Uleman, Newman, & Moskowitz, 1996; Uleman, 1987), which suggest that people reflexively and spontaneously infer trait characteristics about targets based on behaviors performed by the target (e.g., inferring that a target is extraverted when they engage in extraverted behaviors). After forming impressions of targets in our self-similarity procedures, participants then complete a memory test for details associated with the target, such as the impression they formed of the social target (i.e., positive or negative impression). Specifically, in the *memory test* phase of the self-similarity procedures, participants are shown the social target (just the face or name of the target depending on the experiment) and are asked to report the impression they formed of that specific social target (positive or negative). After the memory test, participants then complete the *self-relevant rating* phase, where they are shown the trait word that each behavioral sentence implied (e.g., kind, sad, helpful, etc.) and asked to rate how much that word describes them (e.g., high-, medium-, or low-self-relevance).[2] Importantly, we can then use the self-relevance ratings to backsort the social targets into high-, medium-, and low-self-similarity. As an example,

[2] Having participants directly rate the self-relevance of words follows procedures used in typical self-reference procedures where participants directly rate the extent the word is true of the self (Rogers, et al., 1977). Further, it is worth noting that during the self-relevant rating, participants did not see the behavioral sentences again; instead, they only saw the word (e.g., kind, sad, helpful, etc.) implied by the behaviors.

let us say that during the impression formation/encoding phase, a participant forms a positive impression of a target (e.g., Randibi) associated with the behavior, "enjoys talking to people at parties", which implies the characteristic extraverted. Then let us say that the participant rates the word "extraverted" as highly descriptive of the self in the self-relevant rating phase of the experiment. We can then bin that social target (e.g., Randibi) as a positive high-self-similarity target (again, because the participant formed a positive impression of the target binned as high in self-similarity). Using such a procedure we can then look at memory for social targets who are high-, medium-, and low- in self-similarity (using the memory responses from the memory test phase of the experiment).[3] Now that we have described the general self-similarity experimental procedure, I will now walk through evidence showing self-similarity effects, a type of self-reference-like effect in social episodic memory.

In a functional magnetic resonance imaging (fMRI) experiment, participants formed impressions of 144 social targets (Leshikar, Cassidy, & Gutchess, 2016). During impression formation, participants were shown a picture (i.e., face) of a single target and a behavior the target performed, which implied a single trait about the target (e.g., kind, sad, helpful, etc.). At test, participants rated their ability to remember the impression formed for each social target (e.g., remembering that *this* target was associated with *that* impression). Participants then completed self-relevance ratings (as described in the paragraph above), which allowed us to bin social targets into high-, medium-, and low-self-similarity. Before I reveal the memory results, it is important to remember the primary memory principle described in part one of the current paper: that processing self-relevant information leads to detail-rich memory representations. By analogy, if it is

[3] One point that is worth mentioning is that in these self-similarity experimental procedures we do not explicitly ask participants to compare the self to social targets. This is a departure of sorts from many self-reference experiments in the cognitive literature that generally ask people to explicitly judge the extent studied material is relevant to the self. Interestingly, however, some self-reference work does show that people exhibit self-reference effects in memory even when not explicitly asked to judge incoming information as relevant to the self (Cunningham, Turk, Macdonald, & Macrae, 2008; Kesebir & Oishi, 2010; Turk, Cunningham, & Macrae, 2008; Yaoi, Osaka, & Osaka, 2021). Indeed, some scholars suggest that people habitually default to processing information in relation to self (e.g., using the self-schema), suggesting the self-schema is highly important in processing new information about the world (Meyer & Lieberman, 2018). In line with this idea, it is worth noting that in the one study in the social cognitive domain (that we reviewed above) that has shown evidence of a self-similarity-like effect in social episodic memory (Carpenter, 1988), participants were not explicitly comparing the self to social targets, but instead were simply following impression formation instruction ("form an impression of this target").

the case that there is a self-reference-like effect in social episodic memory, then it should follow that participants should form more detailed social episodic memory representation for targets who are highly similar to the self, compared to targets who are not, as measured by improved ability to remember the impression associated with the target. Now turning to the results, impression memory in Leshikar et al. (2016) yielded exactly what we predicted: memory was best for high-self-similarity targets, and poorest for low-self-similarity targets (memory for the medium-self-similarity targets was in between the high- and low-self-similarity targets). Because this was an fMRI experiment, we could also look at regions of the brain that supported this self-similarity memory effect. We found that regions of the medial prefrontal cortex (both ventral and dorsal mPFC regions) supported enhanced memory for the high-self-similarity targets compared to the medium- and low-self-similarity targets. Specifically, we found that regions of the mPFC showed graded functional activity that tracked self-similarity: activity in these regions was highest for high-self-similarity targets, next highest for the medium-self-similarity targets, and lowest for the low-self-similarity targets. This finding (that mPFC regions show graded functional activity as a function of similarity to the self) is consistent with abundant social neuroscience research that suggest medial prefrontal regions are involved in processes associated with thinking about the self as well as thinking about others (i.e., social targets; Lombardo et al., 2010; Saxe et al., 2006; Sugimoto & Tsukiura, 2018). Overall, Leshikar et al. (2016), showed evidence for a self-similarity effect in social episodic memory as reflected both behaviorally (as measured by impression memory) as well as functionally (as measured by fMRI brain activity). Intriguingly, something quite interesting happens when considering valence (of impressions), which I will describe next.

Before I describe valence effects in our self-similarity work, let us return to the self-similarity experimental procedure to briefly describe how we can sort self-similarity trials into both positive and negative trial types, respectively, to examine valence effects on social episodic memory representations. During impression formation, participants are asked to form either positive or negative impressions of targets. We can use this initial impression to bin trials (or targets) into both positive and negative trial types (while also sorting targets into high-, medium-, and low-self-similarity; for example, two paragraphs above I described that Randibi from the opening vignette can be categorized as a positive, high-self-similarity target). I will now describe findings from two experiments in

Leshikar and Gutchess (2015). I will first start by describing findings for the *positive* trials across Experiments 1 and 2. Experiment 1 used a slight variation of our typical self-similarity experimental procedures: Specifically, participants formed impressions of 144 targets, and for each target we showed both the behavior the target performed ("enjoys talking to people at parties") as well as the trait word that behavior implies ("extraverted").[4] Consistent with the work of Leshikar et al. (2016), we again found a self-similarity effect in impression memory in Experiment 1. Specifically, we found that impression memory showed a graded effect as a function of self-similarity with best memory for the high-self-similarity targets, followed by the medium- targets, and poorest memory for the low-self-similarity targets. In Experiment 2, we used our standard self-similarity procedure, where participants formed impressions of targets based on behaviors. Results of Experiment 2 again showed a self-similarity effect for the positive trials (high-self-similarity > medium-self-similarity > low-self-similarity). Overall, results of both experiments of Leshikar and Gutchess (2015) suggest that similarity to the self has a strong impact on social episodic memory.

In contrast to memory effects we observed for the positive trials, results for the *negative* trials in Leshikar and Gutchess (2015) showed a fundamentally different pattern of results as a function of self-similarity. Results showed that impression memory was poorest for the negative high-self-similarity trials, better for the medium-self-similarity trials, and best for the low-self-similarity, which is in effect a reverse self-reference-like effect in social episodic memory for the negative trials. Since this effect is so different from the self-similarity effect for the positive trials, how can we make sense of this reverse self-reference effect? Interestingly, there is some work in the social domain known as self-protection and self-enhancement effects that can account for this finding for the negative trials (poorest memory for high-self-similarity and best memory for low-self-similarity). The primary idea behind these effects is that people are motivated to form and maintain a positive self-image (e.g., self-schema). To develop and maintain a positive self-schema, work on self-enhancement/self-improvement suggest people are motivated to seek out information that supports a positive self-schema (self-enhancement) and avoid information

[4] This is a slight departure because we included the trait word implied by the behavioral sentence in the impression formation/encoding phase of this Experiment. Generally, we do not show the trait word implied by the sentence in our self-similarity experimental procedures.

that negatively affects self-schema (self-protection; Alicke & Sedikides, 2009; D'Argembeau & Van der Linden, 2008; Sedikides & Alicke, 2012). In terms of memory, work in this domain (self-protection/self-enhancement) suggests that people show strong memory biases to remember positive information about the self. In contrast, people also show strong biases against remembering negative-implying information about the self (e.g., people are much less likely to remember negative information about the self that could negatively impact the self-schema; D'Argembeau & Van der Linden, 2008). Given this work on self-protection/self-enhancement effects, it is possible now to interpret the negative trials from Leshikar and Gutchess (2015). If it is indeed the case that people are motivated to show poorer memory for information that could negatively impact the self-schema, then it makes sense that participants in Leshikar and Gutchess (2015) would show poorest memory for the negative high-self-similarity targets, as a means to protect the self-schema (because remembering negative information about social targets that is also true of the self could negatively affect the self-schema). Overall, the work of Leshikar and Gutchess (2015) show that self-similarity has a strong effect on social episodic memory as measured by impression memory, but that self-similarity interacts with valence, leading to strikingly different memory effects (a self-reference-like effect for targets associated with positive information, and a reverse self-reference-like effect for targets associated with negative information).

Thus far I have described evidence for self-similarity effects in social episodic memory, but all the evidence I have reviewed up to this point used samples of younger adults. What happens, however, when older adults encounter social targets who vary in self-similarity? Will older adults show parallel self-similarity patterns as younger adults, analogous to how older adults show similar/identical self-reference effects compared to younger adults (as reviewed in part one)? Interestingly, work in lifespan development, suggest that people's sense of self is stable over the lifespan (Hazel, 1991; Terracciano, McCrae, Brant, & Costa, 2005; Terracciano, McCrae, & Costa, 2010), thus, it is plausible that self-similarity effects may be as robust in older adults as they are in younger adults. To examine self-similarity age effects, Leshikar, Park, and Gutchess (2014) had younger and older adults form impressions of 144 social targets in our typical self-similarity experimental procedures. Because this was an investigation about aging, we used social targets of various ages (e.g., faces images we used depicted social targets from 20–79 years old that were equally distributed across this age range.) Results showed that for the positive trials, both younger and older adults showed strong self-similarity effects, where memory was highest for high-self-similarity targets, and lowest for low-similarity targets. In addition, older adults showed even better memory performance for the social targets associated with positive impressions compared to younger adults (collapsed across self-similarity). Over the decades of work comparing episodic memory performance between younger and older adults, it is rare to find instances where older adults are out-performing younger adults (Matzen & Benjamin, 2013). We think older adults may show improved memory for the positive trials relative to younger adults for two reasons. First, there is ample evidence that older adults tend to show better memory for positive relative to negative information, whereas younger adults tend not to show such positivity biases in memory (and often show better memory for negative compared to positive information; Barber & Kim, 2021; Carstensen & DeLiema, 2018; Kensinger & Corkin, 2003; Niu et al., 2024). Given this, improved memory for the positive trials in Leshikar et al. (2014), fits with positivity effects seen in older adults. Second, there is growing work suggesting that older adults are especially attentive to social information. Work from Carstensen (and colleagues) as well as others has shown instances where older adults show improved memory for content that contains, or is framed in, social contexts (Carstensen, 1992; Cassidy & Gutchess, 2012; Charles & Carstensen, 2010). It follows then, that older adults may be showing improved memory for the positive trials in Leshikar et al. (2014) due to the social and emotional nature of the to-be-remembered social targets. For the negative trials, both age groups showed a self-similarity effect denoted by poorest memory for high-self-similarity trials, and best memory for the low-self-similarity trials, as we have seen before. More work is necessary to better understand the extent that older adults might use their self-schema when thinking about social targets in service of forming social episodic memory representations.

We have replicated the self-similarity effect many times, across many experiments. The fact that we have seen the self-similarity effect so reliably, suggests that people spontaneously and consistently use their self-schema to think about, form impressions of, and subsequently remember episodic details associated with specific social targets under impression formation experimental procedures (e.g., tasks where participants are simply asked to form generalized positive or negative impressions of targets). Having said that, we have identified one factor that seems to attenuate the self-similarity effect, and that is when participants learn political-ideological information about targets (e.g., whether a target is associated with liberal or conservative political-ideological information). We became interested in the extent that ideological information associated with targets might affect social episodic memory given broader societal trends that we live in an increasingly ideologically polarized era (Bishop & Cushing, 2009; Lütjen & Matschoss, 2015; Motyl, Iyer, Oishi, Trawalter, & Nosek, 2014). To understand how political-implying information affects social episodic memory, we conducted three experiments using self-similarity experimental procedures in Sklenar, Pérez, McCurdy, Frankenstein, and Leshikar (2023). In Experiment 1, we sought to replicate the self-similarity effect as we have seen before (without presenting political-ideological information with targets). As we have seen many times, we found the standard self-similarity effect (for positive trials: high-self-similarity > low-self-similarity; for negative trials: low-self-similarity > high-self-similarity). In Experiment 2, however, we showed participants a target and a trait-implying behavior just as we have done before, but this time we added one additional label to the target: whether the target was "liberal" or "conservative". Interestingly, impression memory results revealed no effect of self-similarity. Instead, we only found a valence effect, where memory was better for targets associated with positive impressions relative to negative impressions. This was our first evidence that the mere presence of political-implying information (in this case a "liberal" or "conservative" label) disrupted the self-similarity effect. In Experiment 3 of Sklenar et al. (2023), we again presented targets associated with the label "liberal" or "conservative", but instead of trait-implying behaviors we showed political-implying belief statements associated with targets (e.g., "believes that health care is a universal right", which implies liberal beliefs). Memory results for Experiment 3 were essentially identical to Experiment 2: there was no self-similarity effect, but there was a valence effect, where impression memory was better for positive than negative trials. Considering all three experiments of Sklenar et al. (2023) together (as well as the work of Leshikar & Gutchess, 2015; Leshikar et al., 2014, 2016 reviewed above), these findings suggest that when people form generalized impressions of targets, they "default" to using the self-schema when thinking about others for a variety of different types of information (various types of behavioral information, various types of trait information, etc.); however, when people learn information about targets that imply political-ideological information, this may cause people to shift away from using the self-schema to process information about targets, and instead use a different type of schematic representation (e.g., political schemas) to process incoming information about social targets. To better situate the findings of Experiment 2 and 3 of Sklenar et al. (2023), let us return once again to the opening vignette. At Terry's social gathering, you formed a positive impression of Patwa who told you about his beliefs that were political in nature. Finding from Sklenar et al. (2023) imply that even if you share some similarity with Patwa, the mere presence of political-ideological-implying information about Patwa makes is less likely that you will experience a self-similarity effect (e.g., improved memory, etc.) for episodic details associated with Patwa. Overall, much more work is necessary to better understand the extent political-ideological information associated with targets affects social episodic memory.

4.4 Interim summary of part two

I have shown evidence of a self-reference-like effect in social episodic memory which we call the self-similarity effect. Perhaps the most captivating component of the self-similarity effect is the strong role that valence (positive or negative) plays on how social targets are processed and subsequently remembered. The idea that remembering affectively positive or negative information associated with social targets is an important factor in part three of the current paper that I describe next. Although I have exclusively focused on the role that self-similarity plays in social episodic memory, we have also articulated other factors that influence social episodic memory (e.g., that participants tend to have better memory for information that is consistent with what they already know about a target relative to inconsistent, Frankenstein et al., 2020; Patel et al., 2022; Udeogu, Frankenstein, Sklenar, Urban Levy, & Leshikar, 2022; that targets who engage in prosocial behaviors are typically remembered better than target who do not, which we call the prosocial advantage in memory, Urban Levy, Sklenar, Frankenstein, & Leshikar, 2023), but those factors are a bit outside of the primary focus for the current paper and so I will not discuss those findings. At this point in the current paper, I will now turn our attention away from self-relevance/self-similarity, and instead focus on how social episodic memories are used in service of social decision-making. In particular, I will focus on the extent social episodic memory representations that contain positive or negative affective details (e.g., impressions) strongly affect decisions to approach or avoid social targets.

5. Part three: Social episodic memory influences approach/avoidance (AA) decisions

Since the start of the modern era of psychology going back to the late 1800's, a useful organizational principle to understand different types of psychological scholarship can be reduced to the terms structuralism and functionalism (Hatfield, 2015; Roback, 1952). Structuralism, at the most fundamental level, is psychological endeavors (e.g., research) to understand the organization, component parts, or structure of different psychological phenomenon, such as memory (e.g., the famous three stage model of memory of Atkinson and Shiffrin (1968) is one such model to explain the component parts, or structure, of memory). Alternatively, functionalism places less emphasis on the structure of different psychological phenomenon, and instead seeks to understand how psychological abilities (like memory) are adaptive and allow an organism to function in day-to-day life. In the first two parts of the current paper, I have taken a structuralist approach to understand different memory phenomena (i.e., that self-referencing yields detail rich episodic memories; that self-similarity strongly affects social episodic memory). From this point on in the current paper, I take more of a functionalist approach to understand *what social episodic memory is good for*, or said differently, how social episodic memory is used in service of making adaptive social decisions. As mentioned in the paragraph immediately above, I will now step away from focus on self-relevance/self-similarity, and instead focus on the extent that social episodic memory representations that contain affectively positive or negative information (positive versus negative impressions) influences decisions to approach or avoid social targets. To help situate the research I describe below, let us return once again to the opening vignette. At Terry's social gathering you met and formed positive impressions of both Nathant and Jennio. Later you come across Nathant and Jennio in your community, and I asked whether you would choose to approach (or interact) with them? I further asked whether your social episodic memory representations (e.g., what you remember about them) would tip your decisions towards approach or towards avoidance? To help give insights into these questions, I provide evidence showing that social episodic memory representations strongly influence subsequent social decisions. To foreshadow that discussion, I show that remembering affectively positive details (e.g., impressions) about targets spurs approach, and remembering affectively negative details (e.g., impressions) induces avoidance. In what follows below, I first begin this section with a highly abbreviated review of work on approach/avoidance (AA). Then I will describe experimental evidence showing that valenced social episodic memory representations, both positive and negative, strongly influence subsequent AA decisions.

5.1 Highly abbreviated review of approach/avoidance (AA) decisions

People are motivated to approach positive or rewarding outcomes and to avoid negative or punishing outcomes (Elliot, 2006; McNaughton, DeYoung, & Corr, 2016; Roth & Cohen, 1986). In the social domain, people seek or approach rewarding social experiences such as social affiliation, and avoid negative social experiences such as social rejection (Elliot, Gable, & Mapes, 2006; Gable, 2006). Some work in the social domain has shown that people use immediately available information about social targets such as physical appearance to inform AA decisions, such as approaching targets that are attractive (Van Straaten, Engels, Finkenauer, & Holland, 2009), or avoiding targets with canonically "untrustworthy" facial features (Todorov, 2008), etc. These lines of work, and others, suggest that factors important in social perception (e.g., physical appearance) play a role in AA decisions for those targets. Relatively less research, however, investigates the extent social episodic memory representations (i.e., memory for specific episodic details associated with specific social targets) influence subsequent AA decisions. In what follows, I present work showing that remembering affectively positive information (e.g., impressions) associated with targets leads to strong approach decisions, whereas remembering affectively negative information (impressions) associated with targets leads to avoidance.

5.2 Social episodic memory representations influence approach/avoidance (AA) decisions

Before showing evidence that valenced social episodic memory influences AA decisions, it is first worth describing the general experimental approach we used as well as describing our primary dependent measure (e.g., AA responses) that we use in all experiments in this section. As in our self-similarity work (reviewed in part two of the current paper), we use a variant of the impression memory procedures, which consists of three phases: impression formation/encoding, memory test, approach/avoidance phase. In the *impression formation/encoding* phase, participants form positive or negative impressions of targets based on behaviors targets perform.

During the *memory test* phase, we measure participants' memory for episodic details they could retrieve for each social target, including the impression (positive or negative) they generated for each target. During the *approach/avoidance* phase, participants are shown just the face of the social target (or name, depending on the experiment) without any other details, and are asked whether they would approach or avoid that specific social target. In all the papers I describe below, our dependent measure of interest is the percent of times participants endorsed an approach response compared against a 50% baseline (for example, for all targets correctly remembered as associated with positive impressions, we looked at the percent of times those targets were given an approach response). The logic behind a 50% baseline is as follows: if participants have no social episodic memory representations of a target (and all social targets physical facial features are carefully controlled), then it should be the case that participants would endorse approach for targets about 50% of the time on average, which would suggest neither an approach or avoidance tendency (and of course, we have normative data showing this). If, however, the approach response for a group of targets (such as correctly remembered positive impression targets), is greater than 50%, this would imply an approach tendency, and alternatively, an approach response lower than 50% for a group of targets (such as correctly remembered negative impression targets) would imply an avoidance tendency.

Our first evidence showing that social episodic memory influences AA decisions was Sklenar, McCurdy, Frankenstein, Motyl, and Leshikar (2021). In Sklenar et al. (2021) participants formed positive or negative impressions of 128 social targets. At test, we measured impression memory for the 128 studied targets as well as 64 novel targets (i.e. targets not seen before). Participants then made AA decisions for all targets (e.g., the 128 studied targets and the 64 novel targets). AA results showed that for correctly remembered positive impression targets, participants endorsed approach for those targets significantly greater than 50% (specifically, 62%), suggesting that remembering an affectively positive detail (impression) leads to an approach tendency. By contrast, results showed that for correctly remembered negative impression targets, participants endorsed approach for those targets significantly less than 50% (specifically, 23%), suggesting that remembering an affectively negative detail (impression) leads to an overall avoidance tendency towards targets. Although past work has hinted that people use the contents of their memory when making social decisions about targets (Murty, FeldmanHall, Hunter, Phelps, & Davachi, 2016; Schaper, Mieth, & Bell, 2019), Sklenar et al. (2021) was the first to directly measure memory for specific social targets (e.g., assess social episodic memory representations for specific social targets) and then show that accurate social episodic memories strongly influence subsequent decisions to approach or avoid targets. Importantly, for targets that were not correctly remembered, participants showed neither approach or avoidance tendencies. Overall, results of Sklenar et al. (2021), suggest that people use the contents of their social episodic memory when deciding whether to approach or avoid other people (e.g., social targets). Something interesting happens, however, when we look more carefully at responses for the novel social targets (e.g., targets not encountered before), which I will describe next.

In Sklenar et al. (2021), participants made approach/avoidance (AA) decisions both for studied targets (that they formed impressions of) and novel targets they had not seen before. For some novel social targets, participants experienced memory errors where they falsely remembered forming either a positive or negative impression (i.e., although they did not see/form an impression of novel targets, they falsely remembered doing so for some targets). Such false memories offer an opportunity to address the following question: do false social episodic memories have an influence on subsequent AA decisions? Starting first with the positive false alarms (i.e., novel targets that were falsely remembered associated with positive impressions), results showed that participants showed neither an approach or avoidance tendency with mean AA ratings of 49%. However, something striking happens to AA decisions for the negative false alarms (i.e., novel targets that were falsely remembered associated with negative impressions). Participants showed strong avoidance tendencies for these targets (specifically 26%). What these data imply is that falsely remembering negative affective information about targets, even targets never encountered before, can have significant effects on later decisions about those same targets. Overall, finding evidence that false (negative) social episodic memory representations leads to avoiding social targets one has never met is a novel phenomenon that joins a rich body of other work showing that false memories can lead to poor real-world outcomes in context such as in therapy (Brainerd & Reyna, 2005; Loftus, 1993) and in the courtroom (Loftus, 1996; Wells & Olson, 2003). Additionally, the fact that we saw an avoidance tendency for the negative false alarms, but no approach or avoidance tendency for the positive false alarms, is aligned with a principle commonly described in the social domain that "bad is stronger than good", where negative social information about targets has a larger or stronger effect on social cognitive processes than positive social information associated with targets (Baumeister, Bratslavsky, Finkenauer, & Vohs, 2001). In line with this idea, it is worth noting that in all our work on understanding the extent social episodic memory influences AA decisions (Kadwe, Sklenar, Frankenstein, Levy, & Leshikar, 2022; Sklenar et al., 2021; Sklenar, Frankenstein, Urban Levy, & Leshikar, 2022), we generally see the pattern that correctly remembered negative impression trials (not false alarm trials, but the correctly remembered trials) lead to stronger AA decision effects than for our correctly remembered positive impression trials, reflected by the findings that negative impression trials generally deviate more from our 50% baseline (i.e., we typically see AA rates of approximately 25%, which is a large deviation [25%] from our 50% baseline) compared to positive impression trials (i.e., we typically see AA rates of 65%, which is smaller deviation [15%] from 50% baseline). Overall, much more work is necessary to understand the extent that false affective social episodic memories affect social decision, such as AA decisions.

Thus far the evidence showing social episodic memory influences subsequent AA decisions has involved stimuli where social targets engage in behaviors, but would these AA findings hold in situations where participants formed impressions based on beliefs that targets held? There is some evidence in the social domain that behaviors that social targets perform may be more predictive or diagnostic of a targets' character than beliefs (i.e., it is more informative to know what a target has done than it is to know what a target believes). Thus, one possibility is that social episodic memory representations based on behaviors may have a stronger effect on subsequent AA decisions than memory representations based on beliefs because behaviors (performed by targets) may be more predictive of future actions of targets. An alternative possibility, however, is that social episodic memory representations based on various types of social information, such as both beliefs and behaviors, would all be important in influencing subsequent AA decisions. To understand how memory for targets' beliefs (and behaviors) influences AA decisions, Sklenar et al. (2022) had participants form positive or negative impressions for targets associated with behaviors (e.g., "enjoys talking to people at parties") or with beliefs (e.g., "thinks it is important to invest in early childhood education"). AA results were identical for targets associated with behaviors as well as beliefs. Specifically, and in line with our prior work (Kadwe et al., 2022; Sklenar et al., 2021), correctly remembered positive impression trials were associated with approach tendencies for targets associated with both behaviors and beliefs (72% for behaviors; 69% for beliefs), and correctly remembered negative impression trials were associated with avoidance tendencies for both behaviors and beliefs (27% for behaviors; 25% for beliefs). The fact that we found essentially identical AA results for social targets associated with beliefs as well as behaviors suggests that social episodic memory representations based on a variety of different types of social information have a strong influence on subsequent AA decisions. Overall, these results suggest the importance of (positive and negative) social episodic memory representations on subsequent social decisions, specifically decisions to approach or avoid targets.

Data presented to this point has shown that social episodic memory representations affect subsequent AA decisions. Interestingly, it is well-known within the memory literature that episodic memories are not all equal in strength, where some memory representations are stronger (e.g., encoded and remembered at higher rates) than other representations (Verde & Rotello, 2007; Yonelinas, 2001). If it is the case that social episodic memories truly influence AA decisions, then it should be that stronger episodic memory representations would have a larger effect on subsequent AA decisions than do weaker episodic memory representations. To investigate this possibility, Sklenar, Frankenstein, Urban Levy, and Leshikar (In Preparation) used our typical approach/avoidance experimental procedure, but, importantly, participants viewed some targets twice during the impression formation/encoding phase, whereas other targets were presented only once. The rationale behind this procedure is that memory for the targets presented twice should be stronger than for the targets presented once, which in turn should have greater impact on subsequent AA decisions. Results showed that memory was indeed better for targets presented twice relative to once. As we have seen repeatedly, we again found that correctly remembered positive trials resulted in approach decisions and that correctly remembered negative trials resulted in avoidance decisions (collapsed across memory strength). Critically, approach and avoidance rates were stronger (e.g., deviated more from baseline) for the targets presented twice relative to the targets presented once. Overall, these results give converging evidence that social episodic memory impacts AA decisions given that targets associated with stronger memory representations led to even stronger/more pronounced approach and avoidance tendencies relative to targets associated with weaker memory representations.

At present, we have replicated the finding that social episodic memory representations strongly influence AA decisions many times, and thus we see this as a reliable psychological phenomenon. Although we have seen this effect repeatedly, an open question is whether there is a single most important factor for how social episodic memories influence AA decisions? To answer this question, it is worth going back to theoretical work on AA decisions. Much of the theoretical work on AA decisions suggest that there must be some source of "pull" to invoke approach behaviors, and, similarly, there must be some source of "push" to induce avoidance behaviors (Elliot et al., 2006; Gable, 2006; McNaughton et al., 2016). This theoretical work generally suggests that positive situations or outcomes induce approach, and that negative situations or outcomes induce avoidance. Given this context, we think that it is the presence of affectively positive or affectively negative social episodic memory details, respectively, that are the primary drivers of the "pull" associated with subsequent social approach decisions, and the "push" associated with subsequent social avoidance decisions. Going further, we also argue that "cold" social episodic memory representations (e.g., memory representations that contain no affective details) should have significantly less, or no impact, on subsequent AA decisions. Consistent with this notion, more recent work shows exactly this. In Urban Levy et al. (In Preparation), participants formed positive, negative, or neutral impressions about social targets. AA decisions for the positive and negative trials showed the same pattern we have observed repeatedly where correctly remembered positive impression trials induced approach tendencies, and correctly remembered negative impressions trials induced avoidance tendencies. Importantly, for the correctly remembered neutral trials we found no evidence of an approach or avoidance tendency. Such findings strongly suggest it is valenced social episodic memory representations of social targets that influence subsequent AA decisions.

5.3 Interim summary of part three

I have shown evidence that affectively positive and negative social episodic memory representations are used in service of subsequent approach/avoidance decisions. I have also shown that falsely remembering negative affective information about social targets, even targets one has never met, can induce strong avoidance tendencies. Collectively this work suggests a central role of social episodic memory representations in social decisions, specifically AA decisions. Of course, there are many types of social decisions humans make about social targets such as seeking romantic relationships, hiring decisions, etc. Thus, future work in this domain should work to better understand how the contents of memory for specific social targets may be used in social decision across many different contexts and situations. I see this domain (e.g., understanding how social episodic memory representations influence social decisions) as a highly fertile and generative area for future research.

6. Part four: Future directions for the role of memory in social decision making

Throughout the current paper, I have mentioned areas for further investigation tied to many topics (e.g., self-reference effects; self-similarity effects; aging effects; effects of political-ideological information; etc.). Looking forward, I think one area that has great potential for future scholarship is a broader push to understand how memory representations about targets affect social decisions. All the work I have presented on the extent social episodic memory influences AA decisions has focused on memory for specific episodic details (e.g., impressions) associated with specific social targets (i.e., social episodic memory). Another way to think about social episodic memory representations, however, is that these are types of memory representations that participants can explicitly bring to mind (e.g., explicit memory representations.) Undoubtedly, however, there are also likely implicit memory processes at play in social decision making. In the cognitive literature, there is extensive work showing that past encounters with information can influence later information processing and decisions, even in instances where a person cannot explicitly retrieve details of prior exposure (e.g., priming, etc. Roediger & McDermott, 1993; Roediger, 1990; Schacter & Buckner, 1998; Schacter, Chiu, & Ochsner, 1993; Schacter, 1987; Turk-Browne, Yi, & Chun, 2006). I strongly suspect that implicit memory representations associated with specific social targets formed from prior encounters has an influence on social decision making. Thus, I think future work should investigate the extent implicit memory representations for specific targets can affect a broad range of social decisions. Of course, there are rich and extensive bodies of work showing implicit (memory) processes that influence social decisions, but much of this work focuses on implicit biases people may develop based on group level characteristics (e.g., biases involving race, age, gender, etc.), but when I talk about implicit social memory representations I mean something different: I mean implicit memory representations tied to specific social targets based on prior encounters that can affect social decisions about those same targets, even in the absence of explicit memory representations. There are many challenges in trying to assess implicit memory representations for specific social targets, and how those social implicit memory representations may in turn affect subsequent decisions. Although it is beyond the scope of the current paper to describe those challenges, we do lay out those challenges, as well as experimental solutions that may overcome those challenges, in understanding the extent implicit memory representations for specific social targets might affect social decisions in a separate paper (Sklenar & Leshikar, 2024). Overall, people make numerous social decisions about social targets on a daily basis that affect both what they do and with whom they do it. Working to better understand those social decisions and how both explicit (e.g., social episodic memory representations) as well as implicit social memory representations will undoubtedly lead to new insights into a range of social cognitive processes that affect social dynamics.

7. Conclusions

In the opening vignette of the current paper, I posed a number of questions. I will now return to those questions and provide some preliminary insights based on the data that I have reviewed in the current paper. In the opening vignette, you met Lauram, Randibi, Nathant, and Jennio. Lauram, Randibi, Nathant, and Jennio all showed characteristics that are true of you (at least true of the self that you were asked to imagine), and importantly, you formed positive impressions of everyone. I asked how likely you are to remember details about Lauram, Randibi, Nathant, and Jennio in the opening vignette. Based on the data that I reviewed on the self-similarity effect, I can give a partial answer to this question and say that you are likely to form enriched social episodic memory representations for each person which will allow you to remember specific details, such as the impression you formed, for Lauram, Randibi, Nathant, and Jennio. I further asked whether there are memory-related principles that might account for your enriched memory for these individuals? Here again I can give a partial answer to this question and say that you are likely to remember episodic details associated with these targets based on principles related to the self-reference effect, which shows that processing information relevant to self leads to formation of detail-rich episodic memory representations. You also met Patwa in the opening vignette who expressed political-ideological information, and I reviewed evidence that political implying information associated with social targets seems to disrupt self-similarity processes. Thus, based on the work I reviewed, you might not have enriched social episodic memory representations for Patwa, given the political ideological information you learned about him.

In the opening vignette I also asked questions related to social decisions you might make about the people that you met at Terry's gathering. After the social gathering you run into Lauram, Randibi, Nathant, and Jennio in your daily life, and I asked whether you would choose to approach them (e.g., engage with them), and if yes, I also asked whether your social episodic memory representations would play a role in such decisions? Evidence that I reviewed in the third part of the current paper, can offer some answers to these questions. You are indeed more likely to choose to interact with (i.e., approach) Lauram, Randibi, Nathant, and Jennio, and you are likely to do so because you remember affectively positive details (e.g., impression) associated with each respective person.

In this paper, I reviewed work showing that information that is relevant to the self can yield especially enriched episodic memory representations. I then showed a self-reference-like effect in social episodic memory that we call the self-similarity effect, where social episodic memory representations for social targets are strongly affected by similarity to the self (e.g., the extent the self and another social target are similar on some characteristic, such as extraverted). I also showed that people use their social episodic memory representations while making approach or avoidance decisions about social targets. Specifically, I showed that if people remember affectively positive details about a social target (e.g., a positive impression) this can induce approach motivations towards that social target. By contrast, if people remember affectively negative details about a social target (e.g., a negative impression) this can induce avoidance motivations for that social target. Taking a bigger picture view, it is self-evident that humans are social organisms that live in enriched and complex social environments. It is clear that people develop social episodic memory representations of social targets around them and use those memory representations in service of successfully navigating their social world.

Acknowledgments

I would like to thank many people who have contributed to this work in some way or another over the years including: Audrey Duarte, Angela Gutchess, Brittany Cassidy, Michael Dulas, Jung Park, Allison Sklenar, Matthew McCurdy, Andrea Frankenstein, Pauline Urban Levy, Jonathan Villasenor, Liat Zabludovsky, Nicole Rosa, and Hikaru Sugimoto.

References

Alicke, M. D., Dunning, D. A., & Krueger, J. (2013). *The self in social judgment*. Psychology Press.

Alicke, M. D., & Sedikides, C. (2009). Self-enhancement and self-protection: What they are and what they do. *European Review of Social Psychology, 20*(1), 1–48.

Anderson, R. C. (2018). *Role of the reader's schema in comprehension, learning, and memory. Theoretical models and processes of literacy*. Routledge, 136–145.

Atkinson, R. C., & Shiffrin, R. M. (1968). *Human memory: A proposed system and its control processes. Psychology of learning and motivation, Vol. 2*, Elsevier, 89–195.

Banaji, M. R., & Prentice, D. A. (1994). The self in social contexts. *Annual Review of Psychology, 45*(1), 297–332.

Barber, S. J., & Kim, H. (2021). The positivity effect. *Multiple Pathways of Cognitive Aging: Motivational and Contextual Influences, 84*.

Bartlett, F. C. (1932). *Remembering: An experimental and social study*. Cambridge: Cambridge University.

Baumeister, R. F., Bratslavsky, E., Finkenauer, C., & Vohs, K. D. (2001). Bad is stronger than good. *Review of General Psychology, 5*(4), 323.

Bishop, B., & Cushing, R. G. (2009). *The big sort: Why the clustering of like-minded America is tearing us apart*. Houghton Mifflin Harcourt.

Bjork, E. L., & Bjork, R. A. (2011). Making things hard on yourself, but in a good way: Creating desirable difficulties to enhance learning. *Psychology and the Real World: Essays Illustrating Fundamental Contributions to Society, 2*, 59–68.

Bower, G. H., & Gilligan, S. G. (1979). Remembering information related to one's self. *Journal of Research in Personality, 13*(4), 420–432.

Brainerd, C. J., & Reyna, V. F. (2005). *The science of false memory*. Oxford University Press.

Brown, P., Keenan, J. M., & Potts, G. R. (1986). The self-reference effect with imagery encoding. *Journal of Personality and Social Psychology, 51*(5), 897.

Burden, C., Leach, R. C., Sklenar, A. M., Urban Levy, P., Frankenstein, A. N., & Leshikar, E. D. (2021). Examining the influence of brain stimulation to the medial prefrontal cortex on the self-reference effect in memory. *Brain and Behavior*, e2368.

Byrne, R. W., & Bates, L. A. (2007). Sociality, evolution and cognition. *Current Biology, 17*(16), R714–R723.

Carpenter, S. L. (1988). Self-relevance and goal-directed processing in the recall and weighting of information about others. *Journal of Experimental Social Psychology, 24*(4), 310–332.

Carstensen, L. L. (1992). Social and emotional patterns in adulthood: Support for socio-emotional selectivity theory. *Psychology and Aging,* 7(3), 331.

Carstensen, L. L., & DeLiema, M. (2018). The positivity effect: A negativity bias in youth fades with age. *Current Opinion in Behavioral Sciences, 19*, 7–12.

Cassidy, B. S., & Gutchess, A. H. (2012). Social relevance enhances memory for impressions in older adults. *Memory (Hove, England), 20*(4), 332–345.

Cassidy, B. S., Leshikar, E. D., Shih, J. Y., Aizenman, A., & Gutchess, A. H. (2013). Valence-based age differences in medial prefrontal activity during impression formation. *Social Neuroscience, 8*(5), 462–473.

Cassidy, B. S., Zebrowitz, L. A., & Gutchess, A. H. (2012). Appearance-based inferences bias source memory. *Memory & Cognition*, 1–11.

Catrambone, R., & Markus, H. (1987). The role of self-schemas in going beyond the information given. *Social Cognition, 5*(4), 349–368.

Charles, S. T., & Carstensen, L. L. (2010). Social and emotional aging. *Annual Review of Psychology, 61*, 383–409.

Colton, G., Leshikar, E. D., & Gutchess, A. H. (2013). Age differences in neural response to stereotype threat and resiliency for self-referenced information. *Frontiers in Human Neuroscience, 7*.

Cunningham, S. J., Brebner, J. L., Quinn, F., & Turk, D. J. (2014). The self-reference effect on memory in early childhood. *Child Development, 85*(2), 808–823.

Cunningham, S. J., Turk, D. J., Macdonald, L. M., & Macrae, C. N. (2008). Yours or mine? Ownership and memory. *Consciousness and Cognition, 17*(1), 312–318.

Cunningham, S. J., Vergunst, F., Macrae, C. N., & Turk, D. J. (2013). Exploring early self-referential memory effects through ownership. *British Journal of Developmental Psychology, 31*(3), 289–301.

D'Argembeau, A., & Van der Linden, M. (2008). Remembering pride and shame: Self-enhancement and the phenomenology of autobiographical memory. *Memory (Hove, England), 16*(5), 538–547 https://doi.org/792623179 [pii]10.1080/09658210802010463.

Dulas, M. R., Newsome, R. N., & Duarte, A. (2011). The effects of aging on ERP correlates of source memory retrieval for self-referential information. *Brain Research, 1377*, 84–100 https://doi.org/S0006-8993(11)00008-4 [pii] 10.1016/j.brainres.2010.12.087.

Durbin, K. A., Mitchell, K. J., & Johnson, M. K. (2017). Source memory that encoding was self-referential: The influence of stimulus characteristics. *Memory (Hove, England), 25*(9), 1191–1200.

Elliot, A. J. (2006). The hierarchical model of approach-avoidance motivation. *Motivation and Emotion, 30*, 111–116.

Elliot, A. J., Gable, S. L., & Mapes, R. R. (2006). Approach and avoidance motivation in the social domain. *Personality and Social Psychology Bulletin, 32*(3), 378–391.

Festinger, L. (1954). A theory of social comparison processes. *Human Relations,* 7(2), 117–140.

Fong, G. T., & Markus, H. (1982). Self-schemas and judgments about others. *Social Cognition, 1*(3), 191–204.

Fossati, P., Hevenor, S. J., Graham, S. J., Grady, C., Keightley, M. L., Craik, F., & Mayberg, H. (2003). In search of the emotional self: an FMRI study using positive and negative emotional words. *American Journal of Psychiatry, 160*(11), 1938–1945. http://www.ncbi.nlm.nih.gov/entrez/query.fcgi?cmd=Retrieve&db=PubMed&dopt=Citation&list_uids=14594739.

Frankenstein, A. N., McCurdy, M. P., Sklenar, A. M., Pandya, R., Szpunar, K. K., & Leshikar, E. D. (2020). Future thinking about social targets: The influence of prediction outcome on memory. *Cognition,* 1–9. https://doi.org/10.1016/j.cognition.2020.104390.

Frankenstein, A. N., Udeogu, O. J., McCurdy, M. P., Sklenar, A. M., & Leshikar, E. D. (2022). Exploring the relationship between retrieval practice, self-efficacy, and memory. *Memory & Cognition, 50*(6), 1299–1318.

Gable, S. L. (2006). Approach and avoidance social motives and goals. *Journal of Personality, 74*(1), 175–222.

Giannakopoulos, K. L., McCurdy, M. P., Sklenar, A. M., Frankenstein, A. N., Levy, P. U., & Leshikar, E. D. (2021). Less constrained practice tests enhance the testing effect for item memory but not context memory. *The American Journal of Psychology, 134*(3), 321–332.

Giannakopoulos, K. L., McCurdy, M. P., Sklenar, A. M., Frankenstein, A. N., Urban Levy, P., & Leshikar, E. D. (2024). Lower constraint testing enhances the testing effect for some contextual details but not others. *Brain and Behavior, 14*(1), e3380.

Gilron, R., & Gutchess, A. H. (2012). Remembering first impressions: Effects of intentionality and diagnosticity on subsequent memory. *Cognitive, Affective & Behavioral Neuroscience, 12*(1), 85–98.

Glisky, E. L., & Marquine, M. J. (2009). Semantic and self-referential processing of positive and negative trait adjectives in older adults. *Memory (Hove, England), 17*(2), 144–157. https://doi.org/792992980 [pii] 10.1080/09658210802077405.

Grilli, M. D., & Glisky, E. L. (2010). Self-imagining enhances recognition memory in memory-impaired individuals with neurological damage. *Neuropsychology, 24*(6), 698.

Gutchess, A. H., Hebrank, A., Sutton, B. P., Leshikar, E., Chee, M. W., Tan, J. C., ... Park, D. C. (2007). Contextual interference in recognition memory with age. *Neuroimage, 35*(3), 1338–1347. https://doi.org/S1053-8119(07)00090-0 [pii] 10.1016/j.neuroimage.2007.01.043.

Gutchess, A. H., Kensinger, E. A., & Schacter, D. L. (2007). Aging, self-referencing, and medial prefrontal cortex. *Social Neuroscience, 2*(2), 117–133. https://doi.org/778890605 [pii] 10.1080/17470910701399029.

Gutchess, A. H., Kensinger, E. A., Yoon, C., & Schacter, D. L. (2007). Ageing and the self-reference effect in memory. *Memory (Hove, England), 15*(8), 822–837. https://doi.org/10.1080/09658210701701394.

Gutchess, A. H., Sokal, R., Coleman, J. A., Gotthilf, G., Grewal, L., & Rosa, N. (2015). Age differences in self-referencing: Evidence for common and distinct encoding strategies. *Brain Research, 1612*, 118–127.

Hamami, A., Serbun, S. J., & Gutchess, A. H. (2011). Self-referencing enhances memory specificity with age. *Psychology and Aging, 26*(3), 636.

Hastie, R., & Kumar, P. A. (1979). Person memory: Personality traits as organizing principles in memory for behaviors. *Journal of Personality and Social Psychology, 37*(1), 25.

Hatfield, G. (2015). Radical empiricism, critical realism, and American functionalism: James and Sellars. *HOPOS: The Journal of the International Society for the History of Philosophy of Science, 5*(1), 129–153.

Hazel, R. (1991). The role of the self-concept in aging. *Annual Review of Gerontology and Geriatrics, 11*, 110.

Heatherton, T. F., Wyland, C. L., Macrae, C. N., Demos, K. E., Denny, B. T., & Kelley, W. M. (2006). Medial prefrontal activity differentiates self from close others. *Social Cognitive and Affective Neuroscience, 1*(1), 18–25. https://doi.org/10.1093/scan/nsl001.

Hou, M., Grilli, M. D., & Glisky, E. L. (2019). Self-reference enhances relational memory in young and older adults. *Aging, Neuropsychology, and Cognition, 26*(1), 105–120.

Hutchison, J., Ross, J., & Cunningham, S. J. (2021). Development of evaluative and incidental self-reference effects in childhood. *Journal of Experimental Child Psychology, 210*, 105197.

Ilenikhena, G. O., Narmawala, H., Sklenar, A. M., McCurdy, M. P., Gutchess, A. H., & Leshikar, E. D. (2021). Stop shouting at me: The influence of case and self-referencing on explicit and implicit memory. *Frontiers in Psychology, 12*, 2063.

Jackson, J. D., Luu, C., Vigderman, A., Leshikar, E. D., St Jacques, P. L., & Gutchess, A. (2019). Reduction of the self-reference effect in younger and older adults. *Psychology & Neuroscience, 12*(2), 257.

Jacobsen, T., Schubotz, R. I., Hofel, L., & Cramon, D. Y. (2006). Brain correlates of aesthetic judgment of beauty. *Neuroimage, 29*(1), 276–285. https://doi.org/S1053-8119(05)00499-4 [pii] 10.1016/j.neuroimage.2005.07.010.

Johnson, M. K., Foley, M. A., Suengas, A. G., & Raye, C. L. (1988). Phenomenal characteristics of memories for perceived and imagined autobiographical events. *Journal of Experimental Psychology: General, 117*(4), 371–376. http://www.ncbi.nlm.nih.gov/pubmed/2974863.

Johnson, M. K., Hashtroudi, S., & Lindsay, D. S. (1993). Source monitoring. *Psychological Review, 114*, 3–28.

Johnson, M. K., & Raye, C. L. (1981). Reality monitoring. *Psychological Review, 88*(1), 67.

Johnson, S. C., Schmitz, T. W., Kawahara-Baccus, T. N., Rowley, H. A., Alexander, A. L., Lee, J., & Davidson, R. J. (2005). The cerebral response during subjective choice with and without self-reference. *Journal of Cognitive Neuroscience, 17*(12), 1897–1906. https://doi.org/10.1162/089892905775008607.

Kadwe, P. P., Sklenar, A. M., Frankenstein, A. N., Levy, P. U., & Leshikar, E. D. (2022). The influence of memory on approach and avoidance decisions: Investigating the role of episodic memory in social decision making. *Cognition, 225*, 105072.

Kensinger, E. A. (2007). Negative emotion enhances memory accuracy behavioral and neuroimaging evidence. *Current Directions in Psychological Science, 16*(4), 213–218.

Kensinger, E. A., & Corkin, S. (2003). Effect of negative emotional content on working memory and long-term memory. *Emotion (Washington, D. C.), 3*(4), 378–393. https://doi.org/10.1037/1528-3542.3.4.378 2003-10417-005 [pii].

Kensinger, E. A., Garoff-Eaton, R. J., & Schacter, D. L. (2007). How negative emotion enhances the visual specificity of a memory. *Journal of Cognitive Neuroscience, 19*(11), 1872–1887. https://doi.org/10.1162/jocn.2007.19.11.1872.

Kesebir, S., & Oishi, S. (2010). A spontaneous self-reference effect in memory: Why some birthdays are harder to remember than others. *Psychological Science, 21*, 1525–1531.

Leach, R. C., McCurdy, M. P., Trumbo, M. C., Matzen, L. E., & Leshikar, E. D. (2019). Differential age effects of transcranial direct current stimulation on associative memory. *The Journals of Gerontology: Series B*.

Leblond, M., Laisney, M., Lamidey, V., Egret, S., de La Sayette, V., Chételat, G., ... Eustache, F. (2016). Self-reference effect on memory in healthy aging, mild cognitive impairment and Alzheimer's disease: Influence of identity valence. *Cortex; A Journal Devoted to the Study of the Nervous System and Behavior, 74*, 177–190.

Leshikar, E. D., Cassidy, B. S., & Gutchess, A. H. (2016). Similarity to the self influences cortical recruitment during impression formation. *Cognitive, Affective & Behavioral Neuroscience, 16*(2), 302–314.

Leshikar, E. D., & Duarte, A. (2014). Medial prefrontal cortex supports source memory for self-referenced materials in young and older adults. *Cognitive, Affective & Behavioral Neuroscience, 14*(1), 236–252.

Leshikar, E. D., Duarte, A., & Hertzog, C. (2012). Task-selective memory effects for successfully implemented encoding strategies. *PLoS One, 7*(5), e38160.

Leshikar, E. D., Dulas, M. R., & Duarte, A. (2015). Self-referencing enhances recollection in both young and older adults. *Aging, Neuropsychology, and Cognition, 22*(4), 388–412.

Leshikar, E. D., Gutchess, A. H., Hebrank, A. C., Sutton, B. P., & Park, D. C. (2010). The impact of increased relational encoding demands on frontal and hippocampal function in older adults. *Cortex; A Journal Devoted to the Study of the Nervous System and Behavior, 46*(4), 507–521. https://doi.org/S0010-9452(09)00225-1 [pii] 10.1016/j.cortex.2009.07.011.

Leshikar, E. D., & Gutchess, A. H. (2015). Similarity to the self affects memory for impressions of others. *Journal of Applied Research in Memory and Cognition, 4*(1), 20–28.

Leshikar, E. D., Leach, R. C., McCurdy, M. P., Trumbo, M. C., Sklenar, A. M., Frankenstein, A. N., & Matzen, L. E. (2017). Transcranial direct current stimulation of dorsolateral prefrontal cortex during encoding improves recall but not recognition memory. *Neuropsychologia, 106*, 390–397.

Leshikar, E. D., Park, J. M., & Gutchess, A. H. (2014). Similarity to the self affects memory for impressions of others in younger and older adults. *Journals of Gerontology Series B: Psychological Sciences and Social Sciences, 70*(5), 737–742.

Liu, Z., Wen, J., Liu, Y., & Hu, C. P. (2023). The effectiveness of self: A meta-analysis of using self-referential encoding techniques in education. *British Journal of Educational Psychology*.

Loftus, E. F. (1993). The reality of repressed memories. *American Psychologist, 48*(5), 518.

Loftus, E. F. (1996). *Eyewitness testimony*. Harvard University Press.

Lombardo, M. V., Chakrabarti, B., Bullmore, E. T., Wheelwright, S. J., Sadek, S. A., Suckling, J., & Baron-Cohen, S. (2010). Shared neural circuits for mentalizing about the self and others. *Journal of Cognitive Neuroscience, 22*(7), 1623–1635.

Lütjen, T., & Matschoss, R. (2015). Ideological migration in partisan strongholds: Evidence from a quantitative case study. *The Forum*.

Macrae, C. N., Moran, J. M., Heatherton, T. F., Banfield, J. F., & Kelley, W. M. (2004). Medial prefrontal activity predicts memory for self. *Cerebral Cortex, 14*(6), 647–654. https://doi.org/10.1093/cercor/bhh025 ([pii]).

Markus, H. (1977). Self-schemata and processing information about the self. *Journal of Personality and Social Psychology; Journal of Personality and Social Psychology, 35*(2), 63.

Markus, H., & Smith, J. (1981). The influence of self-schemata on the perception of others. *Personality, Cognition, and Social Interaction*, 233–262.

Markus, H., Smith, J., & Moreland, R. L. (1985). Role of the self-concept in the perception of others. *Journal of Personality and Social Psychology, 49*(6), 1494.

Matzen, L. E., & Benjamin, A. S. (2013). Older and wiser: Older adults' episodic word memory benefits from sentence study contexts. *Psychology and Aging, 28*(3), 754.

Matzen, L. E., Trumbo, M. C., Leach, R. C., & Leshikar, E. D. (2015). Effects of non-invasive brain stimulation on associative memory. *Brain Research, 1624*, 286–296.

McCurdy, M. P., Frankenstein, A. N., Sklenar, A. M., Levy, P. U., & Leshikar, E. D. (2021). Examining the relationship between generation constraint and memory. *Memory & Cognition*, 1–17.

McCurdy, M. P., Leach, R. C., & Leshikar, E. D. (2017). The generation effect revisited: Fewer generation constraints enhances item and context memory. *Journal of Memory and Language, 92*, 202–216.

McCurdy, M. P., Leach, R. C., & Leshikar, E. D. (2019). Fewer constraints enhance the generation effect for source memory in younger, but not older adults. *Open Psychology, 1*(1), 168–184.

McCurdy, M. P., & Leshikar, E. D. (2022). Contextual framework of the generation effect. *The American Journal of Psychology, 135*(3), 251–270.

McCurdy, M. P., Sklenar, A. M., Frankenstein, A. N., & Leshikar, E. D. (2020). Fewer generation constraints increase the generation effect for item and source memory through enhanced relational processing. *Memory (Hove, England), 28*(5), 598–616.

McCurdy, M. P., Viechtbauer, W., Sklenar, A. M., Frankenstein, A. N., & Leshikar, E. D. (2020). Theories of the generation effect and the impact of generation constraint: A meta-analytic review. *Psychonomic Bulletin & Review*, 1–27.

McElwee, R. O. B., Dunning, D., Tan, P. L., & Hollmann, S. (2001). Evaluating others: The role of who we are versus what we think traits mean. *Basic and Applied Social Psychology, 23*(2), 123–136.

McNaughton, N., DeYoung, C. G., & Corr, P. J. (2016). *Approach/avoidance. Neuroimaging personality, social cognition, and character.* Elsevier, 25–49.

Meyer, M. L., & Lieberman, M. D. (2018). Why people are always thinking about themselves: Medial prefrontal cortex activity during rest primes self-referential processing. *Journal of Cognitive Neuroscience, 30*(5), 714–721.

Meyers, Z. R., McCurdy, M. P., Leach, R. C., Thomas, A. K., & Leshikar, E. D. (2020). Effects of survival processing on item and context memory: Enhanced memory for survival-relevant details. *Frontiers in Psychology, 11.*

Mitchell, K. J., & Johnson, M. K. (2009). Source monitoring 15 years later: What have we learned from fMRI about the neural mechanisms of source memory? *Psychological Bulletin, 135*(4), 638–677. https://doi.org/2009-09537-007 [pii] 10.1037/a0015849.

Moran, J. M., Heatherton, T. F., & Kelley, W. M. (2009). Modulation of cortical midline structures by implicit and explicit self-relevance evaluation. *Social Neuroscience, 4*(3), 197–211. https://doi.org/908135818 [pii] 10.1080/17470910802250519.

Morel, N., Villain, N., Rauchs, G., Gaubert, M., Piolino, P., Landeau, B., ... Chételat, G. (2014). Brain activity and functional coupling changes associated with self-reference effect during both encoding and retrieval. *PLoS One, 9*(3), e90488.

Motyl, M., Iyer, R., Oishi, S., Trawalter, S., & Nosek, B. A. (2014). How ideological migration geographically segregates groups. *Journal of Experimental Social Psychology, 51*, 1–14.

Mueller, J. H., Wonderlich, S., & Dugan, K. (1986). Self-referent processing of age-specific material. *Psychology and Aging, 1*(4), 293–299. http://www.ncbi.nlm.nih.gov/pubmed/3267409.

Murty, V. P., FeldmanHall, O., Hunter, L. E., Phelps, E. A., & Davachi, L. (2016). Episodic memories predict adaptive value-based decision-making. *Journal of Experimental Psychology: General, 145*(5), 548.

Newman, L. S., & Uleman, J. S. (1989). *Spontaneous trait inference.* New York: Guilford, 155–188.

Niu, X., Utayde, M. F., Sanders, K. E., Denis, D., Kensinger, E. A., & Payne, J. D. (2024). Age-related positivity effect in emotional memory consolidation from middle age to late adulthood. *Frontiers in Behavioral Neuroscience.*

Northoff, G., & Bermpohl, F. (2004). Cortical midline structures and the self. *Trends in Cognitive Sciences, 8*(3), 102–107. https://doi.org/10.1016/j.tics.2004.01.004 S136466130400021X [pii].

Northoff, G., Heinzel, A., De Greck, M., Bermpohl, F., Dobrowolny, H., & Panksepp, J. (2006). Self-referential processing in our brain—A meta-analysis of imaging studies on the self. *Neuroimage, 31*(1), 440–457. https://doi.org/S1053-8119(05)02515-2 [pii] 10.1016/j.neuroimage.2005.12.002.

Old, S. R., & Naveh-Benjamin, M. (2008). Differential effects of age on item and associative measures of memory: A meta-analysis. *Psychology and Aging, 23*(1), 104–118. https://doi.org/2008-02853-013 [pii] 10.1037/0882-7974.23.1.104.

Park, D. C., Lautenschlager, G., Hedden, T., Davidson, N. S., Smith, A. D., & Smith, P. K. (2002). Models of visuospatial and verbal memory across the adult life span. *Psychology and Aging, 17*(2), 299–320. http://www.ncbi.nlm.nih.gov/pubmed/12061414.

Patel, S. P., McCurdy, M. P., Frankenstein, A. N., Sklenar, A. M., Urban Levy, P., Szpunar, K. K., & Leshikar, E. D. (2022). The reciprocal relationship between episodic memory and future thinking: How the outcome of predictions is subsequently remembered. *Brain and Behavior, 12*(9), e2603.

Roback, A. A. (1952). In A. A. Roback (Ed.). *The Structuralism of Titchener* (pp. 180–191). Library Publishers. https://doi.org/10.1037/10800-016.

Roediger, H. L. (1990). Implicit memory: Retention without remembering. *American Psychologist, 45*(9), 1043.

Roediger, H. L., & McDermott, K. B. (1993). Implicit memory in normal subjects. *Handbook of Neuropsychology, 8*, 63–131.

Rogers, T. B., Kuiper, N. A., & Kirker, W. S. (1977). Self-reference and the encoding of personal information. *Journal of Personality and Social Psychology, 35*(9), 677–688. http://www.ncbi.nlm.nih.gov/entrez/query.fcgi?cmd=Retrieve&db=PubMed&dopt=Citation&list_uids=909043.

Rosa, N. M., Deason, R. G., Budson, A. E., & Gutchess, A. H. (2016). Source memory for self and other in patients with mild cognitive impairment due to Alzheimer's disease. *Journals of Gerontology Series B: Psychological Sciences and Social Sciences, 71*(1), 59–65.

Roth, S., & Cohen, L. J. (1986). Approach, avoidance, and coping with stress. *American Psychologist, 41*(7), 813.

Saxe, R., Moran, J. M., Scholz, J., & Gabrieli, J. (2006). Overlapping and non-overlapping brain regions for theory of mind and self reflection in individual subjects. *Social Cognitive and Affective Neuroscience, 1*(3), 229–234.

Schacter, D. L. (1987). Implicit memory: History and current status. *Journal of Experimental Psychology: Learning, Memory, and Cognition, 13*(3), 501.

Schacter, D. L., & Buckner, R. L. (1998). Priming and the brain. *Neuron, 20*(2), 185–195. https://doi.org/S0896-6273(00)80448-1 [pii].

Schacter, D. L., Chiu, C.-Y. P., & Ochsner, K. N. (1993). Implicit memory: A selective review. *Annual Review of Neuroscience, 16*(1), 159–182.

Schaper, M. L., Mieth, L., & Bell, R. (2019). Adaptive memory: Source memory is positively associated with adaptive social decision making. *Cognition, 186*, 7–14.

Schneider, F., Bermpohl, F., Heinzel, A., Rotte, M., Walter, M., Tempelmann, C., ... Northoff, G. (2008). The resting brain and our self: Self-relatedness modulates resting state neural activity in cortical midline structures. *Neuroscience, 157*(1), 120–131.

Sedikides, C., & Alicke, M. D. (2012). Self-enhancement and self-protection motives. In R. Ryan (Ed.). *Oxford handbook of motivation*, Oxford University Press [rWvH].

Selfhout, M., Denissen, J., Branje, S., & Meeus, W. (2009). In the eye of the beholder: perceived, actual, and peer-rated similarity in personality, communication, and friendship intensity during the acquaintanceship process. *Journal of Personality and Social Psychology, 96*(6), 1152.

Serbun, S. J., Shih, J. Y., & Gutchess, A. H. (2011). Memory for details with self-referencing. *Memory (Hove, England), 19*(8), 1004–1014.

Sklenar, A. M., Frankenstein, A., Urban Levy, P., & Leshikar, E. D. (In Preparation). *Strength of social episodic memory influences subsequent social decisions*. 1–10.

Sklenar, A., Frankenstein, A., Urban Levy, P., & Leshikar, E. (2022). The influence of memory for impressions based on behaviours and beliefs on approach/avoidance decisions. *Cognition and Emotion, 36*(8), 1491–1508.

Sklenar, A. M., & Leshikar, E. D. (2024). Memory as a foundation for approach and avoidance decisions: A fertile area for research. *Memory and Cognition*, 1–6. https://doi.org/10.3758/s13421-024-01588-7.

Sklenar, A. M., McCurdy, M. P., Frankenstein, A. N., Motyl, M., & Leshikar, E. D. (2021). Person memory mechanism underlying approach and avoidance judgments of social targets. *Social Cognition, 39*(6), 747–772.

Sklenar, A., Pérez, J., McCurdy, M., Frankenstein, A., & Leshikar, E. (2023). Similarity to the self influences memory for social targets. *Cognition and Emotion*, 1–22.

Spencer, W. D., & Raz, N. (1995). Differential effects of aging on memory for content and context: A meta-analysis. *Psychology and Aging, 10*(4), 527–539.

Srull, T. K. (1981). Person memory: Some tests of associative storage and retrieval models. *Journal of Experimental Psychology: Human Learning and Memory*, 7(6), 440.

Srull, T. K., Lichtenstein, M., & Rothbart, M. (1985). Associative storage and retrieval processes in person memory. *Journal of Experimental Psychology: Learning, Memory, and Cognition, 11*(2), 316.

Srull, T. K., & Wyer, R. S. (1989). Person memory and judgment. *Psychological Review, 96*(1), 58.

Sugimoto, H., & Tsukiura, T. (2018). Contribution of the medial prefrontal cortex to social memory. *Brain and Nerve= Shinkei Kenkyu no Shinpo, 70*(7), 753–761.

Sui, J., & Humphreys, G. W. (2015). The integrative self: How self-reference integrates perception and memory. *Trends in Cognitive Sciences, 19*(12), 719–728.

Sui, J., & Zhu, Y. (2005). Five-year-olds can show the self-reference advantage. *International Journal of Behavioral Development, 29*(5), 382–387.

Symons, C. S., & Johnson, B. T. (1997). The self-reference effect in memory: A meta-analysis. *Psychological Bulletin, 121*(3), 371–394. http://www.ncbi.nlm.nih.gov/entrez/query.fcgi?cmd=Retrieve&db=PubMed&dopt=Citation&list_uids=9136641.

Terracciano, A., McCrae, R. R., & Costa, P. T. (2010). Intra-individual change in personality stability and age. *Journal of Research in Personality, 44*(1), 31–37. https://doi.org/10.1016/j.jrp.2009.09.006.

Terracciano, A., McCrae, R. R., Brant, L. J., & Costa, P. T., Jr. (2005). Hierarchical linear modeling analyses of the NEO-PI-R scales in the Baltimore Longitudinal Study of Aging. *Psychology and Aging, 20*(3), 493–506. https://doi.org/2005-13210-012 [pii] 10.1037/0882-7974.20.3.493.

Todorov, A. (2008). Evaluating faces on trustworthiness: An extension of systems for recognition of emotions signaling approach/avoidance behaviors. *Annals of the New York Academy of Sciences, 1124*(1), 208–224.

Tulving, E. (1985). Memory and consciousness. *Canadian Psychology, 26*(1), 1–12.

Turk, D. J., Cunningham, S. J., & Macrae, C. N. (2008). Self-memory biases in explicit and incidental encoding of trait adjectives. *Consciousness and Cognition, 17*(3), 1040–1045.

Turk-Browne, N. B., Yi, D. J., & Chun, M. M. (2006). Linking implicit and explicit memory: Common encoding factors and shared representations. *Neuron, 49*(6), 917–927. https://doi.org/S0896-6273(06)00087-0 [pii] 10.1016/j.neuron.2006.01.030.

Udeogu, O. J., Frankenstein, A. N., Sklenar, A. M., Urban Levy, P., & Leshikar, E. D. (2022). Predicting and remembering the behaviors of social targets: How prediction accuracy affects episodic memory. *BMC Psychology, 10*(1), 96.

Uleman, J. S. (1987). Consciousness and control: The case of spontaneous trait inferences. *Personality and Social Psychology Bulletin, 13*(3), 337–354.

Uleman, J. S., Newman, L. S., & Moskowitz, G. B. (1996). People as flexible interpreters: Evidence and issues from spontaneous trait inference. *Advances in Experimental Social Psychology, 28*, 211–279.

Urban Levy, P., Sklenar, A. M., Frankenstein, A. N., & Leshikar, E. D. (2023). Evidence for a memory advantage for prosocial behaviors. *Brain and Behavior*, e3096.

Urban Levy, P., Tafolla, E., Frankenstein, A., Sklenar, A. M., Villaseñor, J. J., & Leshikar, E. D. (In Preparation). Affective social episodic memory drives approach and avoidance decisions.

Van Kesteren, M. T., Ruiter, D. J., Fernández, G., & Henson, R. N. (2012). How schema and novelty augment memory formation. *Trends in Neurosciences, 35*(4), 211–219.

Van Straaten, I., Engels, R. C., Finkenauer, C., & Holland, R. W. (2009). Meeting your match: How attractiveness similarity affects approach behavior in mixed-sex dyads. *Personality and Social Psychology Bulletin, 35*(6), 685–697.

Verde, M. F., & Rotello, C. M. (2007). Memory strength and the decision process in recognition memory. *Memory & Cognition, 35*(2), 254–262.

Villaseñor, J. J., Sklenar, A. M., Frankenstein, A. N., Levy, P. U., McCurdy, M. P., & Leshikar, E. D. (2021). Value-directed memory effects on item and context memory. *Memory & Cognition*, 1–19.

Wells, G. L., & Olson, E. A. (2003). Eyewitness testimony. *Annual Review of Psychology, 54*(1), 277–295.

Wong, S., Irish, M., Leshikar, E. D., Duarte, A., Bertoux, M., Savage, G., ... Hornberger, M. (2017). The self-reference effect in dementia: Differential involvement of cortical midline structures in Alzheimer's disease and behavioural-variant frontotemporal dementia. *Cortex; A Journal Devoted to the Study of the Nervous System and Behavior, 91*, 169–185.

Wyer, R. S., Jr, Bodenhausen, G. V., & Srull, T. K. (1984). The cognitive representation of persons and groups and its effect on recall and recognition memory. *Journal of Experimental Social Psychology, 20*(5), 445–469.

Yamawaki, R., Nakamura, K., Aso, T., Shigemune, Y., Fukuyama, H., & Tsukiura, T. (2017). Remembering my friends: Medial prefrontal and hippocampal contributions to the self-reference effect on face memories in a social context. *Human Brain Mapping, 38*(8), 4256–4269.

Yaoi, K., Osaka, M., & Osaka, N. (2015). Neural correlates of the self-reference effect: Evidence from evaluation and recognition processes. *Frontiers in Human Neuroscience, 9*, 383.

Yaoi, K., Osaka, M., & Osaka, N. (2021). Does implicit self-reference effect occur by the instantaneous own-name? *Frontiers in Psychology, 12*, 709601.

Yonelinas, A. P. (2001). Components of episodic memory: The contribution of recollection and familiarity. *Philosophical Transactions of the Royal Society of London. Series B: Biological Sciences, 356*(1413), 1363–1374.

Yonelinas, A. P. (2002). The nature of recollection and familiarity: A review of 30 years of research. *Journal of Memory and Language, 46*, 441–517.
Yoshimura, S., Ueda, K., Suzuki, S., Onoda, K., Okamoto, Y., & Yamawaki, S. (2009). Self-referential processing of negative stimuli within the ventral anterior cingulate gyrus and right amygdala. *Brain and Cognition, 69*(1), 218–225. https://doi.org/S0278-2626(08)00234-0 [pii] 10.1016/j.bandc.2008.07.010.
Zysset, S., Huber, O., Ferstl, E., & von Cramon, D. Y. (2002). The anterior frontomedian cortex and evaluative judgment: An fMRI study. *Neuroimage, 15*(4), 983–991. https://doi.org/10.1006/nimg.2001.1008 S1053811901910080 [pii].

CHAPTER FIVE

Listening challenges in children: Comprehension and effort in noisy and voice-degraded conditions

Silvia Murgia*
Department of Speech and Hearing Science, University of Illinois Urbana, Champaign, IL, United States
*Corresponding author. e-mail address: smurgia2@illinois.edu

Contents

Abstract

Listening comprehension and effort in children are critical components of cognitive development, particularly in educational settings where background noise and dysphonia can pose significant challenges. This review examines how environmental

Psychology of Learning and Motivation, Volume 81
ISSN 0079-7421, https://doi.org/10.1016/bs.plm.2024.07.004

factors such as high levels of background noise and dysphonic voices impact children's ability to process auditory information, thereby increasing cognitive load and listening effort. It explores the role of executive function such as working memory and selective attention in managing listening tasks and mitigating the effects of adverse listening conditions. Various assessment methods, including subjective and objective measures, are discussed to evaluate their effectiveness in capturing listening effort. The findings underscore the importance of creating acoustically optimized learning environments and addressing voice quality issues to support children's academic performance and cognitive development.

1. Introduction

Listening and hearing represent distinct processes, where hearing denotes the passive reception of sounds, and listening indicates an active and deliberate engagement with auditory stimuli (Purdy & Borisoff, 1997; Yıldırım & Yıldırım, 2016). Kline (1996) stated: "The difference between hearing and listening can be stated this way: Hearing is the reception of sound, listening is the attachment of meaning to the sound" (Kline, 1996, p. 7). Listening is a dynamic and complex cognitive activity that requires the brain to decode, interpret, and integrate spoken language with attention, memory, and broader cognitive processes (Bodie & Wolvin, 2020). The listening process encompasses multiple steps: receiving, attending, understanding, responding, and remembering (Kline, 1996). Initially, the listener must be open and willing to receive the message. Attention must be actively maintained on the target to ensure the message is not overlooked or ignored. Understanding involves interpreting and fully comprehending the message, often requiring interaction to clarify meanings. Responding, which can be verbal or nonverbal, immediate or delayed, indicates to the speaker that the message has been understood. Finally, remembering involves retaining the information. This structured approach highlights the necessity of active engagement in each step to ensure successful communication.

This differentiation between hearing and listening holds particular relevance in language learning contexts, where challenges in listening to and understanding language can impede effective communication (Petrić, 2000). The development of listening skills is crucial in language acquisition, and it is worth noting that these skills are not only acquirable but also teachable (Petrić, 2000). Effective listening, facilitated by attention, enables individuals to establish meaningful connections with their environment and engage in interactions (Okhunjonov & Shermukhammedova, 2023). In the domain of child development and education, listening plays a critical role in literacy development, academic success, and social interactions (McDevitt, Spivey, Sheehan, Lennon, & Story, 1990). Its significance in language learning lies in facilitating communication and processing input into meaningful output (Kumar & Shankar, 2021; Yıldırım & Yıldırım, 2016), and educators have considerable influence over its development (Ahmadi, 2016). From a young age, children use listening to acquire language, recognize differences in tone and meaning, and develop mental adaptability (Vouloumanos & Waxman, 2014; Vouloumanos & Werker, 2007).

In essence, listening is not merely a passive activity but an active and dynamic process that significantly contributes to children's language development, academic achievement, and social competence. By prioritizing listening skills in educational settings, it is possible to support children's development and prepare them for successful communication in various aspects of their lives.

2. Listening comprehension in child development and education

Listening comprehension, a multifaceted cognitive process involving decoding, interpretation, and assimilation of spoken language (Kim & Pilcher, 2016), relies on a range of cognitive skills beyond hearing. Although hearing is essential for the listening process, effective listening also involves cognitive functions such as executive function, which includes selective attention and working memory. These abilities help listeners focus on specific signals in the presence of distractions and discern speech even amidst competing noises, and temporally retain and manipulate information.

The development of efficient selective attention mechanisms is particularly crucial for children, as argued by Plebanek and Sloutsky (2019). Their work demonstrates that developing strong selective attention skills significantly enhances and predicts working memory capabilities among children aged 4 and 7 years old. The synergy of these cognitive abilities works together to achieve effective listening (O'Neill, Barkhouse, Patro, & Srinivasan, 2023). This underscores the significance of selective attention in listening comprehension, as it involves not only processing auditory information but also efficiently filtering out irrelevant information (Wolfgramm, Suter, & Göksel, 2016). The listening comprehension process encompasses advanced linguistic analysis and interpretation of a sentence's syntactic and semantic features, as well as its vocabulary. Additionally, it requires the incorporation of newly acquired knowledge into existing lexical structures and the drawing of inferences from semantic information retained in long-term memory (Lewis, Vasishth, & Van Dyke, 2006). The process of listening involves complex cognitive activities that are essential for understanding spoken language, which in turn supports the development of broader language abilities and literacy. Children acquire language by engaging in listening and learning to discern and interpret different sounds and voices, which are critical for language development and the acquisition of phonological awareness, leading up to skills necessary for reading (Hogan, Adlof, & Alonzo, 2014; Kim & Pilcher, 2016).

Transforming heard speech into something meaningful begins with the speech input produced by the speaker, recognized as "bottom-up" information. This speech input is processed by the listener's auditory system, utilizing previously acquired linguistic knowledge, such as grammar and vocabulary. This integration is known as "top-down" processing. Various processing mechanisms then operate at different levels. Initially, speech perception and prosodic analysis identify phonetic units and prosodic features like pitch and loudness to grasp the structure and emotional tone of the utterance. Word recognition follows, where the listener activates and selects words from their internal vocabulary based on the incoming sounds. Then, syntactic and semantic processing compute the sentence's structure and assign thematic roles, resulting in a literal mental representation. Pragmatic processing integrates context, previous information, world knowledge, and communication rules to enrich this mental representation. (Grosjean & Byers-Heinlein, 2018, Fig. 1). This complex process highlights the intricate structure of listening comprehension, which is constructed incrementally. The system processes information as it arrives, progressing from speech sounds to syntactic, semantic, and pragmatic elements.

In educational settings, listening comprehension is often overshadowed by more tangible skills like reading and writing. However, its impact on learning is profound, influencing children's ability to process information, engage in effective communication, and perform well academically (Hogan, Bridges, Justice, & Cain, 2011; Kim & Pilcher, 2016). Listening comprehension aids in vocabulary acquisition, as children learn new words and their meanings through exposure to spoken language, especially when listening is combined with reading (Valentini, Ricketts, Pye, & Houston-Price, 2018). Additionally, listening comprehension fosters critical thinking and problem-solving skills, as children must analyze and interpret spoken information to respond appropriately (Díaz-Galaz, 2020).

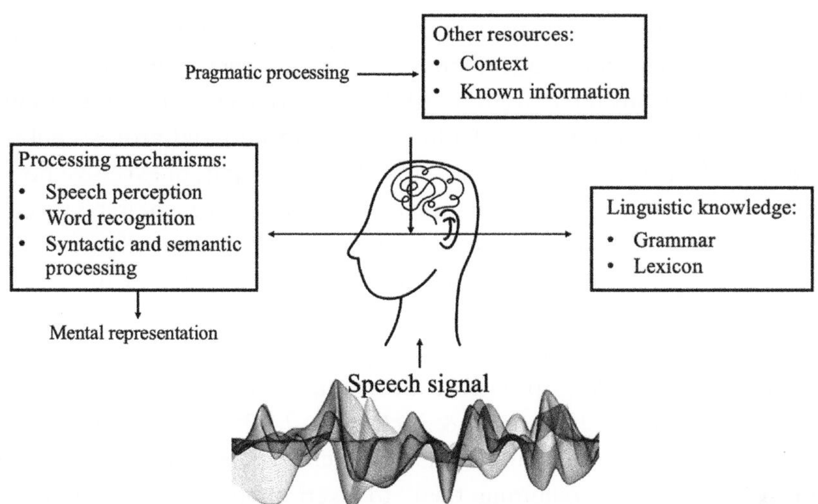

Fig. 1 Speech perception and listening comprehension process.

Understanding the elements that support listening comprehension can provide further insights into its vital role in educational success. Several factors can influence children's listening comprehension abilities, including cognitive, linguistic, environmental, developmental and age- and health-related factors. Cognitive factors such as selective attention, working memory, and processing speed play a significant role in listening comprehension (Kim & Phillips, 2014; Kim & Pilcher, 2016). Selective attention is the ability to focus on relevant information while ignoring distractions. while engaged in one or more tasks. It encompasses the effective distribution of these resources when multitasking. Working memory plays a crucial role in temporarily storing and manipulating information required to execute complex tasks. Additionally, processing speed is directly linked to the task's complexity, with more challenging tasks demanding faster cognitive operations. These cognitive abilities collectively enhance the efficiency and effectiveness of listening comprehension. Children with better working memory and selective attention skills tend to have stronger listening comprehension abilities, as they can retain and process spoken information more effectively (Adams, Bourke, & Willis, 1999; de Bree & Zee, 2021; Finney, Montgomery, Gillam, & Evans, 2014; Florit, Roch, Altoè, & Levorato, 2009; Kim, 2016; Magimairaj & Montgomery, 2012; McInnes, Humphries, Hogg-Johnson, & Tannock, 2003). Additionally, linguistic factors, including vocabulary knowledge and syntactic awareness, also contribute significantly to listening comprehension proficiency (Kim, 2015, 2016).

The physical environment, particularly within educational settings, significantly influences listening comprehension effectiveness (Ameen & Saeed, 2022; Klatte, Lachmann, & Meis, 2010; Picard & Bradley, 2001). Classroom acoustics play a crucial role in children's ability to hear and process spoken language. Challenges arise from poor acoustics resulting from excessive noise and reverberation, which obscure speech sounds, hindering children's speech perception and, consequently, their listening comprehension (Klatte et al., 2010). These effects may be further intensified for children with hearing impairments or language processing disorders. Extensive research has explored the impact of noise on cognitive performance in children (Clark, & Sörqvist, 2012; Gheller, Spicciarelli, Scimemi, & Arfé, 2024; Kamrath & Vigeant, 2014; Klatte, Bergström, & Lachmann, 2013; Zhang & Ma, 2022). Noise can disrupt the auditory signal that children rely on for learning spoken content, thus requiring them to exert more cognitive effort to separate relevant sounds from irrelevant background noise. This increased cognitive load can diminish the mental resources available for processing and understanding the content of what is being said, leading to poorer comprehension outcomes (Klatte et al., 2013).

As detrimental as excessive noise and poor acoustics are, voice disorders introduce an additional obstacle in the auditory challenges of educational settings, affecting children's ability to comprehend spoken language. Dysphonia, characterized by discrepancies in voice quality, pitch, and loudness relative to an individual's age, gender, cultural background, or geographic location (ASHA, 2009), adds complexity to the challenges encountered by children in listening environments. A dysphonic voice can obscure crucial acoustic cues necessary for understanding speech due to the increased intrinsic noise and reduced intensity and frequency range compared to normal speech (Isshiki, Yanagihara, & Morimoto, 1966; Ma & Yiu, 2006). To compensate for these degraded messages, the brain employs top-down mechanisms, which involve using pre-existing knowledge, expectations, and context to interpret and understand the incoming information despite the lack of clear acoustic cues. These mechanisms rely on the listener's familiarity with the language, context of the conversation, and previous experiences to fill in the gaps and make sense of the distorted speech. Consequently, the teacher's voice quality becomes crucial, as vocal impairments notably reduce speech transmission and negatively impact speech perception (Ishikawa, Nudelman, Park, & Ketring, 2021), word recognition (Bottalico, Murgia, Mekus, & Flaherty, 2023), and thus listening comprehension (Chui & Ma, 2019; Morsomme, Minell, & Verduyckt, 2011; Rogerson & Dodd, 2005). In particular, the study of Chui and Ma (2019) involved three and four-grade students and investigated the impact of dysphonic voices on these children's listening comprehension in both Cantonese and English. The test consisted of six passages (three in Cantonese and three in English) read in normal, mildly dysphonic, or severely dysphonic voices. Each passage was followed by six multiple-choice comprehension questions. The main findings revealed that listening comprehension decreased significantly, even with only mildly impaired voice quality. Furthermore, the study emphasized that dysphonic voices demanded more working memory resources for perceptual processing, consequently reducing the resources available for comprehension.

2.1 The cognitive demands of listening effort

Under optimal listening conditions, listening is typically an effortless process. However, when the conversation is degraded, the brain must deploy mechanisms to compensate for missing acoustic cues. In situations with degraded communication environments, such as noisy backgrounds or signal distortion, the brain must engage more intensively to discern relevant speech signals from irrelevant auditory noise. This segregation process is described by Kerlin, Shahin, and Miller (2010) and involves a selective gain mechanism that enhances the perception of important acoustic cues while suppressing non-essential background noise.

Listening effort pertains to a specific domain of cognitive effort where the listener decides to allocate mental resources to complete a listening task (Pichora-Fuller et al., 2016). It encompasses a complex, multidimensional phenomenon (Alhanbali, Dawes, Millman, & Munro, 2019), involving factors such as selective attention, working memory, and processing speed (Pichora-Fuller et al., 2016). A widely accepted definition in the research community characterizes listening effort as "the deliberate allocation of mental resources to overcome obstacles in goal pursuit when carrying out a task, with listening effort applying more specifically when tasks involve listening" (Pichora-Fuller et al., 2016, pp. 10S). This description highlights the willingness of listeners to allocate their cognitive resources during listening tasks.

To further understand the concept of listening effort, it is useful to examine the stages of speech communication, which are delineated in the speech chain. This framework describes the transmission of speech, from creating a message in the brain of the speaker, through transmitting the message, to receiving the message by both the listener and the speaker. When any component of the speech chain is impaired, such as by poor transmission (e.g., background noise), poor voice quality (e.g., voice disorders), or listener's hearing or language ability (e.g. hearing loss, communication disorders)

(Mattys, Davis, Bradlow, & Scott, 2012), listeners need to adapt and compensate for the obscured information. This compensation leads to increased use of cognitive resources, resulting in increased effort (Peelle, 2018). As a result, identifying and understanding speech in such conditions requires more cognitive resources. This increased demand on cognitive systems to manage and resolve more complex auditory inputs directly contributes to higher listening effort (Fig. 2).

Listening effort is grounded in the idea that the brain has a limited capacity for mental resources (Kahneman, 1973). The complexity of listening effort involves three key factors: (1) the inherent demands of the task, (2) the cognitive resources required for the task, and (3) the listener's motivation and engagement in utilizing these resources to successfully complete the task (Alhanbali et al., 2019). It is essential to highlight that listening effort is not merely driven by how much conscious or unconscious effort is required to complete a task, but also by listeners' willingness to allocate mental resources to complete it (Pichora-Fuller et al., 2016). This nuanced understanding is crucial for developing approaches that enhance auditory comprehension in varied settings. Introducing assessments of listening effort is crucial to supplement conventional audiometric

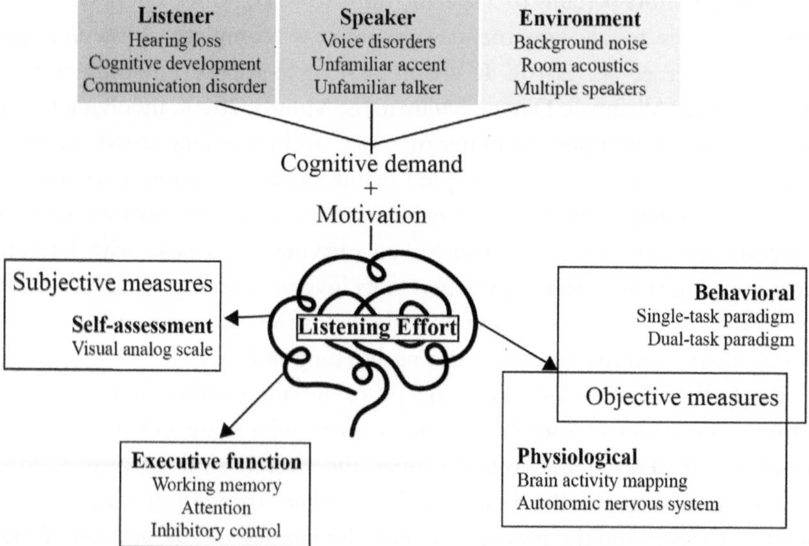

Fig. 2 Acoustic challenges faced by a children in a classroom environment, determined by a combination of their individual hearing ability and the external acoustic environment, including speech quality and background noise.

measurements, which gauge the threshold levels at which a person can detect sounds, providing limited insights into the cognitive aspects of hearing and listening. These measures of listening effort provide the advantage of estimating the resources utilized as task difficulty escalates, until the brain's capacity reaches saturation (Pichora-Fuller et al., 2016). When this situation occurs and the brain has minimal additional resources available, listeners may disengage and abandon the task.

In recent years, there has been a growing focus on listening effort, driven by the necessity to establish reliable measures for characterizing mental exertion in both adults and children (Alhanbali et al., 2019; McGarrigle et al., 2014; Peelle, 2018). This emphasis on measuring listening effort stems from the understanding that accuracy in detecting and comprehending speech alone often fails to convey the full extent of the challenge a listener faces when decoding a distorted speech signal, even when comprehension of the message remains intact (Winn & Teece, 2021). However, frequently, there is a lack of agreement among the findings, and the different measures currently used to gauge listening effort (such as self-reported measures, behavioral measures, and physiological measures) show low correlation (Alhanbali et al., 2019). There is thus a need for a more comprehensive evaluation and application of measurements to address the gap in existing literature regarding the causes of listening effort, particularly in the pediatric population. This is crucial, considering that children reportedly spend 45–65% of their day in classrooms, actively engaging in listening activities such as listening to teachers, interacting with classmates, and learning through communication (Rosenberg et al., 1999). However, in educational settings, the acoustical quality of speech is frequently compromised (Crandell & Smaldino, 2000), and children are required to exert significant listening effort to maintain attention and facilitate learning (Peelle, 2018).

2.2 Listening effort and accuracy

In the classroom environment, students' ongoing listening processes are not restricted to solely decoding speech signals successfully. Different classroom dynamics and interactions, such as simple to complex teacher-centered lectures; interactions between classmates and teachers during discussions; and simultaneous small group work, might have different impacts on listening effort. These varying dynamics warrant exploration to understand their effects, as they can lead to different degrees of listening effort.

Although increased listening effort is often linked to reduced listening task accuracy, these are distinct aspects of listener performance, providing separate insights (Winn & Teece, 2021). The effectiveness of speech communication in classrooms can be compromised by several factors: (1) the transmission channel, which may be affected by long reverberation times and high noise levels; (2) the quality of the signal, which can be degraded by voice disorders such as dysphonia; and (3) the hearing capabilities of the listener (Mattys et al., 2012). Numerous studies have explored the impact of these factors on listening comprehension (Lyberg-Åhlander & Brännström, 2015; Lyberg-Åhlander, Haake, Brännström, Schötz, & Sahlén, 2015; Rudner et al., 2018; Valente, Plevinsky, Franco, Heinrichs-Graham, & Lewis, 2012). However, research focusing on listening effort remains relatively limited.

While a relationship between improved performance and decreased listening effort has been observed, this relationship is not strictly linear. Accuracy scores alone do not fully capture the level of effort expended by individuals. Accuracy refers to the correctness or precision of an individual's responses or performances, typically measured through the proportion of correct answers or tasks completed successfully. Notably, identical scores can result from varying levels of cognitive resource deployment to decode a message (Koelewijn, Zekveld, Festen, & Kramer, 2012). For instance, this could be easily observed in a scenario where both a typical listener and a hard-of-hearing listener are presented with the same auditory task. If disruptive factors like background noise are absent, the individual with typical hearing may comprehend the message effortlessly (Ohlenforst et al., 2017b). However, despite achieving similar accuracy levels, the hard-of-hearing listener may need to exert more effort, employing compensatory strategies to discern useful information and disregard irrelevant details, thus experiencing higher cognitive strain (Winn, Wendt, Koelewijn, & Kuchinsky, 2018). This disparity also manifests in environments where communication is hindered by acoustic challenges, such as background noise, or by compromised signal quality from voice disorders. In these instances, listening effort does not directly correlate with the percentage of the message that is correctly understood (Koeritzer, Rogers, Van Engen, & Peelle, 2018; Krueger et al., 2017). Even with perfect message decoding, the brain might still be required to exert significant effort to overcome the impact of degraded acoustic cues (Peelle, 2018; Rönnberg et al., 2013). This increased cognitive exertion can adversely affect information processing and memory retention, leading to performance variations between individuals exerting greater effort and those who manage the task with minimal effort.

It is worth mentioning that listening effort doesn't stem from misidentifying the target signal, as listeners might not realize the misperception and could feel assured in decoding the message accurately, hence not needing extra effort. Rather, it arises from the exertion required to rectify errors by employing cognitive strategies to restore speech obscured by a degraded communication environment (Winn et al., 2018). For these reasons, even if the maximum accuracy score is achieved, measuring listening effort becomes a valuable tool for describing listeners' performance in challenging listening conditions.

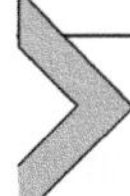

3. Models and frameworks for understanding listening effort

The emerging interdisciplinary field of cognitive hearing science has channeled its research attention to the interaction between cognition, hearing, and communication (Arlinger, Lunner, Lyxell, & Pichora-Fuller, 2009). Cognitive Hearing Science intends to investigate the balance between bottom-up processing, which allows the brain to rebuild the acoustic message thanks to the acoustic cues received from the signal, and top-down processing, where the brain needs higher knowledge of context and language to compensate for a degraded message. As mentioned earlier, the key concept of listening effort assumes that there is a limit on the mental resources that are needed for and that can be freely shared among different tasks to be performed (Kahneman, 1973). Moreover, the maximum mental capacity varies across individuals, and the amount of capacity needed to complete a task increases as the difficulty of the task increases (Wingfield, 2016). Under these premises, a well-established model and an integrative framework have been developed to explain the factors that influence listening effort, including hearing loss, voice disorders, and challenging acoustics. These include (1) the ease of language understanding (ELU) model (Rönnberg et al., 2013) and (2) the Framework for Understanding Effortful Listening (FUEL) (Pichora-Fuller et al., 2016).

The ELU model is based on the assumption that in long-term memory, there is a phonological representation of speech to which information can be linked in a rapid, automatic, multimodal way. If there is an easy match between received language segments and the information stored in long-term memory, the listener will experience no effort in understanding the speech. The listener resorts to what Rönnberg et al. (2013) define as an implicit mechanism since it is activated automatically and quickly. If, on the other hand, an easy correspondence is not found, a compensation mechanism is activated in the brain. The mismatch can be due to a signal degraded by a noisy environment, poor quality of the signal, or hearing impairment. In such cases, the brain will then have to rely on additional memory resources explicitly. Therefore, acoustically challenging situations are expected to lead to an increase in listening effort. (Rönnberg et al., 2013).

The FUEL framework emerged from the need to construct a comprehensive model accommodating various conceptual dimensions drawn from existing models of listening effort. Specifically, it is based on the ELU model integrating factors such as the listener's auditory capacity, their motivation to allocate cognitive resources to the task, and the demands of the task itself to explain the variance in listening effort (Pichora-Fuller et al., 2016). Research indicates that an individual's motivation significantly influences performance, especially in tasks characterized by high cognitive demands stemming from their complexity (Zhang, Siegle, McNeil, Pratt, & Palmer, 2019). If the topic of discussion fails to captivate or engage the listener, they may be disinclined to invest additional mental effort in understanding unclear signals. Moreover, in accordance with the FUEL model, as mental resources become exhausted, the listener necessitates more time to process information, leading to an increased likelihood of errors (Pichora-Fuller et al., 2016).

4. Measures of listening effort assessment

The assessment of listening effort is pivotal for understanding the intricate relationship between auditory perception and cognitive processing. Listening effort itself is a multifaceted phenomenon, encompassing perceptual, cognitive, and physiological elements. It cannot be fully captured by a single parameter or solely through one dimension of analysis. Each type of measure offers distinct insights into how individuals process and respond to auditory information, from their personal experiences to observable behaviors and the underlying biological mechanisms. This comprehensive evaluation includes three types of measures: (1) subjective measures, which offer direct insights into individuals' perceived effort and personal challenges, fostering a comprehensive understanding of their listening experience. (2) behavioral measures, how individuals direct their attention and allocate cognitive resources across various auditory tasks, offering objective data on behavioral responses to different listening demands; and (3) physiological measures, which explore the connections between listening ability and neurological activity, examining how the brain and nervous system respond to auditory inputs. This type of measurement gives a deeper understanding of the biological underpinnings of listening effort. Strengths and limitations of each type of assessment are discussed in the following paragraphs and reported in Table 1.

4.1 Subjective measures

Subjective measures entail the listener's self-assessment of the effort experienced immediately after performing a listening task. These measures rely on the ability of listeners to rate their own effort in performing a listening task and their having the memory to report it. The two most common tools used to self-rate listening effort are visual analog scales (e.g. Rudner, Lunner, Behrens, Thorén, & Rönnberg, 2012) and the speech, spatial, and qualities (SSQ) of hearing rating scale (Gatehouse & Noble, 2004). In visual analog scales, the listener rates on a scale the effort expended (e.g., from 0 – very easy to 10 – very difficult). On the other hand, the SSQ of hearing scale is a multidimensional questionnaire indirectly related to listening effort through its assessment of the qualities of hearing across multiple domains, with a particular focus on listening to speech in a variety of contexts. This concept is particularly relevant for individuals with hearing impairments, as they often need to exert more effort to achieve the same level of understanding as those with normal hearing.

Subjective measures offer important advantages due to the quick administration, intuitiveness, and straightforward interpretation of the data. They do not require researchers to have particular expertise to administrate them. Despite its subjective nature, this measurement provides valuable insights into listener perception. For example, perceived unpleasantness can significantly diminish listener motivation and increase disengagement from the task.

However, the literature has not shown a strong connection between subjective assessments and the objective measures of listening effort (Lemke & Besser, 2016). Research has indicated that self-assessment of listening effort may stem from a tendency to evaluate the accuracy and correctness of responses rather than the true cognitive effort needed to comprehend the stimulus (Moore & Picou, 2018). This challenge arises because participants, particularly children, often struggle to differentiate between these two concepts. The primary drawback of self-rating is its inherent subjectivity, which complicates the ability to make objective comparisons between different individuals. This is because self-rating relies on personal perception

Table 1 Comparison of listening effort measurements.

	LE measure	Tool	Advantages	Disadvantages
Subjective	Self- reported	Visual analog scale and SSQ of hearing scale	No expertise is required to administer; Quick and easy to administrate; Straightforward and intuitive interpretation; Provides insights into listener perception.	Individual threshold of effort not considered; Influenced by the questionnaire interpretation; Influenced by the listener's motivation/engagement; Children might not understand what they need to rate; Often not correlated to objective measures.
Objective	Behavioral	Single-task paradigm Dual-task paradigm	Easy to administrate; Easy to interpret; More ecological validity (e.g., multitasking).	Influenced by the listener's motivation/engagement; Dual-task not reliable for younger children.
	Physiological	EEG	High temporal resolution; Non-invasive; Low cost; Safe (radiation-free); Can be portable.	Poor spatial resolution; Does not allow a lot of motion.
		fMRI	Non-invasive; Safe (radiation free); Excellent spatial resolution (1 mm).	Children may struggle with constrained environment; Expensive; Noisy.

fNIRS	Good temporal resolution; Non-invasive; Safe (radiation-free); Low cost; Allows motion; Portable; Quiet.	Low spatial resolution; Superficial resolution (no deeper than 3 cm); Relatively new in listening effort studies.
Pupillometry	Time-series measurement; Relatively easy and fast to set up; Less expensive compared to others.	Influenced by medication use, eye disease; Dilation due to the effort is minimal; Threshold limit of difficulty; Influenced by the listener's motivation/engagement.
Skin conductance	Non-invasive; Easy to administrate.	Affected by changes in temperature and humidity; Sensitive to emotional factors; Poor temporal resolution.

Note: LE = listening effort; EEG= Electroencephalography; fMRI= Functional magnetic resonance imaging; fNIRS= Functional near-infrared spectroscopy.

and individual experiences of effort, which can vary widely from one person to another. For example, what one individual considers to be a significant effort might be perceived as minimal by someone else. This variation can be influenced by numerous factors such as personal standards, previous experiences, and individual thresholds for discomfort or difficulty. Additionally, younger children may also be more influenced by social desirability bias (King & Bruner, 2000), which could lead them to underreport the listening difficulties they actually face due to a worry about being viewed negatively by researchers. Consequently, when using self-rating methods, it's challenging to establish a consistent and reliable scale of effort across a diverse group of people. This lack of uniformity can lead to inconsistencies in data collection and analysis, making it difficult to draw broad conclusions or apply findings universally across different populations.

4.2 Behavioral measures

Behavioral measures represent another category used to assess the level of listening effort. These measures are intended to measure listening effort in relation to cognitive domains such as attention, working memory, and processing speed (Pichora-Fuller et al., 2016). They rely on the fact that when a task is more difficult and requires greater cognitive capacity, information processing tends to slow down, with a potential increase in error frequency. (Pichora-Fuller et al., 2016). Behavioral measures can be influenced by motivation and a loss in the listener's engagement, and these factors should be carefully considered in the experiment design phase. They can be classified into two subcategories: (1) single-task and (2) dual-task paradigms (McGarrigle et al., 2014).

4.2.1 Single-task paradigm

The single-task paradigm serves as a behavioral measure, commonly entailing the assessment of a listener's response time or reaction time during a listening task. Response time can be gauged through verbal responses, such as in a listen-and-repeat task (Gatehouse & Gordon, 1990), or by pressing a button to indicate the correct response (Houben, van Doorn-Bierman, & Dreschler, 2013). It is computed as the duration between the presentation of the stimulus and the chosen response. In contrast, reaction time does not involve selecting a response but rather reflects a reaction to a stimulus (e.g., light on a screen). These measures are based on the assumption that listeners need more time to give a response if the signal is difficult to decode. This increased response time occurs because the listener must engage in more intensive auditory processing to interpret ambiguous or complex auditory signals. When the clarity or quality of the signal deteriorates, the brain must work harder to reconstruct the intended message, which delays the reaction. The response time is measurable specifically in tasks that necessitate making a choice among options, serving as a quantitative indicator of how swiftly an individual can process speech information. This metric varies depending on the complexity of the speech signal and the listener's auditory and cognitive capacities, illustrating how different levels of signal difficulty impact the speed of cognitive processing.

The link between the listening effort needed to accurately discern an acoustic signal and the time taken to react or respond to a stimulus is not straightforward. According to McGarrigle et al. (2014), findings may be misleading, reflecting the listener's heightened attention rather than the actual effort expended in processing the information. Consequently, a faster response time might occur not only in situations where a listener correctly identifies a word immediately but also in scenarios where frustration and disengagement arise from excessively challenging listening conditions resulting in a typical inverted U-shape function, as noted by Pichora-Fuller et al. (2016). This complexity highlights the nuances in interpreting response times as a direct measure of listening effort. Research using the single-task paradigm to measure listening effort in children revealed that the single-task paradigm is sensitive to changes in signal-to-noise ratio (SNR) in both native and nonnative English-speaking children (Oosthuizen, Picou, Pottas, Myburgh, & Swanepoel, 2020) and that it can effectively measure listening effort in children as young as 6–7-year-old (Prodi, Visentin, Borella, Mammarella, & Di Domenico, 2019).

4.2.2 Dual-task paradigm

Listening effort can also be measured in what is known as a dual-task paradigm. This paradigm consists of a primary task and a secondary task. The primary task typically involves a speech perception task, while the secondary task can encompass either simple tasks, measuring the reaction to a stimulus, such as pressing a button as quickly as possible when a light is illuminated (monitoring visual stimulus), or complex tasks, involving exercises that demand rigorous cognitive processes, such as working memory. During the test execution, the listener is instructed to concentrate on the primary task while simultaneously engaging in the secondary task. The underlying hypothesis of the dual-task paradigm is based on the notion that the brain possesses a limited pool of cognitive resources, and the listener must allocate these resources efficiently across multiple tasks (Kahneman, 1973). As the difficulty of the primary task increases, requiring more resources, fewer resources are available for the secondary task, resulting in decreased performance. It is crucial to calibrate the difficulty of the secondary task for the sensitivity of the outcome. If the task is too simple, it may become an automatic response for the listener, necessitating fewer cognitive resources and showing minimal changes in listening effort. Conversely, if the task is overly complex, it may demand a significant allocation of resources at the expense of the primary task, potentially compromising the sensitivity of the listening effort measure. During test execution, the complexity of the secondary task may escalate, such as by increasing the number of potential responses, decisions, or actions required, without necessarily increasing its difficulty (Picou, Charles, & Ricketts, 2017). Assessing listening effort through a dual-task during a speech recognition test is often considered more ecologically valid than the single-task method. In everyday scenarios, individuals are frequently required to respond to multiple stimuli concurrently, necessitating the distribution of attention across several tasks. This is particularly true in educational settings where students are expected not only to listen but also to engage in other simultaneous activities, such as writing.

Despite its practical relevance, the reliability of the dual-task paradigm for assessing listening effort in children remains a subject of debate. Research indicates that the capability to manage and allocate resources effectively across multiple tasks typically develops in children around the ages of 10–12 (Picou et al., 2017). Indeed, the complexity and depth of the secondary task in a dual-task paradigm can influence the measurement of listening effort in children, potentially leading to less reliable results (Picou et al., 2017). Consequently, the dual-task paradigm may not provide reliable measures for children younger than 12, as they often struggle to prioritize tasks effectively. This inability to allocate cognitive resources efficiently can result in one task being neglected, usually the one perceived as more challenging (Choi, Lotto, Lewis, Hoover, & Stelmachowicz, 2008). Given these complexities, it is essential for researchers to consider these factors carefully when designing experiments to assess listening effort. Addressing these considerations is crucial to avoid inconsistent results and to ensure that the findings are reflective of true listening capabilities in varied real-world conditions.

4.3 Physiological measures

The last group of listening effort measures includes physiological measures. They fall into two major categories: brain activity mapping, which includes electroencephalography (EEG) and functional near-infrared spectroscopy (fNIRS); and autonomic nervous system measures, including pupillometry, heart rate, and skin conductance. These latter measures are based on the assumption that increased listening effort leads to greater stress, which increases sympathetic activity and decreases parasympathetic activity (Rovetti, Goy, Pichora-Fuller, & Russo, 2019).

4.3.1 Electroencephalography

With EEG, the brain's electrical activity is measured through electrodes placed on the scalp, capturing the synchronized activity of large neuronal populations. Oscillatory activity in particular is categorized into frequency bands: delta (0.5–4 Hz), theta (4–8 Hz), alpha (8–12 Hz), and gamma (>40 Hz). The use of EEG in assessing listening effort has been primarily focused on analyzing alpha and theta activity. In fact, the literature indicates that both alpha and theta brain oscillations play significant roles in speech processing. Specifically, theta oscillations have been linked to memory-related processing, reflecting their involvement in managing and recalling information during listening tasks (Wisniewski, Iyer, Thompson, & Simpson, 2018). In particular, the research conducted by Wisniewski et al. (2018) on young adults investigated the role of theta oscillations in relation to listening effort, particularly noting that theta activity is indicative of the cognitive demands placed on memory processes during complex auditory tasks. They highlight that sustained frontal midline theta enhancements are closely associated with increased working memory demands, reflecting the brain's effort to organize and process auditory information effectively. This suggests a direct link between the intensity of theta oscillations and the level of listening effort required to comprehend and remember spoken language under various acoustic conditions. This is crucial in contexts where understanding and retaining speech is necessary.

On the other hand, alpha oscillations are associated with attentional processes related to the suppression of irrelevant information, helping to filter out background noise and non-essential stimuli (Dimitrijevic, Smith, Kadis, & Moore, 2017; Obleser, Wöstmann, Hellbernd, Wilsch, & Maess, 2012; Wisniewski, Thompson, & Iyer, 2017). One study conducted by Dimitrijevic et al. (2017) recruited normal hearing young adults (average age 25.4 years) to investigate the relationship between cortical alpha oscillations and speech intelligibility in noisy settings using the digits-in-noise (DiN) test. Participants engaged in two listening conditions: an active condition where they concentrated on and repeated the heard digits, and a passive condition where they watched a silent video while ignoring the digits. EEG recordings were used to monitor alpha oscillations (8–12 Hz) during these tasks, examining event-related synchronization (ERS) and event-related desynchronization (ERD). Key results showed significant alpha oscillatory activity during active listening, whereas passive listening produced minimal oscillatory changes. Notably, a greater alpha ERD correlated with correct digit identification, indicating that reduced alpha power (increased neural activity) in this region enhances speech processing in noise. In contrast, alpha ERS in the central/parietal areas did not consistently differ between correct and incorrect responses, suggesting that alpha ERD plays a critical role in facilitating auditory attention and processing during difficult listening conditions. The main findings revealed that during active listening, distinct alpha oscillations were observed, whereas during passive listening, there were almost no oscillatory changes. Greater alpha ERD in the left temporal region was associated with correct digit identification, indicating that stronger neural activation (lower alpha power) in these areas supports better speech intelligibility. In contrast, alpha ERS in central/parietal regions did not show consistent differences between correct and incorrect trials. This suggests that alpha ERD is crucial for enhancing auditory processing and attention during challenging listening tasks.

The advantages of EEG become particularly apparent when compared to other neuroimaging techniques. In contrast to other methods such as functional MRI, EEG offers high temporal resolution, capturing brain activity with sensitivity at a fraction of a second. This temporal precision is crucial given the fluctuating nature of listening effort over time (Winn et al., 2018). The ability to track these temporal dynamics with precision, coupled with the non-invasive nature of EEG, renders it invaluable for investigating both the neural underpinnings of effort and cognitive engagement during auditory tasks. However, despite advancements in brain mapping, EEG is still characterized by a limited spatial resolution, hindering precise localization of brain activity. Nonetheless, this limitation may be less critical when probing listening effort. Additionally, EEG has demonstrated its reliability in measuring cognitive load until mental resources are depleted (Petersen, Wöstmann, Obleser, Stenfelt, & Lunner, 2015). It's crucial to acknowledge that while the non-invasive nature of EEG makes it suitable for use with children, interpreting EEG findings in children engaged in tasks may differ from those in adults, due to variations in developmental stages (Clarke, Barry, McCarthy, & Selikowitz, 2001).

4.3.2 Functional magnetic resonance imaging

Functional Magnetic Resonance Imaging (fMRI) is a technique that assesses brain activity by detecting changes in cerebral blood flow, which correlate with neuronal activity. When a person engages in a task, the activated brain regions require more oxygen. The magnetic field created inside a scanner enables the fMRI to monitor fluctuations in blood oxygen levels, serving as a marker of attention during tasks such as listening (Rosemann & Thiel, 2019). fMRI offers outstanding spatial resolution and is non-invasive and free of radiation, making it advantageous for many studies. However, because the process requires lying motionless within a confined space, it can be challenging for studies using younger individuals (Byars et al., 2002).

4.3.3 Functional near-infrared spectroscopy

fNIRS is an optical neuroimaging technique that uses near-infrared light to measure changes in the hemodynamic activity of the brain resulting from neural activity. It provides information on the concentration of oxygenated hemoglobin (HbO) and deoxygenated hemoglobin (HbR). This measurement can be carried out given the transparency of biological tissue under near-infrared light, which is absorbed by hemoglobin at wavelengths between 650 nm and 1 mm. The unabsorbed photons are re-emitted, allowing the assessment of changes in HbO and HbR which have absorption peaks at different wavelengths.

Despite its relatively recent use, fNIRS presents significant advantages that render it a suitable tool for measuring listening effort in children. Notably, it is portable, non-invasive, and free of harmful radiation, offering commendable temporal resolution while allowing freedom of movement. Another significant advantage is its compatibility with hearing devices. Studying hard-of-hearing populations is crucial as they are more likely to experience increased effort compared to their normal-hearing peers. Although fNIRS has yet to be utilized for assessing listening effort in children, previous studies demonstrate its sensitivity to speech, auditory attention, and speech processing (Lloyd-Fox, Blasi, & Elwell, 2010; Nagamitsu, Yamashita, Tanaka, & Matsuishi, 2012). Furthermore, research on hard-of-hearing adults has unveiled a positive correlation between oxyhemoglobin (HbO) concentration in the prefrontal cortex and increased listening effort (Rovetti et al., 2019). However, its correlation with subjective measures and reaction time appears to be weak. In comparison to other neuroimaging techniques like fMRI and EEG, fNIRS offers a balanced compromise: superior spatial resolution (up to 1 cm) compared to EEG and better temporal resolution (up to 250 Hz) than fMRI.

4.3.4 Pupillometry

Pupillometry measures the responsiveness and change in pupil size in response to an external stimulus. The pupil reacts to environmental changes (e.g., changes in brightness) by adapting its size. It also reacts in response to increased effort due to changes in attention, stress, and memory (Laeng, Sirois, & Gredebäck, 2012). Pupil size is a complex parameter to assess. It is not a direct index of listening effort, but rather, it is influenced by a set of variables that reflect the contribution of the autonomic nervous system, which provides a nonlinear response. During the performance of an easy task, the pupil size undergoes minimal changes. The same pattern is found for tasks that are too difficult as the listener loses motivation to finish the task and decides to give up by not employing any mental effort. The study of pupil dilation is largely related to the willingness to use mental resources (Chiew & Braver, 2013) because if the listener is not interested in or is frustrated by the difficulty of the task, the pupil size will remain unchanged. Pupil dilatation has been considered an indicator of more vigilance and greater listener attention rather than actual mental effort (Wendt, Dau, & Hjortkjær, 2016). Pupillometry introduces several advantages over behavioral measures. One of the benefits is that it is a time-series measurement giving an accurate description of listening effort fluctuation. The effort experienced by the listener may not be evenly distributed, and pupillometry has the advantage of showing the distribution over time. Koelewijn et al. (2012) demonstrated that pupillometry is sensitive to changes in masker noises. They tested adults with three types of maskers (stationary noise, fluctuating noise, and single-talker masker), measuring pupil dilatation while performing a speech recognition task. The largest pupil dilation was found for the single-talker masker, while there was no significant difference between the other two noises conditions. The results highlight that a greater vigilance and attention is required when the speech is interfered with by a noise containing speech information.

Pupillometry, while useful, is subject to several limitations. The changes in pupil size attributed to listening effort during speech perception tasks are relatively small, ranging from 0.1 to 0.5 mm. This is minimal compared to the more substantial effects of other external factors, such as changes in brightness, which can induce pupil dilations of 3–4 mm. Pupil dilation continues up to a certain threshold of difficulty; beyond this point, the pupil size rapidly diminishes (Winn & Moore, 2018). Additionally, the reliability of pupillometry can be compromised by variables such as medication use, eye disorders, the emotional state of the listener, their motivation, and the specifics of the test administered. Accurate measurements require maintaining a consistent distance between the eyes and the device, often necessitating the use of a stabilizer like a chin rest, which can be uncomfortable and unnatural, especially in tests that require verbal responses from participants, and it can be challenging for children who may tire quickly and struggle to remain still. Moreover, studies have shown no correlation between pupillometry measurements and subjective assessments of perceived effort (Alhanbali et al., 2019; McGarrigle, Rakusen, & Mattys, 2021).

4.3.5 Skin conductance

Skin conductance is employed to measure the electrical activity on the skin's surface, particularly through eccrine sweat glands predominantly found on the palms. This activity is regulated by the sympathetic nervous system, reflecting changes in arousal (McGarrigle et al., 2014; Pichora-Fuller et al., 2016). To measure skin conductance, two electrodes are placed on the fingers to detect changes in electrical conductivity following the application of a mild 0.5 V current. The non-invasive nature and simplicity of this method make it well-suited for assessing listening effort. However, the reliability of skin conductance as a measure is compromised due to its high sensitivity to the emotional state of the listener, which can lead to significant variability in results (Alhanbali et al., 2019). External factors, including temperature and humidity, significantly influence readings, necessitating strict regulation of room conditions throughout the duration of the experiment. Furthermore, the low temporal resolution, necessitating long stabilization times (around 3 min), limits the method's ability to capture rapid fluctuations in listening effort during brief speech recognition tasks such as word or vowel recognition.

Using skin conductance to measure listening effort in children is beneficial because it requires minimal cooperation from the participants and is easy to measure, which is particularly useful in studies involving young participants who may not easily comply with more complex requirements (Shibagaki, Yamanaka, & Furuya, 1992). Additionally, it allows researchers to study physiological responses with minimal explanation needed for the children, simplifying the data collection process (Shibagaki et al., 1992). However, skin conductance response amplitude has shown to be neither sensitive nor reliable in detecting listening effort during tasks, as demonstrated by significant changes in amplitude across different sessions (Giuliani, Brown, & Wu, 2021). Moreover, the method has achieved mixed results regarding its sensitivity to changes in speech recognition abilities, which questions its effectiveness in reliably measuring cognitive load in children (Giuliani et al., 2021).

5. The interplay of executive function and auditory processing

Listening comprehension is a complex cognitive activity that requires the active processing of auditory information to extract meaning and relevance. This process becomes especially intricate in environments where noise, multiple speakers, or complex information are present. The efficiency and effectiveness of listening in such conditions center significantly on the proficiency of executive function. Executive function encompasses high-level cognitive processes that enable an individual to engage in goal-oriented performance by managing thoughts, actions, and emotions. They are crucial for planning, decision-making, problem-solving, controlling impulses, and executing complex tasks (Diamond, 2013). Additionally, they are also essential for academic success, with a strong link between executive function and educational outcomes (Huizinga, Baeyens, & Burack, 2018).

In children, executive function is still in the developmental stage, which influences their ability to process auditory information, understand spoken language, and manage the cognitive load that comes with listening in complex auditory environments (Diamond, 2013). Executive function includes a set of core skills, including working memory and selective attention/inhibitory control. Working memory allows individuals to hold and manipulate information in their minds over short periods, which is crucial for following conversations and recalling past auditory information (Baddeley, 2010). Inhibitory control and attention, on the other hand, involves the ability to concentrate on relevant stimuli and ignore distractions, which is critical for learning and performing tasks efficiently (Posner & Petersen, 1990). As executive function develops, it significantly impacts children's listening comprehension and the effort they must exert to understand speech, especially in challenging situations.

In the auditory processing domain, executive function is not an isolated operation; these cognitive skills interact closely with each other and with sensory inputs to enhance listening comprehension and reduce listening effort. Understanding the roles and interplay of executive function in listening and their typical development in children is clinically relevant. For individuals with hearing impairments or cognitive deficits, such as hard-of-hearing children or those with neurodevelopmental disorders, mastering these skills can significantly impact daily communications and quality of life (Beer, Kronenberger, & Pisoni, 2011; Figueras, Edwards, & Langdon, 2008; Lemke & Scherpiet, 2015). Moreover, advancements in this field can help researchers and clinician to enhance typical cognitive development in children and lead to better design and development of auditory aids, educational strategies, and therapeutic interventions.

5.1 Role of executive function in listening comprehension

The critical role of working memory and selective attention are at the heart of listening comprehension process. Working memory is essential for retaining and processing spoken words and phrases long enough to extract meaningful content and construct coherent understanding (Daneman & Hannon, 2007; Finney et al., 2014; Lewis et al., 2006; Pichora-Fuller, 1996; Was & Woltz, 2007). This capacity extends to the semantic integration of spoken language, where working memory supports the manipulation and integration of linguistic elements across sentences and contexts, thus enabling listeners to construct meaning from continuous speech (Ericsson & Kintsch, 1995). Simultaneously, selective attention enhances listening comprehension by enabling listeners to concentrate on the speech stream, filter out irrelevant background noise, and dynamically shift focus as needed to follow the evolving threads of conversation (Wild et al., 2012). This integration of working memory and attention is particularly crucial when listeners engage with complex narratives; working memory retains earlier parts of the story, facilitating a comprehensive understanding as the narrative unfolds, while attention filters and prioritizes information, focusing on relevant details and disregarding distractions (Rönnberg et al., 2013).

Moreover, the adaptability and flexibility provided by selective attention are necessary in dynamic listening environments. This ability enables listeners to switch their focus between different speakers or topics and adjust their listening strategies based on the context. Such skills are crucial in places like classrooms or crowded areas, where the focal point of listening often shifts rapidly (Shinn-Cunningham & Best, 2008). The need for rapid attentional shifting and the suppression of potential distractions from competing auditory streams are particularly pronounced in multi-talker scenarios or noisy educational settings, where executive function governs the selection of relevant information sources (Shinn-Cunningham & Best, 2008). Children, especially, depend on their developing working memory and attentional capabilities to integrate semantic content and anticipate linguistic cues, which assists them in navigating educational settings where they must often listen to a teacher while ignoring side conversations, thus supporting effective listening and learning.

5.2 Role of executive function in listening effort

Listening effort in children encompasses the cognitive resources required to process auditory information effectively, especially in challenging environments. This effort is intricately linked to executive function, with working memory and selective attention playing crucial roles in managing the cognitive load necessary for successful auditory processing. In noisy or crowded classrooms, children utilize their executive function skills to dynamically allocate cognitive resources, enabling them to focus on relevant speech while filtering out irrelevant sounds, a process that can be mentally exhausting for young listeners (Pichora-Fuller et al., 2016). The flexibility to adapt listening strategies in response to difficult conditions is a critical aspect where children might emphasize listening for keywords or reposition themselves to better hear the sound source, thus reducing cognitive load (Francis & Love, 2020).

The effort exerted can be observed through behaviors such as the time taken to respond to questions or the ability to follow multi-step instructions, while subjective assessments often involve personal evaluations of the difficulty experienced in understanding spoken communication (McGarrigle et al., 2014). Neurophysiological studies, such as EEG examinations, provide insights into the role of executive function during listening tasks. Essential areas like the prefrontal and parietal cortex, crucial for working memory and selective attention, display activation patterns linked to listening effort. Specifically, increased theta activity signals higher cognitive loads, while reductions in alpha power indicate focused attention essential for processing speech amidst distractions (Kerlin et al., 2010; Strauß, Wöstmann, & Obleser, 2014, Wisniewski et al., 2017, 2018). This neural activity is crucial for effective auditory processing under strain, as evidenced by EEG oscillations showing that increased theta and reduced alpha activities correlate with greater memory encoding and the inhibition of irrelevant information, respectively (Obleser & Weisz, 2012, Wisniewski et al., 2017, 2018). These findings, together with behavioral data, underscore how a child's executive function supports their listening activities, especially in challenging environments.

Ultimately, the management of cognitive load through executive function is vital in controlling listening effort. When auditory input is unclear or obscured by noise, the increased cognitive load demands greater deployment of working memory and attentional resources to maintain comprehension. This heightened engagement can lead to faster fatigue and increased subjective listening effort, particularly for children whose executive function skills are still developing, making certain listening environments, characterized by poor speech transmission, particularly demanding (Francis & Love, 2020). Those with higher working memory capacity may experience lower subjective effort, as their cognitive resources are more efficiently managed, allowing them to better navigate the complexities of listening and learning in diverse acoustic environments (Koelewijn et al., 2012).

6. The impact of noise and dysphonia on listening comprehension and cognitive development in children

As discussed so far, listening comprehension is an essential cognitive skill that significantly influences successful communication, academic learning, and social interaction in elementary school children (Backlund, 1985). Effective listening skills are directly correlated with children's improved academic performance, reading comprehension, and language development (Hogan et al., 2014). These foundational language skills are pivotal for overall educational success. Understanding spoken instructions and verbal content is critical across all students, enabling children to follow lessons, engage in discussions, and retain crucial information. Moreover, listening comprehension plays a key role in social development, helping children to interact with peers, resolve conflicts, and build relationships. Recognizing that traditional listening test scores may not fully capture the cognitive resources children employ during auditory tasks (Winn & Teece, 2021), recent research has shifted attention toward studying listening effort, although such investigations remain relatively limited. There is a particular need to assess both listening comprehension and listening effort under adverse conditions, such as in the presence of noise or voice quality issues (dysphonia).

The presence of noise in learning environments can severely compromise comprehension by introducing a cognitive strain that leads to overload, diminishes attention, and impairs working memory retention (Gheller, Lovo, Arsie, & Bovo, 2020; Klatte et al., 2010, 2013; Lyberg-Åhlander & Brännström, 2015; Lyberg-Åhlander et al., 2015; Osman & Sullivan, 2014; Sullivan, Osman, & Schafer, 2015). This strain significantly affects children's ability to process information efficiently and is particularly detrimental to young children who have not yet fully developed their executive function skills (Leon-Carrion, García-Orza, & Pérez-Santamaría, 2004). A systematic review by Klatte et al. (2013) indicated that while children's ability to comprehend speech in noisy environments gradually improves until adolescence, it remains less efficient than that of adults until about age 10, especially with fluctuating noise sources. Younger children require higher signal-to-noise ratios (5–7 dB) compared to adults to achieve similar levels of accuracy and struggle more with using phonological knowledge and contextual cues to interpret noise-masked speech. Additionally, their reduced capacity to selectively focus attention on relevant auditory information increases their susceptibility to interference from background speech noise in noisy environments. Furthermore, studies have highlighted how noise impacts students' learning, with findings demonstrating that road traffic noise can impair reading speed and basic mathematics (Ljung, Sörqvist, & Hygge, 2009), higher background noise levels can lower language and reading test scores (Connolly et al., 2019), and increased background noise and reverberation time can reduce comprehension performance (Lamotte, Essadek, Shadili, Perez, & Raft, 2021). These findings underscore the importance of creating quiet, acoustically-friendly learning environments to support students' academic success. Expanding on these insights, Hygge, Evans, and Bullinger (2002) found that chronic exposure to noise could lead to broader educational delays with negative effects on long- and short-term memory, emphasizing the need for quiet learning environments to support cognitive development.

Quiet learning environments are crucial for supporting children's cognitive development. Research consistently demonstrates that continuous exposure to noise detrimentally affects children's psychological well-being, manifesting in increased stress, anxiety, and hyperactivity, which in turn can impair cognitive performance, motivation, and overall mental health (Haines, Brentnall, Stansfeld, & Klineberg, 2003; Sakhvid, Sakhvid, Mehrparvar, & Dzhambov, 2018; Schubert et al., 2019; Stansfeld & Clark, 2015). Additionally, the impact of noise is not uniform; intermittent noises, in particular, have been shown to disrupt children's learning significantly by causing repeated distractions (Clark & Sörqvist, 2012; Söderlund & Sikström, 2012; Wetzel, Scharf, & Widmann, 2019). These distractions have been shown to not only increase reaction times but also decrease performance accuracy in adults (Gumenyuk, Korzyukov, Alho, Escera, & Näätänen, 2004), potentially having an even greater negative impact on children. The challenges are further exacerbated in urban educational settings, where managing noise distractions becomes particularly challenging, making it difficult for teachers to provide optimal learning experiences. (Pervaiz, Lashari, Khan, & Bushra, 2024). This evidence underscores the necessity of establishing and maintaining acoustically-friendly environments in schools to safeguard and enhance the educational outcomes of children.

6.1 Noise

School settings often feature less-than-ideal acoustics that are not beneficial to effective learning. One of the main disruptors of speech comprehension in classrooms is typically a low signal-to-noise ratio (SNR) (Bradley, Reich, & Norcross, 1999; Houtgast, 1981). The SNR serves as an index of the relative power of a target auditory signal against the power of the background noise. A low SNR is indicative of a scenario in which the noise is at a level similar to or greater than the signal, leading to the masking of critical acoustic cues that listeners rely on to process speech (Bradley et al., 1999), leading to an increase in listening effort (Krueger et al., 2017; Picou, Gordon, & Ricketts, 2016). Although the minimum SNR recommended for educational settings is +15 dB (American National Standards Institute, 2010), typical values measured in classrooms range from −7 dB to + 6 dB (Arnold & Canning, 1999; Crandell & Smaldino, 2000).

Students in classrooms are subjected to noise from various sources, including peers speaking simultaneously, noises from neighboring classrooms or hallways, traffic, HVAC systems, among others. These noises can be steady or fluctuating and affect listening on two levels: (1) energetic masking that occurs when noise and speech signals overlap in their acoustic features, thereby disrupting the signal's energetic content and reducing its clarity (Mattys, Brooks, & Cooke, 2009), and (2) informational masking that arises in scenarios where the background noise includes competing speech, which can confuse the listener's auditory perception (Cooke, Garcia Lecumberri, & Barker, 2008). These diverse noise types influence listening comprehension in various ways. Studies indicate that the noise generated by just a few talkers can create more disruption to children's listening comprehension than a steady background noise (Klatte et al., 2010; Rudner et al., 2018). This effect is especially pronounced in children, who are more susceptible to interference from background speech than adults. Indeed, children necessitate an additional 5–7 dB SNR over adults to attain equivalent amount of speech understood (Klatte et al., 2013). Therefore, understanding the diverse acoustic challenges in classrooms is crucial, as these can significantly tax cognitive processing, leading to increased cognitive effort.

So far, studies investigating listening effort in children have predominantly utilized speech recognition tests as the primary listening task. The intricate relationship between acoustical environments and listening effort among school-aged children highlights the challenges of educational settings. Over the years, various studies employing different methodologies have produced inconsistent results regarding how noise affects listening effort. Behavioral measures used to assess listening effort during speech-in-noise tests did not consistently reveal significant increases in effort among children aged 5–14, even with decreasing SNRs (Choi et al., 2008; Hick & Tharpe, 2002; McFadden & Pittman, 2008; McGarrigle, Dawes, Stewart, Kuchinsky, & Munro, 2017; Stelmachowicz, Lewis, Choi, & Hoover, 2007). These studies employed a dual-task paradigm to test children between 5 and 14 years old. They administered word recognition tasks as primary tasks and varied secondary tasks (such as reaction time to light appearance, dot-to-dot puzzle completion, and digit recall), which were hypothesized to intensify cognitive load and impact performance. However, the selection of SNRs, ranging from 10 to 20 dB and close to the optimal classroom listening range of 15 dB as recommended by American National Standards Institute (2010), might have been too mild to significantly affect response accuracy or increase cognitive effort required for message decoding. Similarly, Stelmachowicz et al. (2007) and Choi et al. (2008) utilized a single noise condition with an SNR of +8 dB on 7–14-year-old children performing a monosyllabic word recognition task. However, the SNR used was insufficient to cause notable decrements in performance. This suggests that the SNRs used in these studies may not fully capture the acoustical challenges present in real classroom environments, thus not providing a true reflection of real-life scenarios.

Conversely, several studies have demonstrated the sensitivity of both single- and dual-task paradigms to changes in noise levels (Gustafson, McCreery, Hoover, Kopun, & Stelmachowicz, 2014; Howard, Munro, & Plack, 2010; Hsu, Vanpoucke, & van Wieringen, 2017; Hsu, Vanpoucke, Langereis, Dierckx, & van Wieringen, 2020; Lewis et al., 2016; McCreery

& Stelmachowicz, 2013; McGarrigle, Gustafson, Hornsby, & Bess, 2019; Oosthuizen et al., 2020; Picou et al., 2017; Picou, Bean, Marcrum, Ricketts, & Hornsby, 2019; Prodi et al., 2019; Schiller, Morsomme, Kob, & Remacle, 2020). For instance, Howard et al. (2010) implemented a dual-task paradigm involving a primary word recognition task and a secondary recall task among 9 to 12-year-old children. They introduced three noise conditions at SNRs of +4 dB, 0 dB, and −4 dB, compared to a quiet environment, which resulted in diminished recall performance due to the reallocation of cognitive resources towards the primary task. Hsu et al. (2017, 2020) explored the depth of processing in 7–12- and 6 to 18-year-old children respectively, within a dual-task framework, using speech recognition as the primary task and categorization as the secondary task to evaluate listening effort through both bottom-up and top-down processing, recording response times. They configured typical classroom acoustics with SNRs of 0 dB and 5 dB in the 2017 study and −3 dB and +3 dB in the 2020 study. Although Hsu et al.'s (2017) study did not find differences in listening effort across categories (e.g., color, animal, dangerous), both studies observed performance declines in the secondary task as noise levels increased, indicating heightened effort due to the depletion of mental resources needed to manage the more challenging primary task. Moreover, Hsu et al. (2020) noted a developmental increase in the ability to understand speech amid background noise with age.

The literature lacks consensus on which paradigm (between the single- and dual-task) is more reliable for assessing listening effort during the performance of a speech recognition task in the presence of noise (McGarrigle et al., 2019; Oosthuizen et al., 2020). McGarrigle et al. (2019) tested the sensitivity of both a single-task paradigm (verbal response time) and a dual-task paradigm (visual response time to a target on screen). 6–13-year-old children performed a speech recognition task at different SNRs (−4 dB, 0 dB, +4 dB), and they were asked to respond as quickly as possible in both the single-task paradigm and the dual-task paradigm. Although both paradigms showed an increase in listening effort as the noise increased, the verbal response time measured with the single-task paradigm revealed higher sensitivity and proved to be a more reliable tool than the dual-task paradigm. These results contradict the findings of Oosthuizen et al. (2020). In their study, 7–12-years old children were administered a digit triplet recognition test at three conditions: quiet, SNR at −10 dB, and SNR at −15 dB. The test was repeated twice, using first a single-task paradigm (listen and repeat) and then a secondary task paradigm (listen and repeat –

primary task-, and response time to a visual stimulus on a screen – secondary task-). As opposed to McGarrigle et al.'s (2019) results, the response time obtained with both paradigms showed a clear change in listening effort between both the quiet and noise conditions, as well as between the two noise conditions, showing a similar sensitivity to noise changes.

The conflicting results may be due to a different design of the dual-task paradigm since, according to the theory of limited cognitive resources (Pichora-Fuller et al., 2016), when the brain reaches the threshold of listening effort due to a task being too difficult, there is a loss of motivation resulting in a decrease in the response time. The dual-task paradigm can be a valuable tool in order to assess changes in the listening effort. However, the primary and secondary tasks need to be designed so that the task is challenging enough to demand the allocation of cognitive resources without children reaching the maximum threshold. Reaching resource saturation would result in a ceiling effect. When this occurs, children lose motivation to perform the tasks, with shorter response times that do not reflect the true effect of noise on listening effort (Nakeva von Mentzer, Sundström, Enqvist, & Hällgren, 2018). Nevertheless, increasing dual-task complexity has been shown to be unsuccessful since children have poor categorization ability, leading to a decrease in dual-task sensitivity (Picou et al., 2017). This trend is especially noticeable when comparing the listening effort experienced by adults versus children (Danneels, Degeest, Dhooge, & Keppler, 2021). While adults experienced a constant use of cognitive resources without significant growth in response to increased noise, children exhibited different configurations depending on age. After age ten, children began to develop adult-like cognitive control, experiencing an increase in cognitive effort as SNR decreases. In contrast, before age ten, lower SNR levels (e.g., −2 dB) led to shorter reaction times. This is due to the disengagement of children whose cognitive resources available to fulfill the task are exhausted (Danneels et al., 2021). Children have not yet mastered a mature attention control, and regardless of what task they are told to prioritize, their greatest attention will be directed to the easiest task (Choi et al., 2008).

6.2 Voice disorders

Dysphonia involves abnormal vocal quality, pitch, loudness, resonance, or duration, which is inappropriate for an individual's age or sex (ASHA, 2009). Dysphonia specifically manifests as a rougher, breathier, and more strained voice, often resulting from recurrent and high vocal load. Such alterations in voice quality can obscure critical acoustic cues that are vital for students to accurately perceive and understand spoken messages, ultimately diminishing speech communication quality (Porcaro et al., 2020).

In educational settings, the impact of voice disorders must be considered, especially given the high lifetime prevalence of dysphonia among teachers, which ranges from 51% to 69% (Cutiva, Vogel, & Burdorf, 2013). The teaching profession inherently places high demands on vocal usage, as teachers frequently need to use their voices in the classroom throughout the day to deliver lessons. This extensive use increases their susceptibility to developing voice disorders. Additionally, the acoustics of a classroom can exacerbate these risks, potentially leading to voice disorders (Cutiva & Burdorf, 2015). In a poor acoustic environment, teachers often have to alter their vocal characteristics, such as increasing the fundamental frequency, sound pressure level, and segment duration, to be heard. Such prolonged vocal strain can result in voice fatigue and subsequent signal degradation. Heightening the issue, only about half of the teachers affected by dysphonia seek medical intervention for their condition (Van Houtte, Claeys, Wuyts, & Van Lierde, 2011). Consequently, students are frequently subjected to lectures delivered in compromised acoustic conditions that can impede their ability to understand speech clearly, thereby obstructing their learning process.

Despite the recognized importance of considering voice disorders when discussing listening effort in children within educational settings, the literature on this topic remains limited, with most research focusing on speech recognition and only a few studies addressing listening comprehension. The study of speech intelligibility in classrooms, particularly when impacted by dysphonia, has recently attracted increased attention from researchers. Dysphonic speech, characterized by vocal strain or weakness, presents unique challenges beyond mere intelligibility. Bottalico et al. (2023) and Rudner et al. (2018) found that even in acoustically optimal conditions, elementary school children from second to fourth grade can achieve intelligibility scores comparable to those when listening to a typical speech, the cognitive effort required is significantly higher. This increase in perceived listening effort is crucial as it affects the listener's overall experience and learning potential. Moreover, dysphonia not only impacts signal quality but also adversely affects student motivation. Schiller, Morsomme, Kob, and Remacle (2021) noted a decline in motivation in first graders, attributing it to the unpleasantness of listening to a dysphonic voice, which subsequently increases the perceived difficulty of the task

(Morsomme et al., 2011; Rudner et al., 2018). This relationship between dysphonia, listening effort, and its broader implications in educational settings is a topic that needs more exploration. To delve deeper into these effects, Schiller et al. (2020) conducted an experiment involving children aged 5 to 6 performing a Sentence-picture matching task in quiet and noisy environment (+2 dB and 0 dB SNR). They assessed the impact of an imitated dysphonic voice on speech perception tasks. Findings revealed that dysphonia led to an increase in the children's response time by approximately 100 ms. To simulate a realistic school environment, the study was also performed under conditions of noise. Here, the presence of both noise and dysphonic voice decreased response times by 270 ms, indicating that the combination of these factors exacerbates the negative impact without one overshadowing the other. These studies collectively underscore the need for a comprehensive understanding of how dysphonia affects students in educational environments. Investigating the interplay between dysphonia and listening effort could provide valuable insights into designing more effective educational strategies and interventions, ensuring all students have access to clear and comprehensible instruction.

The interplay between listening effort and voice quality during listening comprehension tasks in elementary school children is a crucial but often overlooked area of research. Studies indicate that although voice quality may not directly impact comprehension scores, it significantly increases perceived difficulty and cognitive load. For instance, Rudner et al. (2018) found that dysphonic voices are perceived as more unpleasant and harder to understand, which can reduce children's motivation to listen and increase their listening effort. This effect is exacerbated by background noise, further straining the children's cognitive resources.

6.3 Listening effort and listening accuracy under noise and dysphonia

In recent years, the literature has increasingly explored the relationship between listening effort and listening comprehension in children. Despite this emerging focus, there remains a significant need for further research to fully understand these dynamics. As previously mentioned, the majority of studies assessing listening effort in children have relied on word or sentence recognition tests. However, these tests might not adequately reflect the complexities of listening comprehension within real-world classroom environments. Listening effort in children during listening comprehension tasks is significantly impacted by the presence of noise, and individual differences in executive function can further influence this dynamic. In noisy classroom environments, children's ability to comprehend spoken language is often compromised, requiring greater cognitive resources to process auditory information. This cognitive effort resulting from challenging listening is caused by factors such as background noise and the quality of the speaker's voice.

The literature so far has revealed a complex interaction between auditory conditions, executive function, and individual differences such as age and language proficiency. Prodi et al. (2019) tested children aged 11–13 who performed sentence comprehension tasks under three listening conditions: quiet, traffic noise, and classroom noise. The experiment took place in real classrooms where task performance accuracy and response times were measured to assess listening effort. The study found that children performed best and had the fastest response times in quiet conditions. Classroom noise significantly increased response times and listening effort, especially for younger children, while traffic noise had a less pronounced effect. The results indicate that older children (13-year-olds) were quicker in processing sentences, suggesting a developmental improvement in coping with background noise.

Similarly, Rudner et al. (2018) conducted a study involving 8-year-old children who participated in four separate experiments designed to simulate elementary school classroom conditions. The main task used to assess listening comprehension was the passage comprehension module of the Clinical Evaluation of Language Fundamentals (CELF 4), where children listened to short narrative texts and answered related questions. Listening effort was measured through subjective ratings of perceived difficulty, where children rated how difficult they found listening under different conditions. The four experiments were as follows: (1) evaluating the effectiveness of a digitally animated virtual talker versus a natural talker in +10 dB signal-to-noise ratio (SNR) conditions; (2) assessing the impact of multi-talker babble noise at +10 dB SNR with and without visual support; (3) investigating the effect of a dysphonic voice on comprehension with and without visual support in quiet and noisy conditions; and (4) exploring the impact of audio-visual multi-talker babble noise on comprehension with congruent and incongruent visual information Additionally, executive function was assessed using Elithorn's Mazes, a test suitable for children, to explore its relationship with listening comprehension under varying levels of background noise, voice quality, and visual support. The main findings revealed that low levels of background babble noise interfered with listening comprehension, which could be somewhat mitigated by visual cues. Although a dysphonic voice did not significantly reduce comprehension scores, it was perceived as unpleasant and increased the effort perceived by the children. The study also found that better executive function was associated with better listening comprehension under adverse conditions.

In terms of executive function, studies such as the one of Nirme, Haake, Lyberg Åhlander, Brännström, and Sahlén (2019) suggest that greater executive capabilities are particularly beneficial in noise-free settings for 8–9-years old children during the performance of short passage comprehension but do not necessarily confer an advantage in noisy conditions. This is supported by findings from Brännström et al. (2021) and Visentin, Pellegatti, Garraffa, Di Domenico, and Prodi (2023), showing varying degrees of effort and comprehension success based on children's native language status and executive function like inhibitory control, especially under challenging auditory conditions. In particular, the study of Brännström et al. (2021) involved elementary school children aged 7 to 9 years, both native and non-native speakers, and investigated listening effort and fatigue using pupillometry while children performed a narrative speech–picture verification task under two listening conditions: typical (0 dB SNR) and favorable (+10 dB SNR). The study used a response time limit of 10 s for the narrative speech–picture verification task. If no response was given within the 10-s limit, the trial was considered incorrect. A backward digit span test was used to assess working memory capability. Pupillometry measured changes in pupil size to evaluate listening effort and fatigue, with greater pupil dilation indicating higher effort and reduced baseline pupil size over time indicating increased fatigue. The main findings showed that children, particularly non-native speakers, exhibited greater pupil dilation in the typical listening condition, indicating higher listening effort. Native speakers demonstrated greater pupil dilation during successful trials, whereas non-native speakers showed increased dilation during unsuccessful trials, suggesting an effort ceiling. Baseline pupil size decreased more steeply over trials in the typical condition, potentially indicating increased listening-related fatigue. In terms of executive function, the study found that working memory, did not differ significantly between native and non-native speakers. However, working memory was a crucial factor in listening comprehension, with children who had higher working memory capacity showing better performance overall. The results indicated that children with stronger working memory were better able to cope with challenging listening conditions, although this effect was more pronounced in native speakers compared to non-native speakers.

Another study by Visentin et al. (2023) involved children aged 8–11 years from elementary school classes and examined the impact of a two-talker masker on listening comprehension, effort, and motivation. The methodology included a sentence comprehension task with varying syntactic complexity under two listening conditions (easy: +9 dB SNR, hard: +1 dB SNR), along with assessments of reading comprehension, inhibitory control, and noise sensitivity. The main findings revealed that higher levels of background noise (hard condition) significantly impaired listening comprehension accuracy and increased response times, particularly for children with high inhibitory control. Additionally, self-reported listening effort was higher in noise-sensitive children in the hard listening condition.

In a study on 8–11-years old children performing a speech-picture verification task during two listening conditions: "ideal" (+15 dB SNR) and "typical" (−2 dB SNR), McGarrigle et al. (2017) highlighted that increased effort, measured through pupillometry, did not always correlate with performance differences. Response times were recorded as the duration between the presentation of the visual image and the child's button press response, with a 10-s limit set for each response. The main findings indicated that children exhibited larger task-evoked pupil dilation in the typical listening condition compared to the ideal condition, reflecting increased listening effort. However, no significant differences were found between listening conditions in terms of performance accuracy or response times. These results indicated that children's adaptation to noise can be complex and not directly observable through traditional performance metrics. Brännström et al. (2021; Brännström, Lyberg-Åhlander, & Sahlén, 2022) further explored these dynamics in 7–9-year-old native and non-native speakers and 6–13-year-old children with hearing aids or cochlear implants, respectively. The children completed a picture verification task and a short passage comprehension task, respectively. The results suggested that while native speakers may utilize their listening effort more effectively to boost comprehension, non-native speakers and those with hearing impairments may encounter limits to their listening effort, especially in noisy environments, resulting in poorer comprehension outcomes.

The relationship between children's executive function and listening comprehension and listening effort requires further investigation. Adults with stronger executive function have been shown to be generally better equipped to allocate cognitive resources effectively in speech recognition tasks, allowing them to maintain understanding and recall even under adverse conditions. For example, a study by Zekveld, Rudner, Johnsrude, and Rönnberg (2013) conducted on young adults highlights the significance of working memory, showing that understanding in noisy settings is significantly improved by cues related to speech. This benefit is particularly pronounced in the presence of competing talker noise, illustrating how individuals with robust working memory can use contextual hints more effectively to overcome difficulties resulting from noise and understand speech. Among the executive function tests, Elithorn's Mazes has been shown to predict better performance in listening comprehension tasks, especially in quiet settings. Elithorn's Mazes evaluates children's executive functioning and general cognitive abilities. This test involves tasks that require self-monitoring, strategic planning, and the ability to inhibit impulsive actions. However, its predictive power diminishes in noisy conditions, suggesting that noise imposes an additional cognitive load that can overwhelm children's executive capacities (Nirme et al., 2019). Additionally, Visentin et al. (2023) found that children with better inhibitory control showed longer response times in the hard listening condition, indicating higher effort, suggesting that only children with sufficient cognitive resources experience increased effort during challenging conditions.

Brännström et al. (2022) conducted a study with children aged 6–13 years who are hard of hearing and use cochlear implants (CI) and/or hearing aids (HA). The research examined how voice quality (typical versus dysphonic) and background noise affect perceived listening effort during a passage comprehension task. The test included four listening conditions, combining typical and dysphonic voices with two noise levels (quiet and 10 dB SNR). Additionally, the children completed the Elithorn Mazes test to assess executive function, focusing on organization, planning skills, inhibitory control, and processing. The main findings showed that poor voice quality and background noise significantly increased perceived listening effort. However, there was no significant link between perceived listening effort and executive function, indicating that despite the higher cognitive demands from degraded listening conditions, the executive function measures did not predict the children's ability to handle increased listening effort.

Table 2 provides a comprehensive summary of research on listening effort in school-age children during listening comprehension tasks in noisy environments and when the speech is dysphonic. Collectively, these findings emphasize the need for effective educational strategies that consider environmental noise, voice quality, and individual cognitive differences. Improving classroom acoustics, using visual aids, and supporting the development of executive function are crucial for optimizing children's listening and comprehension skills in noisy settings.

Table 2 Listening effort studies conducted on school-age normal hearing children during the performance of a speech recognition task.

References	Participants	Acoustics	Speaker voice	Listening task	LE measure	Executive function	Results
Prodi et al. (2019)	159 children 11–13 y.o.	Quiet, SNR near 0 dB (classroom and traffic noise)	Typical	5-word sentences	Response time	None	• Classroom noise reduced accuracy and increased response times (RTs). • Developmental effect across age, varying depending on the task and the listening condition. • Generally higher accuracy and faster response times for girls • Significant interaction between the type of noise and age, particularly affecting the response times.
Rudner et al. (2018)	245 children 8 y.o.	Multi-talker babble noise +10 dB SNR	Typical and dysphonic	Clinical evaluation of language fundamentals (CELF 4)-short passages	Self-rated LE	Elithorn's Mazes (EM)	• Even low levels of babble noise significantly disrupted listening comprehension and increase listening effort • A visible talker's face seemed to mitigate the negative effects of background noise on listening comprehension. • Dysphonic voice did not significantly lower comprehension scores but it increased listening effort, and was perceived as unpleasant • Executive function had a positive correlation with comprehension scores in quiet but not in noise

(continued)

Table 2 Listening effort studies conducted on school-age normal hearing children during the performance of a speech recognition task. *(cont'd)*

References	Participants	Acoustics	Speaker voice	Listening task	LE measure	Executive function	Results
McGarrigle et al. (2017)	41 children 8–11 y.o.	Multi-talker babble noise +15 dB SNR; −2 dB SNR	Typical	Speech–picture verification task	Response times pupillometry	None	• Increased pupil dilation (increased effort) with −2 dB SNR • No significant differences in task performance or response time between the two conditions
Nirme et al. (2019)	55 children 8–9 y.o.	Quiet; Multi-talker babble noise +10 dB SNR	Typical + visual speaker	CELF 4 - short passages	Self-rated LE	EM	• Multi-talker babble noise impaired children's performance on listening comprehension content questions. • The presence of noise made children perceive the task as more difficult. • Decreased performance due to noise was mitigated by audio-visual presentation. • Children with high EM scores performed better on content questions, but only in the absence of noise. • High EM-scoring children also performed better on inference questions with audio-only presentation.

Brännström et al. (2021)	63 children native and non-native 7–9 y.o.	Multi-talker child babble noise + 10 dB SNR; 0 dB SNR	Typical	Speech–picture verification task	10 s time limit of response for correct answer Pupillometry	None	• Non-native speakers show greater pupil dilation (higher listening effort) in 0 dB SNR. • Native speakers display greater pupil dilation during successful trials, indicating effective use of listening effort to improve comprehension. • Non-native speakers exhibit the most significant pupil dilation during unsuccessful trials, especially in noisier environments. They might reach an effort limit, leading to poorer comprehension.
Brännström et al. (2022)	24 children with cochlear implant (CI) or hearing aids (HA) 6–13 y.o.	Quiet, 10 dB SNR	Typical and Dysphonic	CELF 4 - short passages	Self-rated LE	EM	• Dysphonia and background noise increased perceived listening effort in children with CI and HA. • No interaction with executive function.

(continued)

Table 2 Listening effort studies conducted on school-age normal hearing children during the performance of a speech recognition task. (*cont'd*)

References	Participants	Acoustics	Speaker voice	Listening task	LE measure	Executive function	Results
Visentin et al. (2023)	104 children 8–12 y.o.	Two-talker masker +9 dB SNR; +1 dB SNR	Typical	Sentence comprehension	Self-rated LE Self-rated motivation Response time	Inhibitory control	• Speech comprehension accuracy significantly improved in easier listening conditions and with simpler syntactic complexity. • Children with lower inhibitory control perceived more effort, particularly in harder listening conditions. • Motivation showed a slight decrease in harder conditions. • No direct effect of noise on self-listening effort but children with higher noise sensitivity perceived more effort • Faster response times in simpler syntactic conditions and easier listening settings. Better inhibitory control correlated with longer response times (more effort) in more challenging conditions.
Schiller et al. (2020)	53 children 5–6 y.o.	Quiet 0 dB SNR; +2 dB SNR	Typical and dysphonic	Elo material - sentence-picture matching	Response time	None	• Equal performance in quiet and noise for the typical voice quality but a decrease in noise for the dysphonic voice quality. • The presence of both noise and dysphonic voice did not affected response time

7. Advancements in physiological measures for assessing listening effort in children: pupillometry and EEG insights

The use of physiological measures to assess listening effort in children is limited but growing in importance. Research on physiological measures of listening effort in children has primarily focused on pupillometry, a method that measures pupil dilation in response to cognitive load (Gómez-Merino, Gheller, Spicciarelli, & Trevisi, 2020; McGarrigle et al., 2017). This method has been used to demonstrate increased listening effort during a listening comprehension task in children in noisy environments (McGarrigle et al., 2017) and to compare listening effort between children who are native and non-native speakers (Brännström et al., 2021). McGarrigle et al. (2017) focused on normal-hearing children aged 8–11 years in classroom-like conditions using a narrative speech–picture verification task and pupillometry to assess the mental effort exerted. They demonstrated that while performance accuracy showed no significant differences, the typical classroom noise (−2 dB SNR) led to significantly increased pupil dilation compared to ideal conditions (+15 dB SNR), indicating greater listening effort. However, no significant differences in task performance accuracy or self-reported fatigue were observed between conditions. Another study on Swedish 7–9 years old school children found similar results. (Brännström et al., 2021). Their study examined the effects of classroom-like SNR on children's listening effort and including both native and non-native speakers of Swedish, using a narrative speech–picture verification task and pupillometry. The children performed tasks under typical (0 dB SNR) and favorable (+10 dB SNR) listening conditions, with results showing greater pupil dilation indicating more listening effort in the typical condition, especially for non-native speakers, and a decrease in baseline pupil size over trials suggesting increased listening-related fatigue in the typical condition. These findings highlight the physiological strain of noisy environments on children, particularly those with non-native language backgrounds, underscoring the importance of managing classroom acoustics to support effective learning and reduce fatigue. Understanding these physiological mechanisms is crucial for developing interventions aimed at mitigating listening difficulties and enhancing the academic performance and well-being of school-aged children (Bess & Hornsby, 2014).

EEG has also become a pivotal tool in understanding the cognitive processes underlying listening effort, particularly in challenging auditory environments. The measurement of EEG power, specifically in the alpha

(8–12 Hz) and theta (4–8 Hz) frequency bands, has provided significant insights into how the brain manages listening effort under varying noise conditions. Alpha power is closely linked to attentional processes and cognitive control. Several studies have demonstrated that alpha power decreases as the listening task becomes more demanding, reflecting increased cognitive effort. For instance, Ala et al. (2022) investigated listening effort measured through EEG alpha oscillations and pupil dilation in hearing-aid users while listening to continuous speech. Eight adults were exposed to continuous speech streams with varying SNRs of 0 dB and −5 dB. The study found that during more effortful listening conditions (i.e., −5 dB SNR), there was a significant decrease in alpha power in the parietal lobe. This reduction in alpha power suggests that the brain is allocating more cognitive resources to process the auditory information, thereby indicating higher listening effort. Similarly, Wisniewski et al. (2017) explored the dynamics of alpha power in different listening conditions. The study utilized a standard auditory-oddball paradigm where young adults had to detect deviant tones amid standard ones. The results indicated that alpha power decreased significantly in more challenging listening conditions, such as those with lower SNRs. This finding aligns with the notion that alpha oscillations play a crucial role in sensory inhibition, helping to focus attention on relevant auditory signals while suppressing irrelevant noise.

Theta power, on the other hand, is associated with working memory and cognitive load. Enhanced theta power is often observed in tasks that require significant cognitive effort with the involvement of working memory. In Wisniewski et al. (2017), a study was conducted on young adults to examine theta power during a delayed pitch discrimination task. Participants were required to remember and compare pitch intervals under two conditions: a 'Fixed' condition, where the lower pitch was constant, and a 'Roving' condition, where the lower pitch varied randomly. The results showed that theta power increased significantly during the 'Roving' condition, which demanded higher working memory due to the need to retain the first tone for comparison with the second. This increase in theta power during the inter-stimulus interval (ISI) underscores the role of theta oscillations in supporting working memory and indicates elevated listening effort in more complex auditory tasks. Further supporting this, Wisniewski et al. (2018) noted that frontal midline theta power increased as SNR decreased in a sentence-recognition task, paralleling self-reports of increased effort. This suggests that theta power enhancements are closely linked to the cognitive control processes required to manage challenging listening conditions.

The combined analysis of alpha and theta power provides a comprehensive view of the neural mechanisms involved in listening effort. While alpha power reductions indicate increased attentional engagement and sensory inhibition, theta power enhancements reflect the cognitive load and memory demands of the task. For instance, in tasks where participants had to identify words in noise, theta power increased with the difficulty of the task, indicating higher cognitive load, whereas alpha power decreased, highlighting the need for greater attentional control (Wisniewski et al., 2017). The relationship between alpha and theta power can vary depending on the specific cognitive demands of the task. For example, in tasks that require significant working memory, theta power enhancements are more pronounced, whereas tasks that demand attentional focus and sensory inhibition may show greater reductions in alpha power. This complementary relationship helps to capture the full spectrum of cognitive processes involved in managing listening effort under different auditory conditions.

The relationship between listening effort and EEG activity has been minimally investigated in children. Marsella et al. (2017) conducted a study on hard-of-hearing pediatric individuals, identifying increased cognitive load through EEG alpha power levels. This study involved seven hard-of-hearing 8–16-years-old children performing a forced-choice word identification task. Throughout the experiment, the sound level was maintained at 65 dB HL, while the SNR adjusted based on whether the word was identified correctly (decreasing SNR by 2 dB HL) or incorrectly (increasing SNR by 2 dB HL). The study aimed to determine which EEG frequency band, theta or alpha, better reflected changes in listening effort. The findings indicated that theta power oscillations remained stable regardless of the listening challenge, whereas alpha power activity increased in some difficult listening situations, although it showed no variation in the most challenging condition.

Finally, the relationship between pupillometry and EEG in assessing listening effort is complex, with some studies suggesting that they may reflect different cognitive processes (Miles et al., 2017). Pupil dilation could be related to true performance levels and task accuracy, while alpha power change is not significantly associated with these factors. These findings underscore the importance of using multiple physiological measures to capture the complexity of listening effort, particularly in children. By integrating pupillometry and EEG, researchers can develop a more comprehensive understanding of the cognitive processes underlying listening effort and develop interventions to support children with listening difficulties, ultimately improving their academic performance and overall well-being.

8. The interaction of working memory, selective attention, and listening comprehension

In examining the complex connection between working memory, attention and listening, it becomes evident that these cognitive processes interact in complex ways, particularly in challenging acoustic environments. Pichora-Fuller et al. (2016) shed light on the crucial role of working memory and selective attention in modulating listening effort. Their research suggests that individuals with better working memory skills can have the ability to effectively retain and process speech temporarily, which aids speech understanding in adverse acoustic conditions. This implies that the capacity to hold onto and manipulate speech information in the mind, even momentarily, can significantly alleviate the cognitive load associated with understanding speech in noisy or challenging auditory settings. Moreover, Brännström, Karlsson, Waechter, and Kastberg (2018) emphasize the importance of selective attention in enhancing listening comprehension and influencing listening effort. Their findings suggest that selective attention enables individuals to focus on relevant auditory stimuli while simultaneously filtering out distractions. By directing cognitive resources towards target speech signals and suppressing irrelevant background noise, selective attention plays a crucial role in optimizing speech perception, thereby reducing the perceived effort required for listening.

The interaction between working memory and selective attention also plays a crucial role in the auditory experience, especially in environments where competing sounds and distractions are prevalent. Individuals with strong working memory capabilities may exhibit greater ability in utilizing selective attention to concentrate on relevant speech cues while disregarding competing auditory inputs (Dalton, Santangelo, & Spence, 2009). This skill to prioritize essential auditory information and exclude extraneous noise underscores the vital connection between working memory and attentional processes. Not only does this connection enhance listening comprehension, but it also conserves cognitive resources, thereby reducing the effort required to listen and understand in noisy settings. Moreover, the efficient coordination of working memory and selective attention facilitates adaptation to variable acoustic environments, ensuring that communication remains effective even amid auditory challenges. It enables a more targeted and efficient use of mental energy, crucial during prolonged periods of listening or when needing to swiftly shift focus among different sound sources. Better understanding this interaction could lead to more effective strategies for training cognitive skills, ultimately improving auditory processing and reducing the cognitive demands of listening in everyday life—particularly beneficial for children who are still developing these capabilities.

This concept is further exemplified in research by Visentin et al. (2023), which highlights how attention influences children's responses to changes in listening conditions. Their study suggests that children with better inhibitory control exert more effort when transitioning from easier to more challenging listening conditions, indicating a dynamic interplay between attentional processes and listening effort. However, no differences were found among children with low inhibitory control which might suggest that they reach the available resources to perform the task. Additionally, Dhamani, Leung, Carlile, and Sharma (2013) point out the difficulties children face in managing recurring listening challenges, particularly in terms of attention switching. Their findings reveal that struggles with processing both expected and unexpected auditory information can impede children's ability to effectively listen in noisy environments. This underscores the importance of understanding the developmental trajectory of attentional processes in children and its implications for their auditory capabilities, enhancing our approach to fostering these critical skills in younger populations.

When examining the correlation between cognitive abilities, comprehension, and listening effort, it becomes increasingly apparent that age plays a crucial role in shaping these dynamics. Children's working memory and attentional capacities are still maturing, creating additional challenges compared to adults and older peers who have better-developed cognitive abilities. Osman and Sullivan (2014) demonstrate how background noise significantly impacts children's auditory working memory, suggesting that noise produces greater cognitive demands beyond task complexity. This could be attributed to children's limited experience in handling contextual cues in noisy settings compared to adults, emphasizing the need for tailored interventions to support children's speech perception in adverse listening conditions. Moreover, Carlie et al. (2024) highlight the importance of development across 7- to 9-year-old children's cognitive abilities. Their research suggests that older children demonstrate better-coping strategies and utilize memory more effectively compared to their younger counterparts. This developmental progression highlights the interplay between cognitive maturation and comprehension abilities in children. Understanding these developmental contrasts is crucial for implementing effective interventions and support strategies to optimize comprehension and minimize listening effort in children, particularly in educational settings.

9. Conclusion

This chapter underscores a significant gap between the theoretical understanding of children's listening effort in challenging acoustic environments and the practical implications for classroom settings. This disparity often stems from underestimating the impact of poor classroom acoustics and dysphonic voices on children's cognitive load and listening effort. The implications of this literature review on the effects of noise and dysphonia on listening comprehension are profound. In fact, it must be noted that the considered studies often reflect actual classroom acoustic conditions (McGarrigle et al., 2017; Prodi et al., 2019; Schiller et al., 2020; Visentin et al., 2023), where SNR range between +6 and −7 dB (Arnold & Canning, 1999; Crandell & Smaldino, 2000). Additionally, dysphonia is a common disorder among teachers, with a lifetime prevalence ranging from 51% to 69% (Cutiva et al., 2013). Consequently, children often have to learn in environments where they are exposed to impaired voices and significant background noise. Moreover, even studies presenting ideal conditions (Brännström et al., 2021, 2022; Nirme et al., 2019; Rudner et al., 2018) have shown that even low levels of noise can detrimentally affect children's ability to effectively comprehend spoken words and increase the effort required for listening. These conditions can severely limit children's access to speech, deeply affecting their comprehension and potentially causing delays in learning. This highlights the urgent need to develop standards and interventions to protect and enhance the learning experiences of children.

Exploring the effects of degraded acoustic environments through the lens of cognitive load management can help identify specific conditions and tasks that most impact children's listening effort and comprehension. This knowledge can inform the creation of more effective educational strategies and interventions to support children's cognitive and academic development. However, the lack of standardized measures that directly link classroom acoustics to long-term academic outcomes indicates the need for more sensitive and comprehensive assessment techniques. Physiological measures can provide more information on the neural mechanisms underlying listening effort and how this relates to language development and cognitive function. However, there is a notable gap in the literature applying these measurements with children. Studies have predominantly used pupillometry (Brännström et al., 2021; Gómez-Merino et al., 2020; McGarrigle et al., 2017), with only one study using EEG (Marsella et al., 2017). EEG, particularly alpha and theta band activities, has shown relevance to speech processing, particularly in relation to attentional and memory processing, respectively (Dimitrijevic et al., 2017; Obleser et al., 2012; Wisniewski et al., 2017, 2018). Applying this technique in children would provide better insight into the role of executive function and language development in supporting listening comprehension and managing listening effort.

The literature suggests that children's developing executive function, such as working memory and selective attention, are crucial in managing the increased cognitive load caused by challenging acoustic conditions. Children may compensate for auditory challenges by reallocating cognitive resources, similar to how adults handle complex tasks, though they do not yet have full control over these functions (Diamond, 2013). This compensation often results in greater cognitive strain, especially in demanding environments like noisy classrooms or when processing dysphonic speech. This "cognitive load management" hypothesis provides insight into why younger children and those with weaker executive function are more affected by long-term listening comprehension issues, which can lead to poorer academic performance. The varied inclusion of noise types and voice qualities in studies can obscure the nuanced impacts on listening effort, given children's different developmental stages and cognitive capacities. This also explains why interventions aimed at enhancing executive function and improving classroom acoustics are crucial for reducing listening effort and improving comprehension outcomes. Furthermore, considering children with auditory impairments or communication disorders is especially crucial, as these groups may exhibit unique responses to auditory challenges not fully captured in smaller or less varied study cohorts. Expanding the scope of research in this way will help develop more effective interventions and support mechanisms tailored to the needs of all children, regardless of their auditory and language capabilities. Additionally, it is essential to consider these results in the context of children's developmental stages. Understanding how children of different ages respond to auditory challenges could provide critical insights into developmental trajectories and the maturation of auditory processing capabilities.

Although this chapter does not cover all aspects of the extensive literature on acoustic challenges in educational settings, given the substantial impact of poor acoustics and dysphonic voices on children's learning, there is a strong argument for incorporating more sensitive measures into classroom assessments and teacher training programs. This approach would provide a more detailed understanding of the chronic effects of acoustic challenges, prompting a shift from general classroom improvements to targeted interventions addressing specific cognitive and auditory processing needs. The evidence pointing to the significant impact of degraded acoustic environments on children's listening comprehension and cognitive effort is compelling. Moving forward, it is vital to recognize the limitations of current assessment methods, potential biases in study designs, and the challenge of isolating the effects of poor acoustics from other classroom variables. Further research into the impacts of acoustic environments on children's cognitive and academic outcomes is encouraged, aiming to shed light on this critical topic through rigorous investigation and innovative and standardized solutions. Additionally, the study underscores the importance of vocal health among teachers. By improving teacher vocal health through training and preventive strategies, the prevalence of dysphonic voices in classrooms can be reduced. This improvement not only benefits the teachers but also enhances the auditory environment for the students, facilitating better comprehension and reducing the cognitive load required to understand dysphonic speech.

In conclusion, this chapter emphasizes the need for optimal acoustic management in educational settings. It advocates for classroom designs that enhance acoustic conditions, facilitating more effective learning. The literature review highlights the impacts of dysphonia and background noise on children's educational experiences, promoting policies that improve classroom acoustics and encourage vocal health training for teachers. The findings also point to the extra cognitive effort required by children to process speech under these conditions, emphasizing the necessity of supportive learning environments, especially for children with pre-existing auditory or cognitive challenges. Addressing both environmental and individual cognitive factors is crucial for creating effective learning environments that support all students, particularly those more vulnerable to the adverse effects of noise and dysphonia.

References

Adams, A. M., Bourke, L., & Willis, C. (1999). Working memory and spoken language comprehension in young children. *International Journal of Psychology, 34*(5-6), 364–373. https://doi.org/10.1080/002075999399701.

Ahmadi, S. M. (2016). The importance of listening comprehension in language learning. *International Journal of Research in English Education, 1*(1), 7–10.

Ala, T. S., Alickovic, E., Cabrera, A. F., Whitmer, W. M., Hadley, L. V., Rank, M. L., ... Graversen, C. (2022). Alpha oscillations during effortful continuous speech: From scalp EEG to ear-EEG. *IEEE Transactions on Biomedical Engineering, 70*(4), 1264–1273. https://doi.org/10.1109/TBME.2022.3214428.

Alhanbali, S., Dawes, P., Millman, R. E., & Munro, K. J. (2019). Measures of listening effort are multidimensional. *Ear and Hearing, 40*(5), 1084–1097. https://doi.org/10.1097/AUD.0000000000000697.

Ameen, B., & Saeed, S. A. (2022). The effects of the physical setting on students' listening comprehension. *International Journal of Language and Literary Studies, 4*(4), 39–51. https://doi.org/10.36892/ijlls.v4i4.1080.

American National Standards Institute. (2010). ANSI S12.60: American national standard acoustical performance criteria, design requirements, and guidelines for schools (American National Standards Institute, New York).

ASHA. (2009). Voice disorders: Overview. Asha.org. https://www.asha.org/PRPSpecificTopic.aspx?folderid=8589942600 (Last viewed May, 2024).

Arlinger, S., Lunner, T., Lyxell, B., & Pichora-Fuller, M. K. (2009). The emergence of cognitive hearing science. *Scandinavian Journal of Psychology, 50*(5), 371–384. https://doi.org/10.1111/j.1467-9450.2009.00753.x.

Arnold, P., & Canning, D. (1999). Does classroom amplification aid comprehension? *British Journal of Audiology, 33*(3), 171–178. https://doi.org/10.3109/03005369909090096.

Backlund, P. (1985). Essential speaking and listening skills for elementary school students. *Communication Education, 34*(3), 185–195. https://doi.org/10.1080/03634528509378606.

Baddeley, A. (2010). Working memory. *Current Biology, 20*(4), R136–R140. https://doi.org/10.1016/j.cub.2009.12.014.

Beer, J., Kronenberger, W. G., & Pisoni, D. B. (2011). Executive function in everyday life: Implications for young cochlear implant users. *Cochlear Implants International, 12*(sup1), S89–S91. https://doi.org/10.1179/146701011X13001035752570.

Bess, F. H., & Hornsby, B. W. (2014). Commentary: Listening can be exhausting—Fatigue in children and adults with hearing loss. *Ear and Hearing, 35*(6), 592–599. https://doi.org/10.1097/AUD.0000000000000099.

Bodie, G. D., & Wolvin, A. D. (2020). The psychobiology of listening: Why listening is more than meets the ear. In L. S. Aloia, A. Denes, & J. P. Crowley. (Eds.). *The Oxford handbook of the physiology of interpersonal communication* (pp. 288–307). Oxford University Press. https://doi.org/10.1093/oxfordhb/9780190679446.013.16.

Bottalico, P., Murgia, S., Mekus, T., & Flaherty, M. (2023). Classroom acoustics for enhancing students' understanding when a teacher suffers from a dysphonic voice. *Language, Speech, and Hearing Services in Schools, 54*(4), 1195–1207. https://doi.org/10.1044/2023_LSHSS-22-00158.

Bradley, J. S., Reich, R. D., & Norcross, S. G. (1999). On the combined effects of signal-to-noise ratio and room acoustics on speech intelligibility. *The Journal of the Acoustical Society of America, 106*(4), 1820–1828. https://doi.org/10.1121/1.427932.

Brännström, J., Rudner, M., Carlie, J., Sahlén, B., Gulz, A., Andersson, K., & Johansson, R. (2021). Listening effort and fatigue in native and non-native primary school children. *Journal of Experimental Child Psychology, 210*, 105203. https://doi.org/10.1016/j.jecp.2021.105203.

Brännström, K. J., Karlsson, E., Waechter, S., & Kastberg, T. (2018). Listening effort: Order effects and core executive functions. *Journal of the American Academy of Audiology, 29*(08), 734–747. https://doi.org/10.3766/jaaa.17024.

Brännström, K. J., Lyberg-Åhlander, V., & Sahlén, B. (2022). Perceived listening effort in children with hearing loss: Listening to a dysphonic voice in quiet and in noise. *Logopedics, Phoniatrics, Vocology, 47*(1), 1–9. https://doi.org/10.1080/14015439.2020.1794030.

Byars, A. W., Holland, S. K., Strawsburg, R. H., Bommer, W., Dunn, R. S., Schmithorst, V. J., & Plante, E. (2002). Practical aspects of conducting large-scale functional magnetic resonance imaging studies in children. *Journal of Child Neurology, 17*(12), 885–889. https://doi.org/10.1177/08830738020170122201.

Carlie, J., Sahlén, B., Johansson, R., Andersson, K., Whitling, S., & Brännström, K. J. (2024). The effect of background noise, bilingualism, socioeconomic status, and cognitive functioning on primary school children's narrative listening comprehension. *Journal of Speech, Language, and Hearing Research, 67*(3), 960–973. https://doi.org/10.1044/2023_JSLHR-22-00637.

Chiew, K. S., & Braver, T. S. (2013). Temporal dynamics of motivation-cognitive control interactions revealed by high-resolution pupillometry. *Frontiers in Psychology, 4.* https://doi.org/10.3389/fpsyg.2013.00015.

Choi, S., Lotto, A., Lewis, D., Hoover, B., & Stelmachowicz, P. (2008). Attentional modulation of word recognition by children in a dual-task paradigm. *Journal of Speech, Language, and Hearing Research, 51*(4), 1042–1054. https://doi.org/10.1044/1092-4388(2008/076).

Chui, J. C. H., & Ma, E. P. M. (2019). The impact of dysphonic voices on children's comprehension of spoken language. *Journal of Voice, 33*(5), 801–e7. https://doi.org/10.1016/j.jvoice.2018.03.004.

Clark, C., & Sörqvist, P. (2012). A 3 year update on the influence of noise on performance and behavior. *Noise and Health, 14*(61), 292–296. https://doi.org/10.4103/1463-1741.104896.

Clarke, A. R., Barry, R. J., McCarthy, R., & Selikowitz, M. (2001). Age and sex effects in the EEG: Development of the normal child. *Clinical Neurophysiology, 112*(5), 806–814. https://doi.org/10.1016/S1388-2457(01)00488-6.

Connolly, D., Dockrell, J., Shield, B., Conetta, R., Mydlarz, C., & Cox, T. (2019). The effects of classroom noise on the reading comprehension of adolescents. *The Journal of the Acoustical Society of America, 145*(1), 372–381. https://doi.org/10.1121/1.5087126.

Cooke, M., Garcia Lecumberri, M. L., & Barker, J. (2008). The foreign language cocktail party problem: Energetic and informational masking effects in non-native speech perception. *The Journal of the Acoustical Society of America, 123*(1), 414–427. https://doi.org/10.1121/1.2804952.

Crandell, C. C., & Smaldino, J. J. (2000). Classroom acoustics for children with normal hearing and with hearing impairment. *Language, Speech, and Hearing Services in Schools, 31*(4), 362–370. https://doi.org/10.1044/0161-1461.3104.362.

Cutiva, L. C. C., & Burdorf, A. (2015). Effects of noise and acoustics in schools on vocal health in teachers. *Noise & Health, 17*(74), 17–22. https://doi.org/10.4103/1463-1741.149569.

Cutiva, L. C. C., Vogel, I., & Burdorf, A. (2013). Voice disorders in teachers and their associations with work-related factors: A systematic review. *Journal of Communication Disorders, 46*(2), 143–155. https://doi.org/10.1016/j.jcomdis.2013.01.001.

Dalton, P., Santangelo, V., & Spence, C. (2009). The role of working memory in auditory selective attention. *Quarterly Journal of Experimental Psychology, 62*(11), 2126–2132. https://doi.org/10.1080/17470210903023646.

Danneels, M., Degeest, S., Dhooge, I., & Keppler, H. (2021). Central auditory processing and listening effort in normal-hearing children: A pilot study. *International Journal of Audiology, 60*(10), 739–746. https://doi.org/10.1080/14992027.2021.1877365.

Daneman, M., & Hannon, B. (2007). What do working memory span tasks like reading span really measure. In N. Osaka, R. H. Logie, & M. D'Esposito (Eds.). *The cognitive neuroscience of working memory* (pp. 21–42). Oxford university press.

de Bree, E., & Zee, M. (2021). The unique role of verbal memory, vocabulary, concentration and self-efficacy in children's listening comprehension in upper elementary grades. *First Language, 41*(2), 129–153. https://doi.org/10.1177/0142723720941680.

Dhamani, I., Leung, J., Carlile, S., & Sharma, M. (2013). Switch attention to listen. *Scientific reports, 3*(1), 1297. https://doi.org/10.1038/srep01297.

Diamond, A. (2013). Executive functions. *Annual Review of Psychology, 64*, 135–168. https://doi.org/10.1146/annurev-psych-113011-143750.

Díaz-Galaz, S. (2020). Listening and comprehension in interpreting: Questions that remain open. *Translation and Interpreting Studies, 15*(2), 304–323. https://doi.org/10.1075/tis.20074.dia.

Dimitrijevic, A., Smith, M. L., Kadis, D. S., & Moore, D. R. (2017). Cortical alpha oscillations predict speech intelligibility. *Frontiers in Human Neuroscience, 11*, 88. https://doi.org/10.3389/fnhum.2017.00088.

Ericsson, K. A., & Kintsch, W. (1995). Long-term working memory. *Psychological Review, 102*(2), 211. https://doi.org/10.1037/0033-295x.102.2.211.

Figueras, B., Edwards, L., & Langdon, D. (2008). Executive function and language in deaf children. *Journal of Deaf Studies and Deaf Education, 13*(3), 362–377. https://doi.org/10.1093/deafed/enm067.

Finney, M. C., Montgomery, J. W., Gillam, R. B., & Evans, J. L. (2014). Role of working memory storage and attention focus switching in children's comprehension of spoken object relative sentences. *Child Development Research, 2014*(1), 450734. https://doi.org/10.1155/2014/450734.

Florit, E., Roch, M., Altoè, G., & Levorato, M. C. (2009). Listening comprehension in preschoolers: The role of memory. *British Journal of Developmental Psychology, 27*(4), 935–951. https://doi.org/10.1348/026151008X397189.

Francis, A. L., & Love, J. (2020). Listening effort: Are we measuring cognition or affect, or both? *Wiley Interdisciplinary Reviews: Cognitive Science, 11*(1), e1514. https://doi.org/10.1002/wcs.1514.

Gatehouse, S., & Gordon, J. (1990). Response times to speech stimuli as measures of benefit from amplification. *British Journal of Audiology, 24*(1), 63–68. https://doi.org/10.3109/03005369009077843.

Gatehouse, S., & Noble, W. (2004). The speech, spatial and qualities of hearing scale (SSQ). *International Journal of Audiology, 43*(2), 85–99. https://doi.org/10.1080/14992020400050014.

Gheller, F., Lovo, E., Arsie, A., & Bovo, R. (2020). Classroom acoustics: Listening problems in children. *Building Acoustics, 27*(1), 47–59. https://doi.org/10.1177/1351010X19886035.

Gheller, F., Spicciarelli, G., Scimemi, P., & Arfé, B. (2024). The effects of noise on children's cognitive performance: A systematic review. *Environment and Behavior*, 00139165241245823. https://doi.org/10.1177/00139165241245823.

Giuliani, N. P., Brown, C. J., & Wu, Y. H. (2021). Comparisons of the sensitivity and reliability of multiple measures of listening effort. *Ear and Hearing, 42*(2), 465–474. https://doi.org/10.1097/AUD.0000000000000950.

Gómez-Merino, N., Gheller, F., Spicciarelli, G., & Trevisi, P. (2020). Pupillometry as a measure for listening effort in children: A review. *Hearing, Balance and Communication, 18*(3), 152–158. https://doi.org/10.1080/21695717.2020.1807256.

Grosjean, F., & Byers-Heinlein, K. (2018). *The listening bilingual: Speech perception, comprehension, and bilingualism*. Wiley-Blackwell.

Gumenyuk, V., Korzyukov, O., Alho, K., Escera, C., & Näätänen, R. (2004). Effects of auditory distraction on electrophysiological brain activity and performance in children aged 8–13 years. *Psychophysiology, 41*(1), 30–36. https://doi.org/10.1111/1469-8986.00123.

Gustafson, S., McCreery, R., Hoover, B., Kopun, J. G., & Stelmachowicz, P. (2014). Listening effort and perceived clarity for normal-hearing children with the use of digital noise reduction. *Ear and Hearing, 35*(2), 183–194. https://doi.org/10.1097/01.aud.0000440715.85844.b8.

Haines, M. M., Brentnall, S. L., Stansfeld, S. A., & Klineberg, E. (2003). Qualitative responses of children to environmental noise. *Noise and Health, 5*(19), 19–30.

Hick, C. B., & Tharpe, A. M. (2002). Listening effort and fatigue in school-age children with and without hearing loss. *Journal of Speech, Language, and Hearing Research, 45*(3), 573–584. https://doi.org/10.1044/1092-4388(2002/046).

Hogan, T., Bridges, M. S., Justice, L. M., & Cain, K. (2011). Increasing higher level language skills to improve reading comprehension. *Focus on Exceptional Children, 44*(3), 1–20. https://doi.org/10.17161/foec.v44i3.6688.

Hogan, T. P., Adlof, S. M., & Alonzo, C. N. (2014). On the importance of listening comprehension. *International Journal of Speech-Language Pathology, 16*(3), 199–207. https://doi.org/10.3109/17549507.2014.904441.

Houben, R., van Doorn-Bierman, M., & Dreschler, W. A. (2013). Using response time to speech as a measure for listening effort. *International Journal of Audiology, 52*(11), 753–761. https://doi.org/10.3109/14992027.2013.832415.

Houtgast, T. (1981). The effect of ambient noise on speech intelligibility in classrooms. *Applied Acoustics, 14*(1), 15–25. https://doi.org/10.1016/0003-682X(81)90040-2.

Howard, C. S., Munro, K. J., & Plack, C. J. (2010). Listening effort at signal-to-noise ratios that are typical of the school classroom. *International Journal of Audiology, 49*(12), 928–932. https://doi.org/10.3109/14992027.2010.520036.

Hsu, B. C.-L., Vanpoucke, F., & van Wieringen, A. (2017). Listening effort through depth of processing in school-age children. *Ear and Hearing, 38*(5), 568–576. https://doi.org/10.1097/AUD.0000000000000436.

Hsu, B. C.-L., Vanpoucke, F., Langereis, M., Dierckx, A., & van Wieringen, A. (2020). Age-related changes in listening effort for children and teenagers with normal hearing and cochlear implants. *Ear and Hearing, 42*(3), 506–519. https://doi.org/10.1097/AUD.0000000000000953.

Huizinga, M., Baeyens, D., & Burack, J. A. (2018). Executive function and education. *Frontiers in Psychology, 9*, 388544. https://doi.org/10.3389/fpsyg.2018.01357.

Hygge, S., Evans, G. W., & Bullinger, M. (2002). A prospective study of some effects of aircraft noise on cognitive performance in schoolchildren. *Psychological Science, 13*(5), 469–474. https://doi.org/10.1111/1467-9280.00483.

Ishikawa, K., Nudelman, C., Park, S., & Ketring, C. (2021). Perception and acoustic studies of vowel intelligibility in dysphonic speech. *Journal of Voice, 35*(4), 659–e11. https://doi.org/10.1016/j.jvoice.2019.12.022.

Isshiki, N., Yanagihara, N., & Morimoto, M. (1966). Approach to the objective diagnosis of hoarseness. *Folia Phoniatrica et Logopaedica, 18*(6), 393–400. https://doi.org/10.1159/000263069.

Kahneman, D. (1973). *Attention and effort.* Englewood Cliffs, NJ: Prentice-Hall.

Kamrath, M., & Vigeant, M. C. (2014). Gaps in the literature on the effects of aircraft noise on children's cognitive performance. -2304 *The Journal of the Acoustical Society of America, 136*(4_Supplement), 2304. https://doi.org/10.1121/1.4900337.

Kerlin, J. R., Shahin, A. J., & Miller, L. M. (2010). Attentional gain control of ongoing cortical speech representations in a "cocktail party". *The Journal of Neuroscience, 30*(2), 620–628. https://doi.org/10.1523/JNEUROSCI.3631-09.2010.

Kim, Y. S. (2015). Language and cognitive predictors of text comprehension: Evidence from multivariate analysis. *Child Development, 86*(1), 128–144. https://doi.org/10.1111/cdev.12293.

Kim, Y. S. G. (2016). Direct and mediated effects of language and cognitive skills on comprehension of oral narrative texts (listening comprehension) for children. *Journal of Experimental Child Psychology, 141*, 101–120. https://doi.org/10.1016/j.jecp.2015.08.003.

Kim, Y. S. G., & Pilcher, H. (2016). What is listening comprehension and what does it take to improve listening comprehension? In R. Schiff, & R. M. Joshi (Vol. Eds.), *Interventions in learning disabilities: A handbook on systematic training programs for individuals with learning disabilities: 13*, (pp. 159–173). Cham: Springer. https://doi.org/10.1007/978-3-319-31235-4_10.

Kim, Y. S., & Phillips, B. (2014). Cognitive correlates of listening comprehension. *Reading Research Quarterly, 49*(3), 269–281. https://doi.org/10.1002/rrq.74.

King, M. F., & Bruner, G. C. (2000). Social desirability bias: A neglected aspect of validity testing. *Psychology & Marketing, 17*(2), 79–103. https://doi.org/10.1002/(SICI)1520-6793(200002)17:2<79::AID-MAR2>3.0.CO;2-0.

Klatte, M., Bergström, K., & Lachmann, T. (2013). Does noise affect learning? A short review on noise effects on cognitive performance in children. *Frontiers in Psychology, 4*, 55965. https://doi.org/10.3389/fpsyg.2013.00578.

Klatte, M., Lachmann, T., & Meis, M. (2010). Effects of noise and reverberation on speech perception and listening comprehension of children and adults in a classroom-like setting. *Noise & Health, 12*(49), 270–282. https://doi.org/10.4103/1463-1741.70506.

Kline, J. A. (1996). *Listening effectively*. Air University Press.

Koelewijn, T., Zekveld, A. A., Festen, J. M., & Kramer, S. E. (2012). Pupil dilation uncovers extra listening effort in the presence of a single-talker masker. *Ear and Hearing, 33*(2), 291–300. https://doi.org/10.1097/AUD.0b013e3182310019.

Koeritzer, M. A., Rogers, C. S., Van Engen, K. J., & Peelle, J. E. (2018). The impact of age, background noise, semantic ambiguity, and hearing loss on recognition memory for spoken sentences. *Journal of Speech, Language, and Hearing Research, 61*(3), 740–751. https://doi.org/10.1044/2017_JSLHR-H-17-0077.

Krueger, M., Schulte, M., Zokoll, M. A., Wagener, K. C., Meis, M., Brand, T., & Holube, I. (2017). Relation between listening effort and speech intelligibility in noise. *American Journal of Audiology, 26*(3S), 378–392. https://doi.org/10.1044/2017_AJA-16-0136.

Kumar, F. N., & Shankar, L. R. (2021). The importance of listening skill in language acquisition-the problems experienced & strategies adopted in teaching listening skill. *International Journal of Innovative Research,* 7(12), 309–314.

Laeng, B., Sirois, S., & Gredebäck, G. (2012). Pupillometry: A window to the preconscious? *Perspectives on Psychological Science: A Journal of the Association for Psychological Science,* 7(1), 18–27. https://doi.org/10.1177/1745691611427305.

Lamotte, A. S., Essadek, A., Shadili, G., Perez, J. M., & Raft, J. (2021). The impact of classroom chatter noise on comprehension: A systematic review. *Perceptual and Motor Skills, 128*(3), 1275–1291. https://doi.org/10.1177/00315125211005935.

Lemke, U., & Besser, J. (2016). Cognitive load and listening effort: Concepts and age-related considerations. *Ear and Hearing, 37*(Suppl 1), 77S–84S. https://doi.org/10.1097/AUD.0000000000000304.

Lemke, U., & Scherpiet, S. (2015). Oral communication in individuals with hearing impairment—Considerations regarding attentional, cognitive and social resources. *Frontiers in Psychology, 6*, 998. https://doi.org/10.3389/fpsyg.2015.00998.

Leon-Carrion, J. O. S. E., García-Orza, J., & Pérez-Santamaría, F. J. (2004). Development of the inhibitory component of the executive functions in children and adolescents. *International Journal of Neuroscience, 114*(10), 1291–1311. https://doi.org/10.1080/00207450490476066.

Lewis, D., Schmid, K., O'Leary, S., Spalding, J., Heinrichs, Graham, E., & High, R. (2016). Effects of noise on speech recognition and listening effort in children with normal hearing and children with mild bilateral or unilateral hearing loss. *Journal of Speech, Language, and Hearing Research, 59*(5), 1218–1232. https://doi.org/10.1044/2016_JSLHR-H-15-0207.

Lewis, R. L., Vasishth, S., & Van Dyke, J. A. (2006). Computational principles of working memory in sentence comprehension. *Trends in Cognitive Sciences, 10*(10), 447–454. https://doi.org/10.1016/j.tics.2006.08.007.

Ljung, R., Sörqvist, P., & Hygge, S. (2009). Effects of road traffic noise and irrelevant speech on children' s reading and mathematical performance. *Noise and Health, 11*(45), 194–198. https://doi.org/10.4103/1463-1741.56212.

Lloyd-Fox, S., Blasi, A., & Elwell, C. E. (2010). Illuminating the developing brain: The past, present and future of functional near infrared spectroscopy. *Neuroscience and Biobehavioral Reviews, 34*(3), 269–284. https://doi.org/10.1016/j.neubiorev.2009.07.008.

Lyberg-Åhlander, V., & Brännström, K. J. (2015). On the interaction of speakers' voice quality, ambient noise and task complexity with children's listening comprehension and cognition. *Frontiers in Psychology, 6*, 139560. https://doi.org/10.3389/fpsyg.2015.00871.

Lyberg-Åhlander, V., Haake, M., Brännström, J., Schötz, S., & Sahlén, B. (2015). Does the speaker's voice quality influence children's performance on a language comprehension test? *International Journal of Speech-language Pathology, 17*(1), 63–73. https://doi.org/10.3109/17549507.2014.898098.

Ma, E. P. M., & Yiu, E. M. L. (2006). Multiparametric evaluation of dysphonic severity. *Journal of Voice, 20*(3), 380–390. https://doi.org/10.1016/j.jvoice.2005.04.007.

Magimairaj, B. M., & Montgomery, J. W. (2012). Children's verbal working memory: Role of processing complexity in predicting spoken sentence comprehension. *Journal of Speech, Language, and Hearing Research, 55*(3), 669–682. https://doi.org/10.1044/1092-4388(2011/11-0111).

Marsella, P., Scorpecci, A., Cartocci, G., Giannantonio, S., Maglione, A. G., Venuti, I., ... Babiloni, F. (2017). EEG activity as an objective measure of cognitive load during effortful listening: A study on pediatric subjects with bilateral, asymmetric sensorineural hearing loss. *International Journal of Pediatric Otorhinolaryngology, 99*, 1–7. https://doi.org/10.1016/j.ijporl.2017.05.006.

Mattys, S. L., Brooks, J., & Cooke, M. (2009). Recognizing speech under a processing load: Dissociating energetic from informational factors. *Cognitive Psychology, 59*(3), 203–243. https://doi.org/10.1016/j.cogpsych.2009.04.001.

Mattys, S. L., Davis, M. H., Bradlow, A. R., & Scott, S. K. (2012). Speech recognition in adverse conditions: A review. *Language and Cognitive Processes, 27*(7–8), 953–978. https://doi.org/10.1080/01690965.2012.705006.

McCreery, R. W., & Stelmachowicz, P. G. (2013). The effects of limited bandwidth and noise on verbal processing time and word recall in normal-hearing children. *Ear and Hearing, 34*(5), 585–591. https://doi.org/10.1097/AUD.0b013e31828576e2.

McDevitt, T. M., Spivey, N., Sheehan, E. P., Lennon, R., & Story, R. (1990). Children's beliefs about listening: Is it enough to be still and quiet? *Child Development, 61*(3), 713–721. https://doi.org/10.1111/j.1467-8624.1990.tb02814.x.

McFadden, B., & Pittman, A. (2008). Effect of minimal hearing loss on children's ability to multitask in quiet and in noise. *Language, Speech, and Hearing Services in Schools, 39*(3), 342–351. https://doi.org/10.1044/0161-1461(2008/032).

McGarrigle, R., Dawes, P., Stewart, A. J., Kuchinsky, S. E., & Munro, K. J. (2017). Measuring listening-related effort and fatigue in school-aged children using pupillometry. *Journal of Experimental Child Psychology, 161*, 95–112. https://doi.org/10.1016/j.jecp.2017.04.006.

McGarrigle, R., Gustafson, S. J., Hornsby, B. W. Y., & Bess, F. H. (2019). Behavioral measures of listening effort in school-age children: Examining the effects of signal-to-noise ratio, hearing loss, and amplification. *Ear and Hearing, 40*(2), 381–392. https://doi.org/10.1097/AUD.0000000000000623.

McGarrigle, R., Munro, K. J., Dawes, P., Stewart, A. J., Moore, D. R., Barry, J. G., & Amitay, S. (2014). Listening effort and fatigue: What exactly are we measuring? A British Society of Audiology Cognition in Hearing Special Interest Group' white paper. *International Journal of Audiology, 53*(7), 433–445. https://doi.org/10.3109/14992027.2014.890296.

McGarrigle, R., Rakusen, L., & Mattys, S. (2021). Effortful listening under the microscope: Examining relations between pupillometric and subjective markers of effort and tiredness from listening. *Psychophysiology, 58*(1), e13703. https://doi.org/10.1111/psyp.13703.

McInnes, A., Humphries, T., Hogg-Johnson, S., & Tannock, R. (2003). Listening comprehension and working memory are impaired in attention-deficit hyperactivity disorder irrespective of language impairment. *Journal of Abnormal Child Psychology, 31*, 427–443. https://doi.org/10.1023/A:1023895602957.

Miles, K., McMahon, C., Boisvert, I., Ibrahim, R., De Lissa, P., Graham, P., & Lyxell, B. (2017). Objective assessment of listening effort: Coregistration of pupillometry and EEG. *Trends in Hearing, 21*, 1–13. https://doi.org/10.1177/2331216517706396.

Moore, T. M., & Picou, E. M. (2018). A potential bias in subjective ratings of mental effort. *Journal of Speech, Language, and Hearing Research, 61*(9), 2405–2421. https://doi.org/10.1044/2018_JSLHR-H-17-0451.

Morsomme, D., Minell, L., & Verduyckt, I. (2011). Impact of teachers' voice quality on children's language processing skills. *Vocology: Stem En Stemstoornissen*, 9–15.

Nagamitsu, S., Yamashita, Y., Tanaka, H., & Matsuishi, T. (2012). Functional near-infrared spectroscopy studies in children. *Biopsychosocial Medicine, 6*(1), 1–7. https://doi.org/10.1186/1751-0759-6-7.

Nakeva von Mentzer, C., Sundström, M., Enqvist, K., & Hällgren, M. (2018). Assessing speech perception in Swedish school-aged children: Preliminary data on the Listen-Say test. *Logopedics, Phoniatrics, Vocology, 43*(3), 106–119. https://doi.org/10.1080/14015439.2017.1380076.

Nirme, J., Haake, M., Lyberg Åhlander, V., Brännström, J., & Sahlén, B. (2019). A virtual speaker in noisy classroom conditions: Supporting or disrupting children's listening comprehension? *Logopedics, Phoniatrics, Vocology, 44*(2), 79–86. https://doi.org/10.1080/14015439.2018.1455894.

O'Neill, S., Barkhouse, M., Patro, C., & Srinivasan, N. K. (2023). Interplay between attention, working memory, and cognition to speech understanding in noise. -A157 *The Journal of the Acoustical Society of America, 153(3_supplement),* A157. https://doi.org/10.1121/10.0018494.

Obleser, J., Wöstmann, M., Hellbernd, N., Wilsch, A., & Maess, B. (2012). Adverse listening conditions and memory load drive a common alpha oscillatory network. *Journal of Neuroscience, 32*(36), 12376–12383. https://doi.org/10.1523/JNEUROSCI.4908-11.2012.

Obleser, J., & Weisz, N. (2012). Suppressed alpha oscillations predict intelligibility of speech and its acoustic details. *Cerebral Cortex, 22*(11), 2466–2477. https://doi.org/10.1093/cercor/bhr325.

Ohlenforst, B., Zekveld, A. A., Lunner, T., Wendt, D., Naylor, G., Wang, Y., ... Kramer, S. E. (2017b). Impact of stimulus-related factors and hearing impairment on listening effort as indicated by pupil dilation. *Hearing Research, 351*, 68–79. https://doi.org/10.1016/j.heares.2017.05.012.

Okhunjonov, A., & Shermukhammedova, A. (2023). Top 7 listening tactics for effective communication. *Fergana State University Conference, 196.* https://conf.fdu.uz/index.php/conf/article/view/2936.

Oosthuizen, I., Picou, E. M., Pottas, L., Myburgh, H. C., & Swanepoel, D. W. (2020). Listening effort in native and nonnative English-speaking children using low linguistic single- and dual-task paradigms. *Journal of Speech, Language, and Hearing Research: JSLHR, 63*(6), 1979–1989. https://doi.org/10.1044/2020_JSLHR-19-00330.

Osman, H., & Sullivan, J. R. (2014). Children's auditory working memory performance in degraded listening conditions. *Journal of Speech, Language, and Hearing Research, 57*(4), 1503–1511. https://doi.org/10.1044/2014_JSLHR-H-13-0286.

Peelle, J. E. (2018). Listening effort: How the cognitive consequences of acoustic challenge are reflected in brain and behavior. *Ear and Hearing, 39*(2), 204–214. https://doi.org/10.1097/AUD.0000000000000494.

Pervaiz, A., Lashari, A. A., Khan, A., & Bushra, A. (2024). Exploring the challenges of noisy areas faced by teachers in teaching and learning in urban schools. *Pakistan Journal of Humanities and Social Sciences, 12*(1), 525–536. https://doi.org/10.52131/pjhss.2024.v12i1.2045.

Petersen, E. B., Wöstmann, M., Obleser, J., Stenfelt, S., & Lunner, T. (2015). Hearing loss impacts neural alpha oscillations under adverse listening conditions. *Frontiers in Psychology, 6*, 177. https://doi.org/10.3389/fpsyg.2015.00177.

Petrić, B. (2000). The effect of listening instruction on the development of listening skills of university students of English. *Novelty*, 7(3), 15–29. https://doi.org/10.3109/00206090109073117.

Picard, M., & Bradley, J. S. (2001). Revisiting speech interference in classrooms: Revisando la interferencia en el habla dentro del salón de clases. *Audiology: Official Organ of the International Society of Audiology, 40*(5), 221–244.

Pichora-Fuller, M. K. (1996). Speechreading and working memory. In D. Stork, & M. Hennecke (Eds.). *Speechreading by humans and machines: Models, systems and applications* (pp. 257–274). Berlin, Heidelberg: Springer. https://doi.org/10.1007/978-3-662-13015-5_20.

Pichora-Fuller, M. K., Kramer, S. E., Eckert, M. A., Edwards, B., Hornsby, B. W., Humes, L. E., ... Wingfield, A. (2016). Hearing impairment and cognitive energy: The framework for understanding effortful listening (FUEL). *Ear and Hearing, 37*, 5S–27S. https://doi.org/10.1097/AUD.0000000000000312.

Picou, E. M., Bean, B., Marcrum, S. C., Ricketts, T. A., & Hornsby, B. W. Y. (2019). Moderate reverberation does not increase subjective fatigue, subjective listening effort, or behavioral listening effort in school-aged children. *Frontiers in Psychology, 10*, 1749. https://doi.org/10.3389/fpsyg.2019.01749.

Picou, E. M., Charles, L. M., & Ricketts, T. A. (2017). Child–adult differences in using dual-task paradigms to measure listening effort. *American Journal of Audiology, 26*(2), 143–154. https://doi.org/10.1044/2016_AJA-16-0059.

Picou, E. M., Gordon, J., & Ricketts, T. A. (2016). The effects of noise and reverberation on listening effort in adults with normal hearing. *Ear and Hearing, 37*(1), 1–13. https://doi.org/10.1097/AUD.0000000000000222.

Plebanek, D. J., & Sloutsky, V. M. (2019). Selective attention, filtering, and the development of working memory. *Developmental Science, 22*(1), e12727. https://doi.org/10.1111/desc.12727.

Porcaro, C. K., Evitts, P. M., King, N., Hood, C., Campbell, E., White, L., & Veraguas, J. (2020). Effect of dysphonia and cognitive-perceptual listener strategies on speech intelligibility. *Journal of Voice, 34*(5), 806.e7–806.e18. https://doi.org/10.1016/j.jvoice.2019.03.013.

Posner, M. I., & Petersen, S. E. (1990). The attention system of the human brain. *Annual Review of Neuroscience, 13*(1), 25–42. https://doi.org/10.1146/annurev.ne.13.030190.000325.

Prodi, N., Visentin, C., Borella, E., Mammarella, I. C., & Di Domenico, A. (2019). Noise, age, and gender effects on speech intelligibility and sentence comprehension for 11- to 13-year-old children in real classrooms. *Frontiers in Psychology, 10*. https://doi.org/10.3389/fpsyg.2019.02166.

Purdy, M., & Borisoff, D. (1997). *Listening in everyday life: A personal and professional approach* (2nd edn.). University Press of America.

Rogerson, J., & Dodd, B. (2005). Is there an effect of dysphonic teachers' voices on children's processing of spoken language? *Journal of Voice, 19*(1), 47–60. https://doi.org/10.1016/j.jvoice.2004.02.007.

Rönnberg, J., Lunner, T., Zekveld, A., Sörqvist, P., Danielsson, H., Lyxell, B., ... Rudner, M. (2013). The ease of language understanding (ELU) model: Theoretical, empirical, and clinical advances. *Frontiers in Systems Neuroscience,* 7, 31. https://doi.org/10.3389/fnsys.2013.00031.

Rosemann, S., & Thiel, C. M. (2019). The effect of age-related hearing loss and listening effort on resting state connectivity. *Scientific Reports, 9*(1), 2337. https://doi.org/10.1038/s41598-019-38816-z.

Rosenberg, G., Blake-Rahter, P., Heavner, J., Allen, L., Redmond, B. M., Phillips, J., & Stigers, K. (1999). Improving classroom acoustics (ICA): A three-year FM sound field classroom amplification study. *Journal of Educational Audiology,* 7, 8–28.

Rovetti, J., Goy, H., Pichora-Fuller, M. K., & Russo, F. A. (2019). Functional near-infrared spectroscopy as a measure of listening effort in older adults who use hearing aids. *Trends in Hearing, 23*, 2331216519886722. https://doi.org/10.1177/2331216519886722.

Rudner, M., Lyberg-Åhlander, V., Brännström, J., Nirme, J., Pichora-Fuller, M. K., & Sahlén, B. (2018). Listening comprehension and listening effort in the primary school classroom. *Frontiers in Psychology, 9*, 1193. https://doi.org/10.3389/fpsyg.2018.01193.

Rudner, M., Lunner, T., Behrens, T., Thorén, E. S., & Rönnberg, J. (2012). Working memory capacity may influence perceived effort during aided speech recognition in noise. *Journal of the American Academy of Audiology, 23*(8), 577–589. https://doi.org/10.3766/jaaa.23.7.7.

Sakhvid, F. Z., Sakhvid, M. J. Z., Mehrparvar, A. H., & Dzhambov, A. M. (2018). Environmental noise exposure and neurodevelopmental and mental health problems in children: A systematic review. *Current Environmental Health Reports, 5*, 365–374. https://doi.org/10.1007/s40572-018-0208-x.

Schiller, I. S., Morsomme, D., Kob, M., & Remacle, A. (2020). Noise and a speaker's impaired voice quality disrupt spoken language processing in school-aged children: Evidence from performance and response time measures. *Journal of Speech, Language, and Hearing Research, 63*(7), 2115–2131. https://doi.org/10.1044/2020_JSLHR-19-00348.

Schiller, I. S., Morsomme, D., Kob, M., & Remacle, A. (2021). Listening to a dysphonic speaker in noise may impede children's spoken language processing in a realistic classroom setting. *Language, Speech, and Hearing Services in Schools, 52*(1), 396–408. https://doi.org/10.1044/2020_LSHSS-20-00078.

Schubert, M., Hegewald, J., Freiberg, A., Starke, K. R., Augustin, F., Riedel-Heller, S. G., ... Seidler, A. (2019). Behavioral and emotional disorders and transportation noise among children and adolescents: A systematic review and meta-analysis. *International Journal of Environmental Research and Public Health, 16*(18), 3336. https://doi.org/10.3390/ijerph16183336.

Shibagaki, M., Yamanaka, T., & Furuya, T. (1992). Effects of attention state on electrodermal activity during auditory stimulation of children. *Perceptual and Motor Skills, 75*(1), 35–43. https://doi.org/10.2466/pms.1992.75.1.

Shinn-Cunningham, B. G., & Best, V. (2008). Selective attention in normal and impaired hearing. *Trends in Amplification, 12*(4), 283–299. https://doi.org/10.1177/1084713808325306.

Söderlund, G. B. W., & Sikström, S. (2012). Distractor or noise?: The influence of different sounds on cognitive performance in inattentive and attentive children. *IntechOpen.* https://doi.org/10.5772/29657.

Stansfeld, S., & Clark, C. (2015). Health effects of noise exposure in children. *Current Environmental Health Reports, 2*, 171–178. https://doi.org/10.1007/s40572-015-0044-1.

Stelmachowicz, P. G., Lewis, D. E., Choi, S., & Hoover, B. (2007). The effect of stimulus bandwidth on auditory skills in normal-hearing and hearing-impaired children. *Ear and Hearing, 28*(4), 483–494. https://doi.org/10.1097/AUD.0b013e31806dc265.

Strauß, A., Wöstmann, M., & Obleser, J. (2014). Cortical alpha oscillations as a tool for auditory selective inhibition. *Frontiers in Human Neuroscience, 8*, 350. https://doi.org/10.3389/fnhum.2014.00350.

Sullivan, J. R., Osman, H., & Schafer, E. C. (2015). The effect of noise on the relationship between auditory working memory and comprehension in school-age children. *Journal of Speech, Language, and Hearing Research, 58*(3), 1043–1051. https://doi.org/10.1044/2015_JSLHR-H-14-0204.

Valente, D. L., Plevinsky, H. M., Franco, J. M., Heinrichs-Graham, E. C., & Lewis, D. E. (2012). Experimental investigation of the effects of the acoustical conditions in a simulated classroom on speech recognition and learning in children. *The Journal of the Acoustical Society of America, 131*(1), 232–246. https://doi.org/10.1121/1.3662059.

Valentini, A., Ricketts, J., Pye, R. E., & Houston-Price, C. (2018). Listening while reading promotes word learning from stories. *Journal of Experimental Child Psychology, 167*, 10–31. https://doi.org/10.1016/j.jecp.2017.09.022.

Van Houtte, E., Claeys, S., Wuyts, F., & Van Lierde, K. (2011). The impact of voice disorders among teachers: Vocal Complaints, treatment-seeking behavior, knowledge of vocal care, and voice-related absenteeism. *Journal of Voice, 25*(5), 570–575. https://doi.org/10.1016/j.jvoice.2010.04.008.

Visentin, C., Pellegatti, M., Garraffa, M., Di Domenico, A., & Prodi, N. (2023). Individual characteristics moderate listening effort in noisy classrooms. *Scientific Reports, 13*(1), 14285. https://doi.org/10.1038/s41598-023-40660-1.

Vouloumanos, A., & Waxman, S. R. (2014). Listen up! Speech is for thinking during infancy. *Trends in Cognitive Sciences, 18*(12), 642–646. https://doi.org/10.1016/j.tics.2014.10.001.

Vouloumanos, A., & Werker, J. F. (2007). Listening to language at birth: Evidence for a bias for speech in neonates. *Developmental Science, 10*(2), 159–164. https://doi.org/10.1111/j.1467-7687.2007.00549.x.

Was, C. A., & Woltz, D. J. (2007). Reexamining the relationship between working memory and comprehension: The role of available long-term memory. *Journal of Memory and Language, 56*(1), 86–102. https://doi.org/10.1016/j.jml.2006.07.008.

Wendt, D., Dau, T., & Hjortkjær, J. (2016). Impact of background noise and sentence complexity on processing demands during sentence comprehension. *Frontiers in Psychology*, 7, 1–12. https://doi.org/10.3389/fpsyg.2016.00345.

Wetzel, N., Scharf, F., & Widmann, A. (2019). Can't ignore—Distraction by task-irrelevant sounds in early and middle childhood. *Child Development, 90*(6), e819–e830. https://doi.org/10.1111/cdev.13109.

Wild, C. J., Yusuf, A., Wilson, D. E., Peelle, J. E., Davis, M. H., & Johnsrude, I. S. (2012). Effortful listening: The processing of degraded speech depends critically on attention. *Journal of Neuroscience, 32*(40), 14010–14021. https://doi.org/10.1523/JNEUROSCI.1528-12.2012.

Wingfield, A. (2016). Evolution of models of working memory and cognitive resources. *Ear and Hearing, 37*, 35S. https://doi.org/10.1097/AUD.0000000000000310.

Winn, M. B., & Moore, A. N. (2018). Pupillometry reveals that context benefit in speech perception can be disrupted by later-occurring sounds, especially in listeners with cochlear implants. *Trends in Hearing, 22*, 1–22. https://doi.org/10.1177/2331216518808962.

Winn, M. B., & Teece, K. H. (2021). Listening effort is not the same as speech intelligibility score. *Trends in Hearing, 25*. 23312165211027690. https://doi.org/10.1177/23312165211027688.

Winn, M. B., Wendt, D., Koelewijn, T., & Kuchinsky, S. E. (2018). Best practices and advice for using pupillometry to measure listening effort: An introduction for those who want to get started. *Trends in Hearing, 22*, 2331216518800869. https://doi.org/10.1177/2331216518800869.

Wisniewski, M. G., Iyer, N., Thompson, E. R., & Simpson, B. D. (2018). Sustained frontal midline theta enhancements during effortful listening track working memory demands. *Hearing Research, 358*, 37–41. https://doi.org/10.1016/j.heares.2017.11.009.

Wisniewski, M. G., Thompson, E. R., & Iyer, N. (2017). Theta-and alpha-power enhancements in the electroencephalogram as an auditory delayed match-to-sample task becomes impossibly difficult. *Psychophysiology, 54*(12), 1916–1928. https://doi.org/10.1111/psyp.12968.

Wolfgramm, C., Suter, N., & Göksel, E. (2016). Examining the role of concentration, vocabulary and self-concept in listening and reading comprehension. *International Journal of Listening, 30*(1-2), 25–46. https://doi.org/10.1080/10904018.2015.1065746.

Yıldırım, S., & Yıldırım, Ö. (2016). The importance of listening in language learning and listening comprehension problems experienced by language learners: A literature review. *Abant İzzet Baysal Üniversitesi Eğitim Fakültesi Dergisi, 16*(4), 2094–2110.

Zekveld, A. A., Rudner, M., Johnsrude, I. S., & Rönnberg, J. (2013). The effects of working memory capacity and semantic cues on the intelligibility of speech in noise. *The Journal of the Acoustical Society of America, 134*(3), 2225–2234. https://doi.org/10.1121/1.4817926.

Zhang, L., & Ma, H. (2022). The effects of environmental noise on children's cognitive performance and annoyance. *Applied Acoustics, 198*, 108995. https://doi.org/10.1016/j.apacoust.2022.108995.

Zhang, M., Siegle, G. J., McNeil, M. R., Pratt, S. R., & Palmer, C. (2019). The role of reward and task demand in value-based strategic allocation of auditory comprehension effort. *Hearing Research, 381*, 107775. https://doi.org/10.1016/j.heares.2019.107775.

CHAPTER SIX

More than a bump to the head: An overview of the long-term effects of concussion

Colt A. Coffman, Tracey Covassin, and Matthew B. Pontifex*
Department of Kinesiology, Michigan State University, East Lansing, MI, United States
*Corresponding author. e-mail address: pontifex@msu.edu

Contents

Abstract

Concussion is often depicted as a short-term injury whereby symptoms assessed in the clinical setting typically resolve within two to four weeks. Recent high-profile cases involving post-concussion syndrome, chronic traumatic encephalopathy, and disturbing behavioral alterations in veterans and athletes participating in high-impact sports have begun a new discussion within both the general public and research community centered around the potential long-term effects of concussion. Innovative research, employing experimental measures of neural and behavioral function, have begun to contradict this notion of transience and suggests that concussed individuals can have lasting effects for years following initial injury. This chapter will provide context for this new perspective. We start by providing a brief description of concussion, outlining its symptomology and the existing guidelines for assessing clinical "recovery". Additionally, to help clarify their distinction from the evidence herein, we find it crucial to define two disorders commonly linked to long-term concussion effects: Post-Concussion Syndrome and Chronic Traumatic Encephalopathy. Fundamental to this chapter, we will review the evidence of subtle yet persistent functional alterations in

Psychology of Learning and Motivation, Volume 81
ISSN 0079-7421, https://doi.org/10.1016/bs.plm.2024.06.003

individuals with a history of concussion, expanding upon the insights provided by neurophysiological techniques and highlighting their implications for clinical recovery and future research directions.

1. Introduction

The brain's ability to maintain functionality throughout a human's lifespan, despite its delicate structure and the near-constant biomechanical forces exerted upon it, emphasizes its remarkable nature. Such resilience is aided by surrounding anatomical defenses (i.e., the skull, meninges, and cerebrospinal fluid) which help redistribute and absorb external forces transmitted toward the brain (Sakka, Coll, & Chazal, 2011; Walsh et al., 2021; Yoganandan et al., 1994). However, when biomechanical forces exceed the capacity of endogenous protective mechanisms to mitigate damage, traumatic brain injury (TBI) occurs, disrupting functionality (Werner & Engelhard, 2007). Estimating the true incidence of TBI is challenging, but it is believed that annually 64–74 million cases occur worldwide (Dewan et al., 2018). Distinct from moderate to severe TBI—which is associated with protracted loss of consciousness, altered mental status, and structural pathology (e.g., intracranial hemorrhage, lesions, or edema) or penetrating injury (e.g., skull fracture) (Maas, Stocchetti, & Bullock, 2008); the term "concussion" is used to refer to the substantial percentage of TBI (70–90%) that are classified as "mild" in severity (Cassidy et al., 2004). Roughly 1 in 5 adolescents report a lifetime prevalence of at least one concussion, with these estimates approaching 1 in 3 individuals in adulthood (Daugherty, DePadilla, Sarmiento, & Breiding, 2020; Veliz, Eckner, Zdroik, & Schulenberg, 2019). Despite significant functional impairment, concussion is described as a "silent" injury due to the general absence of gross structural pathologies or abnormalities and absence of sustained loss of consciousness/altered mental status, rendering it less likely that individuals will seek medical care (Patricios, Schneider, et al., 2023). As clinical symptomology is popularly asserted to resolve within two to four weeks after injury onset (Putukian et al., 2023), the general absence of detectable pathology and transient symptoms has historically shaped the perception that concussion is merely a "bump to the head" with brief and self-resolving symptoms. However, research over the past two decades has revealed that the effects of concussion are less temporary than commonly believed (Martini & Broglio, 2018).

Two of the most concerning long-term outcomes linked to concussion history are post-concussion syndrome, characterized by the persistence of concussion-like symptoms beyond the typical recovery timeframe, and the manifestation of neurodegenerative diseases later in life (Barlow, 2016; Gardner & Yaffe, 2015). While presenting potentially troublesome prognoses, ongoing research has started to identify non-concussion-related factors influencing their likelihood (see Sections 2.2–2.3). Tremendous efforts have been made to enhance concussion prevention strategies and reduce unnecessary exposure to head impacts by developing more advanced equipment technology, implementing safer rules for sport (May et al., 2023), improving education (Feiss, Lutz, Reiche, Moody, & Pangelinan, 2020), and refining diagnostic and management protocols (Broglio et al., 2024; Eliason et al., 2023). Nevertheless, fear of the potential deleterious effects has intensified (Baugh, Kroshus, Kiernan, Mendel, & Meehan, 2017; Walton et al., 2022). Out of an abundance of caution, nearly 1 in 5 of adults now report that they would never allow their children to participate in high-contact sports such as American tackle football (Waltzman, Sarmiento, & Daugherty, 2024). Considerable discourse has arisen regarding whether the potential long-term effects linked to concussion history outweigh the benefits of sport participation (Malcolm, Matthews, & Wiltshire, 2024; Piggin, Parry, & White, 2024). As such, ongoing scientific inquiry has sought to further elucidate the long-term effects of concussion.

Advancements in research methods have uncovered underlying behavioral and physiological differences between individuals with and without a history of concussion, implying residual alterations despite individuals being considered as clinically recovered (Martini & Broglio, 2018). There is growing concern that these alterations, while subtle, may negatively impact daily functioning and quality of life, and contribute to an increased risk of injury (Reneker, Babl, & Flowers, 2019). The present chapter aims to review modern evidence on the long-term effects of concussion, consider their potential impact on functionality throughout the lifespan, and present how neurophysiological approaches can be implemented to further our understanding of these effects. We start by defining concussion and outlining how this injury is typically managed. Additionally, we find it crucial to explain how differences in timelines, clinical burden, and contributing factors necessitate that post-concussion syndrome and neurodegenerative diseases are treated as distinct conditions despite sharing similar symptomology and history of head trauma. We conclude by examining how these emergent findings may guide future research directions. A paucity of data prompts us to periodically reference studies covering a wider spectrum of TBI severity (including concussion) throughout this chapter. We recommend caution when extrapolating these findings to concussion specifically, but this approach may unveil avenues for further exploration.

2. Defining concussion

Historical inconsistencies in the terminology, definitions, and criteria for concussion have made it difficult even for experts to coherently synthesize research findings. Therefore, before proceeding, it is necessary to outline how diverse terminology has been consolidated into the general conceptual definition as it stands today. Colloquial terms such as "ding", "bump", "bell ringer", or "rattled" have generally been deemed as outdated/improper terminology that should be avoided in favor of the terms "mild TBI" and "concussion"—which are generally recognized as interchangeable. Recognizing that certain injury characteristics and return-to-activity/work considerations may be unique to the context in which head trauma occurred, it has been suggested that the use of the term "concussion" be restricted to injuries sustained in a sport-related context. More unitary perspectives of TBI however argue that context does not adequately differentiate concussion from other forms of mild TBI, rather that the term "concussion" may be more appropriately used to denote a subset of mild TBI with relatively minor clinical outcomes (King, 2019; McCrory et al., 2013). As a result, concussive injuries or injuries producing concussion-like symptoms after a single or repeated impact(s) have been historically characterized as minor TBI, minor head trauma, or minor head (brain) (Gronwall, 1991; Kibby & Long, 1996; Weight, 1998). Consistent with such a view, the term "concussion" has been suggested as the preferred term when speaking with patients to avoid perceptions of "permanent brain damage" (Management of Concussion/mTBI Working Group, 2009). However, these terms lack distinct operational definitions and there is no objective test or biomarker that clinicians utilize for diagnosis. Importantly, their injury characteristics and outcomes fall within the broadest criteria set for diagnosing concussion (McCrory et al., 2013). Fundamentally, the lack of a common definition represents a critical failure within this area of research and medicine. It is further important to acknowledge that while concussion reflects the lowest clinical severity from a unitary perspective of TBI, the historical tendency has been to present concussions as "no big deal", something that can be brushed aside or played through, and/or lacking long-term implications—either due to a research emphasis oriented towards more severe head trauma or sporting contexts oriented towards enabling athletes to return to participation. Within the present chapter, the term "concussion" is preferentially used, although studies using related terms may be referenced due to their inherent overlap in diagnostic criteria.

Beyond the limitations in appropriately characterizing the literature in this area, the lack of consistent terminology also has implications for diagnosis and assessment. At least 17 published definitions for concussion and mild TBI requiring blunt head trauma have been proposed (Crowe et al., 2018). Substantial variability in these definitions makes it difficult for clinicians to diagnose the injury with assurance. The Glasgow Coma Scale is the conventional method used to determine a suspected TBI's severity within the first 6 h of injury, with scores ranging from 3 (completely unresponsive) to 15 (fully conscious) (Sternbach, 2000). A person with a concussion would obtain a score between 13 and 15, indicating mild to no impairment in consciousness, alertness, orientation, and responsiveness to eye-opening and motor commands. However, a high Glasgow Coma Scale score alone does not guarantee the absence of underlying structural pathology and clinical neuroimaging techniques including Computerized Tomography and Magnetic Resonance Imaging may be used at the clinician's discretion.

To confirm head trauma, a plausible mechanism of injury must be first identified whereby acceleration, deceleration, angular, and/or rotational forces were transferred directly or indirectly to the brain—although an important note is that a collision between the brain and the skull (e.g., a coup-countercoup injury) is not necessary. It is generally understood that such forces cause a shearing or stretching of neural tissue, initiating a complex pathophysiological cascade that aligns with concussion's symptomology (Giza & Hovda, 2014). Nonetheless, there is significant ambiguity in asserting the magnitude of forces required to produce these consequences. Therefore, injury characteristics immediately following the event are further utilized to help diagnosis TBI, including loss of consciousness, post-traumatic amnesia, disorientation/confusion, tonic posturing, seizure, and other focal neurologic deficits reported by the patient or witnesses (Silverberg et al., 2023). Generally, loss of consciousness duration must be ≤ 30 min and post-traumatic amnesia duration must be ≤ 24 h to exclude moderate/severe TBI. However, loss of consciousness and post-traumatic amnesia are not required for diagnosing concussion, and more conservative definitions which apply specific duration requirements raise concerns regarding the extent to which the individual can accurately recall the period following injury (Crowe et al., 2018).

The "cornerstone" of concussion diagnosis and management relies on assessing clinical symptoms indicative of neurological dysfunction (see Section 2.1). It is crucial to assess clinical symptoms during the acute period (i.e., within 72 h post-injury) when symptoms are most severe, as they may evolve over hours or days (Patricios, Schneider, et al., 2023). Relying solely on symptom profiles for decision-making can often result in misdiagnosis, as concussion symptomology is non-specific (i.e., not unique to concussion/ TBI). Diagnostic criteria require that clinicians ensure that concussion-like symptoms are not solely attributable to drug, alcohol, or medication usage, cervical injuries, psychological disorders, or other comorbid conditions. The Concussion Recognition Tool-6 combines signs of TBI, injury characteristics, clinical symptoms, and modified Maddocks questions to strengthen diagnostic assurance (Echemendia, Ahmed, et al., 2023).

While consensus groups have moved toward establishing more standardized criteria, we reiterate that there is no unanimous definition for concussion, and its diagnosis relies on the clinician's judgement. For a more accurate diagnosis, the methods detailed above may be utilized but are not explicitly required. Four overlapping criteria consistently appear across the expert consensus derived definitions for concussion/mild TBI: (i) A plausible mechanism of injury resulting in the transfer of biomechanical forces to the brain must have occurred, (ii) Acute symptoms and/or evidence of neurological impairment attributable to the injury must be present upon clinical evaluation, (iii) In the absence of acute symptomology, injury characteristics or neuroimaging must be attributable to the injury, and (iv) Criteria (ii) and (iii) cannot be accounted for by confounding factors or more severe TBI (Davis, Patricios, Schneider, Iverson, & Silverberg, 2023; Harmon et al., 2019; Silverberg et al., 2023).

2.1 Clinical assessment of concussion recovery

Current guidelines on concussion management call for assessment of an individual's recovery progress using a comprehensive multimodal evaluation, preferably conducted by a multidisciplinary team (Broglio et al., 2024; Patricios, Schneider, et al., 2023), in order to suppress any one individual bias or perspective. There is no universal set of assessments for clinicians to use in their evaluation. Instead, clinicians have discretion in selecting which symptom domains to assess and the tools used to evaluate them. Again, such a "wild-west" approach represents a critical failure within this area of research and medicine given that concussion symptomology is non-specific and heterogeneous (i.e., symptoms as well as their onset, duration, and severity can vary widely among individuals). The argument for this approach, however, is that attempting to assess the full breadth of potential concussion symptomology would be costly and potentially burdensome to both the patient and clinician (Broglio et al., 2024).

To reduce assessment redundancy and the need to build individualized assessment plans, clinicians regularly utilize a symptom rating scale within a battery of tools to identify common symptoms profiles and their relative severity (Kontos, Sufrinko, Sandel, Emami, & Collins, 2019; Kontos et al., 2020; Lempke et al., 2023). Popular standardized assessment batteries, such as the Sport Concussion Assessment Tool-6 (SCAT6) and the Sport Concussion Office Assessment Tool-6 (SCOAT6)—which offer child (8–12 years) and adolescent/adult (≥13 years) versions—are valuable in discriminating between concussed and non-concussed individuals during the acute and subacute (i.e., 72 h to weeks postinjury) periods, respectively (Echemendia, Brett, et al., 2023; Patricios, Davis, et al., 2023; Patricios, Schneider, et al., 2023). Clinicians may seek to further enhance decision-making by employing neurocognitive test batteries (Alsalaheen, Stockdale, Pechumer, & Broglio, 2016), coordination/balance assessments (Buckley, Munkasy, & Clouse, 2018), measurements of heart rate, blood pressure, and symptoms in response to postural change or physical exertion (Haider et al., 2021), cervical spine and neurological evaluation (Mohai et al., 2022), Vestibular-Ocular Motor Screening (Mucha et al., 2014), and/or validated mental health or sleep screening instruments (Patricios, Schneider, et al., 2023).

Once the clinical assessment of a concussion is made, the current standard of practice is to address the symptoms which manifest following the injury. Although historical strict rest protocols such as 'dark room" or "cocoon" therapy are no longer recommended, consensus statements emphasize a relative rest period within the first 24–48 h postinjury (Broglio et al., 2024; Patricios, Schneider, et al., 2023). During this period, relative rest protocols often encourage individuals to maintain activities of daily living to the best of their ability, rest physically—to address dysfunctions associated with postural/motor control and perceptual sensitivities and avoid tasks which require cognitive engagement (such as screen time, school, and work)—to address dysfunctions associated with high level cognitive operations and memory (Patricios, Schneider, et al., 2023).

Beyond this, the standard of practice encourages a graduated return-to-activity/work protocol, where individuals progressively return to doing those activities that do not exacerbate their symptoms while avoiding high-risk activities (such as contact, collision, or falls) to mitigate the risk of reinjury (Leddy et al., 2023; Putukian et al., 2023). To aid this protocol, clinicians may choose to employ graded aerobic exercise testing—such as the Buffalo Concussion Treadmill or Bike Tests—which gradually increase exercise intensity up until the point at which concussion symptoms are exacerbated or re-manifest, as exercise intolerance due to symptom exacerbation may indicate persistent physiological dysfunction (Haider et al., 2019; Leddy & Willer, 2013). Even "cutting edge" therapeutic practices still utilize a concussion symptom abatement approach, focusing only on addressing symptomologies, having patients undergo balance, vision, and cognitive training to minimize symptom presentation within that domain. Pharmacological treatments for concussion have similarly followed suit with 1 in 10 clinicians prescribing Amantadine—a neurostimulant originally used as an antiviral agent—in an attempt to offset post-injury cognitive impairments (Reddy, Collins, Lovell, & Kontos, 2013). When such a symptom abatement approach is considered in the context of physical injuries such as a broken bone, it is unsurprising that long-term issues persist following concussion. Treating only those symptoms that manifest following a concussion is the equivalent of only using Tylenol to treat a broken bone—the treatment would center around pain reduction but would fail to address the actual injury. While some injuries would heal and go away on their own; a sizable portion of individuals would exhibit persistent limitations or dysfunctions, eventually resulting in an inability to continue their normal activities or even impaired health. Fundamentally, this summarizes the current situation surrounding concussion and the emergence of persistent post-concussion syndrome, along with recognition that concussion is a risk factor for subsequent mental health issues (Guskiewicz et al., 2007; Rice et al., 2016, 2018; Solomon, Kuhn, & Zuckerman, 2016).

Although the determination of clinical recovery varies widely across clinical settings, it is generally based upon: (1) a reduction in symptom ratings to a marginal or pre-injury level, (2) a general absence of neurological dysfunction due to concussion (e.g., normative neurocognitive performance, adequate postural stability, lack of symptom provocation during cognitive/physical exertion or VOMS), and (3) a complete return to learning environments and activity (work/play) (Broglio et al., 2024; Patricios, Schneider, et al., 2023). Thus, a majority of concussed individuals will return to their regular activities and exhibit marginal symptomatology within two to four weeks postinjury (Putukian et al., 2023). While such return to regular activity is popularly asserted as a reflection of clinical recovery—even if the individual still experiences some residual symptomatology; true physiological recovery extends far beyond this timeframe as evidence from more sensitive techniques has consistently observed long-term effects months to years following injury, even in asymptomatic presentations (Kamins et al., 2017). As many of the assessment approaches within this literature are essentially minor evolutions of 1940s era paper-and-pencil screening tools to detect gross-abnormalities in function, the question remains as to the clinical significance of more modern and sensitive assessment techniques. Specifically, if an individual presents with relatively normal functioning but still exhibits impairments on more sensitive assessments, it is unclear how clinical decision-making should change—as well as how willing individuals in sporting contexts may be to delay returning to full participation. The current literature further lacks explicit consideration of temporality, often relying on observed differences between individuals with (i.e., presumably deemed "clinically recovered") and without a history of concussion to extrapolate potential long-term effects, without assessing the persistence of these effects from injury onset. As modern approaches appear to be sensitive to alterations in the brain and cognition in response to a wide array of behaviors (e.g., caffeine, sleep, physical activity, etc.), some caution is warranted in directly attributing differences between groups to a single underlying cause.

2.2 Post-concussion syndrome

Nevertheless, within those individuals who incur a concussion, up to 30% may experience signs of protracted clinical recovery (Voormolen et al., 2018; Yeates et al., 2023). This condition, referred to as persistent post-concussion symptoms or Post-Concussion Syndrome (PCS)—the latter used for consistency herein, is broadly characterized by a symptom course lasting more than three months after initial concussion diagnosis (Mittenberg & Strauman, 2000). While referrals to specialized physicians and targeted interventions may be implemented to better manage PCS, the central assessment remains consistent with assessment recommendations for the subacute period (Yeates et al., 2023). Diagnosing PCS is as challenging as diagnosing concussion itself. As concussion symptoms are non-specific, when these symptoms appear well after the typical recovery timeframe it poses a substantial challenge in determining their biological underpinnings.

Indeed, up to 20% of healthy individuals report concussion-like symptoms consistent with PCS criteria (Asken, Snyder, Smith, Zaremski, & Bauer, 2017). Therefore, PCS diagnosis depends upon clinical discretion when evaluating an individual's recovery progress and confirming that their symptoms are not better explained by an extraneous underlying condition (s) (Harmon et al., 2019).

Extensive research has focused on identifying predictors of PCS and at-risk populations to facilitate earlier intervention, hopefully reducing its prevalence. An elevated risk of PCS is observed in females and older adults (Mavroudis, Balmus, Ciobica, & Hogas, 2024; Varriano et al., 2018), as well as in individuals with pre-existing mental health disorders (Broshek, De Marco, & Freeman, 2015; Morgan et al., 2015; Ponsford et al., 2019), somatization (Root et al., 2016), and headache/migraine disorders (Scott, Uomoto, & Barry, 2020). However, it should be noted that individuals with these risk factors may not necessarily develop PCS, and conversely, PCS may be developed absent these risk factors. In populations experiencing symptomatology which overlaps with that of concussion, clinical decision-making may be made more difficult. It has been suggested that one reason for the elevated risk of PCS in such populations may be a reflection upon individuals being prematurely cleared to return to school, work, or play as residual impairments/symptoms are misattributed (Bullard et al., 2022; Coffman et al., 2023). Importantly however, findings in Attention-Deficit Hyperactivity Disorder (ADHD) populations indicate that although ADHD-related and concussion-related symptomatology are similar, they exhibit distinct factor structures (Bullard et al., 2022). Such findings indicate that the elevated risk of PCS in individuals with ADHD is not a function of overlapping constructs being assessed and confused, but rather may reflect symptom exacerbation as a result of some other means. It has been proposed that concussion may trigger mechanisms in individuals with a natural predisposition to develop symptomatology in these domains, further exacerbating their symptoms (Broshek et al., 2015). Additionally, emotional distress (e.g., anxiety, fear, post-traumatic stress, or depression) associated with changes to habitual activities or injury outcomes may cause patients to attribute their difficulties erroneously to concussion (Wijenberg, Stapert, Verbunt, Ponsford, & Van Heugten, 2017; Wood, McCabe, & Dawkins, 2011).

The pathophysiological consequences associated with clinical symptom presentation generally resolve within the subacute period. Pre-existing characteristics or psychological factors that overlap with or exacerbate symptomatology may contribute to seemingly prolonged concussion effects, representing a distinct syndrome, PCS. In contrast, the long-term effects reviewed herein are not detected by traditional clinical techniques during the subacute period and are presumed to be present even in cases of typical recovery. Nonetheless, our current understanding of what constitutes "typical" recovery is limited outside the context of clinical symptomology. Without extensive longitudinal data, it is difficult to determine whether PCS and the long-term effects of concussion are mutually exclusive from a pathophysiological perspective. Indeed, it may be that all post-concussion presentations exist along the same continuum of pathophysiological and symptomological recovery, influenced by a myriad of factors which determine the chronicity and severity of symptoms. While we believe that such a unified approach warrants further consideration, at present, PCS is viewed as distinct from other long-term effects of concussion and will be described as such our review of the literature.

2.3 Chronic traumatic encephalopathy and other neurodegenerative diseases

If the general public were asked, "What long-term effects do you associate with concussion?", "CTE" would likely be the most common response, with many mistakenly identifying its first letter as "concussion". However, the general public is not at fault for these misconceptions. Over the past decade, perceptions of this concept have been largely influenced by widespread alarming media reports and a blockbuster film titled "Concussion" which dramatized the discovery of Chronic Traumatic Encephalopathy (CTE) in former American Football players. During the same period, researchers failed to establish reliable evidence linking CTE to concussion history (Godbolt et al., 2014; Stein, Alvarez, & McKee, 2015). Considerable refinements have been made to CTE criteria and its proposed etiology in light of this new research (McKee, Stein, et al., 2023), yet nearly 70% of the general public still express concern that a single concussion event could increase one's risk of CTE (Daugherty & Sarmiento, 2018; Merz, Van Patten, & Lace, 2017; Salisbury, Kolessar, Callender, & Bennett, 2017; Zurlinden et al., 2024). As such, we believe it is imperative to describe the current view on CTE and its relationship to concussion to avoid past mistakes in knowledge translation.

Chronic Traumatic Encephalopathy is a rare neurodegenerative disease characterized by the abnormal deposition of tau, an essential structural protein found in neurons, within the frontal and temporal cortices, as well as in crevices of the brain called sulci (McKee, Stein, et al., 2023). While at present CTE can only be diagnosed through post-mortem pathohistological examination, it is associated with a progressive array of nonspecific clinical features typically during mid-to-late adulthood (e.g., behavioral disturbance, suicidal behaviors, cognitive decline, and overt clinical dementia) termed Traumatic Encephalopathy Syndrome (TES) (Katz et al., 2021). Alarmingly, CTE has also been identified in contact-sport athletes who were younger than 30 years old at the time of their death (McKee, Mez, et al., 2023). The causal etiology of CTE is proposed to result from long-term exposure to repetitive head impacts, which may or may not include a history of concussion (McKee, Stein, et al., 2023). Proponents of this hypothesis argue that there is preponderance of evidence supporting it, citing that 97% of CTE cases occur in retired professional athletes from collision/contact sports (McKee, Stein, et al., 2023). However, critics have called for the abandonment of this hypothesis, arguing that it is overly reductionist (Barr, 2020; Carson, 2017; Malcolm et al., 2024), and highlighting the lack of empirical characterization in the diagnostic criteria for CTE and TES (Hazrati et al., 2013; Iverson & Gardner, 2020; Randolph, 2018; Terry et al., 2024). Studies heavily rely on brain donors, often lack control groups, and rarely account for additional lifestyle factors which may occur within these populations (e.g., alcohol, drug, or pain medication overuse, as well as psychiatric conditions) and simultaneously contribute to tau accumulation. Clearly, more diagnostic refinements and investigations into causal criteria are needed before a consensus is reached on whether repeated head impacts or concussion contributes to CTE/TES development.

Epidemiological evidence suggests that a history of concussion may confer an increased risk for other neurodegenerative diseases including amyotrophic lateral sclerosis (ALS) (Chen, Richard, Sandler, Umbach, & Kamel, 2007), Alzheimer's (Fleminger, Oliver, Lovestone, Rabe-Hesketh, & Giora, 2003; Mortimer et al., 1991; Schofield et al., 1997), Parkinson's (Jafari, Etminan, Aminzadeh, & Samii, 2013), and other dementias (Kalkonde et al., 2012; Lee et al., 2013; Rosso et al., 2003). In neurodegenerative tauopathies (e.g., CTE, Alzheimer's, and frontotemporal dementia), the accumulation of tau—and amyloid-β peptides in some diseases—deposits both intracellularly and extracellularly, forming aggregates called neurofibrillary tangles (Lee, Goedert, & Trojanowski, 2001). These aggregates are believed to be neurotoxic, triggering chronic inflammation and subsequent neuronal dysfunction, damage, or death—although it is important to acknowledge growing perspectives that the accumulation of tau and amyloid-β may be physiological markers of neurotoxic environments rather than causal factors (Langworth-Green et al., 2023). Healthy individuals without these neurodegenerative tauopathies maintain functional waste-clearing mechanisms, inhibiting their accumulation (Nedergaard, 2013; Tanaka, Mizushima, & Saeki, 2012). For example, the glymphatic system, preferentially active during sleep, facilitates the clearance of brain waste by a convective flow of interstitial and cerebral spinal fluids through perivascular spaces (Nedergaard, 2013). Researchers have hypothesized that sleep disturbances following concussion can hinder glymphatic clearance, allowing for extracellular tau accumulation to propagate and thereby increasing the risk of developing neurodegenerative tauopathies (Giza & Hovda, 2014; Iliff et al., 2014; Medina & Avila, 2014). However, this theory does not help explain the increased risk of ALS or Parkinson's, and in order for it to be considered viable, further empirical evidence is required. Additionally, the current epidemiological findings are inconsistent in their conclusions (Helmes, Østbye, & Steenhuis, 2011; Mehta et al., 1999) and their studies are considered methodologically limited, as they rarely address other factors known to be important for brain health (Patricios, Schneider, et al., 2023).

3. Evidence of long-term functional alterations

Despite its apparent flaws, the current clinical assessment approach is particularly useful for categorizing symptom profiles following concussion and evaluating their interrelatedness. The clinical profiles model, popularized by Collins and colleagues, categorizes symptoms into five, often co-occurring, clinical profiles: (1) cognitive/fatigue (e.g., difficulty remembering/concentrating, memory problems, feeling 'slow'), (2) vestibular (e.g., dizziness, nausea, balance problems, motion sensitivity), (3) ocular (e.g., blurry vision, difficulty focusing, difficulty reading), (4) migraine (e.g., headache with nausea and/or phono/photosensitivity, visual aura), and (5) anxiety/mood (e.g., depression, irritability, anxiousness), with two modifying factors: (a) sleep (e.g., trouble falling asleep, sleeping more/less than usual) and (b) cervicogenic injury (e.g., neck pain or stiffness, headache originating toward the back of the head, numbness or tingling) (Collins, Kontos, Reynolds, Murawski, & Fu, 2014; Kontos et al., 2019). Such an approach enables clinicians to identify secondary symptom manifestations, allowing resources and therapeutic efforts to be allocated toward addressing the particular symptomological profile. For example, if a patient's symptoms primarily align with the anxiety/mood profile but they also present with exaggerated headaches and sleep disturbance, the clinician may determine that there is a shared psychological explanation for the reported symptoms and focus the patient's treatment accordingly. Nevertheless, the clinical profiles approach is only as sensitive as the assessment tools used to inform it. If the assessment tools chosen to have suboptimal sensitivity, underlying or subclinical symptoms/profiles can go unrecognized, despite their potential to develop into long-term functional impairments if left unaddressed. As such, our review will be framed in the context of this significant gap, focusing on the flaws of more traditional assessment tools and detailing evidence from studies using experimental measures that appear sensitive enough to detect long-term alterations in four often-neglected symptom domains following concussion.

3.1 Mental health

Historically, concussion practices and guidelines have focused on ameliorating physical pain and other somatic symptoms, inadvertently overlooking the assessment of mental health status. An increased emphasis has been placed on mental health assessment more recently as nearly 1 in 4 concussed patients report psycho-affective symptoms (Fish et al., 2023; Iverson, Greenberg, & Cook, 2022; Kontos et al., 2019; Yang, Peek-Asa, Covassin, & Torner, 2015). Further, psychiatric difficulties are among the strongest predictors of protracted recovery and symptom severity following concussion (D'Alonzo et al., 2022; Daley et al., 2024; Iverson et al., 2017, 2022; Ponsford et al., 2012; Weber et al., 2018; Zemek et al., 2016). As such, mental health screening instruments, primarily focusing on the manifestation of anxiety, depression, irritability, and emotional instability, have become some of the most valuable tools within a clinician's arsenal.

Mental health status following a concussion does not solely reflect its pathophysiological consequences but is also influenced by pre-injury psychiatric difficulties (Yang et al., 2015) and non-specific injury effects, such as detraining, boredom, isolation, or other sociocultural factors (Putukian, 2016). Indeed, it is important to consider that secondary effects of injury could even exacerbate underlying mental health concerns as a result of activity restrictions, separation from peers or group members, and concerns about regaining the opportunity to resume typical daily activities. Ideally, psycho-affective symptoms would be treated uniquely based on their causal factors. However, mental health assessment following concussion is often constrained to just a few items on a symptom rating scale or a brief questionnaire (Crawford, Wenden, & Wade, 1996; Echemendia et al., 2023; Kontos et al., 2020; Patricios et al., 2023). While the inclusion of such items reflects a considerable improvement over historic standards of care and can serve as an initial trigger for referring a patient for more focused follow-up assessment and care; such a limited characterization makes it challenging for clinicians to disentangle the heterogeneous factors contributing to psycho-affective symptomology. This approach ultimately contributes to inadequate treatment for a subset of patients, risking symptom persistence, exacerbation, or even temporary masking, with symptoms reemerging after patients are deemed "clinically recovered".

If one were to focus within the typical clinical recovery period (i.e., injury onset to full medical clearance), psycho-affective symptoms would appear to be transient, following a similar but slightly extended time course to other concussion symptoms (Covassin et al., 2023; Mainwaring et al., 2004; Sicard, Harrison, & Moore, 2021). However, higher rates of mental health disturbances are observed in individuals with a history of concussion, even years after the initial injury (Brett, Nelson, & Meier, 2022; Burns et al., 2024; Chrisman & Richardson, 2014; Izzy et al., 2021; Keightley et al., 2014; Ledoux et al., 2022; Russell, Walld, Bolton, Chateau, & Ellis, 2023). A recent meta-analysis found that individuals with a history of concussion had nearly 3.3 times greater odds of being diagnosed with depression compared to their non-concussed counterparts (Hellewell, Beaton, Welton, & Grieve, 2020). These increased odds were stable from 6 months to more than 10 years post-injury and consistent across biological sex, age at injury/ assessment, and injury etiology. Thus, the trajectory of psycho-affective symptoms following concussion may not be transient; rather, it may follow a biphasic pattern, with symptom regression during the acute and subacute periods and reemergence around 6 months post-injury.

While this evidence certainly points toward an association between concussion history and mental health disturbance, much of the available research is limited by its cross-sectional design, and the presence of pre-injury mental health diagnoses cannot be ruled out, making it challenging to infer causality. Nonetheless, there is limited evidence supporting the notion that concussion is indeed a significant risk factor for depression and other affective disorders. Delmonico and colleagues, using a longitudinal matched cohort design, demonstrated that even concussed individuals with no prior history of affective disorders had greater odds of developing depressive disorders (OR = 1.9) and anxiety disorders (OR = 1.7) up to 48 months post-injury compared to uninjured controls (Delmonico, Theodore, Sandel, Armstrong, & Camicia, 2022).

Furthermore, select studies have observed a frequency-response relationship in contact sport athletes, where a greater lifetime history of concussion is associated with increased depressive symptom severity (Brett, Kerr, et al., 2022; Didehbani, Munro Cullum, Mansinghani, Conover, & Hart, 2013; Gouttebarge, Aoki, Lambert, Stewart, & Kerkhoffs, 2017; Kerr, Thomas, Simon, McCrea, & Guskiewicz, 2018; Pryor, Larson, & DeBeliso, 2016; Walton et al., 2021). The precise number of concussions required to produce a clinically significant increase in depressive symptom severity remains unknown. Generally, studies note that while one or two concussions marginally increase the likelihood of a concurrent depression diagnosis, the likelihood becomes significantly greater with three or more concussions (Guskiewicz et al., 2007; Kennedy et al., 2024; Kerr, Marshall, Harding, & Guskiewicz, 2012; Kerr et al., 2014). Such evidence could be interpreted by instead suggesting that a history of repetitive non-concussive head trauma is the true underlying cause; however, former contact athletes across all levels of competition do not exhibit an increased risk of psychiatric disorder (Bohr, Boardman, & McQueen, 2019; Deshpande et al., 2017; Deshpande, Hasegawa, Weiss, & Small, 2020; Iverson & Terry, 2022; Iverson, Merz, & Terry, 2021; Russell et al., 2020). The collective findings indicate that experiencing multiple concussions may have a cumulative and detrimental effect on mental health; yet it is important to note that not all studies observe such an effect (Hellewell et al., 2020; Kay et al., 2022) and athletes exhibit poorer recall of concussion history when they experience greater mental health difficulties (Brett, Kerr, et al., 2022). This phenomenon likely represents a more complex interaction between concussion history and pre-existing risk factors (Moore et al., 2023).

Moreover, depression does not manifest in isolation but is accompanied by other psycho-affective and neurocognitive changes following concussion. For example, impulsivity, either as a risk factor or a long-term effect, is correlated with concussion history (Beidler et al., 2021). Researchers have posited that impulsivity moderates the relationship between depression and suicidal behaviors, suggesting that while severely depressed individuals may report suicidal ideation, those who are both depressed and impulsive are at the greatest risk of attempting suicide (Dumais et al., 2005; Mann et al., 2009; Wang, Jiang, Cheung, Sun, & Chan, 2015). A recent meta-analysis found that individuals with a history of concussion were twice as likely to commit suicide compared to those without a history of concussion (Fralick, Thiruchelvam, Tien, & Redelmeier, 2016). Nevertheless, suicide remains relatively rare, as absolute risk ranged from 0.28%

to 0.59% among concussed individuals (Fralick et al., 2016). In the United States, middle school and high school students who sustained at least one concussion had 1.69- and 1.60-times greater odds of attempting suicide within the same year, respectively (Mantey, Omega-Njemnobi, Barroso, & Kelder, 2020; Mantey, Omega-Njemnobi, & Kelder, 2021). More recent analysis of the high school data indicates that these risks become more meaningful when accounting for concussion frequency and demographic risk factors (e.g., race, ethnicity, and biological sex) (Eagle et al., 2022; Kay et al., 2022). For example, Kay and colleagues found that male students with two or more concussions in the past year had double the odds of attempting suicide compared to those with a single concussion, however, a frequency-response relationship was not observed for female students (Kay et al., 2022). While an increased risk of suicide represents a particularly concerning long-term consequence of concussion, we reiterate that much of the current literature is still limited to cross-sectional studies.

Some researchers have hypothesized that post-concussion factors act as stressors for individuals with a diathesis toward psycho-affective disturbance, enabling the development of clinically significant mental health disorders after injury (Moore, Kay, & Ellemberg, 2018). While this potentially explains the association between concussion and the development of depression, anxiety, and other affective disorders, it does not account for the biphasic trajectory of psycho-affective symptoms. In addition to suboptimal assessment sensitivity and inadequate treatment, this unique time course may reflect that concussed patients are temporarily concealing their psycho-affective symptoms to expedite medical clearance. Of course, we cannot discount the additional possibility that participants recruited in these cross-sectional studies may have undiagnosed PCS, making them unrepresentative of most individuals with a history of concussion. Without more extensive longitudinal data, extant literature offers limited guidance for clinical practice in mental health assessment and treatment following concussion. At the moment, it is imperative to prioritize concussion prevention and ensure that individuals struggling with mental health issues following a concussion are provided with a comprehensive support system.

3.2 Sleep

Within the broader discussion of concussive injuries, a particularly dominant perspective is the view that "too much sleep" contributes toward worse outcomes following a concussion. Such views reflect pervasive misconceptions that sleep must be avoided or periodically interrupted to prevent deterioration shortly after a concussion (Rieger et al., 2018). Yet, the extant evidence in this area has largely dispelled such ideas. In fact, acute pleiosomnia (i.e., requiring more sleep than before injury) has been proposed as a necessary behavior following concussion to maximize recovery processes and glymphatic clearance (Imbach et al., 2016; Sommerauer, Valko, Werth, & Baumann, 2013). Problematically, sleep-wake disturbances also occur with concussion, partially due to disruption of orexin/wake-promoting pathways following injury (Baumann et al., 2009; Maerlender et al., 2020). These interconnected factors and inconsistencies in communicating the importance of maintaining healthy sleep habits likely not only impair recovery but could also contribute to a cycle of long-term issues (Kureshi, Stowe, Francis, & Djalilian, 2023).

A common research approach to assess post-concussion sleep health involves using various symptom rating scales and questionnaires to evaluate dimensions such as **S**atisfaction with sleep, **A**lertness during waking hours, **T**iming of sleep, sleep **E**fficiency, and sleep **D**uration, together known as **SATED** (Buysse, 2014). As such, studies have consistently found that individuals with a history of concussion report poorer sleep quality, excessive daytime sleepiness, insomnia, and altered sleep duration; with prevalence ranging from 28% to 41% (Gosselin et al., 2009; Pillar et al., 2003; Theadom et al., 2015). Similar reports of sleep disturbances are observed at high rates (~29–72%) during the symptomatic period as well (Chan & Feinstein, 2015; Fisher, Wiseman-Hakes, Obeid, & DeMatteo, 2022; Hoffman, O'Connor, Schmidt, Lynall, & Schmidt, 2019; Howell, Oldham, Brilliant, & Meehan, 2019). Furthermore, prevalence appears to increase with prior concussion history (Blake, McVicar, Retino, Hall, & Ketcham, 2019; Bryan, 2013; Oyegbile, Dougherty, Tanveer, Zecavati, & Delasobera, 2020; Schatz, Moser, Covassin, & Karpf, 2011). These findings indicate that underlying sleep disturbances are inadequately addressed in clinical assessments. There may be several explanations for this oversight. First, inconsistent incorporation of all five SATED dimensions could contribute to ineffective management, as it would overlook the heterogeneity of sleep symptoms, allowing certain sleep-wake disturbances to remain untreated. Additionally, behavioral techniques, medications, and/or supplements (e.g., melatonin) prescribed by the clinician to abate symptoms associated with difficulty sleeping may temporarily alleviate sleep disturbances during the clinical recovery phase, only for these disturbances to resurface upon discontinuation. Whether these interventions continue to alleviate sleep-wake disturbances long-term is currently unknown.

Identifying which long-term sleep complaints are linked to objective changes in sleep-wake behavior is essential for determining necessary additions to clinical assessments and tailoring interventions to effectively address sleep-related issues. However, research utilizing actigraphy, a method for quantifying sleep-wake behavior through movement changes, indicates that longer total sleep time, prolonged nighttime sleep onset latency, and greater wake after sleep onset observed during the symptomatic period do not seem to persist past the typical recovery timeframe (Fisher et al., 2022; Hoffman et al., 2019; Khoury et al., 2013; Maerlender et al., 2020; Raikes & Schaefer, 2016; Stevens, Appleton, Bickley, Holtzhausen, & Adams, 2023). Indeed, individuals with a history of concussion exhibit only slightly lower sleep efficiency (~4%) compared to controls, along with small, inconsistent alterations in total sleep time, sleep onset latency, and wake after sleep onset (Barlow et al., 2020; Kaufman et al., 2001; Williams, Lazic, & Ogilvie, 2008). Multiple sleep latency tests, an objective measure of daytime sleepiness, do reveal quicker daytime sleep onset latency in those with a history of concussion regardless of subjective sleepiness (Imbach et al., 2015, 2016; Schreiber et al., 2008). The absence of objective differences in sleep-wake behavior, coupled with the presence of sleep complaints and increased daytime sleepiness, aligns with the features of nonrestorative sleep (Stone, Taylor, McCrae, Kalsekar, & Lichstein, 2008).

Undoubtedly, a lack of longitudinal research on the subject prevents inference as to whether these sleep-wake disturbances originate due to concussion itself or are exacerbated by other long-term sequelae, such as psycho-affective disturbances (Alvaro, Roberts, & Harris, 2013; Reynolds & Banks, 2010). Unfortunately, the poor alignment between subjective complaints and objective sleep-wake behavior may indicate poor sensitivity in detecting subtle, long-term effects of concussion with the current techniques (Allan et al., 2017; Barlow et al., 2020; Berger, Obeid, Timmons, & DeMatteo, 2017; Lan Chun Yang, Colantonio, & Mollayeva, 2021). As such, delving into the intricacies of the neurophysiological organization and structure of sleep (i.e., sleep architecture) throughout the night may provide a deeper understanding of concussion's long-term impact on sleep-wake processes and neurological function.

Polysomnography (PSG; a comprehensive sleep analysis utilizing EEG, actigraphy, muscle activity, and other physiological parameters) or EEG alone can capture the gradual transition of predominant patterns of sustained oscillatory brain activity and specific EEG events to classify stages and features of sleep architecture (Berry et al., 2015). A number of investigations have begun to utilize such approaches to characterize patterns of sleep architecture related to TBI, with meta-analytic reviews indicating that reduced duration of NREM sleep stage 2 (N2) and increased duration of NREM sleep stage 3 (N3 or slow wave sleep) are observable more than 6 months after moderate to severe TBI (Mantua, Henry, Garskovas, & Spencer, 2017). Although such investigations have generally failed to observe consistent alterations in sleep architecture in individuals with a history of concussion, it is important to note the general paucity of evidence specific to concussion and that much of the literature is plagued by problematically small sample sizes which contribute to inconsistent findings.

Nevertheless, the pattern of sleep architecture observed following injury is consistent with restorative theories of sleep which suggest that the brain preferentially adopts greater time in slow wave sleep to support cellular repair and renewal processes. Synchronous firing of neurons during slow wave sleep is also associated with an influx of glymphatic fluids enlarging the perivascular spaces in the brain, facilitating waste clearance (Hablitz et al., 2020). Recent work has observed the presence of enlarged perivascular spaces in veterans with a history of TBI—including concussion, with their severity (i.e., number and volume) notably correlated with sleep complaints, diminished total sleep time, and reduced NREM sleep (Opel et al., 2019; Piantino et al., 2021). As enlarged perivascular spaces are thought to be a marker of impaired glymphatic clearance contributing to a potentially neurotoxic environment through the accumulation of interstitial solutes and waste; then the alterations in sleep architecture (i.e., greater time spent within slow wave sleep) may be an adaptive response or at least mechanistically linked to such impairments (Opel et al., 2019). Of course, replication is necessary, but exploring these associations may offer deeper insight into the pathogenesis of a variety of long-term consequences following concussion, particularly in relation to neurodegenerative processes.

Refined quantification techniques of sleep EEG enable researchers to examine the duration, frequency, and spatial distribution of oscillatory activities and EEG features within specific sleep stages, known as sleep microarchitecture. Sleep microarchitecture and its distinct features, such as k-complex and sleep spindle density, are thought to play a vital role in cognitive processing and sleep-dependent memory consolidation but have been minimally investigated following concussion (Astori, Wimmer, &

Lüthi, 2013; Cote et al., 2015; Djonlagic et al., 2021). Of the research conducted, individuals with a history of concussion exhibit subtle alterations in beta and delta power during sleep (Arbour et al., 2015; Khoury et al., 2013; Rao, Bergey, Hill, Efron, & McCann, 2011; Mantua, Mahan, Henry, & Spencer, 2015). The conflicting nature of these findings across different brain regions and sleep stages makes it challenging to ascertain whether changes in sleep microarchitecture are inherent to concussion or even linked to its cognitive deficits. The study of long-term effects of concussion on sleep is certainly in its infancy, necessitating extensive replication and further characterization; however, its potential insights into cognition and neurodegenerative disease underscore its importance as a pivotal area of research moving forward.

3.3 Cognition

Prominent dysfunctions with cognitive abilities, difficulty sustaining attention, and exacerbated symptoms associated with cognitive engagement have made the assessment of cognition following concussion a particularly popular area of study (Walton et al., 2022). Individuals with a history of concussion report heightened cognitive symptomology, showing an apparent dose-response relationship (i.e., more concussions sustained result in greater reported dysfunction) (Brooks et al., 2013; Cunningham, Broglio, O'Grady, & Wilson, 2020; Kaye et al., 2019; Register-Mihalik, Mihalik, & Guskiewicz, 2009; Walton et al., 2022). Yet, such cognitive complaints are non-specific and remain poorly characterized (Vynorius, Paquin, & Seichepine, 2016; Weber et al., 2018), making the use of symptom rating scales particularly ineffective for detecting objective cognitive impairment in the presence of more dominant comorbid factors such as elevated psychological distress or fatigue (Brett et al., 2023; Bryant et al., 2023).

To introduce objectivity, commercialized cognitive batteries or select neuropsychological measures are frequently integrated as central components of the clinical evaluation during the acute and subacute periods. The Immediate Post-Concussion Assessment and Cognitive Test (ImPACT) is among the most widely used computerized cognitive battery for concussion evaluation; however, concerns regarding its reliability and sensitivity beyond the acute period are warranted (Bruce, Echemendia, Meeuwisse, Comper, & Sisco, 2014; Kontos, Sufrinko, Womble, & Kegel, 2016). Indeed, extensive research demonstrates that individuals with and without a history of concussion generally perform similarly on the ImPACT and other computerized batteries, regardless of number of prior concussions (Alsalaheen et al., 2017; Broglio, Pontifex, O'Connor, & Hillman, 2009; Brooks et al., 2016; Bruce & Echemendia, 2009; Collie, McCrory, & Makdissi, 2006; Dretsch, Silverberg, & Iverson, 2015; Martini, Eckner, Meehan, & Broglio, 2017; Olson, Brush, Ehmann, Buckman, & Alderman, 2018; Pontifex, O'Connor, Broglio, & Hillman, 2009; Rosenblum et al., 2020; Singh et al., 2014; Tsushima, Geling, Arnold, & Oshiro, 2016). A critical issue in this area is that although such measures provide standardized approaches, they often rely upon a very small number of trials to assess a given cognitive domain. Also, they often assess performance across a wide range of cognitive domains while also suiting individuals with varying cognitive abilities (e.g., 12 years old to 80 years old). As a result, such assessments compromise their ability to detect more subtle changes in performance in favor of identifying gross-level differences. Indeed, evidence indicates that the ImPACT fails to detect well-established diurnal variation in cognitive performance (Anderson, Elbin, Schatz, Henry, & Covassin, 2021). Despite their widespread popularity and adoption, it is important to acknowledge that it is unclear if such computerized cognitive batteries provide utility for clinical decision-making beyond detecting egregious performance degradation—which likely could be detected by clinical staff without such assessments, raising questions about their comparative value against cheaper and less burdensome symptom rating scales.

Such null findings within individuals with a history of concussion seem to extend to many traditional neuropsychological assessments as well (Bruce & Echemendia, 2009; Clough et al., 2018; Cunningham et al., 2020; De Beaumont, Brisson, Lassonde, & Jolicoeur, 2007; De Souza et al., 2021). While Moore and colleagues have identified that some standardized neuropsychological tests (e.g., Raven's Coloured Progressive Matrices, Wide Range Achievement Test-3, and Comprehensive Trail Making Test—trials requiring interference control) may be sensitive enough to detect cognitive alterations in children with a history of concussion (Moore et al., 2019), even these measures produce mixed findings (Little et al., 2016; Moser, Schatz, & Jordan, 2005). Importantly, domain-specific alterations across these studies demonstrate that higher-order cognitive processes such as executive control appear most likely to manifest with residual impairments associated with a history of concussion (Cunningham et al., 2020).

In particular, a number of investigations have detected persistent impairments associated with concussion across classic domains of executive control. Specifically, impairments in inhibitory control (De Beaumont et al., 2009; Ellemberg, Leclerc, Couture, & Daigle, 2007; McGowan et al., 2019; Moore, Hillman, & Broglio, 2014; Moore et al., 2015; Ornstein, Haden, & Hedrick, 2004; Parks et al., 2015; Pontifex et al., 2009; Pontifex et al., 2012), working memory (Elbin et al., 2012; Hudac, Cortesa, Ledwidge, & Molfese, 2018; Ozen, Itier, Preston, & Fernandes, 2013; Sicard & Moore, 2022; Sicard, Moore, & Ellemberg, 2018; Sicard, Moore, & Ellemberg, 2019), and cognitive flexibility (McGowan et al., 2018; Redlinger, Sicard, Caron, & Ellemberg, 2022) have been observed months to years following injury. However, it is important to note that despite these findings' relative consistency, if the task is not carefully considered, even assessments of these domains of executive control may fail to detect these persistent cognitive deficits. Interestingly, two perspectives have been put forward in this regard to explain why utilization of a particular task might be sensitive while other similar tasks might fail to detect differences. Simply put, tasks which are not sufficiently difficult may enable the use of alternative strategies, processes, and even neural degeneracy to compensate for underlying cognitive difficulty (Parks et al., 2015). As a result, performance in an impaired individual is indistinguishable from that of a healthy individual. Tasks which require lower-order cognitive operations and tasks which are not adequately calibrated to avoid ceiling effects (performance at or near perfect/maximal levels) are unlikely to provide utility in understanding the long-term effects of concussion. While tasks that are inherently more effortful—such as executive control tasks—serve to tax neural resources fundamentally limiting the extent to which compensatory processing could suitably mask residual impairments in cognition; such tasks can also fail to observe effects if they are not sufficiently challenging for the population. This concept makes it difficult to implement measures of executive control within clinical batteries as tasks must be tailored to the population of interest. Critically, within the present literature and diagnostic battery approach, assessments of executive control often neglect such tailoring in favor of adopting a one-size fits all approach.

Alternatively, the failure of some executive control tasks to detect persistent impairments associated with concussion may be the result of the extent to which the task relies upon visuospatial attention (McGowan et al., 2018). Tasks such as the flanker task, attentional network task, spatial working memory tasks, and perceptually based cognitive flexibility tasks all rely upon intact visuospatial attention and are those tasks most commonly utilized within investigations observing long-term impairments; whereas tasks such as the Stroop task, serial working memory tasks, and rule-based cognitive flexibility tasks—tasks which tap the same underlying aspects of cognition without being dependent upon visuospatial attention—have been observed to fail to detect residual impairments beyond the acute phase of concussion (McGowan et al., 2018). Accordingly, it is critically important to consider not just the overall domain of cognition being assessed, but also to consider the way in which the assessment is tapping that domain. Such an idea is not mutually exclusive with consideration of cognitive difficulty and sensitivity; but rather these perspectives align to reflect important aspects of the way assessments are designed that may impact upon their utility in this area of research.

Beyond the assessment of overt behavioral performance, event-related brain potentials (ERPs) offer insight into covert cognitive operations which appear sensitive to the long-term effects of concussion. The vast majority of research in this area has focused upon the P3 (also known as the P300 or P3b), which provides a neural index of the allocation of attentional resources during stimulus engagement (i.e., P3 amplitude) and stimulus classification and processing speed (i.e., P3 latency). Even when behavioral performance is equivalent between individuals with and without a history of concussion, studies consistently find that persistent reductions in the allocation of attentional resources, as indexed by decreased P3 amplitude (Baillargeon, Lassonde, Leclerc, & Ellemberg, 2012; Broglio et al., 2009; De Beaumont et al., 2007, 2009; Dupuis, Johnston, Lavoie, Lepore, & Lassonde, 2000; Gosselin, Theriault, Leclerc, Montplaisier, & Lassonde, 2006; Gosselin et al., 2012; Lavoie, Dupuis, Johnston, Leclerc, & Lassonde, 2004; Moore et al., 2014, 2015, 2016; Ozen et al., 2013; Parks et al., 2015; Theriault, de Beaumont, Gosselin, Filipinni, & Lassonde, 2009), and delays in stimulus classification and processing speed, as indexed by P3 latency (De Beaumont et al., 2009; Gaetz, Goodman, & Weinberg, 2000; Gosselin et al., 2006; Ledwidge & Molfese, 2016), are apparent even years post-injury. Within a four-year longitudinal design, Clayton and colleagues observed that alterations in P3 amplitude were most dramatic during the acute phase of concussion and gradually diminished during the graded return-to-activity phase. Interestingly however, not only were alterations in the P3 still apparent when behavioral patterns had returned to pre-injury levels; but those individuals who failed to show normalization of the amplitude of the P3 following injury were also more likely to exhibit persistent symptomatology and were more prone to repeated concussions (Clayton et al., 2020).

Another prominent ERP component of interest is the error related negativity (ERN) which provides a neural index of action-monitoring processes signaling the need for further control (Falkenstein, Hohnsbein, Hoormann, & Blanke, 1991; Gehring, Goss, Coles, Meyer, & Donchin, 1993; Miltner et al., 2003). However, there is a paucity of investigations assessing this component within concussed individuals, and the studies that have been conducted present conflicting findings. While some evidence appears to indicate that persistent reductions in action monitoring as indexed by smaller ERN amplitude are apparent even years following a concussion (De Beaumont, Beauchemin, Beaulieu, & Jolicoeur, 2013; Moore et al., 2015; Pontifex et al., 2009), other findings have failed to observe any relationship (Larson, Clayson, & Farrer, 2012), or have observed greater action monitoring as indexed by larger ERN amplitude for individuals with a history of concussion (Olson et al., 2018). Although it is unclear what methodological differences in studies may have contributed to such discrepant findings, it is important to acknowledge that the ERN component has been observed to be particularly alterable in response to strategic initiatives. Thus, even minor alterations in instruction (e.g., emphasizing speed vs accuracy) and adaptative strategic control (e.g., proactive vs reactive control) can drastically alter how this component may manifest. Nevertheless, future investigation may benefit by assessing the extent to which this ERP component may exhibit diminished modulation in response to such goal representations in individuals with a history of concussion.

Although ERPs such as the P3 component appear particularly sensitive to the residual effects of a concussion, a critical question that has yet to be resolved is to what extent this information is clinically relevant. As articulated by Clayton and colleagues (2020), absent any other behavioral or symptom manifestation, should altered P3 amplitude be sufficient cause to delay returning an individual to work/play contexts? Arguably, at present there is little compelling evidence for such a perspective given the relative dearth of longitudinal evidence. However, as the ERP approach enables assessment of neural processes underlying our behavioral interactions with the environment, there may well be key relationships such as risk of subsequent reinjury or neurodegenerative implications that warrant careful consideration in such discussions.

3.4 Motor performance

Gross deficits in motor control (e.g., balance and gait difficulties, motor incoordination, and ataxia) are among the most immediate signs and quickest resolving symptoms of a concussion (Guskiewicz, Ross, & Marshall, 2001; Patricios, Schneider, et al., 2023). While recent efforts have been made to enhance the clinical assessment of motor control following concussion, these assessments remain focused on identifying prominent balance and gait impairments and evaluating closely related sensory and vestibular dysfunction (Echemendia, Brett, et al., 2023; Mucha et al., 2014; Patricios, Schneider, et al., 2023). Given that many guidelines are oriented toward returning athletes or military personnel to their pre-injury performance levels with minimal risk of re-injury, healthcare practitioners are tasked with ensuring that patients can maintain sufficient motor performance during both physical and cognitive exertion throughout the return-to-activity phase (Patricios, Schneider, et al., 2023). Yet, evidence of an elevated risk of injury among individuals with a history of concussion would indicate that current practices are inadequate in identifying more subtle, persistent motor deficits (Gardner et al., 2024; McPherson, Nagai, Webster, & Hewett, 2019; Reneker et al., 2019; Wilkerson et al., 2021, 2024); and unfortunately, there is a dearth of literature in this area.

Of the research available, dynamic stability and gait parameters are the most well-studied and have been shown to be altered well beyond clinical recovery (Baker & Cinelli, 2014; Fino, Nussbaum, & Brolinson, 2016; Martini et al., 2011; Sosnoff, Broglio, Shin, & Ferrara, 2011). Although these findings provide valuable insight into long-term motor control after concussion, the clinical relevance of the complex measures needed to produce consistent findings (e.g., center of mass parameters and non-linear dynamics)—while promising (Chou et al., 2023; Johnston et al., 2019)—requires further investigation. Recent studies, utilizing tasks that more closely resemble the movement demands of sport (i.e., jump cut maneuvers and drop-landing maneuvers), observe distinct biomechanical patterns associated with a greater risk of lower extremity injury in individuals with a history of concussion (DuBose et al., 2017; Lapointe et al., 2018; Avedesian, Covassin, & Dufek, 2020). Although such tasks require advanced techniques, they could be particularly useful in clinical settings and additional research aimed at developing tasks that mimic the specific movement demands of various patient populations would further enhance their utility.

One hypothesis as to why traditional clinical tasks may fail to detect persistent motor control deficits is that concussed individuals can compensate for compromised neural efficiency when tasks impose little demand on the motor system. Indeed, dual gait tasks requiring divided attention and those necessitating cognitive-motor integration are more likely to elicit observable motor control impairments in individuals with a history of concussion (Brown, Dalecki, Hughes, Macpherson, & Sergio, 2015; Howell, Beasley, Vopat, & Meehan, 2017; Howell, Osternig, & Chou, 2018; Howell et al., 2020; Hurtubise, Gorbet, Hamandi, Macpherson, & Sergio, 2016; Ketcham et al., 2019; Lapointe et al., 2018). In an effort to detect these alterations earlier in recovery, the SCAT-6 and SCOAT-6 have recently added a timed tandem gait task, as well as optional complex tandem gait and dual tasks, into their assessment batteries (Echemendia, Brett, et al., 2023; Patricios, Davis, et al., 2023). At present, it remains too early to determine whether the incorporation of these tools in their current form will lead to extended recovery times or even impose sufficient demand to capture more subtle motor control deficits. Additional longitudinal research will provide an opportunity to integrate higher-order measures of motor control into clinical settings and return-to-activity protocols. While this research will be crucial for understanding the chronicity and breadth of behavioral alterations in motor control following concussion, it lacks the ability to probe neurophysiological etiology.

Transcranial Magnetic Stimulation (TMS) is a unique neurophysiological approach to motor assessment that has greatly enhanced our understanding of the functional alterations within and between the primary motor cortices following concussion. While TMS is primarily known for its versatile therapeutic applications as non-invasive brain modulation technique, it is also capable of providing reliable measures of corticomotor function by assessing muscle activity in response to stimulation of the primary motor cortex (Lefaucheur, 2019). As such, TMS research has greatly enhanced our understanding of the functional alterations within and between the primary motor cortices following concussion. Such evidence has generally failed to observe any differences in the excitability of corticomotor pathways after injury (Davidson & Tremblay, 2016; King et al., 2019; Pauhl, Yasen, & Christie, 2022; Pearce et al., 2015; Pearce, Rist, Fraser, Cohen, & Maller, 2018; Stokes et al., 2020). That is, when a single TMS pulse is applied, the magnitude of responses to proportionally identical intensities and the minimum intensity needed to elicit a muscular response are comparable between previously concussed individuals and their healthy counterparts. However, a relatively consistent feature in individuals with a history of concussion is prolonged duration of the corticospinal silent period (cSP; i.e., the succeeding, brief interruption in muscle activity opposite the stimulated hemisphere), which indicates increased intracortical inhibition (De Beaumont et al., 2009, 2011; King et al., 2019; Pearce et al., 2018; Tremblay, de Beaumont, Lassonde, & Théoret, 2011). Interestingly, when concussed individuals are symptomatic such alterations are not consistently observed (Pauhl et al., 2022; Pearce et al., 2015; Schmidt et al., 2021; Seeger et al., 2017).

Paired-pulse paradigms, which use two TMS pulses delivered at set intervals to the same location, help confirm these findings while offering a more nuanced view. Specifically, short- (2–3 ms) and long-interval (~100 ms) paradigms index different intracortical inhibitory mechanisms mediated by γ-aminobutyric acid (GABA) type A and B receptor activity, respectively (Sanger, Garg, & Chen, 2001). With the exception of a few studies conducted with PCS patients (Pearce, Tommerdahl, & King, 2019; Pearce et al., 2021), null findings in short-interval paradigms are quite common following concussion (Lewis, Hume, Stavric, Brown, & Taylor, 2017; Meehan, Mirdamadi, Martini, & Broglio, 2017; Pearce et al., 2015; Schmidt et al., 2021; Seeger et al., 2017). In contrast, long-interval paradigms demonstrate a similar pattern to cSP findings—both mediated by GABA type B receptor activity—whereby enhanced intracortical inhibition is exhibited in individuals with a history of concussion but not in earlier, more symptomatic periods (De Beaumont, Tremblay, Poirier, Lassonde, & Théoret, 2012; Lewis, Hume, Stavric, Brown, & Taylor, 2017; Pearce et al., 2015; Pearce, Rist, Fraser, Cohen, & Maller, 2018; Powers, Cinelli, & Kalmar, 2014; Tremblay, de Beaumont, Lassonde, & Théoret, 2011). While it is possible these results reflect a delayed manifestation of corticomotor effects, pathophysiological factors associated with clinical symptomology may instead have a masking effect, inhibiting consistent observation in recently concussed individuals and those with PCS (King et al., 2019; Pearce et al., 2020). Unfortunately, research early after concussion is fairly limited, as TMS can be particularly challenging for reliable clinical use due to its sensitivity to inter-individual variability and nuances in technique. More consistent deviations are evident in those with a history of multiple concussions and older individuals—or are at least more challenging to capture in youth—indicating that these effects may also be cumulative and impacted by age-related changes in neural reserve (De Beaumont et al., 2011; Stokes et al., 2020).

Inhibitory modulation does not appear to be confined to intracortical pathways either. Limited yet consistent findings reveal that interhemispheric processes are functionally altered in individuals with a history of concussion, as they display prolonged transcallosal conduction time (i.e., duration for neural signals to propagate from the stimulated hemisphere across the corpus callosum to the opposite hemisphere) and reduced duration of the ipsilateral silent period (iSP; i.e., the succeeding, brief interruption in muscle activity on the same side of the stimulated hemisphere) (Davidson & Tremblay, 2016; King et al., 2019; Locke et al., 2020; Schmidt et al., 2021). Such findings may be unsurprising given the existing evidence of long-term microstructural alterations in the corpus callosum (Churchill et al., 2017a; Churchill, Caverzasi, Graham, Hutchison, & Schweizer, 2017b; Dean, Sato, Vieira, McNamara, & Sterr, 2015; Henry et al., 2011), but together suggest that transcallosal integrity is compromised both structurally and functionally in the long-term following concussion.

The extant TMS literature provides convincing evidence that enhanced GABAergic activity, particularly linked to type B receptor activity within the primary motor cortex, as well as inefficiencies in interhemispheric communication, are long-term effects of concussion. Yet, further investigations are required to determine whether these effects truly impair interrelated behaviors or simply represent compensatory mechanisms. Indeed, some studies note correlations among corticomotor metrics, task kinematics, and reaction time following concussion (De Beaumont et al., 2009; Pearce et al., 2015, 2020; Schmidt et al., 2021). However, their potential associations with motor control, motor learning, and bimanual or gait coordination (Fling & Seidler, 2012; Paci, Di Cosmo, Perrucci, Ferri, & Costantini, 2021; Sarwary, Wischnewski, Schutter, Selen, & Medendorp, 2018; Swanson & Fling, 2018), particularly in the context of increased injury risk, have not been examined. While this may seem to reiterate our calls for inquiry into the relationship between underlying physiological alterations and measurable behavioral outcomes, it is important to note that TMS techniques are uniquely capable of answering such research questions while also offering therapeutic applications as a neuromodulation tool, broadening its potential for use in our field.

4. Conclusion

This chapter highlights a clear misalignment between the clinical perception of concussion transience and the chronicity of its effects as documented in the current literature. The field is familiar with translational lapses between research, clinical, and public perception. However, in this case, we posit that such misalignment likely stems from the poor sensitivity of traditional clinical measures in detecting subtle, long-term alterations following concussion. While we have reviewed studies on four important symptom domains, it's essential to acknowledge that long-term functional alterations extend beyond these domains and the techniques discussed herein. Indeed, a number of neuroimaging techniques (e.g., diffusion tensor imaging, magnetic resonance imaging, positron emission tomography, etc.), which were not covered in the current review, have also demonstrated sensitivity to persistent changes in individuals with a history of concussion (Henry, Elbin, Collins, Marchetti, & Kontos, 2016; Manley et al., 2017). While neurophysiological techniques are undoubtedly valuable from a research perspective for identifying the underlying pathophysiological consequences of concussion, they lack the standardization required for clinical decision-making. Furthermore, positive neurophysiological findings following concussion are often presented without any associated behavioral or symptomatic manifestations, rendering them clinically irrelevant within the current treatment approach.

One possible explanation for these seemingly inconsistent findings could be that the brain compensates for neurological inefficiencies following concussion, similar to how we compensate for declining cognitive efficiency as we reach older age (Reuter-Lorenz & Cappell, 2008). That is, the brain has the ability, through physical and functional redundancies which constitute an individual's reserve capacity (Stern, 2002), to reorganize or recruit alternate neural resources in response to brain damage, utilizing additional resources that might not typically be engaged to meet task demands. In many cases, neural compensation does not result in any behavioral alterations, and performance is maintained as it would be in a non-concussed individual. However, in situations where task demands require the recruitment of a sufficiently damaged network (e.g., the fronto-executive network) or need to be completed under resource-demanding conditions (e.g., high-intensity exercise, sleep deprivation, increased states of anxiety, or divided attention tasks), behavioral alterations and performance deficits can manifest (Ledwidge & Molfese, 2016; Sicard, Caron, Moore, & Ellemberg, 2021). This "Reorganization/Compensation" hypothesis explains why older adults often exhibit more frequent long-term effects of concussion compared to younger individuals. As age-related neurodegeneration advances, older adults with a history of concussion must compensate not only for the neural inefficiencies caused by the concussion but also those associated with aging. The inclusion of adolescent or young adult samples in many reviewed studies may mask long-term behavioral alterations due to concussion, given their enhanced reserve capacity. Similarly, it explains why individuals with a history of multiple concussions may show a higher likelihood of long-term behavioral alterations. With each additional concussion, their reserve capacity diminishes, leaving fewer resources available for compensation. Examining the long-term effects of concussion under this model of reserve capacity can help us understand the conditions, tasks, and populations in which a history of concussion is most likely to result in clinically significant functional alterations. Nonetheless, the absence of clear causative indicators linking concussion directly to these long-term effects suggests that neurophysiological techniques may not be immediately necessary outside of research settings.

While the chapter does not cover the entire breadth of existing literature on concussion's long-term effects, it effectively underscores the importance of further investigation before considering significant changes to clinical concussion management. Yet, given the significant public fear surrounding the long-term effects of concussion and the imperative to address patients' desire for symptom relief regardless of the burden imposed, there may be a case for incorporating more sensitive techniques into clinical assessment as a supplemental tool or within targeted interventions as the outcome of interest. Such an approach would enable a more nuanced understanding of the chronicity of concussion effects, prompting a shift from symptom abatement to the implementation of more targeted treatments. The evidence of long-term effects following concussion is convincing, however, moving forward it is crucial to acknowledge the limitations inherent in defining causality, potential selection biases, and the challenge of disentangling effects directly caused by concussion from contaminate effects of other long-term sequelae. We encourage our readers to continue pursuing research avenues related to the long-term effects of concussion within their respective specialties, striving to illuminate this topic through rigorous investigation.

References

Allan, A. C., Edmed, S. L., Sullivan, K. A., Karlsson, L. J. E., Lange, R. T., & Smith, S. S. (2017). Actigraphically measured sleep-wake behavior after mild traumatic brain injury: A case-control study. *The Journal of Head Trauma Rehabilitation, 32*(2), E35. https://doi.org/10.1097/HTR.0000000000000222.

Alsalaheen, B., Stockdale, K., Pechumer, D., & Broglio, S. P. (2016). Validity of the immediate post concussion assessment and cognitive testing (ImPACT). *Sports Medicine, 46*(10), 1487–1501. https://doi.org/10.1007/s40279-016-0532-y.

Alsalaheen, B., Stockdale, K., Pechumer, D., Giessing, A., He, X., & Broglio, S. P. (2017). Cumulative effects of concussion history on baseline computerized neurocognitive test scores: Systematic review and meta-analysis. *Sports Health, 9*(4), 324–332. https://doi.org/10.1177/1941738117713974.

Alvaro, P. K., Roberts, R. M., & Harris, J. K. (2013). A systematic review assessing bidirectionality between sleep disturbances, anxiety, and depression. *Sleep, 36*(7), 1059–1068. https://doi.org/10.5665/sleep.2810.

Anderson, M., Elbin, R. J., Schatz, P., Henry, L., & Covassin, T. (2021). Comparing before- and after-school neurocognitive performance in high school athletes: Implications for concussion management. *Clinical Journal of Sport Medicine, 31*(1), 31. https://doi.org/10.1097/JSM.0000000000000685.

Arbour, C., Khoury, S., Lavigne, G. J., Gagnon, K., Poirier, G., Montplaisir, J. Y., ... Gosselin, N. (2015). Are NREM sleep characteristics associated to subjective sleep complaints after mild traumatic brain injury? *Sleep Medicine, 16*(4), 534–539. https://doi.org/10.1016/j.sleep.2014.12.002.

Asken, B. M., Snyder, A. R., Smith, M. S., Zaremski, J. L., & Bauer, R. M. (2017). Concussion-like symptom reporting in non-concussed adolescent athletes. *The Clinical Neuropsychologist, 31*(1), 138–153. https://doi.org/10.1080/13854046.2016.1246672.

Astori, S., Wimmer, R. D., & Lüthi, A. (2013). Manipulating sleep spindles—Expanding views on sleep, memory, and disease. *Trends in Neurosciences, 36*(12), 738–748. https://doi.org/10.1016/j.tins.2013.10.001.

Avedesian, J. M., Covassin, T., & Dufek, J. S. (2020). Landing biomechanics in adolescent athletes with and without a history of sports-related concussion. *Journal of Applied Biomechanics, 36*(5), 313–318. https://doi.org/10.1123/jab.2020-0034.

Baillargeon, A., Lassonde, M., Leclerc, S., & Ellemberg, D. (2012). Neuropsychological and neurophysiological assessment of sport concussion in children, adolescents and adults. *Brain Injury, 26*(3), 211–220. https://doi.org/10.3109/02699052.2012.654590.

Baker, C. S., & Cinelli, M. E. (2014). Visuomotor deficits during locomotion in previously concussed athletes 30 or more days following return to play. *Physiological Reports, 2*(12), e12252. https://doi.org/10.14814/phy2.12252.

Barlow, K. M. (2016). Postconcussion syndrome: A review. *Journal of Child Neurology, 31*(1), 57–67. https://doi.org/10.1177/0883073814543305.

Barlow, K. M., Girgulis, K. A., Goldstein, G., Crowe, E. G., Vo, M. K., Su, P., ... Kirk, V. G. (2020). Sleep parameters and overnight urinary melatonin production in children with persistent post-concussion symptoms. *Pediatric Neurology, 105*, 27–34. https://doi.org/10.1016/j.pediatrneurol.2019.11.006.

Barr, W. B. (2020). Believers versus deniers: The radicalization of sports concussion and chronic traumatic encephalopathy (CTE) science. *Canadian Psychology, 61*(2), 151–162. https://doi.org/10.1037/cap0000210.

Baugh, C. M., Kroshus, E., Kiernan, P. T., Mendel, D., & Meehan, W. P. (2017). Football players' perceptions of future risk of concussion and concussion-related health outcomes. *Journal of Neurotrauma, 34*(4), 790–797. https://doi.org/10.1089/neu.2016.4585.

Baumann, C. R., Bassetti, C. L., Valko, P. O., Haybaeck, J., Keller, M., Clark, E., ... Scammell, T. E. (2009). Loss of hypocretin (orexin) neurons with traumatic brain injury. *Annals of Neurology, 66*(4), 555–559. https://doi.org/10.1002/ana.21836.

Beidler, E., Donnellan, M. B., Kontos, A., Pontifex, M., Nogle, S., & Covassin, T. (2021). The relationship between impulsivity, sensation seeking, and concussion history in collegiate student-athletes. *Athletic Training & Sports Health Care, 13*(6), e402–e412. https://doi.org/10.3928/19425864-20210519-01.

Berger, I., Obeid, J., Timmons, B. W., & DeMatteo, C. (2017). Exploring accelerometer versus self-report sleep assessment in youth with concussion. *Global Pediatric Health, 4*. https://doi.org/10.1177/2333794X17745973.

Berry, R. B., Brooks, R., Gamaldo, C. E., Harding, S. M., Lloyd, R. M., Marcus, C. L., & Vaughn, B. V. (2015). *The AASM manual for the scoring of sleep and associated events: Rules, terminology and technical specifications, version 2.2.* American Academy of Sleep Medicine.

Blake, A. L., McVicar, C. L., Retino, M., Hall, E. E., & Ketcham, C. J. (2019). Concussion history influences sleep disturbances, symptoms, and quality of life in collegiate student-athletes. *Sleep Health, 5*(1), 72–77. https://doi.org/10.1016/j.sleh.2018.10.011.

Bohr, A. D., Boardman, J. D., & McQueen, M. B. (2019). Association of adolescent sport participation with cognition and depressive symptoms in early adulthood. 2325967119868658 *Orthopaedic Journal of Sports Medicine,* 7(9), https://doi.org/10.1177/2325967119868658.

Brett, B. L., Kerr, Z. Y., Chandran, A., Walton, S., Aggarwal, N. T., Gifford, K., ... McCrea, M. A. (2023). A dominance analysis of subjective cognitive complaint comorbidities in former professional football players with and without mild cognitive impairment. *Journal of the International Neuropsychological Society, 29*(6), 582–593. https://doi.org/10.1017/S135561772200056X.

Brett, B. L., Kerr, Z. Y., Walton, S. R., Chandran, A., Defreese, J. D., Mannix, R., ... McCrea, M. (2022). Longitudinal trajectory of depression symptom severity and the influence of concussion history and physical function over a 19-year period among former National Football League (NFL) players: An NFL-LONG study. *Journal of Neurology, Neurosurgery & Psychiatry, 93*(3), 272–279. https://doi.org/10.1136/jnnp-2021-326602.

Brett, B. L., Nelson, L. D., & Meier, T. B. (2022). The association between concussion history and increased symptom severity reporting is independent of common medical comorbidities, personality factors, and sleep quality in collegiate athletes. *The Journal of Head Trauma Rehabilitation, 37*(4), E258. https://doi.org/10.1097/HTR.0000000000000724.

Broglio, S. P., Pontifex, M. B., O'Connor, P., & Hillman, C. H. (2009). The persistent effects of concussion on neuroelectric indices of attention. *Journal of Neurotrauma, 26*(9), 1463–1470. https://doi.org/10.1089/neu.2008.0766.

Broglio, S. P., Register-Mihalik, J. K., Guskiewicz, K. M., Leddy, J. J., Merriman, A., & Valovich McLeod, T. C. (2024). National athletic trainers' association bridge statement: Management of sport-related concussion. *Journal of Athletic Training, 59*(3), 225–242. https://doi.org/10.4085/1062-6050-0046.22.

Brooks, B. L., Mannix, R., Maxwell, B., Zafonte, R., Berkner, P. D., & Iverson, G. L. (2016). Multiple past concussions in high school football players: Are there differences in cognitive functioning and symptom reporting? *The American Journal of Sports Medicine, 44*(12), 3243–3251. https://doi.org/10.1177/0363546516655095.

Brooks, B. L., McKay, C. D., Mrazik, M., Barlow, K. M., Meeuwisse, W. H., & Emery, C. A. (2013). Subjective, but not objective, lingering effects of multiple past concussions in adolescents. *Journal of Neurotrauma, 30*(17), 1469–1475. https://doi.org/10.1089/neu.2012.2720.

Broshek, D. K., De Marco, A. P., & Freeman, J. R. (2015). A review of post-concussion syndrome and psychological factors associated with concussion. *Brain Injury, 29*(2), 228–237. https://doi.org/10.3109/02699052.2014.974674.

Brown, J. A., Dalecki, M., Hughes, C., Macpherson, A. K., & Sergio, L. E. (2015). Cognitive-motor integration deficits in young adult athletes following concussion. *BMC Sports Science, Medicine and Rehabilitation,* 7(1), 25. https://doi.org/10.1186/s13102-015-0019-4.

Bruce, J., Echemendia, R., Meeuwisse, W., Comper, P., & Sisco, A. (2014). 1 year test–retest reliability of ImPACT in professional ice hockey players. *The Clinical Neuropsychologist, 28*(1), 14–25. https://doi.org/10.1080/13854046.2013.866272.

Bruce, J. M., & Echemendia, R. J. (2009). History of multiple self-reported concussions is not associated with reduced cogntiive abilities. *Neurosurgery, 64*(1), 100. https://doi.org/10.1227/01.NEU.0000336310.47513.C8.

Bryan, C. J. (2013). Repetitive traumatic brain injury (or concussion) increases severity of sleep disturbance among deployed military personnel. *Sleep, 36*(6), 941–946. https://doi.org/10.5665/sleep.2730.

Bryant, A. M., Kerr, Z. Y., Walton, S. R., Barr, W. B., Guskiewicz, K. M., McCrea, M. A., & Brett, B. L. (2023). Investigating the association between subjective and objective performance-based cognitive function among former collegiate football players. *The Clinical Neuropsychologist, 37*(3), 595–616. https://doi.org/10.1080/13854046.2022.2083021.

Buckley, T. A., Munkasy, B. A., & Clouse, B. P. (2018). Sensitivity and specificity of the modified balance error scoring system in concussed collegiate student athletes. *Clinical Journal of Sport Medicine, 28*(2), 174. https://doi.org/10.1097/JSM.0000000000000426.

Bullard, L. E., Coffman, C. A., Kay, J. J. M., Holloway, J. P., Moore, R. D., & Pontifex, M. B. (2022). Attention-deficit/hyperactivity disorder-related self-reported symptoms are associated with elevated concussion symptomatology. *Journal of Sport and Exercise Psychology, 1*(aop), 1–11. https://doi.org/10.1123/jsep.2021-0225.

Burns, C., Jo, J., Williams, K., Davis, P., Amedy, A., Anesi, T. J., ... Zuckerman, S. L. (2024). Subclinical, long-term psychological symptoms following sport-related concussion: Are athletes more depressed than we think? *Brain Injury, 38*(8), 637–644. https://doi.org/10.1080/02699052.2024.2334352.

Buysse, D. J. (2014). Sleep health: Can we define it? Does it matter? *Sleep, 37*(1), 9–17. https://doi.org/10.5665/sleep.3298.

Carson, A. (2017). Concussion, dementia and CTE: Are we getting it very wrong? *Journal of Neurology, Neurosurgery & Psychiatry, 88*(6), 462–464. https://doi.org/10.1136/jnnp-2016-315510.

Cassidy, J. D., Carroll, L., Peloso, P., Borg, J., Von Holst, H., Holm, L., ... Coronado, V. (2004). Incidence, risk factors and prevention of mild traumatic brain injury: Results of the who collaborating centre task force on mild traumatic brain injury. *Journal of Rehabilitation Medicine, 36*(0), 28–60. https://doi.org/10.1080/16501960410023732.

Chan, L. G., & Feinstein, A. (2015). Persistent sleep disturbances independently predict poorer functional and social outcomes 1 year after mild traumatic brain injury. *The Journal of Head Trauma Rehabilitation, 30*(6), E67. https://doi.org/10.1097/HTR.0000000000000119.

Chen, H., Richard, M., Sandler, D. P., Umbach, D. M., & Kamel, F. (2007). Head injury and amyotrophic lateral sclerosis. *American Journal of Epidemiology, 166*(7), 810–816. https://doi.org/10.1093/aje/kwm153.

Chou, T.-Y., Huang, Y.-L., Leung, W., Brown, C. N., Kaminski, T. W., & Norcross, M. F. (2023). Does prior concussion lead to biomechanical alterations associated with lateral ankle sprain and anterior cruciate ligament injury? A systematic review and meta-analysis. *British Journal of Sports Medicine, 57*(23), 1509–1515. https://doi.org/10.1136/bjsports-2023-106980.

Chrisman, S. P. D., & Richardson, L. P. (2014). Prevalence of diagnosed depression in adolescents with history of concussion. *Journal of Adolescent Health, 54*(5), 582–586. https://doi.org/10.1016/j.jadohealth.2013.10.006.

Churchill, N. W., Caverzasi, E., Graham, S. J., Hutchison, M. G., & Schweizer, T. A. (2017b). White matter microstructure in athletes with a history of concussion: Comparing diffusion tensor imaging (DTI) and neurite orientation dispersion and density imaging (NODDI). *Human Brain Mapping, 38*(8), 4201–4211. https://doi.org/10.1002/hbm.23658.

Churchill, N., Hutchison, M., Richards, D., Leung, G., Graham, S., & Schweizer, T. A. (2017a). Brain structure and function associated with a history of sport concussion: A multi-modal magnetic resonance imaging study. *Journal of Neurotrauma, 34*(4), 765–771. https://doi.org/10.1089/neu.2016.4531.

Clayton, G., Davis, N., Holliday, A., Joffe, D., Oakley, D. S., Palermo, F. X., ... Rueda, M. (2020). In-clinic event related potentials after sports concussion: A 4-year study. *Journal of Pediatric Rehabilitation Medicine, 13*(1), 81–92. https://doi.org/10.3233/PRM-190620.

Clough, M., Mutimer, S., Wright, D. K., Tsang, A., Costello, D. M., Gardner, A. J., ... Shultz, S. R. (2018). Oculomotor cognitive control abnormalities in Australian rules football players with a history of concussion. *Journal of Neurotrauma, 35*(5), 730–738. https://doi.org/10.1089/neu.2017.5204.

Coffman, C. A., Gunn, B. S., Pasquina, P. F., McCrea, M. A., McAllister, T. W., Broglio, S. P., ... Pontifex, M. B. (2023). Concussion risk and recovery in athletes with psychostimulant-treated attention-deficit/hyperactivity disorder: Findings from the NCAA-DOD CARE consortium. *Journal of Sport and Exercise Psychology, 45*(6), 337–346. https://doi.org/10.1123/jsep.2023-0038.

Collie, A., McCrory, P., & Makdissi, M. (2006). Does history of concussion affect current cognitive status? *British Journal of Sports Medicine, 40*(6), 550–551. https://doi.org/10.1136/bjsm.2005.019802.

Collins, M. W., Kontos, A. P., Reynolds, E., Murawski, C. D., & Fu, F. H. (2014). A comprehensive, targeted approach to the clinical care of athletes following sport-related concussion. *Knee Surgery, Sports Traumatology, Arthroscopy, 22*(2), 235–246. https://doi.org/10.1007/s00167-013-2791-6.

Cote, K. A., Milner, C. E., Speth, T. A., Cote, K. A., Milner, C. E., & Speth, T. A. (2015). Altered sleep mechanisms following traumatic brain injury and relation to waking function. *AIMS Neuroscience, 2*(4), 203–228. https://doi.org/10.3934/Neuroscience.2015.4.203.

Covassin, T., Zynda, A. J., Loftin, M. C., Pollard-McGrandy, A. M., Tracey, A. J., & Tomczyk, C. P. (2023). Changes in state and trait anxiety throughout concussion recovery in high school and college-aged individuals. *Journal of Athletic Training*. https://doi.org/10.4085/1062-6050-0536.22.

Crawford, S., Wenden, F. J., & Wade, D. T. (1996). The Rivermead head injury follow up questionnaire: A study of a new rating scale and other measures to evaluate outcome after head injury. *Journal of Neurology, Neurosurgery & Psychiatry, 60*(5), 510–514. https://doi.org/10.1136/jnnp.60.5.510.

Crowe, L. M., Hearps, S., Anderson, V., Borland, M. L., Phillips, N., Kochar, A., ... Babl, F. E. (2018). Investigating the variability in mild traumatic brain injury definitions: A prospective cohort study. *Archives of Physical Medicine and Rehabilitation, 99*(7), 1360–1369. https://doi.org/10.1016/j.apmr.2017.12.026.

Cunningham, J., Broglio, S. P., O'Grady, M., & Wilson, F. (2020). History of sport-related concussion and long-term clinical cognitive health outcomes in retired athletes: A systematic review. *Journal of Athletic Training, 55*(2), 132–158. https://doi.org/10.4085/1062-6050-297-18.

Daley, M. M., Howell, D. R., Lanois, C. J., Berkner, P. D., Mannix, R. C., Oldham, J. R., & Meehan, W. P. (2024). Concussion symptoms and neurocognitive performance of children and adolescents on antidepressants. *Medicine and Science in Sports and Exercise, 56*(6), 1018–1025. https://doi.org/10.1249/mss.0000000000003383.

Daugherty, J., DePadilla, L., Sarmiento, K., & Breiding, M. J. (2020). Self-reported lifetime concussion among adults: Comparison of 3 different survey questions. *The Journal of Head Trauma Rehabilitation, 35*(2), E136–E143. https://doi.org/10.1097/HTR.0000000000000534.

Daugherty, J., & Sarmiento, K. (2018). Chronic traumatic encephalopathy: What do parents of youth athletes know about it? *Brain Injury, 32*(13–14), 1773–1779. https://doi.org/10.1080/02699052.2018.1530801.

Davidson, T. W., & Tremblay, F. (2016). Evidence of alterations in transcallosal motor inhibition as a possible long-term consequence of concussions in sports: A transcranial magnetic stimulation study. *Clinical Neurophysiology, 127*(10), 3364–3375. https://doi.org/10.1016/j.clinph.2016.07.012.

Davis, G. A., Patricios, J., Schneider, K. J., Iverson, G. L., & Silverberg, N. D. (2023). Definition of sport-related concussion: The 6th International Conference on Concussion in Sport. *British Journal of Sports Medicine, 57*(11), 617–618. https://doi.org/10.1136/bjsports-2022-106650.

De Beaumont, L., Beauchemin, M., Beaulieu, C., & Jolicoeur, P. (2013). Long-term attenuated electrophysiological response to errors following multiple sports concussions. *Journal of Clinical and Experimental Neuropsychology, 35*(6), 596–607. https://doi.org/10.1080/13803395.2013.800023.

De Beaumont, L., Brisson, B., Lassonde, M., & Jolicoeur, P. (2007). Long-term electrophysiological changes in athletes with a history of multiple concussions. *Brain Injury, 21*(6), 631–644. https://doi.org/10.1080/02699050701426931.

De Beaumont, L., Mongeon, D., Tremblay, S., Messier, J., Prince, F., Leclerc, S., ... Théoret, H. (2011). Persistent motor system abnormalities in formerly concussed athletes. *Journal of Athletic Training, 46*(3), 234–240. https://doi.org/10.4085/1062-6050-46.3.234.

De Beaumont, L., Théoret, H., Mongeon, D., Messier, J., Leclerc, S., Tremblay, S., ... Lassonde, M. (2009). Brain function decline in healthy retired athletes who sustained their last sports concussion in early adulthood. *Brain, 132*(3), 695–708. https://doi.org/10.1093/brain/awn347.

De Beaumont, L., Tremblay, S., Poirier, J., Lassonde, M., & Théoret, H. (2012). Altered bidirectional plasticity and reduced implicit motor learning in concussed athletes. *Cerebral Cortex, 22*(1), 112–121. https://doi.org/10.1093/cercor/bhr096.

De Souza, N. L., Buckman, J. F., Dennis, E. L., Parrott, J. S., Velez, C., Wilde, E. A., ... Esopenko, C. (2021). Association between white matter organization and cognitive performance in athletes with a history of sport-related concussion. *Journal of Clinical and Experimental Neuropsychology, 43*(7), 704–715. https://doi.org/10.1080/13803395.2021.1991893.

Dean, P. J. A., Sato, J. R., Vieira, G., McNamara, A., & Sterr, A. (2015). Long-term structural changes after mTBI and their relation to post-concussion symptoms. *Brain Injury, 29*(10), 1211–1218. https://doi.org/10.3109/02699052.2015.1035334.

Delmonico, R. L., Theodore, B. R., Sandel, M. E., Armstrong, M. A., & Camicia, M. (2022). Prevalence of depression and anxiety disorders following mild traumatic brain injury. *PM&R, 14*(7), 753–763. https://doi.org/10.1002/pmrj.12657.

Deshpande, S. K., Hasegawa, R. B., Rabinowitz, A. R., Whyte, J., Roan, C. L., Tabatabaei, A., ... Small, D. S. (2017). Association of playing high school football with cognition and mental health later in life. *JAMA Neurology, 74*(8), 909–918. https://doi.org/10.1001/jamaneurol.2017.1317.

Deshpande, S. K., Hasegawa, R. B., Weiss, J., & Small, D. S. (2020). The association between adolescent football participation and early adulthood depression. *PLoS One, 15*(3), e0229978. https://doi.org/10.1371/journal.pone.0229978.

Dewan, M. C., Rattani, A., Gupta, S., Baticulon, R. E., Hung, Y.-C., Punchak, M., ... Park, K. B. (2018). Estimating the global incidence of traumatic brain injury. *Journal of Neurosurgery, 130*(4), 1080–1097. https://doi.org/10.3171/2017.10.JNS17352.

Didehbani, N., Munro Cullum, C., Mansinghani, S., Conover, H., & Hart, J., Jr. (2013). Depressive symptoms and concussions in aging retired NFL players. *Archives of Clinical Neuropsychology, 28*(5), 418–424. https://doi.org/10.1093/arclin/act028.

Djonlagic, I., Mariani, S., Fitzpatrick, A. L., Van Der Klei, V. M. G. T. H., Johnson, D. A., Wood, A. C., ... Purcell, S. M. (2021). Macro and micro sleep architecture and cognitive performance in older adults. *Nature Human Behaviour, 5*(1), 123–145. https://doi.org/10.1038/s41562-020-00964-y.

Dretsch, M. N., Silverberg, N. D., & Iverson, G. L. (2015). Multiple past concussions are associated with ongoing post-concussive symptoms but not cognitive impairment in active-duty army soldiers. *Journal of Neurotrauma, 32*(17), 1301–1306. https://doi.org/10.1089/neu.2014.3810.

DuBose, D. F., Herman, D. C., Jones, D. L., Tillman, S. M., Clugston, J. R., Pass, A., ... Chmielewski, T. L. (2017). Lower extremity stiffness changes following concussion in collegiate football players. *Medicine and Science in Sports and Exercise, 49*(1), 167–172. https://doi.org/10.1249/MSS.0000000000001067.

Dumais, A., Lesage, A. d, Alda, M., Rouleau, G., Dumont, M., Chawky, N., ... Turecki, G. (2005). Risk factors for suicide completion in major depression: A case-control study of impulsive and aggressive behaviors in men. *American Journal of Psychiatry, 162*(11), 2116–2124. https://doi.org/10.1176/appi.ajp.162.11.2116.

Dupuis, F., Johnston, K. M., Lavoie, M., Lepore, F., & Lassonde, M. (2000). Concussions in athletes produce brain dysfunction as revealed by event-related potentials. *Neuroreport, 11*(18), 4087–4092.

D'Alonzo, B. A., Bretzin, A. C., Wiebe, D. J., Fiore, R., VanPatten, B., Levine, W. N., ... Arlis-Mayor, S. (2022). The role of reported affective symptoms and anxiety in recovery trajectories after sport-related concussion. *The American Journal of Sports Medicine, 50*(8), 2258–2270. https://doi.org/10.1177/03635465221098112.

Eagle, S. R., Brent, D., Covassin, T., Elbin, R. J., Wallace, J., Ortega, J., ... Kontos, A. P. (2022). Exploration of race and ethnicity, sex, sport-related concussion, depression history, and suicide attempts in US youth. *JAMA Network Open, 5*(7), e2219934. https://doi.org/10.1001/jamanetworkopen.2022.19934.

Echemendia, R. J., Ahmed, O. H., Bailey, C. M., Bruce, J. M., Burma, J. S., Davis, G. A., ... Patricios, J. (2023). Introducing the concussion recognition tool 6 (CRT6). *British Journal of Sports Medicine, 57*(11), 689–691. https://doi.org/10.1136/bjsports-2023-106851.

Echemendia, R. J., Brett, B. L., Broglio, S., Davis, G. A., Giza, C. C., Guskiewicz, K. M., ... Bruce, J. M. (2023). Introducing the sport concussion assessment tool 6 (SCAT6). *British Journal of Sports Medicine, 57*(11), 619–621. https://doi.org/10.1136/bjsports-2023-106849.

Elbin, R. J., Covassin, T., Hakun, J., Kontos, A. P., Berger, K., Pfeiffer, K., & Ravizza, S. (2012). Do brain activation changes persist in athletes with a history of multiple concussions who are asymptomatic? *Brain Injury, 26*(10), 1217–1225. https://doi.org/10.3109/02699052.2012.672788.

Eliason, P. H., Galarneau, J.-M., Kolstad, A. T., Pankow, M. P., West, S. W., Bailey, S., ... Emery, C. A. (2023). Prevention strategies and modifiable risk factors for sport-related concussions and head impacts: A systematic review and meta-analysis. *British Journal of Sports Medicine, 57*(12), 749–761. https://doi.org/10.1136/bjsports-2022-106656.

Ellemberg, D., Leclerc, S., Couture, S., & Daigle, C. (2007). Prolonged neuropsychological impairments following a first concussion in female university soccer athletes. *Clinical Journal of Sport Medicine, 17*(5), 369–374.

Falkenstein, M., Hohnsbein, J., Hoormann, J., & Blanke, L. (1991). Effects of crossmodal divided attention on late ERP components. II. Error processing in choice reaction tasks. *Electroencephalography and Clinical Neurophysiology, 78*(6), 447–455. https://doi.org/10.1016/0013-4694(91)90062-9.

Feiss, R., Lutz, M., Reiche, E., Moody, J., & Pangelinan, M. (2020). A systematic review of the effectiveness of concussion education programs for coaches and parents of youth athletes. Article 8 *International Journal of Environmental Research and Public Health, 17*(8), https://doi.org/10.3390/ijerph17082665.

Fino, P. C., Nussbaum, M. A., & Brolinson, P. G. (2016). Decreased high-frequency center-of-pressure complexity in recently concussed asymptomatic athletes. *Gait & Posture, 50*, 69–74. https://doi.org/10.1016/j.gaitpost.2016.08.026.

Fisher, M., Wiseman-Hakes, C., Obeid, J., & DeMatteo, C. (2022). Examining the trajectory and predictors of post-concussion sleep quality in children and adolescents. *Brain Injury, 36*(2), 166–174. https://doi.org/10.1080/02699052.2022.2043439.

Fish, A. M., Vanni, J., Mohammed, F. N., Fedonni, D., Metzger, K. B., Shoop, J., ... McDonald, C. C. (2023). Comparison of anxiety and depression symptoms in concussed and nonconcussed adolescents. *Sports Health, 15*(2), 185–191. https://doi.org/10.1177/19417381221113840.

Fleminger, S., Oliver, D. L., Lovestone, S., Rabe-Hesketh, S., & Giora, A. (2003). Head injury as a risk factor for Alzheimer's disease: The evidence 10 years on; a partial replication. *Journal of Neurology, Neurosurgery & Psychiatry, 74*(7), 857–862. https://doi.org/10.1136/jnnp.74.7.857.

Fling, B. W., & Seidler, R. D. (2012). Task-dependent effects of interhemispheric inhibition on motor control. *Behavioural Brain Research, 226*(1), 211–217. https://doi.org/10.1016/j.bbr.2011.09.018.

Fralick, M., Thiruchelvam, D., Tien, H. C., & Redelmeier, D. A. (2016). Risk of suicide after a concussion. *CMAJ: Canadian Medical Association Journal, 188*(7), 497–504. https://doi.org/10.1503/cmaj.150790.

Gaetz, M., Goodman, D., & Weinberg, H. (2000). Electrophysiological evidence for the cumulative effects of concussion. *Brain Injury, 14*, 1077–1088.

Gardner, C. H., Kotlier, J. L., Fathi, A., Castonguay, J., Thompson, A. A., Bolia, I. K., ... Gamradt, S. C. (2024). NCAA football players are at higher risk of upper extremity injury after first-time concussion. *The Physician and Sportsmedicine*, 1–5. https://doi.org/10.1080/00913847.2024.2327275.

Gardner, R. C., & Yaffe, K. (2015). Epidemiology of mild traumatic brain injury and neurodegenerative disease. *Molecular and Cellular Neuroscience, 66*, 75–80. https://doi.org/10.1016/j.mcn.2015.03.001.

Gehring, W. J., Goss, B., Coles, M. G. H., Meyer, D. E., & Donchin, E. (1993). A neural system for error detection and compensation. *Psychological Science, 4*(6), 385–390. https://doi.org/10.1111/j.1467-9280.1993.tb00586.x.

Giza, C. C., & Hovda, D. A. (2014). The new neurometabolic cascade of concussion. *Neurosurgery, 75*(0 4), S24–S33. https://doi.org/10.1227/NEU.0000000000000505.

Godbolt, A. K., Cancelliere, C., Hincapié, C. A., Marras, C., Boyle, E., Kristman, V. L., ... Cassidy, J. D. (2014). Systematic review of the risk of dementia and chronic cognitive impairment after mild traumatic brain injury: Results of the international collaboration on mild traumatic brain injury prognosis. *Archives of Physical Medicine and Rehabilitation, 95*(3, Supplement), S245–S256. https://doi.org/10.1016/j.apmr.2013.06.036.

Gosselin, N., Chen, J. K., Bottari, C., Petrides, M., Jubault, T., Tinawi, S., ... Ptito, A. (2012). The influence of pain on cerebral functioning after mild traumatic brain injury. *Journal of Neurotrauma, 29*, 2625–2634.

Gosselin, N., Lassonde, M., Petit, D., Leclerc, S., Mongrain, V., Collie, A., & Montplaisir, J. (2009). Sleep following sport-related concussions. *Sleep Medicine, 10*(1), 35–46. https://doi.org/10.1016/j.sleep.2007.11.023.

Gosselin, N., Theriault, M., Leclerc, S., Montplaisier, J., & Lassonde, M. (2006). Neurophysiological anomalies in symptomatic and asymptomatic concussed athletes. *Neurosurgery, 58*, 1151–1161.

Gouttebarge, V., Aoki, H., Lambert, M., Stewart, W., & Kerkhoffs, G. (2017). A history of concussions is associated with symptoms of common mental disorders in former male professional athletes across a range of sports. *The Physician and Sportsmedicine, 45*(4), 443–449. https://doi.org/10.1080/00913847.2017.1376572.

Gronwall, D. (1991). Minor head injury. *Neuropsychology, 5*(4), 253–265. https://doi.org/10.1037/0894-4105.5.4.253.

Guskiewicz, K. M., Marshall, S. W., Bailes, J., Mccrea, M., Harding, H. P., Matthews, A., ... Cantu, R. C. (2007). Recurrent concussion and risk of depression in retired professional football players. *Medicine & Science in Sports & Exercise, 39*(6), 903–909. https://doi.org/10.1249/mss.0b013e3180383da5.

Guskiewicz, K. M., Ross, S. E., & Marshall, S. W. (2001). Postural stability and neuropsychological deficits after concussion in collegiate athletes. *Journal of Athletic Training, 36*(3), 263–273.

Hablitz, L. M., Plá, V., Giannetto, M., Vinitsky, H. S., Stæger, F. F., Metcalfe, T., ... Nedergaard, M. (2020). Circadian control of brain glymphatic and lymphatic fluid flow. *Nature Communications, 11*(1), 4411. https://doi.org/10.1038/s41467-020-18115-2.

Haider, M. N., Johnson, S. L., Mannix, R., Macfarlane, A. J., Constantino, D., Johnson, B. D., ... Leddy, J. (2019). The buffalo concussion bike test for concussion assessment in adolescents. *Sports Health, 11*(6), 492–497. https://doi.org/10.1177/1941738119870189.

Haider, M. N., Patel, K. S., Willer, B. S., Videira, V., Wilber, C. G., Mayer, A. R., ... Leddy, J. J. (2021). Symptoms upon postural change and orthostatic hypotension in adolescents with concussion. *Brain Injury, 35*(2), 226–232. https://doi.org/10.1080/02699052.2021.1871951.

Harmon, K. G., Clugston, J. R., Dec, K., Hainline, B., Herring, S., Kane, S. F., ... Roberts, W. O. (2019). American medical society for sports medicine position statement on concussion in sport. *British Journal of Sports Medicine, 53*(4), 213–225. https://doi.org/10.1136/bjsports-2018-100338.

Hazrati, L.-N., Tartaglia, M. C., Diamandis, P., Davis, K., Green, R. E. A., Wennberg, R., ... Tator, C. H. (2013). Absence of chronic traumatic encephalopathy in retired football players with multiple concussions and neurological symptomatology. *Frontiers in Human Neuroscience,* 7. https://doi.org/10.3389/fnhum.2013.00222.

Hellewell, S. C., Beaton, C. S., Welton, T., & Grieve, S. M. (2020). Characterizing the risk of depression following mild traumatic brain injury: A meta-analysis of the literature comparing chronic mTBI to non-mTBI populations. *Frontiers in Neurology, 11*. https://doi.org/10.3389/fneur.2020.00350.

Helmes, E., Østbye, T., & Steenhuis, R. E. (2011). Incremental contribution of reported previous head injury to the prediction of diagnosis and cognitive functioning in older adults. *Brain Injury, 25*(4), 338–347. https://doi.org/10.3109/02699052.2011.556104.

Henry, L. C., Elbin, R., Collins, M. W., Marchetti, G., & Kontos, A. P. (2016). Examining recovery trajectories following sport-related concussion using a multi-modal clinical assessment approach. *Neurosurgery, 78*(2), 232–241. https://doi.org/10.1227/NEU.0000000000001041.

Henry, L. C., Tremblay, J., Tremblay, S., Lee, A., Brun, C., Lepore, N., ... Lassonde, M. (2011). Acute and chronic changes in diffusivity measures after sports concussion. *Journal of Neurotrauma, 28*(10), 2049–2059. https://doi.org/10.1089/neu.2011.1836.

Hoffman, N. L., O'Connor, P. J., Schmidt, M. D., Lynall, R. C., & Schmidt, J. D. (2019). Differences in sleep between concussed and nonconcussed college students: A matched case–control study. *Sleep, 42*(2), https://doi.org/10.1093/sleep/zsy222.

Howell, D. R., Beasley, M., Vopat, L., & Meehan, W. P. (2017). The effect of prior concussion history on dual-task gait following a concussion. *Journal of Neurotrauma, 34*(4), 838–844. https://doi.org/10.1089/neu.2016.4609.

Howell, D. R., Oldham, J. R., Brilliant, A. N., & Meehan, W. P. (2019). Trouble falling asleep after concussion is associated with higher symptom burden among children and adolescents. *Journal of Child Neurology, 34*(5), 256–261. https://doi.org/10.1177/0883073818824000.

Howell, D. R., Oldham, J., Lanois, C., Koerte, I., Lin, A. P., Berkstresser, B., ... Meehan, W. P. (2020). Dual-task gait recovery after concussion among female and male collegiate athletes. *Medicine and Science in Sports and Exercise, 52*(5), 1015–1021. https://doi.org/10.1249/MSS.0000000000002225.

Howell, D. R., Osternig, L. R., & Chou, L.-S. (2018). Detection of acute and long-term effects of concussion: Dual-task gait balance control versus computerized neurocognitive test. *Archives of Physical Medicine and Rehabilitation, 99*(7), 1318–1324. https://doi.org/10.1016/j.apmr.2018.01.025.

Hudac, C. M., Cortesa, C. S., Ledwidge, P. S., & Molfese, D. L. (2018). History of concussion impacts electrophysiological correlates of working memory. *International Journal of Psychophysiology, 132*, 135–144. https://doi.org/10.1016/j.ijpsycho.2017.09.020.

Hurtubise, J., Gorbet, D., Hamandi, Y., Macpherson, A., & Sergio, L. (2016). The effect of concussion history on cognitive-motor integration in elite hockey players. *Concussion, 1*(3), CNC17. https://doi.org/10.2217/cnc-2016-0006.

Iliff, J. J., Chen, M. J., Plog, B. A., Zeppenfeld, D. M., Soltero, M., Yang, L., ... Nedergaard, M. (2014). Impairment of glymphatic pathway function promotes tau pathology after traumatic brain injury. *The Journal of Neuroscience, 34*(49), 16180–16193. https://doi.org/10.1523/JNEUROSCI.3020-14.2014.

Imbach, L. L., Büchele, F., Valko, P. O., Li, T., Maric, A., Stover, J. F., ... Baumann, C. R. (2016). Sleep–wake disorders persist 18 months after traumatic brain injury but remain underrecognized. *Neurology, 86*(21), 1945–1949. https://doi.org/10.1212/WNL.0000000000002697.

Imbach, L. L., Valko, P. O., Li, T., Maric, A., Symeonidou, E.-R., Stover, J. F., ... Baumann, C. R. (2015). Increased sleep need and daytime sleepiness 6 months after traumatic brain injury: A prospective controlled clinical trial. *Brain, 138*(3), 726–735. https://doi.org/10.1093/brain/awu391.

Iverson, G. L., & Gardner, A. J. (2020). Risk of misdiagnosing chronic traumatic encephalopathy in men with depression. *The Journal of Neuropsychiatry and Clinical Neurosciences, 32*(2), 139–146. https://doi.org/10.1176/appi.neuropsych.19010021.

Iverson, G. L., Gardner, A. J., Terry, D. P., Ponsford, J. L., Sills, A. K., Broshek, D. K., & Solomon, G. S. (2017). Predictors of clinical recovery from concussion: A systematic review. *British Journal of Sports Medicine, 51*(12), 941–948. https://doi.org/10.1136/bjsports-2017-097729.

Iverson, G. L., Greenberg, J., & Cook, N. E. (2022). Anxiety is associated with diverse physical and cognitive symptoms in youth presenting to a multidisciplinary concussion clinic. *Frontiers in Neurology, 12*. https://doi.org/10.3389/fneur.2021.811462.

Iverson, G. L., Merz, Z. C., & Terry, D. P. (2021). Playing high school football is not associated with an increased risk for suicidality in early adulthood. *Clinical Journal of Sport Medicine, 31*(6), 469. https://doi.org/10.1097/JSM.0000000000000890.

Iverson, G. L., & Terry, D. P. (2022). High school football and risk for depression and suicidality in adulthood: Findings from a national longitudinal study. *Frontiers in Neurology, 12*. https://doi.org/10.3389/fneur.2021.812604.

Izzy, S., Tahir, Z., Grashow, R., Cote, D. J., Jarrah, A. A., Dhand, A., ... Zafonte, R. (2021). Concussion and risk of chronic medical and behavioral health comorbidities. *Journal of Neurotrauma, 38*(13), 1834–1841. https://doi.org/10.1089/neu.2020.7484.

Jafari, S., Etminan, M., Aminzadeh, F., & Samii, A. (2013). Head injury and risk of Parkinson disease: A systematic review and meta-analysis. *Movement Disorders, 28*(9), 1222–1229. https://doi.org/10.1002/mds.25458.

Johnston, W., O'Reilly, M., Duignan, C., Liston, M., McLoughlin, R., Coughlan, G. F., & Caulfield, B. (2019). Association of dynamic balance with sports-related concussion: A prospective cohort study. *The American Journal of Sports Medicine, 47*(1), 197–205. https://doi.org/10.1177/0363546518812820.

Kalkonde, Y. V., Jawaid, A., Qureshi, S. U., Shirani, P., Wheaton, M., Pinto-Patarroyo, G. P., & Schulz, P. E. (2012). Medical and environmental risk factors associated with frontotemporal dementia: A case-control study in a veteran population. *Alzheimer's & Dementia, 8*(3), 204–210. https://doi.org/10.1016/j.jalz.2011.03.011.

Kamins, J., Bigler, E., Covassin, T., Henry, L., Kemp, S., Leddy, J. J., ... Giza, C. C. (2017). What is the physiological time to recovery after concussion? A systematic review. *British Journal of Sports Medicine, 51*(12), 935–940. https://doi.org/10.1136/bjsports-2016-097464.

Katz, D. I., Bernick, C., Dodick, D. W., Mez, J., Mariani, M. L., Adler, C. H., ... Stern, R. A. (2021). National institute of neurological disorders and stroke consensus diagnostic criteria for traumatic encephalopathy syndrome. *Neurology, 96*(18), 848–863. https://doi.org/10.1212/WNL.0000000000011850.

Kaufman, Y., Tzischinsky, O., Epstein, R., Etzioni, A., Lavie, P., & Pillar, G. (2001). Long-term sleep disturbances in adolescents after minor head injury. *Pediatric Neurology, 24*(2), 129–134. https://doi.org/10.1016/S0887-8994(00)00254-X.

Kaye, S., Sundman, M. H., Hall, E. E., Williams, E., Patel, K., & Ketcham, C. J. (2019). Baseline neurocognitive performance and symptoms in those with attention deficit hyperactivity disorders and history of concussion with previous loss of consciousness. *Frontiers in Neurology, 10.* https://doi.org/10.3389/fneur.2019.00396.

Kay, J. J. M., Coffman, C. A., Tavakoli, A. S., Torres-McGehee, T. M., Broglio, S. P., & Moore, R. D. (2022). Frequency of concussion exposure modulates suicidal ideation, planning, and attempts among U.S. high school students. *Journal of Athletic Training, 58*(9), 751–758. https://doi.org/10.4085/1062-6050-0117.22.

Keightley, M. L., Côté, P., Rumney, P., Hung, R., Carroll, L. J., Cancelliere, C., & Cassidy, J. D. (2014). Psychosocial consequences of mild traumatic brain injury in children: Results of a systematic review by the international collaboration on mild traumatic brain injury prognosis. *Archives of Physical Medicine and Rehabilitation, 95*(3, Supplement), S192–S200. https://doi.org/10.1016/j.apmr.2013.12.018.

Kennedy, E., Ozmen, M., Bouldin, E. D., Panahi, S., Mobasher, H., Troyanskaya, M., ... Pugh, M. J. (2024). Phenotyping depression after mild traumatic brain injury: Evaluating the impact of multiple injury, gender, and injury context. *Journal of Neurotrauma, 41*(7–8), 924–933. https://doi.org/10.1089/neu.2023.0381.

Kerr, Z. Y., Evenson, K. R., Rosamond, W. D., Mihalik, J. P., Guskiewicz, K. M., & Marshall, S. W. (2014). Association between concussion and mental health in former collegiate athletes. *Injury Epidemiology, 1,* 28. https://doi.org/10.1186/s40621-014-0028-x.

Kerr, Z. Y., Marshall, S. W., Harding, H. P., & Guskiewicz, K. M. (2012). Nine-year risk of depression diagnosis increases with increasing self-reported concussions in retired professional football players. *The American Journal of Sports Medicine, 40*(10), 2206–2212. https://doi.org/10.1177/0363546512456193.

Kerr, Z. Y., Thomas, L. C., Simon, J. E., McCrea, M., & Guskiewicz, K. M. (2018). Association between history of multiple concussions and health outcomes among former college football players: 15-Year follow-up from the NCAA concussion study (1999–2001). *The American Journal of Sports Medicine, 46*(7), 1733–1741. https://doi.org/10.1177/0363546518765121.

Ketcham, C. J., Cochrane, G., Brown, L., Vallabhajosula, S., Patel, K., & Hall, E. E. (2019). Neurocognitive performance, concussion history, and balance performance during a distraction dual-task in collegiate student-athletes. *Athletic Training & Sports Health Care, 11*(2), 90–96. https://doi.org/10.3928/19425864-20180313-02.

Khoury, S., Chouchou, F., Amzica, F., Giguère, J.-F., Denis, R., Rouleau, G. A., & Lavigne, G. J. (2013). Rapid EEG activity during sleep dominates in mild traumatic brain injury patients with acute pain. *Journal of Neurotrauma, 30*(8), 633–641. https://doi.org/10.1089/neu.2012.2519.

Kibby, M. Y., & Long, C. J. (1996). Minor head injury: Attempts at clarifying the confusion. *Brain Injury, 10*(3), 159–186. https://doi.org/10.1080/026990596124494.

King (2019). 'Mild traumatic brain injury' and 'sport-related concussion': Different languages and mixed messages? *Brain Injury, 33*(12), 1556–1563. https://doi.org/10.1080/02699052.2019.1655794.

King, R., Kirton, A., Zewdie, E., Seeger, T. A., Ciechanski, P., & Barlow, K. M. (2019). Longitudinal assessment of cortical excitability in children and adolescents with mild traumatic brain injury and persistent post-concussive symptoms. *Frontiers in Neurology, 10.* https://doi.org/10.3389/fneur.2019.00451.

Kontos, A. P., Elbin, R. J., Trbovich, A., Womble, M., Said, A., Sumrok, V. F., ... Collins, M. (2020). Concussion clinical profiles screening (CP screen) tool: Preliminary evidence to inform a multidisciplinary approach. *Neurosurgery, 87*(2), 348. https://doi.org/10.1093/neuros/nyz545.

Kontos, A. P., Sufrinko, A., Sandel, N., Emami, K., & Collins, M. W. (2019). Sport-related concussion clinical profiles: Clinical characteristics, targeted treatments, and preliminary evidence. *Current Sports Medicine Reports, 18*(3), 82. https://doi.org/10.1249/JSR.0000000000000573.

Kontos, A. P., Sufrinko, A., Womble, M., & Kegel, N. (2016). Neuropsychological assessment following concussion: An evidence-based review of the role of neuropsychological assessment pre- and post-concussion. *Current Pain and Headache Reports, 20*(6), 38. https://doi.org/10.1007/s11916-016-0571-y.

Kureshi, S., Stowe, C., Francis, J., & Djalilian, H. (2023). Circadian therapy interventions for glymphatic dysfunction in concussions injuries: A narrative review. *Science Progress, 106*(3), https://doi.org/10.1177/00368504231189536.

Lan Chun Yang, T., Colantonio, A., & Mollayeva, T. (2021). Misperception of sleep duration in mild traumatic brain injury/concussion: A preliminary report. *Brain Injury, 35*, 1–11. https://doi.org/10.1080/02699052.2020.1863468.

Langworth-Green, C., Patel, S., Jaunmuktane, Z., Jabbari, E., Morris, H., Thom, M., ... Duff, K. (2023). Chronic effects of inflammation on tauopathies. *The Lancet Neurology, 22*(5), 430–442. https://doi.org/10.1016/S1474-4422(23)00038-8.

Lapointe, A. P., Nolasco, L. A., Sosnowski, A., Andrews, E., Martini, D. N., Palmieri-Smith, R. M., ... Broglio, S. P. (2018). Kinematic differences during a jump cut maneuver between individuals with and without a concussion history. *International Journal of Psychophysiology, 132*, 93–98. https://doi.org/10.1016/j.ijpsycho.2017.08.003.

Larson, M. J., Clayson, P. E., & Farrer, T. J. (2012). Performance monitoring and cognitive control in individuals with mild traumatic brain injury. *Journal of the International Neuropsychological Society, 18*(2), 323–333. https://doi.org/10.1017/S1355617711001779.

Lavoie, M. E., Dupuis, F., Johnston, K. M., Leclerc, S., & Lassonde, M. (2004). Visual P300 effects beyond symptoms in concussed college athletes. *Journal of Clinical and Experimental Neuropsychology, 26*(1), 55–73. https://doi.org/10.1076/jcen.26.1.55.23936.

Leddy, J. J., Burma, J. S., Toomey, C. M., Hayden, A., Davis, G. A., Babl, F. E., ... Schneider, K. J. (2023). Rest and exercise early after sport-related concussion: A systematic review and meta-analysis. *British Journal of Sports Medicine, 57*(12), 762–770. https://doi.org/10.1136/bjsports-2022-106676.

Leddy, J. J., & Willer, B. (2013). Use of graded exercise testing in concussion and return-to-activity management. *Current Sports Medicine Reports, 12*(6), 370. https://doi.org/10.1249/JSR.0000000000000008.

Ledoux, A.-A., Webster, R. J., Clarke, A. E., Fell, D. B., Knight, B. D., Gardner, W., ... Zemek, R. (2022). Risk of mental health problems in children and youths following concussion. *JAMA Network Open, 5*(3), e221235. https://doi.org/10.1001/jamanetworkopen.2022.1235.

Ledwidge, P. S., & Molfese, D. L. (2016). Long-term effects of concussion on electrophysiological indices of attention in varsity college athletes: An event-related potential and standardized low-resolution brain electromagnetic tomography approach. *Journal of Neurotrauma, 33*(23), 2081–2090. https://doi.org/10.1089/neu.2015.4251.

Lee, V. M.-Y., Goedert, M., & Trojanowski, J. Q. (2001). Neurodegenarative tauopathies. *Annual Review of Neuroscience, 24*, 1121–1159.

Lee, Y.-K., Hou, S.-W., Lee, C.-C., Hsu, C.-Y., Huang, Y.-S., & Su, Y.-C. (2013). Increased risk of dementia in patients with mild traumatic brain injury: A nationwide cohort study. *PLoS One, 8*(5), e62422. https://doi.org/10.1371/journal.pone.0062422.

Lefaucheur, J.-P. (2019). Chapter 37—Transcranial magnetic stimulation. In K. H. Levin, & P. Chauvel (Vol. Eds.), *Handbook of clinical neurology: Vol. 160*, (pp. 559–580). Elsevier. https://doi.org/10.1016/B978-0-444-64032-1.00037-0.

Lempke, L. B., Boltz, A. J., Garcia, G.-G. P., Syrydiuk, R. A., Pandey, H. S., Pasquina, P. F., ... Broglio, S. P. (2023). Optimizing baseline and post-concussion assessments through identification, confirmation, and equivalence of latent factor structures: Findings from the NCAA-DoD CARE Consortium. *The Clinical Neuropsychologist, 38*(5), 1156–1174. https://doi.org/10.1080/13854046.2023.2271614.

Lewis, G. N., Hume, P. A., Stavric, V., Brown, S. R., & Taylor, D. (2017). New Zealand rugby health study: Motor cortex excitability in retired elite and community level rugby players. *The New Zealand Medical Journal, 130*(1448), 34–44.

Little, C. E., Emery, C., Scott, S. H., Meeuwisse, W., Palacios-Derflingher, L., & Dukelow, S. P. (2016). Do children and adolescent ice hockey players with and without a history of concussion differ in robotic testing of sensory, motor and cognitive function? *Journal of Neuroengineering and Rehabilitation, 13*(1), 89. https://doi.org/10.1186/s12984-016-0195-9.

Locke, M. B., Toepp, S. L., Turco, C. V., Harasym, D. H., Rathbone, M. P., Noseworthy, M. D., & Nelson, A. J. (2020). Altered motor system function in post-concussion syndrome as assessed via transcranial magnetic stimulation. *Clinical Neurophysiology Practice, 5*, 157–164. https://doi.org/10.1016/j.cnp.2020.07.004.

Maas, A. I., Stocchetti, N., & Bullock, R. (2008). Moderate and severe traumatic brain injury in adults. *The Lancet Neurology*, 7(8), 728–741. https://doi.org/10.1016/S1474-4422(08)70164-9.

Maerlender, A., Masterson, C., Calvi, J. L., Caze, T., Mathiasen, R., & Molfese, D. (2020). Sleep and stress in the acute phase of concussion in youth. *Sports Medicine and Health Science, 2*(2), 109–114. https://doi.org/10.1016/j.smhs.2020.06.003.

Mainwaring, L. M., Bisschop, S. M., Green, R. E. A., Antoniazzi, M., Comper, P., Kristman, V., ... Richards, D. W. (2004). Emotional reaction of varsity athletes to sport-related concussion. *Journal of Sport and Exercise Psychology, 26*(1), 119–135. https://doi.org/10.1123/jsep.26.1.119.

Malcolm, D., Matthews, C. R., & Wiltshire, G. (2024). Concussion in sport: It's time to drop the tobacco analogy. *Journal of Science and Medicine in Sport, 0*(0), https://doi.org/10.1016/j.jsams.2024.01.009.

Management of Concussion/mTBI Working Group. (2009). VA/DOD clinical practice guideline for management of concussion/mild traumatic brain injury. *Journal of Rehabilitation Research and Development, 46*(6), CP1–CP68.

Manley, G., Gardner, A. J., Schneider, K. J., Guskiewicz, K. M., Bailes, J., Cantu, R. C., ... Iverson, G. L. (2017). A systematic review of potential long-term effects of sport-related concussion. *British Journal of Sports Medicine, 51*(12), 969–977. https://doi.org/10.1136/bjsports-2017-097791.

Mann, J. J., Arango, V. A., Avenevoli, S., Brent, D. A., Champagne, F. A., Clayton, P., ... Wenzel, A. (2009). Candidate endophenotypes for genetic studies of suicidal behavior. *Biological Psychiatry, 65*(7), 556. https://doi.org/10.1016/j.biopsych.2008.11.021.

Mantey, D. S., Omega-Njemnobi, O., Barroso, C. S., & Kelder, S. H. (2020). Self-reported history of concussions is associated with risk factors for suicide completion among high school students. *Journal of Affective Disorders, 263*, 684–691. https://doi.org/10.1016/j.jad.2019.11.047.

Mantey, D. S., Omega-Njemnobi, O., & Kelder, S. H. (2021). Self-reported history of concussions is associated with risk factors for suicide completion among middle school students: A cross-sectional study. *Journal of Psychiatric Research, 132*, 191–194. https://doi.org/10.1016/j.jpsychires.2020.10.022.

Mantua, J., Henry, O. S., Garskovas, N. F., & Spencer, R. M. C. (2017). Mild traumatic brain injury chronically impairs sleep- and wake-dependent emotional processing. *Sleep, 40*(6), https://doi.org/10.1093/sleep/zsx062.

Mantua, J., Mahan, K. M., Henry, O. S., & Spencer, R. M. C. (2015). Altered sleep composition after traumatic brain injury does not affect declarative sleep-dependent memory consolidation. *Frontiers in Human Neuroscience, 9*. https://doi.org/10.3389/fnhum.2015.00328.

Martini, D. N., & Broglio, S. P. (2018). Long-term effects of sport concussion on cognitive and motor performance: A review. *International Journal of Psychophysiology, 132*, 25–30. https://doi.org/10.1016/j.ijpsycho.2017.09.019.

Martini, D. N., Eckner, J. T., Meehan, S. K., & Broglio, S. P. (2017). Long-term effects of adolescent sport concussion across the age spectrum. *The American Journal of Sports Medicine, 45*(6), 1420–1428. https://doi.org/10.1177/0363546516686785.

Martini, D. N., Sabin, M. J., DePesa, S. A., Leal, E. W., Negrete, T. N., Sosnoff, J. J., & Broglio, S. P. (2011). The chronic effects of concussion on gait. *Archives of Physical Medicine and Rehabilitation, 92*(4), 585–589. https://doi.org/10.1016/j.apmr.2010.11.029.

Mavroudis, I., Balmus, I.-M., Ciobica, A., & Hogas, M. (2024). A narrative review of risk factors and predictors for poor outcome and prolonged recovery after a mild traumatic brain injury. *International Journal of Neuroscience*, 1–10. https://doi.org/10.1080/00207454.2024.2328710.

May, J. M., Angileri, H. S., McLoughlin, D. E., Owen, M. M., Terry, M., & Tjong, V. (2023). Decreased concussion incidence following the implementation of the targeting rules: An updated epidemiology of national football league concussions From 2017 to 2022. *Cureus*. https://doi.org/10.7759/cureus.50997.

McCrory, P., Meeuwisse, W. H., Echemendia, R. J., Iverson, G. L., Dvořák, J., & Kutcher, J. S. (2013). What is the lowest threshold to make a diagnosis of concussion? *British Journal of Sports Medicine, 47*(5), 268–271. https://doi.org/10.1136/bjsports-2013-092247.

McGowan, A. L., Bretzin, A. C., Savage, J. L., Petit, K. M., Covassin, T., & Pontifex, M. B. (2019). Acute and protracted disruptions to inhibitory control following sports-related concussion. *Neuropsychologia, 131*, 223–232. https://doi.org/10.1016/j.neuropsychologia.2019.05.026.

McGowan, A. L., Bretzin, A. C., Savage, J. L., Petit, K. M., Parks, A. C., Covassin, T., & Pontifex, M. B. (2018). Preliminary evidence for differential trajectories of recovery for cognitive flexibility following sports-related concussion. *Neuropsychology, 32*(5), 564–574. https://doi.org/10.1037/neu0000475.

McKee, A. C., Mez, J., Abdolmohammadi, B., Butler, M., Huber, B. R., Uretsky, M., ... Alosco, M. L. (2023). Neuropathologic and clinical findings in young contact sport athletes exposed to repetitive head impacts. *JAMA Neurology, 80*(10), 1037–1050. https://doi.org/10.1001/jamaneurol.2023.2907.

McKee, A. C., Stein, T. D., Huber, B. R., Crary, J. F., Bieniek, K., Dickson, D., ... Daneshvar, D. H. (2023). Chronic traumatic encephalopathy (CTE): Criteria for neuropathological diagnosis and relationship to repetitive head impacts. *Acta Neuropathologica, 145*(4), 371–394. https://doi.org/10.1007/s00401-023-02540-w.

McPherson, A. L., Nagai, T., Webster, K. E., & Hewett, T. E. (2019). Musculoskeletal injury risk after sport-related concussion: A systematic review and meta-analysis. *The American Journal of Sports Medicine, 47*(7), 1754–1762. https://doi.org/10.1177/0363546518785901.

Medina, M., & Avila, J. (2014). The role of extracellular Tau in the spreading of neurofibrillary pathology. *Frontiers in Cellular Neuroscience, 8*. https://doi.org/10.3389/fncel.2014.00113.

Meehan, S. K., Mirdamadi, J. L., Martini, D. N., & Broglio, S. P. (2017). Changes in cortical plasticity in relation to a history of concussion during adolescence. *Frontiers in Human Neuroscience, 11*. https://doi.org/10.3389/fnhum.2017.00005.

Mehta, K. M., Ott, A., Kalmijn, S., Slooter, A. J. C., van Duijn, C. M., Hofman, A., & Breteler, M. M. B. (1999). Head trauma and risk of dementia and Alzheimer's disease. *Neurology, 53*(9), 1959. https://doi.org/10.1212/WNL.53.9.1959.

Merz, Z. C., Van Patten, R., & Lace, J. (2017). Current public knowledge pertaining to traumatic brain injury: Influence of demographic factors, social trends, and sport concussion experience on the understanding of traumatic brain injury sequelae. *Archives of Clinical Neuropsychology, 32*(2), 155–167. https://doi.org/10.1093/arclin/acw092.

Miltner, W. H. R., Lemke, U., Weiss, T., Holroyd, C., Scheffers, M. K., & Coles, M. G. H. (2003). Implementation of error-processing in the human anterior cingulate cortex: A source analysis of the magnetic equivalent of the error-related negativity. *Biological Psychology, 64*, 157–166. https://doi.org/10.1016/S0301-0511(03)00107-8.

Mittenberg, W., & Strauman, S. (2000). Diagnosis of mild head injury and the post-concussion syndrome. *The Journal of Head Trauma Rehabilitation, 15*(2), 783.

Mohai, A., Gifford, J., Herkt, R., Parker, A., Toder, A., Dixon, D., & Kennedy, E. (2022). A scoping review of cervical spine evaluation in standardised clinical concussion evaluation tools. *Physical Therapy in Sport, 57*, 95–104. https://doi.org/10.1016/j.ptsp.2022.07.010.

Moore, R. D., Hillman, C. H., & Broglio, S. P. (2014). The persistent influence of concussive injuries on cognitive control and neuroelectric function. *Journal of Athletic Training, 49*(1), 24–35. https://doi.org/10.4085/1062-6050-49.1.01.

Moore, R. D., Kay, J. J., & Ellemberg, D. (2018). The long-term outcomes of sport-related concussion in pediatric populations. *International Journal of Psychophysiology, 132*, 14–24. https://doi.org/10.1016/j.ijpsycho.2018.04.003.

Moore, R. D., Kay, J. J. M., Gunn, B., Harrison, A. T., Torres-McGehee, T., & Pontifex, M. B. (2023). Increased anxiety and depression among collegiate athletes with comorbid ADHD and history of concussion. *Psychology of Sport and Exercise, 68*, 102418. https://doi.org/10.1016/j.psychsport.2023.102418.

Moore, R. D., Pindus, D. M., Drolette, E. S., Scudder, M. R., Raine, L. B., & Hillman, C. H. (2015). The persistent influence of pediatric concussion on attention and cognitive control during flanker performance. *Biological Psychology, 109*, 93–102. https://doi.org/10.1016/j.biopsycho.2015.04.008.

Moore, R. D., Pindus, D. M., Raine, L. B., Drollette, E. S., Scudder, M. R., Ellemberg, D., & Hillman, C. H. (2016). The persistent influence of concussion on attention, executive control and neuroelectric function in preadolescent children. *International Journal of Psychophysiology: Official Journal of the International Organization of Psychophysiology, 99*, 85–95. https://doi.org/10.1016/j.ijpsycho.2015.11.010.

Moore, R. D., Sicard, V., Pindus, D., Raine, L. B., Drollette, E. S., Scudder, M. R., ... Hillman, C. H. (2019). A targeted neuropsychological examination of children with a history of sport-related concussion. *Brain Injury, 33*(3), 291–298. https://doi.org/10.1080/02699052.2018.1546408.

Morgan, C. D., Zuckerman, S. L., Lee, Y. M., King, L., Beaird, S., Sills, A. K., & Solomon, G. S. (2015). Predictors of postconcussion syndrome after sports-related concussion in young athletes: A matched case-control study. *Journal of Neurosurgery: Pediatrics, 15*(6), 589–598. https://doi.org/10.3171/2014.10.PEDS14356.

Mortimer, J. A., Van Duijn, C. M., Chandra, V., Fratiglioni, L., Graves, A. B., Heyman, A., ... Soininen, H. A Hofman for the Eurodem Risk Factors Research Group. (1991). Head trauma as a risk factor for Alzheimer's disease: A collaborative re-analysis of case-control studies. *International Journal of Epidemiology, 20*(Supplement_2), S28–S35. https://doi.org/10.1093/ije/20.Supplement_2.S28.

Moser, R. S., Schatz, P., & Jordan, B. D. (2005). Prolonged effects of concussion in high school athletes. *Neurosurgery, 57*(2), 300. https://doi.org/10.1227/01.NEU.0000166663.98616.E4.

Mucha, A., Collins, M. W., Elbin, R. J., Furman, J. M., Troutman-Enseki, C., DeWolf, R. M., ... Kontos, A. P. (2014). A brief vestibular/ocular motor screening (VOMS) assessment to evaluate concussions: Preliminary findings. *The American Journal of Sports Medicine, 42*(10), 2479–2486. https://doi.org/10.1177/0363546514543775.

Nedergaard, M. (2013). Garbage truck of the brain. *Science (New York, N. Y.), 340*(6140), 1529–1530. https://doi.org/10.1126/science.1240514.

Olson, R. L., Brush, C. J., Ehmann, P. J., Buckman, J. F., & Alderman, B. L. (2018). A history of sport-related concussion is associated with sustained deficits in conflict and error monitoring. *International Journal of Psychophysiology, 132*, 145–154. https://doi.org/10.1016/j.ijpsycho.2018.01.006.

Opel, R. A., Christy, A., Boespflug, E. L., Weymann, K. B., Case, B., Pollock, J. M., ... Lim, M. M. (2019). Effects of traumatic brain injury on sleep and enlarged perivascular spaces. *Journal of Cerebral Blood Flow & Metabolism, 39*(11), 2258–2267. https://doi.org/10.1177/0271678X18791632.

Ornstein, P. A., Haden, C. A., & Hedrick, A. M. (2004). Learning to remember: Social-communicative exchanges and the development of children's memory skills. *Developmental Review, 24*(4), 374–395. https://doi.org/10.1016/j.dr.2004.08.004.

Oyegbile, T. O., Dougherty, A., Tanveer, S., Zecavati, N., & Delasobera, B. E. (2020). High sleep disturbance and longer concussion duration in repeat concussions. *Behavioral Sleep Medicine, 18*(2), 241–248. https://doi.org/10.1080/15402002.2019.1578223.

Ozen, L. J., Itier, R. J., Preston, F. F., & Fernandes, M. A. (2013). Long-term working memory deficits after concussion: Electrophysiological evidence. *Brain Injury, 27*(11), 1244–1255. https://doi.org/10.3109/02699052.2013.804207.

Paci, M., Di Cosmo, G., Perrucci, M. G., Ferri, F., & Costantini, M. (2021). Cortical silent period reflects individual differences in action stopping performance. *Scientific Reports, 11*(1), 15158. https://doi.org/10.1038/s41598-021-94494-w.

Parks, A. C., Moore, R. D., Wu, C.-T., Broglio, S. P., Covassin, T., Hillman, C. H., & Pontifex, M. B. (2015). The association between a history of concussion and variability in behavioral and neuroelectric indices of cognition. *International Journal of Psychophysiology, 98*(3, Part 1), 426–434. https://doi.org/10.1016/j.ijpsycho.2015.08.006.

Patricios, J. S., Davis, G. A., Ahmed, O. H., Blauwet, C., Schneider, G. M., Purcell, L. K., ... Schneider, K. J. (2023). Introducing the sport concussion office assessment tool 6 (SCOAT6). *British Journal of Sports Medicine, 57*(11), 648–650. https://doi.org/10.1136/bjsports-2023-106860.

Patricios, J. S., Schneider, K. J., Dvorak, J., Ahmed, O. H., Blauwet, C., Cantu, R. C., ... Meeuwisse, W. (2023). Consensus statement on concussion in sport: The 6th International Conference on Concussion in Sport–Amsterdam, October 2022. *British Journal of Sports Medicine, 57*(11), 695–711. https://doi.org/10.1136/bjsports-2023-106898.

Pauhl, A., Yasen, A., & Christie, A. (2022). Corticospinal excitability and inhibition are not different between concussed males and females. Article 7 *Brain Sciences, 12*(7), https://doi.org/10.3390/brainsci12070824.

Pearce, A. J., Hoy, K., Rogers, M. A., Corp, D. T., Davies, C. B., Maller, J. J., & Fitzgerald, P. B. (2015). Acute motor, neurocognitive and neurophysiological change following concussion injury in Australian amateur football. A prospective multimodal investigation. *Journal of Science and Medicine in Sport, 18*(5), 500–506. https://doi.org/10.1016/j.jsams.2014.07.010.

Pearce, A. J., Kidgell, D. J., Frazer, A. K., King, D. A., Buckland, M. E., & Tommerdahl, M. (2020). Corticomotor correlates of somatosensory reaction time and variability in individuals with post concussion symptoms. *Somatosensory & Motor Research, 37*(1), 14–21. https://doi.org/10.1080/08990220.2019.1699045.

Pearce, A. J., Kidgell, D. J., Tommerdahl, M. A., Frazer, A. K., Batchelor, J., & Buckland, M. E. (2021). Chronic neurophysiological effects of repeated head trauma in retired Australian male sport athletes. *Frontiers in Neurology, 12*. https://doi.org/10.3389/fneur.2021.633320.

Pearce, A. J., Rist, B., Fraser, C. L., Cohen, A., & Maller, J. J. (2018). Neurophysiological and cognitive impairment following repeated sports concussion injuries in retired professional rugby league players. *Brain Injury, 32*(4), 498–505. https://doi.org/10.1080/02699052.2018.1430376.

Pearce, A. J., Tommerdahl, M., & King, D. A. (2019). Neurophysiological abnormalities in individuals with persistent post-concussion symptoms. *Neuroscience, 408*, 272–281. https://doi.org/10.1016/j.neuroscience.2019.04.019.

Piantino, J., Schwartz, D. L., Luther, M., Newgard, C., Silbert, L., Raskind, M., ... Peskind, E. (2021). Link between mild traumatic brain injury, poor sleep, and magnetic resonance imaging: Visible perivascular spaces in veterans. *Journal of Neurotrauma, 38*(17), 2391–2399. https://doi.org/10.1089/neu.2020.7447.

Piggin, J., Parry, K. D., & White, A. J. (2024). Conceptualising brainwashing: Corporate communication in a concussion crisis. *International Journal of Sport Policy and Politics, 0*(0), 1–15. https://doi.org/10.1080/19406940.2024.2312813.

Pillar, G., Averbooch, E., Katz, N., Peled, N., Kaufman, Y., & Shahar, E. (2003). Prevalence and risk of sleep disturbances in adolescents after minor head injury. *Pediatric Neurology, 29*(2), 131–135. https://doi.org/10.1016/S0887-8994(03)00149-8.

Ponsford, J., Cameron, P., Fitzgerald, M., Grant, M., Mikocka-Walus, A., & Schönberger, M. (2012). Predictors of postconcussive symptoms 3 months after mild traumatic brain injury. *Neuropsychology, 26*(3), 304–313. https://doi.org/10.1037/a0027888.

Ponsford, J., Nguyen, S., Downing, M., Bosch, M., McKenzie, J., Turner, S., ... Green, S. (2019). Factors associated with persistent post-concussion symptoms following mild traumatic brain injury in adults. *Journal of Rehabilitation Medicine, 51*(1), 32–39. https://doi.org/10.2340/16501977-2492.

Pontifex, M. B., Broglio, S. P., Drollette, E. S., Scudder, M. A., Johnson, C. R., O'Connor, P. M., & Hillman, C. H. (2012). The relation of mild traumatic brain injury to chronic lapses of attention. *Research Quarterly for Exercise and Sport, 83*, 553–559. https://doi.org/10.5641/027013612804582605.

Pontifex, M. B., O'Connor, P. M., Broglio, S. P., & Hillman, C. H. (2009). The association between mild traumatic brain injury history and cognitive control. *Neuropsychologia, 47*(14), 3210–3216. https://doi.org/10.1016/j.neuropsychologia.2009.07.021.

Powers, K. C., Cinelli, M. E., & Kalmar, J. M. (2014). Cortical hypoexcitability persists beyond the symptomatic phase of a concussion. *Brain Injury, 28*(4), 465–471. https://doi.org/10.3109/02699052.2014.888759.

Pryor, J., Larson, A., & DeBeliso, M. (2016). The prevalence of depression and concussions in a sample of active North American semi-professional and professional football players. *Journal of Lifestyle Medicine, 6*(1), 7–15. https://doi.org/10.15280/jlm.2016.6.1.7.

Putukian, M. (2016). The psychological response to injury in student athletes: A narrative review with a focus on mental health. *British Journal of Sports Medicine, 50*(3), 145. https://doi.org/10.1136/bjsports-2015-095586.

Putukian, M., Purcell, L., Schneider, K. J., Black, A. M., Burma, J. S., Chandran, A., ... Broglio, S. (2023). Clinical recovery from concussion–return to school and sport: A systematic review and meta-analysis. *British Journal of Sports Medicine, 57*(12), 798–809. https://doi.org/10.1136/bjsports-2022-106682.

Raikes, A. C., & Schaefer, S. Y. (2016). Sleep quantity and quality during acute concussion: A pilot study. *Sleep, 39*(12), 2141–2147. https://doi.org/10.5665/sleep.6314.

Randolph, C. (2018). Chronic traumatic encephalopathy is not a real disease. *Archives of Clinical Neuropsychology, 33*(5), 644–648. https://doi.org/10.1093/arclin/acy063.

Rao, V., Bergey, A., Hill, H., Efron, D., & McCann, U. (2011). Sleep disturbance after mild traumatic brain injury: Indicator of injury? *The Journal of Neuropsychiatry and Clinical Neurosciences, 23*(2), 201–205. https://doi.org/10.1176/jnp.23.2.jnp201.

Reddy, C. C., Collins, M., Lovell, M., & Kontos, A. P. (2013). Efficacy of amantadine treatment on symptoms and neurocognitive performance among adolescents following sports-related concussion. *The Journal of Head Trauma Rehabilitation, 28*(4), 260–265. https://doi.org/10.1097/HTR.0b013e318257fbc6.

Redlinger, F., Sicard, V., Caron, G., & Ellemberg, D. (2022). Long-term cognitive impairments of sports concussions in college-aged athletes: A meta-analysis. *Translational Journal of the American College of Sports Medicine,* 7(2), e000193. https://doi.org/10.1249/TJX.0000000000000193.

Register-Mihalik, J. K., Mihalik, J. P., & Guskiewicz, K. M. (2009). Association between previous concussion history and symptom endorsement during preseason baseline testing in high school and collegiate athletes. *Sports Health, 1*(1), 61–65. https://doi.org/10.1177/1941738108325920.

Reneker, J. C., Babl, R., & Flowers, M. M. (2019). History of concussion and risk of subsequent injury in athletes and service members: A systematic review and meta-analysis. *Musculoskeletal Science and Practice, 42,* 173–185. https://doi.org/10.1016/j.msksp.2019.04.004.

Reuter-Lorenz, P. A., & Cappell, K. A. (2008). Neurocognitive aging and the compensation hypothesis. *Current Directions in Psychological Science, 17*(3), 177–182. https://doi.org/10.1111/j.1467-8721.2008.00570.x.

Reynolds, A. C., & Banks, S. (2010). Total sleep deprivation, chronic sleep restriction and sleep disruption. In G. A. Kerkhof, & H. P. A. Van Dongen (Vol. Eds.), *Progress in brain research: Vol. 185,* (pp. 91–103). Elsevier. https://doi.org/10.1016/B978-0-444-53702-7.00006-3.

Rice, S. M., Parker, A. G., Rosenbaum, S., Bailey, A., Mawren, D., & Purcell, R. (2018). Sport-related concussion and mental health outcomes in elite athletes: A systematic review. *Sports Medicine (Auckland, N. Z.), 48*(2), 447–465. https://doi.org/10.1007/s40279-017-0810-3.

Rice, S. M., Purcell, R., De Silva, S., Mawren, D., McGorry, P. D., & Parker, A. G. (2016). The mental health of elite athletes: A narrative systematic review. *Sports Medicine (Auckland, N. Z.), 46*(9), 1333–1353. https://doi.org/10.1007/s40279-016-0492-2.

Rieger, B., Lewandowski, L., Potts, H., Potter, K., & Chin, L. S. (2018). Parent knowledge and perceptions of concussion related to youth football. *Cureus, 10*(3), e2268. https://doi.org/10.7759/cureus.2268.

Root, J. M., Zuckerbraun, N. S., Wang, L., Winger, D. G., Brent, D., Kontos, A., & Hickey, R. W. (2016). History of somatization is associated with prolonged recovery from concussion. *The Journal of Pediatrics, 174,* 39–44.e1. https://doi.org/10.1016/j.jpeds.2016.03.020.

Rosenblum, D. J., Walton, S. R., Erdman, N. K., Broshek, D. K., Hart, J. M., & Resch, J. E. (2020). If not now, when? An absence of neurocognitive and postural stability deficits in collegiate athletes with one or more concussions. *Journal of Neurotrauma, 37*(10), 1211–1220. https://doi.org/10.1089/neu.2019.6813.

Rosso, S. M., Landweer, E.-J., Houterman, M., Kaat, L. D., Duijn, C. M. V., & Swieten, J. C. V. (2003). Medical and environmental risk factors for sporadic frontotemporal dementia: A retrospective case–control study. *Journal of Neurology, Neurosurgery & Psychiatry, 74*(11), 1574–1576. https://doi.org/10.1136/jnnp.74.11.1574.

Russell, E. R., McCabe, T., Mackay, D. F., Stewart, K., MacLean, J. A., Pell, J. P., & Stewart, W. (2020). Mental health and suicide in former professional soccer players. *Journal of Neurology, Neurosurgery & Psychiatry, 91*(12), 1256–1260. https://doi.org/10.1136/jnnp-2020-323315.

Russell, K., Walld, R., Bolton, J. M., Chateau, D., & Ellis, M. J. (2023). Incidence of subsequent mental health disorders and social adversity following pediatric concussion: A longitudinal, population-based study. *The Journal of Pediatrics, 259*, 113436. https://doi.org/10.1016/j.jpeds.2023.113436.

Sakka, L., Coll, G., & Chazal, J. (2011). Anatomy and physiology of cerebrospinal fluid. *European Annals of Otorhinolaryngology, Head and Neck Diseases, 128*(6), 309–316. https://doi.org/10.1016/j.anorl.2011.03.002.

Salisbury, D., Kolessar, M., Callender, L., & Bennett, M. (2017). Concussion knowledge among rehabilitation staff. *Baylor University Medical Center Proceedings, 30*(1), 33–37. https://doi.org/10.1080/08998280.2017.11929519.

Sanger, T. D., Garg, R. R., & Chen, R. (2001). Interactions between two different inhibitory systems in the human motor cortex. *The Journal of Physiology, 530*(Pt 2), 307–317. https://doi.org/10.1111/j.1469-7793.2001.0307l.x.

Sarwary, A. M. E., Wischnewski, M., Schutter, D. J. L. G., Selen, L. P. J., & Medendorp, W. P. (2018). Corticospinal correlates of fast and slow adaptive processes in motor learning. *Journal of Neurophysiology, 120*(4), 2011–2019. https://doi.org/10.1152/jn.00488.2018.

Schatz, P., Moser, R. S., Covassin, T., & Karpf, R. (2011). Early indicators of enduring symptoms in high school athletes with multiple previous concussions. *Neurosurgery, 68*(6), 1562. https://doi.org/10.1227/NEU.0b013e31820e382e.

Schmidt, J., Brown, K. E., Feldman, S. J., Babul, S., Zwicker, J. G., & Boyd, L. A. (2021). Evidence of altered interhemispheric communication after pediatric concussion. *Brain Injury, 35*(10), 1143–1161. https://doi.org/10.1080/02699052.2021.1929485.

Schofield, P. W., Tang, M., Marder, K., Bell, K., Dooneief, G., Chun, M., ... Mayeux, R. (1997). Alzheimer's disease after remote head injury: An incidence study. *Journal of Neurology, Neurosurgery & Psychiatry, 62*(2), 119–124. https://doi.org/10.1136/jnnp.62.2.119.

Schreiber, S., Barkai, G., Gur-Hartman, T., Peles, E., Tov, N., Dolberg, O. T., & Pick, C. G. (2008). Long-lasting sleep patterns of adult patients with minor traumatic brain injury (mTBI) and non-mTBI subjects. *Sleep Medicine, 9*(5), 481–487. https://doi.org/10.1016/j.sleep.2007.04.014.

Scott, B. R., Uomoto, J. M., & Barry, E. S. (2020). Impact of pre-existing migraine and other co-morbid or co-occurring conditions on presentation and clinical course following deployment-related concussion. *Headache: The Journal of Head and Face Pain, 60*(3), 526–541. https://doi.org/10.1111/head.13709.

Seeger, T. A., Kirton, A., Esser, M. J., Gallagher, C., Dunn, J., Zewdie, E., ... Barlow, K. M. (2017). Cortical excitability after pediatric mild traumatic brain injury. *Brain Stimulation, 10*(2), 305–314. https://doi.org/10.1016/j.brs.2016.11.011.

Sicard, V., Caron, G., Moore, R. D., & Ellemberg, D. (2021). Post-exercise cognitive testing to assess persisting alterations in athletes with a history of concussion. *Brain Injury, 35*(8), 978–985. https://doi.org/10.1080/02699052.2021.1944668.

Sicard, V., Harrison, A. T., & Moore, R. D. (2021). Psycho-affective health, cognition, and neurophysiological functioning following sports-related concussion in symptomatic and asymptomatic athletes, and control athletes. *Scientific Reports, 11*(1), 13838. https://doi.org/10.1038/s41598-021-93218-4.

Sicard, V., & Moore, R. D. (2022). The relation of learning disabilities to the long-term outcomes of concussion. *Psychology of Sport and Exercise, 58*, 102101. https://doi.org/10.1016/j.psychsport.2021.102101.

Sicard, V., Moore, R. D., & Ellemberg, D. (2018). Long-term cognitive outcomes in male and female athletes following sport-related concussions. *International Journal of Psychophysiology, 132*, 3–8. https://doi.org/10.1016/j.ijpsycho.2018.03.011.

Sicard, V., Moore, R. D., & Ellemberg, D. (2019). Sensitivity of the cogstate test battery for detecting prolonged cognitive alterations stemming from sport-related concussions. *Clinical Journal of Sport Medicine, 29*(1), 62. https://doi.org/10.1097/JSM.0000000000000492.

Silverberg, N. D., Iverson, G. L., Cogan, A., Dams-O-Connor, K., Delmonico, R., Graf, M. J. P., ... Zemek, R. (2023). The American congress of rehabilitation medicine diagnostic criteria for mild traumatic brain injury. *Archives of Physical Medicine and Rehabilitation, 104*(8), 1343–1355. https://doi.org/10.1016/j.apmr.2023.03.036.

Singh, R., Meier, T. B., Kuplicki, R., Savitz, J., Mukai, I., Cavanagh, L., ... Bellgowan, P. S. F. (2014). Relationship of collegiate football experience and concussion with hippocampal volume and cognitive outcomes. *JAMA: The Journal of the American Medical Association, 311*(18), 1883–1888. https://doi.org/10.1001/jama.2014.3313.

Solomon, G. S., Kuhn, A. W., & Zuckerman, S. L. (2016). Depression as a modifying factor in sport-related concussion: A critical review of the literature. *The Physician and Sportsmedicine, 44*(1), 14–19. https://doi.org/10.1080/00913847.2016.1121091.

Sommerauer, M., Valko, P. O., Werth, E., & Baumann, C. R. (2013). Excessive sleep need following traumatic brain injury: A case–control study of 36 patients. *Journal of Sleep Research, 22*(6), 634–639. https://doi.org/10.1111/jsr.12068.

Sosnoff, J. J., Broglio, S. P., Shin, S., & Ferrara, M. S. (2011). Previous mild traumatic brain injury and postural-control dynamics. *Journal of Athletic Training, 46*(1), 85–91. https://doi.org/10.4085/1062-6050-46.1.85.

Stein, T. D., Alvarez, V. E., & McKee, A. C. (2015). Concussion in chronic traumatic encephalopathy. *Current Pain and Headache Reports, 19*(10), 47. https://doi.org/10.1007/s11916-015-0522-z.

Stern, Y. (2002). What is cognitive reserve? Theory and research application of the reserve concept. *Journal of the International Neuropsychological Society, 8*(3), 448–460. https://doi.org/10.1017/S1355617702813248.

Sternbach, G. L. (2000). The glasgow coma scale. *The Journal of Emergency Medicine, 19*(1), 67–71. https://doi.org/10.1016/S0736-4679(00)00182-7.

Stevens, D. J., Appleton, S., Bickley, K., Holtzhausen, L., & Adams, R. (2023). Electroencephalographic changes in sleep during acute and subacute phases after sports-related concussion. *Nature and Science of Sleep, 15*, 267–273. https://doi.org/10.2147/NSS.S397900.

Stokes, W., Runnalls, K., Choynowki, J., St. Pierre, M., Anaya, M., Statton, M. A., ... Cantarero, G. (2020). Altered corticomotor latencies but normal motor neuroplasticity in concussed athletes. *Journal of Neurophysiology, 123*(5), 1600–1605. https://doi.org/10.1152/jn.00774.2019.

Stone, K. C., Taylor, D. J., McCrae, C. S., Kalsekar, A., & Lichstein, K. L. (2008). Nonrestorative sleep. *Sleep Medicine Reviews, 12*(4), 275–288. https://doi.org/10.1016/j.smrv.2007.12.002.

Swanson, C. W., & Fling, B. W. (2018). Associations between gait coordination, variability and motor cortex inhibition in young and older adults. *Experimental Gerontology, 113*, 163–172. https://doi.org/10.1016/j.exger.2018.10.002.

Tanaka, K., Mizushima, T., & Saeki, Y. (2012). The proteasome: Molecular machinery and pathophysiological roles. *393*(4), 217–234. https://doi.org/10.1515/hsz-2011-0285.

Terry, D. P., Jo, J., Williams, K., Davis, P., Iverson, G. L., & Zuckerman, S. L. (2024). Examining the new consensus criteria for traumatic encephalopathy syndrome in community-dwelling older adults. *Journal of Neurotrauma*. https://doi.org/10.1089/neu.2023.0601.

Theadom, A., Cropley, M., Parmar, P., Barker-Collo, S., Starkey, N., Jones, K., & Feigin, V. L. (2015). Sleep difficulties one year following mild traumatic brain injury in a population-based study. *Sleep Medicine, 16*(8), 926–932. https://doi.org/10.1016/j.sleep.2015.04.013.

Theriault, M., de Beaumont, L., Gosselin, N., Filipinni, M., & Lassonde, M. (2009). Electrophysiological abnormalities in well functioning multiple concussed athletes. *Brain Injury, 23*, 899–906.

Tremblay, S., de Beaumont, L., Lassonde, M., & Théoret, H. (2011). Evidence for the specificity of intracortical inhibitory dysfunction in asymptomatic concussed athletes. *Journal of Neurotrauma, 28*(4), 493–502. https://doi.org/10.1089/neu.2010.1615.

Tsushima, W. T., Geling, O., Arnold, M., & Oshiro, R. (2016). Effects of two concussions on the neuropsychological functioning and symptom reporting of high school athletes. *Applied Neuropsychology: Child, 5*(1), 9–13. https://doi.org/10.1080/21622965.2014.902762.

Varriano, B., Tomlinson, G., Tarazi, A., Wennberg, R., Tator, C., & Tartaglia, M. C. (2018). Age, gender and mechanism of injury interactions in post-concussion syndrome. *Canadian Journal of Neurological Sciences/Journal Canadien Des Sciences Neurologiques, 45*(6), 636–642. https://doi.org/10.1017/cjn.2018.322.

Veliz, P., Eckner, J. T., Zdroik, J., & Schulenberg, J. E. (2019). Lifetime prevalence of self-reported concussion among adolescents involved in competitive sports: A National U.S. Study. *Journal of Adolescent Health, 64*(2), 272–275. https://doi.org/10.1016/j.jadohealth.2018.08.023.

Voormolen, D. C., Cnossen, M. C., Polinder, S., von Steinbuechel, N., Vos, P. E., & Haagsma, J. A. (2018). Divergent classification methods of post-concussion syndrome after mild traumatic brain injury: Prevalence rates, risk factors, and functional outcome. *Journal of Neurotrauma, 35*(11), 1233–1241. https://doi.org/10.1089/neu.2017.5257.

Vynorius, K. C., Paquin, A. M., & Seichepine, D. R. (2016). Lifetime multiple mild traumatic brain injuries are associated with cognitive and mood symptoms in young healthy college students. *Frontiers in Neurology, 7*. https://doi.org/10.3389/fneur.2016.00188.

Walsh, D. R., Zhou, Z., Li, X., Kearns, J., Newport, D. T., & Mulvihill, J. J. E. (2021). Mechanical properties of the cranial meninges: A systematic review. *Journal of Neurotrauma, 38*(13), 1748–1761. https://doi.org/10.1089/neu.2020.7288.

Walton, S. R., Kerr, Z. Y., Brett, B. L., Chandran, A., DeFreese, J. D., Smith-Ryan, A. E., ... Guskiewicz, K. M. (2021). Health-promoting behaviours and concussion history are associated with cognitive function, mood-related symptoms and emotional–behavioural dyscontrol in former NFL players: An NFL-LONG Study. *British Journal of Sports Medicine, 55*(12), 683–690. https://doi.org/10.1136/bjsports-2020-103400.

Walton, S. R., Kerr, Z. Y., Mannix, R., Brett, B. L., Chandran, A., DeFreese, J. D., ... Echemendia, R. J. (2022). Subjective concerns regarding the effects of sport-related concussion on long-term brain health among former NFL players: An NFL-LONG Study. *Sports Medicine, 52*(5), 1189–1203. https://doi.org/10.1007/s40279-021-01589-5.

Waltzman, D., Sarmiento, K., & Daugherty, J. (2024). Factors that may influence Americans' views on when children should start playing tackle football. *Journal of Athletic Training, 59*(1), 22–29. https://doi.org/10.4085/1062-6050-0004.23.

Wang, Y., Jiang, N., Cheung, E. F. C., Sun, H., & Chan, R. C. K. (2015). Role of depression severity and impulsivity in the relationship between hopelessness and suicidal ideation in patients with major depressive disorder. *Journal of Affective Disorders, 183*, 83–89. https://doi.org/10.1016/j.jad.2015.05.001.

Weber, M. L., Dean, J.-H. L., Hoffman, N. L., Broglio, S. P., McCrea, M., McAllister, T. W., ... Dykhuizen, B. H. (2018). Influences of mental illness, current psychological state, and concussion history on baseline concussion assessment performance. *The American Journal of Sports Medicine, 46*(7), 1742–1751. https://doi.org/10.1177/0363546518765145.

Weight, D. G. (1998). Minor head trauma. *Psychiatric Clinics of North America, 21*(3), 609–624. https://doi.org/10.1016/S0193-953X(05)70026-5.

Werner, C., & Engelhard, K. (2007). Pathophysiology of traumatic brain injury. *BJA: British Journal of Anaesthesia, 99*(1), 4–9. https://doi.org/10.1093/bja/aem131.

Wijenberg, M. L. M., Stapert, S. Z., Verbunt, J. A., Ponsford, J. L., & Van Heugten, C. M. (2017). Does the fear avoidance model explain persistent symptoms after traumatic brain injury? *Brain Injury, 31*(12), 1597–1604. https://doi.org/10.1080/02699052.2017.1366551.

Wilkerson, G. B., Bruce, J. R., Wilson, A. W., Huang, N., Sartipi, M., Acocello, S. N., ... Mansouri, M. (2021). Perceptual-motor efficiency and concussion history are prospectively associated with injury occurrences among high school and collegiate American football players. *Orthopaedic Journal of Sports Medicine, 9*(10), https://doi.org/10.1177/23259671211051722.

Wilkerson, G. B., Wynn, K. R., Dill, P. W., Acocello, S., Carlson, L. M., & Hogg, J. (2024). Concussion history and virtual reality metrics predict core or lower extremity injury occurrence among high school athletes. *Frontiers in Sports and Active Living, 6*. https://doi.org/10.3389/fspor.2024.1374772.

Williams, B. R., Lazic, S. E., & Ogilvie, R. D. (2008). Polysomnographic and quantitative EEG analysis of subjects with long-term insomnia complaints associated with mild traumatic brain injury. *Clinical Neurophysiology, 119*(2), 429–438. https://doi.org/10.1016/j.clinph.2007.11.003.

Wood, R. L., McCabe, M., & Dawkins, J. (2011). The role of anxiety sensitivity in symptom perception after minor head injury: An exploratory study. *Brain Injury, 25*(13–14), 1296–1299. https://doi.org/10.3109/02699052.2011.624569.

Yang, J., Peek-Asa, C., Covassin, T., & Torner, J. C. (2015). Post-concussion symptoms of depression and anxiety in division I collegiate athletes. *Developmental Neuropsychology, 40*(1), 18–23. https://doi.org/10.1080/87565641.2014.973499.

Yeates, K. O., Räisänen, A. M., Premji, Z., Debert, C. T., Frémont, P., Hinds, S., ... Schneider, K. J. (2023). What tests and measures accurately diagnose persisting post-concussive symptoms in children, adolescents and adults following sport-related concussion? A systematic review. *British Journal of Sports Medicine, 57*(12), 780–788. https://doi.org/10.1136/bjsports-2022-106657.

Yoganandan, N., Sances, A., Pintar, F. A., Walsh, P. R., Ewing, C. L., Thomas, D. J., ... Droese, K. (1994). Biomechanical tolerance of the cranium. *SAE Transactions, 103*, 184–189.

Zemek, R., Barrowman, N., Freedman, S. B., Gravel, J., Gagnon, I., McGahern, C., ... for the Pediatric Emergency Research Canada (PERC) Concussion Team. (2016). Clinical risk score for persistent postconcussion symptoms among children with acute concussion in the ED. *JAMA: The Journal of the American Medical Association, 315*(10), 1014–1025. https://doi.org/10.1001/jama.2016.1203.

Zurlinden, T., Falletta, G., Schneider, K., Sorrell, A. E., Savransky, A., & Everhart, D. E. (2024). Public chronic traumatic encephalopathy knowledge: Sources, accuracy and confidence. *Current Sports Medicine Reports, 23*(1), 23. https://doi.org/10.1249/JSR.0000000000001131.

CHAPTER SEVEN

Individual child characteristics underlie differential engagement of neural oscillations during sentence processing

Julie M. Schneider*
Louisiana State University, Baton Rouge, LA, United States
*Corresponding author. e-mail address: juschnei@lsu.edu

Contents

Abstract

Although young children process sentences quickly and effortlessly, research indicates that the development of adult-like sentence processing abilities is prolonged, continuing into adolescence. This ongoing development suggests children may engage somewhat different skills than adults during sentence comprehension. Through a series of empirical research studies examining neural oscillations, we have identified different brain signatures underlying cognitive skills engaged by children during processing of naturally paced, auditory sentences. Our findings indicate that (a) children in late childhood and early adolescence rely more heavily on semantics for sentence comprehension than adults, and that (b) topographical and temporal changes in theta are sensitive to age differences, while changes in beta are associated with language abilities. Thus, ongoing neural specialization is influenced by individual child characteristics and underlies differences in the cognitive skills children engage during auditory sentence processing.

Psychology of Learning and Motivation, Volume 81
ISSN 0079-7421, https://doi.org/10.1016/bs.plm.2024.06.002

1. Introduction

Comprehension of language relies upon the ability to generate predictions about the sentence's intended meaning as it unfolds in real time (e.g., Altmann & Steedman, 1988; Frazier & Rayner, 1982; Marslen-Wilson, 1973; Trueswell, Sekerina, Hill, & Logrip, 1999). Specifically, one must transform the acoustic input into a phonological representation, identify each word that is spoken, integrate these words into a structured syntactic and semantic representation and use that representation to determine what the speaker is intending to convey (Snedeker & Huang, 2009). While a wealth of research has examined how adults incrementally process sentences (Bastiaansen & Hagoort, 2006; Bonhage, Meyer, Gruber, Friederici, & Mueller, 2017; Lam, Schoffelen, Uddén, Hultén, & Hagoort, 2016; Peña & Melloni, 2012; Prystauka & Lewis, 2019), relatively less is known about how children process language in real time and how they coordinate multiple sources of information during interpretation (Snedeker & Huang, 2009; Trueswell et al., 1999). The examination of neural oscillations has provided scientists with new ways to investigate various cognitive and linguistic processes necessary for successful language comprehension across the course of development. This is because neural oscillations allow for the investigation of simultaneous cognitive processes across longer time windows than traditional Event Related Potentials (ERPs). Despite the utility of studying neural oscillations in children, extant research has primarily focused on adults. The current review highlights the utility of examining neural oscillations during sentence processing in children, with a focus on integration of semantic and syntactic information, as well as the origin of individual differences in language processing.

2. The relationship between event-related potentials (ERPs) and event-related spectral perturbations (ERSPs) in studies of sentence processing

Human developmental neuroanatomy has firmly established that maturational trajectories differ across cortical regions, underlying developmental differences in how children process semantic and syntactic information (for review, see Morgan, Van der Meer, Vulchanova, Blasi, & Baggio, 2020). Research using ERPs consistently reports that semantic and syntactic abilities continue to develop through early adolescence to support language comprehension (e.g., Atchley et al., 2006; Hahne & Friederici, 2002). Although study specifics vary, children generally display an N400 that is later, larger and more broadly distributed and a P600 that is larger and later compared to adults (Benau, Morris, & Couperus, 2011; Friederici & Männel, 2013; Friederici, 2006; Friedrich & Friederici, 2004; Hahne, Eckstein, & Friederici, 2004). These developmental differences are thought to reflect higher cognitive processing demands, related to semantic retrieval (N400) and integration of syntactic information (P600), when children perform the same language task as adults.

These aforementioned ERP findings are informative about the development of early language skills. However, because ERPs are phase-locked neural responses, they fail to capture other relevant, non-phase locked neural activity—which can provide additional important information about different mechanisms that support language processing. Event-Related Spectral Perturbations (ERSPs) can identify induced, non-phase-locked neural responses across multiple frequencies by revealing changes in the amplitude of oscillatory dynamics induced by stimuli (Kielar, Meltzer, Moreno, Alain, & Bialystok, 2014; Lewis, Schoffelen, Bastiaansen, & Schriefers, 2014; Pfurtscheller & Da Silva, 1999). Studies of sentence processing commonly report changes in five discrete frequency bands of interest: delta (1–3 Hz), theta (4–8 Hz), alpha (9–12 Hz), beta (13–30 Hz) and gamma (30–80 Hz; Lam et al., 2016; Lewis, Schoffelen, Schriefers, & Bastiaansen, 2016; Meyer, 2018; Meyer, Obleser, & Friederici, 2013; Prystauka & Lewis, 2019; Weiss & Mueller, 2012). Across these studies, different frequency bands have been associated with various functional explanations. For example, changes in delta power have been related to speech perception (Mai, Minett, & Wang, 2016; Meyer, 2018). Increases in theta power are often associated with retrieval of semantic information, as increases in theta power are elicited in response to processing of individual words, especially those which carry meaning (i.e., open-class words like nouns, verbs, and adjectives; Bastiaansen, Van Der Linden, Ter Keurs, Dijkstra, & Hagoort, 2005; Bastiaansen, Oostenveld, Jensen, & Hagoort, 2008; Maguire, Brier, & Ferree, 2010; Maguire et al., 2022). Increases in alpha power correspond to increased verbal working memory load and attention (Klimesch, 1999; Meyer et al., 2013; Wianda & Ross, 2019), and increases in beta and gamma power are thought to reflect unification of the syntactic and semantic information as the sentence unfolds, respectively (Bastiaansen & Hagoort, 2015; Bastiaansen, Magyari, & Hagoort, 2010;

Behboudi, Castro, Chalamalasetty, & Maguire, 2023; Hald, Bastiaansen, & Hagoort, 2006; Wang Hagoort & Jensen, 2018; Wang, Zhu, & Bastiaansen, 2012). In the current review unification refers to the understanding of sentence meaning via a bottom-up process, wherein the meanings of individual words are combined and integrated through the combinatorial machinery of syntax (Hagoort, Baggio, & Willems, 2009).

Despite a wealth of research utilizing ERSPs to identify the neural correlates of sentence processing, the majority of studies in this area have been primarily focused on adult populations. Adult studies of sentence processing have suggested that ERP components may measure the same cognitive processes as ERSPs, but in somewhat different ways (Hagoort, Hald, Bastiaansen, & Petersson, 2004; Roehm, Bornkessel-Schlesewsky, & Schlesewsky, 2007; Schneider et al., 2016; Bastiaansen, Van Berkum, & Hagoort, 2002; Davidson & Indefrey, 2007). Researchers have argued that the lack of clear association between ERPs and ERSPs suggest that oscillatory dynamics are more than just time frequency representations of the ERP component (Bastiaansen & Hagoort, 2015; Bastiaansen et al., 2008; Wang et al., 2012). Evidence of this understanding comes from research comparing ERP and ERSP components within adults when completing the same task (Schneider et al., 2016; Davidson & Indefrey, 2007). Across these studies, a relationship between the N400 and theta band is observed: the N400 waveform is more negative in response to semantic violations, while theta power increases. Meanwhile, in the presence of a syntactic violation, there is an increase in the P600 component and a decrease in beta power (Schneider et al., 2016). While both ERPs and ERSPs are correlated within an individual in these studies, substantial variability remains unaccounted for. This unaccounted for variance has therefore been taken as evidence that oscillatory dynamics measure neural processes beyond those identified by ERP components (Bastiaansen & Hagoort, 2015; Bastiaansen et al., 2008; Wang et al., 2012). For example, while the N400 and theta power both gauge processing of a semantic violation, increases in theta may be indicative of increased demands to integrate the meaning of the violation into the sentence. Similarly, the presence of a P600 in response to syntactic violations may be related to re-analysis of the syntactic error, while beta power changes may reflect more complex processing skills necessary for unifying syntactic information to reanalyze the error.

By age five, children have mastered the basics of their native language and amassed a substantial vocabulary, yet we know relatively little about how they employ this knowledge as they are listening (Snedeker & Huang, 2009).

Furthermore, children continue to mature in their language skills beyond age five, often continuing their refinement through adolescence. During this prolonged development, children likely engage the same basic cognitive processes and neural mechanisms to perform language tasks as adults, but in somewhat different ways. For example, given there is a steady improvement in working memory performance from 4 to 15 years (Cowan, 2016; Gathercole, Pickering, Ambridge, & Wearing, 2004), children may be less effective in maintaining sentence level information in memory than adults, reflected by increases alpha power. Addressing these shortcomings can inform our understanding of the cognitive architecture underlying sentence processing, establish a comparison point for children with developmental disorders, and reveal the origin of individual differences in language comprehension.

3. How does the ability to process sentences develop?

Successful sentence comprehension is highly reliant on semantic and syntactic processing skills; however, the development of each of these skills, and their role in sentence processing throughout childhood, remains relatively unknown. We have conducted a series of empirical investigations examining the development of neural oscillatory dynamics during processing of sentences containing semantic and syntactic errors compared to correct sentences. Errors place higher demands on the features of language we seek to understand, and as such, can pinpoint which neural oscillatory dynamics underpin developmental differences in semantic and syntactic processing. From these empirical studies we have found evidence that adults engage higher-level unification processes, seamlessly integrating semantic and syntactic information into a cohesive message, while children rely more heavily on retrieval of individual word meanings to comprehend the sentence.

In one of the earliest studies examining the neural basis of auditory sentence processing during development (Schneider et al., 2016), children (10–12 years) and adults participated in a grammaticality judgement task in which they heard a sentence and indicated via button press whether the sentence was grammatical or ungrammatical. Each sentence began with a prepositional phrase, followed by either a plural (we/they) or singular (he/she) pronoun subject, followed by an action verb (e.g., jump; jumps). In ungrammatical sentences, the grammatical violation was a noun–verb

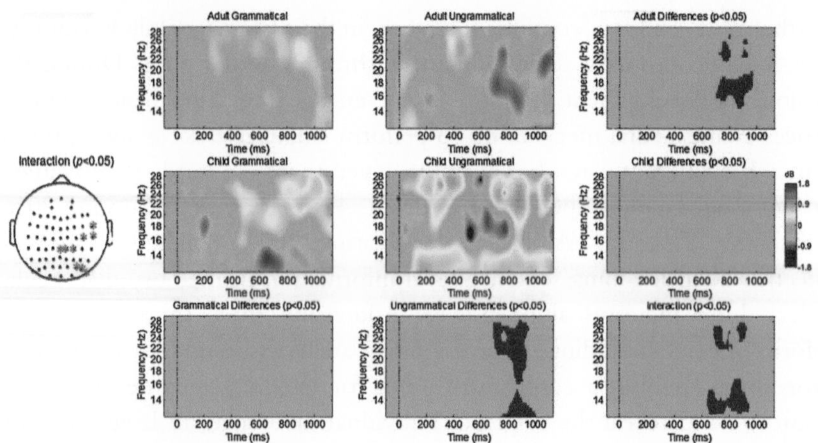

Fig. 1 Developmental differences in beta at CPz from 700 to 900 ms. This figure illustrates the increases/decreases in beta power between conditions from −100 to 1200 ms. Masking was used to highlight the significant interaction of age and grammaticality from 700 to 900 ms pulled out in the first analysis. The blue in the top box highlights beta power decreases for ungrammatical sentences in adults, that was lacking in children. The red in the bottom, right box highlights the significant interaction of age and grammaticality between 12 and 30 Hz ($p < 0.05$). *Reproduced from Schneider, J. M., Abel, A. D., Ogiela, D. A., Middleton, A. E., & Maguire, M. J. (2016). Developmental differences in beta and theta power during sentence processing. Developmental Cognitive Neuroscience, 19, 19–30 (CC BY).*

agreement error occurring at the verb (e.g., he walk, they walks). Children were significantly worse than adults at accurately identifying the grammaticality of sentences across conditions. These behavioral differences were represented neurally as well—in adults, grammatical violations were associated with a P600 effect and beta power decrease, both of which have been related to effective syntactic processing (Hahne et al., 2004; Bastiaansen et al., 2010; Davidson & Indefrey, 2007; Fig. 1). On the other hand, children demonstrated a different pattern of engagement from adults, including a smaller, later P600 effect, an N400 effect, and an increase in theta power in the presence of grammatical violations (Fig. 2).

Given the N400 and increases in theta have been associated with semantic retrieval (Kutas & Federmeier, 2011; Davidson & Indefrey, 2007; Hald et al., 2006; Maguire et al., 2010), we sought to clarify whether children were relying on semantic knowledge during processing of grammatical errors. In a sample of 8–9-year-olds, 12–13-year-olds, and adults we examined neural responses to both semantic and syntactic errors

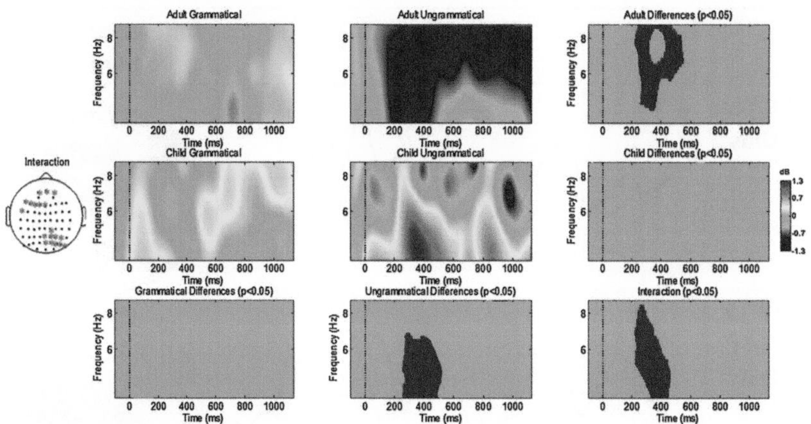

Fig. 2 Developmental differences in theta at F1 from 350 to 450 ms. This figure illustrates the increases/decreases in theta power between conditions from −100 to 1200 ms. Masking was used to highlight the significant interaction of age and grammaticality from 350 to 450 ms pulled out in first analysis. The blue in the top box highlights adult theta power decreases for ungrammatical sentences, which were not evident in children's processing of ungrammatical sentences. The red in the bottom right box highlights the significant interaction of age and grammaticality between 4 and 8 Hz ($p < 0.05$). *Reproduced from Schneider, J. M., Abel, A. D., Ogiela, D. A., Middleton, A. E., & Maguire, M. J. (2016). Developmental differences in beta and theta power during sentence processing. Developmental Cognitive Neuroscience, 19, 19–30 (CC BY).*

embedded in auditory, naturally paced sentences (Schneider & Maguire, 2019). All sentence types included a "target agent-action pairing" in which an inanimate agent (noun) was paired with a modal verb and action verb. In correct sentences, the target agent-action pairing was both possible and grammatically correct (i.e., *Outside in the garden, the hose can spray water on the flowers.*) The grammatically incorrect sentences included the target agent-action pairing, but the action included either the intrusion or omission of a present participle (-ing) form of the verb (i.e., *Outside in the garden, the hose can spraying water on the flowers/Around dinnertime, the oven will be bake the turkey to eat*). The semantic violation also included the target agent-action pairing and was grammatically plausible but introduced an unsuitable pairing of actions with agents (i.e., *Outside in the garden, the hose can bake water on the flowers*).

When identifying a semantic error, 8–9-year-olds performed significantly worse than 12–13 year-olds and adults, and when identifying a syntactic error, both groups of children performed significantly worse than

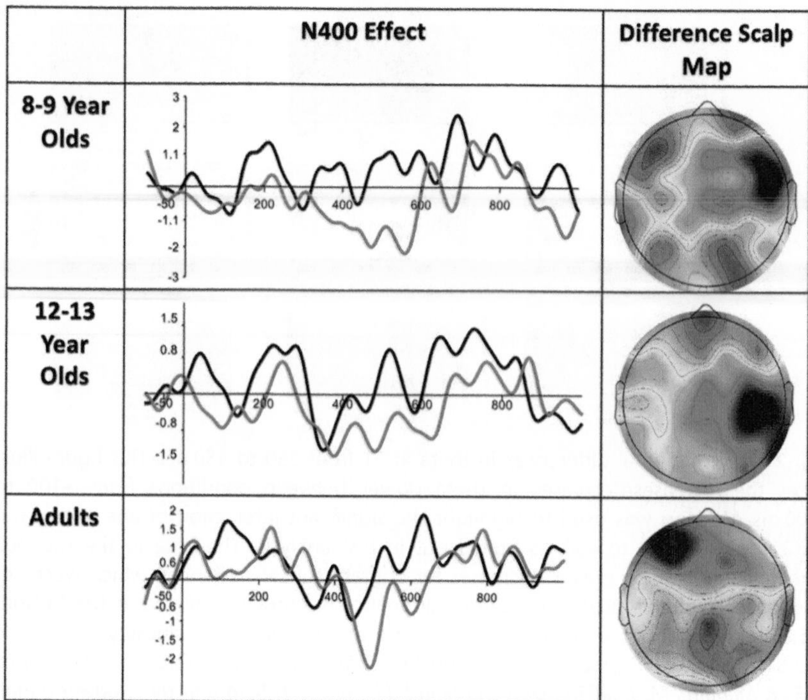

Fig. 3 ERPs for semantic error (red line) and correct sentences (black line) across all three age groups at left-central electrodes. Scalp maps represent the difference between conditions, in that red indicates the areas where an N400 effect was largest. All left-central electrodes were averaged together to produce the ERP for each age group. *Reproduced from Schneider, J. M., & Maguire, M. J. (2019). Developmental differences in the neural correlates supporting semantics and syntax during sentence processing. Developmental Science, 22(4), e12782. https://doi.org/10.1111/desc.12782 (CC BY).*

adults. In the presence of a semantic error, younger children showed a larger N400 and increase in theta compared to older children and adults (Figs. 3 and 4). Importantly, these ERP and ERSP markers were similar to those engaged during processing of a syntactic error in the previous study.

In the presence of a syntactic error, younger children once again exhibited a smaller, later P600 and lacked a decrease in beta compared to older children and adults. Older children, while more similar to adults than younger children, also exhibited a smaller, later P600 and diminished suppression of beta compared to adults (Figs. 5 and 6).

Interestingly, differences in the N400 and theta observed among children in the previous study during processing of syntactic errors were less

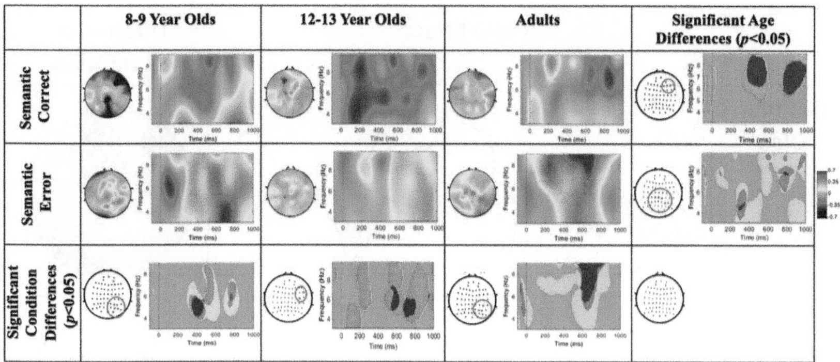

Fig. 4 Developmental changes in theta during processing of semantically correct and incorrect sentences (350–550 ms). Increases in theta power (red) were greater for errors than semantically correct sentences. Red dots on the scalp maps denote electrodes identified as significantly different by the cluster correction analysis ($p < 0.05$). The event-related spectral perturbations (ERSP) represent the average amplitude change across the significant cluster of electrodes circled in each corresponding scalpmap. Decreases are represented by blue and increases by red. Significant differences across the −100 to 1000 ms time window are plotted in the far right spectrograms, as well as the spectrograms along the bottom row. *Reproduced from Schneider, J. M., & Maguire, M. J. (2019). Developmental differences in the neural correlates supporting semantics and syntax during sentence processing. Developmental Science, 22(4), e12782. https://doi.org/10.1111/desc.12782 (CC BY).*

apparent in the current paradigm. The lack of N400 and theta power increase in response to syntactic errors may be attributed to differences in the type of syntactic errors introduced across studies: the omission or intrusion of the third person singular *-s* is less overt than the intrusion or omission of a present participle (-ing) form of the verb. In turn, the subtle nature of the third person singular *-s* may have placed higher processing demands on children, requiring them to engage semantic skills when processing this type of syntactic error. Taken together, these findings indicate that, during auditory sentence processing, children older than age 12 and adults activate unification processes, seamlessly integrating and binding semantic and syntactic information, associated with the P600 and beta, while children under the age of 12 may rely more heavily on retrieval of individual word meanings, associated with the N400 and theta, especially when sentence processing skills are taxed.

Although the investigation of errors allows us to better isolate the independent influence of semantics and syntax during sentence processing, it is also important to consider whether the same cognitive processes are engaged during processing of naturally paced, grammatically correct

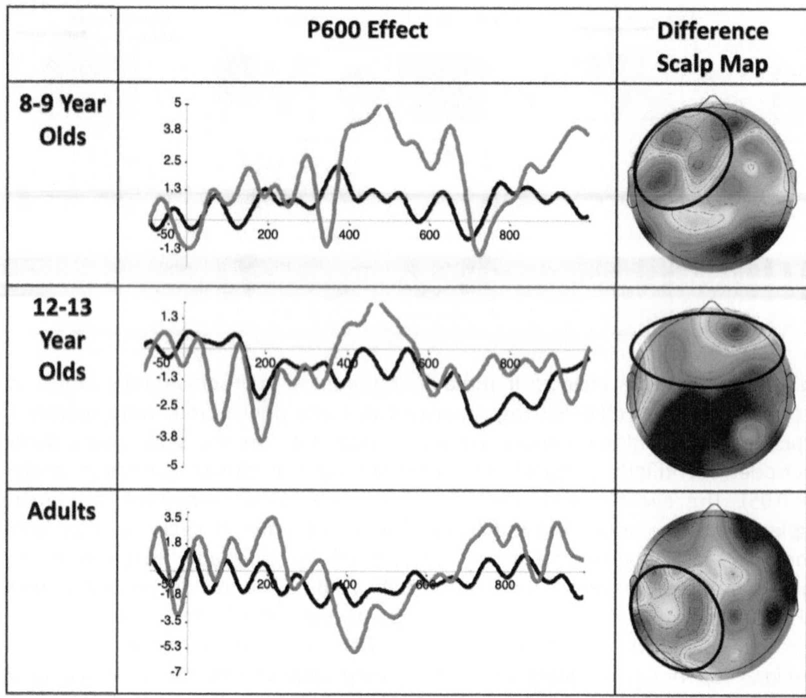

Fig. 5 ERPs for syntactic correct (black line) and syntactic error (red line) conditions across all three age groups. Scalp maps represent the difference between conditions, in that red indicates the areas where a P600 effect was largest. ERPs were plotted based on the location where effects were most robust. The black circles on each scalpmap represent which locations were averaged for the ERP. In 8–9 year olds, left frontal and central regions were collapsed and plotted in the ERP. In 12–13 year olds, left and right frontal regions were collapsed and plotted in the ERP. In adults, left central and parietal regions were collapsed and plotted in the ERP. *Reproduced from Schneider, J. M., & Maguire, M. J. (2019). Developmental differences in the neural correlates supporting semantics and syntax during sentence processing. Developmental Science, 22(4), e12782. https://doi.org/10.1111/desc.12782 (CC BY).*

sentences. If it is in fact the case that children rely more heavily than adults on semantic information to process naturally paced, grammatically and semantically correct language, we would expect to observe a developmental shift in the engagement of theta and beta, such that over the course of a sentence children will exhibit a more broadly distributed and larger theta increase than adults, while adults exhibit larger and more consistent changes in beta. On the other hand, if sentence processing is simply more effortful for children than adults, requiring higher levels of attention and working memory, we would expect children to exhibit increases in alpha power.

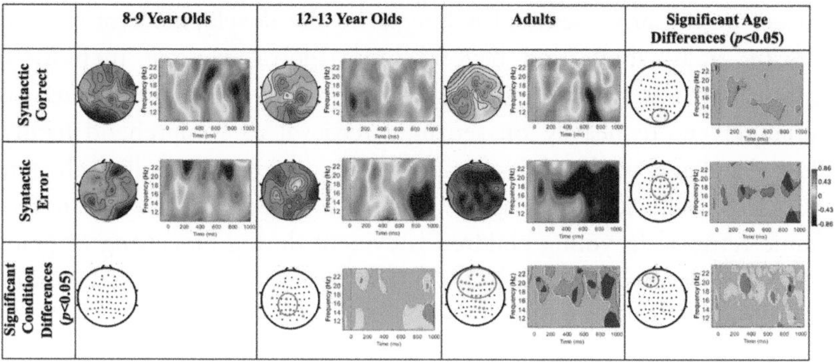

Fig. 6 Developmental changes in beta for syntactic correct and syntactic error conditions from 750 to 950 ms. Decreases in beta power (blue) were greater for errors than syntactically correct sentences and decreased as a function of age. Red dots on the scalp maps denote electrodes identified as significantly different by the cluster correction analysis ($p < 0.05$). The event-related spectral perturbations (ERSP) represent the average amplitude change across the significant cluster of electrodes circled in each corresponding scalpmap. Decreases are represented by blue and increases by red. Significant differences across the −100 to 1000 ms time window are plotted in the far right spectrograms, as well as the spectrograms along the bottom row. *Reproduced from Schneider, J. M., & Maguire, M. J. (2019). Developmental differences in the neural correlates supporting semantics and syntax during sentence processing. Developmental Science, 22(4), e12782. https://doi.org/10.1111/desc.12782 (CC BY).*

A follow-up study examining the neural underpinnings of processing grammatically correct sentences provides support for the first hypothesis (Schneider, Abel, Ogiela, McCord, & Maguire, 2018). Adults showed a consistent and robust increase in beta power throughout the course of the sentence; however, children (ages 10–12 years) did not show these same increases in beta, but instead demonstrated engagement of theta across frontal and right central electrode sites. Frontal theta activation has been shown to be greater when both children and adults are engaged in a task compared to when they are not involved in a task, suggesting theta activation may underlie more domain-general skills, such as working memory and content monitoring (Meyer, Endedijk, Van Ede, & Hunnius, 2019). However, additional research has suggested that theta band engagement over fronto-central electrode sites in childhood may underlie language-specific skills (Meyer et al., 2019; Bosseler et al., 2024; Kikuchi et al., 2011). We provide further evidence for this account, in that alpha engagement, which has also been shown to be greater when individuals are engaged in a task, did not differ between children and adults in the current study. Thus, developmental differences in theta, but not alpha, may suggest theta is more sensitive to language-specific processes, and is integral to the development of sentence processing skills, above and beyond more global working memory or attentional processes. These findings support our earlier arguments that children rely more heavily on semantic retrieval to comprehend natural, auditory language, while adults engage syntactic unification skills (Schneider et al., 2016; Schneider & Maguire, 2018). Furthermore, this reliance on semantic retrieval in young children is evident during processing of grammatically correct language and is not simply attributed to increased working memory demands.

4. What developmental factors underlie individual differences in sentence processing?

There are clear developmental differences in how children process spoken language relative to adults, with clear neural evidence underlying these differences in behavior. What remains unknown is why these differences between children and adults exist: Are differences in sentence processing skills simply a function of brain maturation, or is it that differences in other cognitive faculties related to their existing language abilities limits children's ability to process information in the same way as adults? To address these questions, we launched another series of empirical investigations examining the neural correlates of both auditory and visual sentence processing in children. In these studies, we investigated whether children's age or existing language knowledge predict their engagement of theta and beta during sentence processing throughout the school years. Our cumulative findings provide evidence that beta engagement is modulated by language abilities, while theta changes are sensitive to maturation.

The first investigation in this line of research examined how oscillatory activity is differentially engaged during processing of words, and the sentence context preceding them, when meaning was and was not mapped to a semantic representation (Momsen, Schneider, & Abel, 2022). In this study, children (ages 8–16 years) listened to 100 sentence triplets, each ending in a pseudoword that either supported mapping of a semantic representation or did not. In the Meaning Supportive condition, the target pseudoword stood to represent the same real word across all three sentences within the triplet, whereas in the Meaning Unsupportive condition the target pseudoword represented different real words within the trial, and thus the sentence contexts did not support meaning acquisition (see Table 1). At the end of

Table 1 Example stimuli from task where the final pseudoword either supported mapping of a semantic representation or did not.

	Meaning Supportive Condition	**Meaning Unsupportive Condition**
Sentence 1	Her parents bought her a *pav.*	Her favorite toy of all time is a *zat.*
Sentence 2	The sick child spent the day in his *pav.*	He had a lot of food in his *zat.*
Sentence 3	Mom piled the pillows on the *pav.*	Before bed I have to take a *zat.*

each sentence triplet, children were asked whether the pseudoword represented a real word and, if so, what the real word was. Binomial accuracy was determined by either providing the correct (1) or incorrect (1) meaning for the pseudoword in the Meaning Supportive condition, and by stating there was (0) or was not (1) a meaning for the pseudoword in the Meaning Unsupportive condition. Children's language abilities were also measured using the Clinical Evaluation of Language Fundamentals (CELF-5; Wiig, Semel, & Secord, 2013). We found that better task performance (i.e., accuracy when identifying the meaning of the pseudoword) was driven by greater theta band power and beta band suppression prior to pseudoword onset. However, the way that neural activity was associated with meaning identification performance varied substantially on the basis of age and language ability (as measured by the CELF-5). Our analysis revealed that language abilities, over and above age, influenced the way that beta activity contributed to accuracy when learning new words from linguistic context. Specifically, children with higher language scores, based on the CELF-5, were more likely to exhibit the expected pattern of beta band suppression when accurately identifying the meaning of the pseudoword compared to children with lower language scores. There were also important hemispheric differences in beta activation related to language ability: task-related differences in left hemispheric beta band activity were more pronounced in children with lower language scores, while those with higher language scores exhibited more pronounced task-related changes over right hemisphere sites, particularly frontal and parietal regions. Given changes in beta related to language abilities are not only the result of amplitude differences but differences in scalp distribution as well, our findings provide evidence that there are different neural generators underlying task-relevant beta band activity attributed to variability in children's language abilities.

Adding to evidence that beta activation during sentence processing is sensitive to individual differences in language ability we also found that, on this same task in the written modality, school-aged children (8–16 years) demonstrated a similar pattern of beta activation: children who were better at identifying the meaning of the pseudoword using the surrounding sentence context were more likely to demonstrate greater beta engagement during learning than children who performed more poorly on this task; however, the same asymmetry of beta activation in the previous study was not observed in this study (Schneider et al., 2021). Importantly, greater engagement of beta, but not changes in theta and alpha, positively predicted children's vocabulary outcome. Taken together, across multiple studies, modalities, and populations, changes in beta during sentence processing appear to be intimately linked to children's language abilities.

Using this same paradigm in the auditory modality, we also uncovered an interaction between age and theta band enhancement prior to pseudoword onset. Counter to the positive relationship between beta and language abilities, our data suggest that greater theta band power is less ideal for task performance as children get older, while it is more ideal for task performance among younger children. Support for this finding comes from studies of visual sentence processing in school-aged children (ages 8–16 years; Schneider, Poudel, Abel, & Maguire, 2023; Maguire et al., 2022), wherein theta power activation decreases as a function of increasing age. Across all of these studies changes in theta band activity were greatest over left-hemisphere regions, which aligns with many studies of language processing in adults (e.g., Hald et al., 2006). Drawing on the temporal and topographical patterns of theta responses, and in alignment with prior studies associating theta oscillations with semantic retrieval in adults (Bastiaansen et al., 2005, 2008; Bastiaansen & Hagoort, 2015; Meyer, 2018; Hald et al., 2006; Schneider et al., 2016, 2018; Lam et al., 2016; Schneider & Maguire, 2018), we interpret these developmental variances as being indicative of semantic retrieval processes and broader developmental shifts within the underlying language network. These findings add mounting evidence to previous arguments (Brauer & Friederici, 2007; Friederici et al., 2011; Schneider et al., 2016, 2018) that school-aged children engage a language network that is structurally and functionally different than adults during sentence processing in both the auditory and visual domains.

5. Future directions for considering the generalizability of these claims

The aforementioned series of empirical investigations focus on the development of semantic and syntactic skills underlying successful sentence comprehension. Although these skills are most important in school-aged children, there are other critical aspects of language that support successful comprehension, such as phonology, orthography, and pragmatics. Examining the development of these skills and how the neural signatures underlying these skills relate uniquely to language abilities and age will provide us with a more comprehensive understanding of natural language processing across the course of development. Another important consideration is that the syntactic errors examined in many of these studies are rooted in patterns that are specific to Mainstream American English (MAE); however, for speakers of other language variations, including African American English (AAE) these "errors" are considered a stable, high-frequency, and widely used dialect-specific feature. For example, AAE speakers often do not use the uninflected form of the 3rd person present tense singular verb (i.e., she go-es or he run-s), making it a particularly robust and consistent feature of AAE usage across regional populations (De Villiers & Johnson, 2007). When examining differences in neural activation between MAE and AAE speakers during processing of sentences containing these morphosyntactic forms, Garcia et al. (2022) found that bidialectal speakers of MAE and AAE did not demonstrate the expected P600 ERP pattern present among monodialectal MAE speakers. These findings suggest that dialectal language varieties are distinctly processed, and as such, the findings presented in the current review may not be generalized to speakers of other language variations. Incorporating greater attention to AAE language processing would enhance equity in the study of sentence processing on a broader scale, in turn elevating the effectiveness of clinicians, researchers, educators, and policymakers in their respective fields.

6. Conclusions

In conclusion, our research illuminates the intricate relationship between oscillatory brain activity, language ability, and age, underscoring the nuanced interplay between these factors that influences the acquisition of sentence processing skills among children. Our findings suggest that to comprehend sentences during the school years, children focus more on the retrieval of meaning from individual words in the sentence, as the combinatorial machinery of syntax is still developing. Brain maturation leads to a decline in their reliance on single word meanings, and as their language abilities strengthen, children become more capable of integrating both meaning and structure into a cohesive understanding of the sentence, similar to adults. It is important to note that children's early reliance on word meaning does not indicate a complete lack of syntactic understanding, given that their accuracy in identifying syntactic errors was still relatively high, but rather that their syntactic skills simply continue to develop as they approach and progress through adolescence. In unraveling this intricate interplay between maturation and linguistic proficiency, our ongoing empirical investigations into the neural correlates of auditory and visual sentence processing in children promise to shed light on the fundamental mechanisms shaping cognitive development, thus paving the way for a deeper understanding of the complexities underlying language acquisition and cognitive processing across the developmental spectrum.

References

Altmann, G., & Steedman, M. (1988). Interaction with context during human sentence processing. *Cognition, 30*(3), 191–238.

Atchley, R. A., Rice, M. L., Betz, S. K., Kwasny, K. M., Sereno, J. A., & Jongman, A. (2006). A comparison of semantic and syntactic event related potentials generated by children and adults. *Brain and Language, 99*(3), 236–246.

Bastiaansen, M. C., Oostenveld, R., Jensen, O., & Hagoort, P. (2008). I see what you mean: Theta power increases are involved in the retrieval of lexical semantic information. *Brain and Language, 106*(1), 15–28.

Bastiaansen, M. C., Van Berkum, J. J., & Hagoort, P. (2002). Syntactic processing modulates the θ rhythm of the human EEG. *Neuroimage, 17*(3), 1479–1492.

Bastiaansen, M. C., Van Der Linden, M., Ter Keurs, M., Dijkstra, T., & Hagoort, P. (2005). Theta responses are involved in lexical—Semantic retrieval during language processing. *Journal of Cognitive Neuroscience, 17*(3), 530–541.

Bastiaansen, M., & Hagoort, P. (2006). Oscillatory neuronal dynamics during language comprehension. *Progress in Brain Research, 159*, 179–196.

Bastiaansen, M., & Hagoort, P. (2015). Frequency-based segregation of syntactic and semantic unification during online sentence level language comprehension. *Journal of Cognitive Neuroscience, 27*(11), 2095–2107.

Bastiaansen, M., Magyari, L., & Hagoort, P. (2010). Syntactic unification operations are reflected in oscillatory dynamics during on-line sentence comprehension. *Journal of Cognitive Neuroscience, 22*(7), 1333–1347.

Behboudi, M. H., Castro, S., Chalamalasetty, P., & Maguire, M. J. (2023). Development of gamma oscillation during sentence processing in early adolescence: Insights into the maturation of semantic processing. *Brain Sciences, 13*(12), 1639.

Benau, E. M., Morris, J., & Couperus, J. W. (2011). Semantic processing in children and adults: Incongruity and the N400. *Journal of Psycholinguistic Research, 40*, 225–239.

Bonhage, C. E., Meyer, L., Gruber, T., Friederici, A. D., & Mueller, J. L. (2017). Oscillatory EEG dynamics underlying automatic chunking during sentence processing. *Neuroimage, 152*, 647–657.

Bosseler, A. N., Meltzoff, A. N., Bierer, S., Huber, E., Mizrahi, J. C., Larson, E., ... Kuhl, P. K. (2024). Infants' brain responses to social interaction predict future language growth. *Current Biology, 34*(8), 1731–1738.

Cowan, N. (2016). Working memory maturation: Can we get at the essence of cognitive growth? *Perspectives on Psychological Science, 11*(2), 239–264.

Davidson, D. J., & Indefrey, P. (2007). An inverse relation between event-related and time–frequency violation responses in sentence processing. *Brain Research, 1158*, 81–92.

De Villiers, J. G., & Johnson, V. E. (2007). The information in third-person/s: Acquisition across dialects of American English. *Journal of Child Language, 34*(1), 133–158.

Frazier, L., & Rayner, K. (1982). Making and correcting errors during sentence comprehension: Eye movements in the analysis of structurally ambiguous sentences. *Cognitive Psychology, 14*(2), 178–210.

Friederici, A. D. (2006). The neural basis of language development and its impairment. *Neuron, 52*(6), 941–952.

Friederici, A. D., & Männel, C. (2013). Neural correlates of the development of speech perception and comprehension. *The Oxford Handbook of Cognitive Neuroscience: Core Topics, 1*, 171–192.

Friedrich, M., & Friederici, A. D. (2004). N400-like semantic incongruity effect in 19-month-olds: Processing known words in picture contexts. *Journal of Cognitive Neuroscience, 16*(8), 1465–1477.

Garcia, F. M., Shen, G., Avery, T., Green, H. L., Godoy, P., Khamis, R., & Froud, K. (2022). Bidialectal and monodialectal differences in morphosyntactic processing of AAE and MAE: Evidence from ERPs and acceptability judgments. *Journal of Communication Disorders, 100*, 106267.

Gathercole, S. E., Pickering, S. J., Ambridge, B., & Wearing, H. (2004). The structure of working memory from 4 to 15 years of age. *Developmental Psychology, 40*(2), 177.

Hagoort, P., Baggio, G., & Willems, R. M. (2009). *Semantic unificationThe cognitive neurosciences* (4th ed.). MIT Press, 819–836.

Hagoort, P., Hald, L., Bastiaansen, M., & Petersson, K. M. (2004). Integration of word meaning and world knowledge in language comprehension. *Science (New York, N. Y.), 304*(5669), 438–441.

Hahne, A., & Friederici, A. D. (2002). Differential task effects on semantic and syntactic processes as revealed by ERPs. *Cognitive Brain Research, 13*(3), 339–356.

Hahne, A., Eckstein, K., & Friederici, A. D. (2004). Brain signatures of syntactic and semantic processes during children's language development. *Journal of Cognitive Neuroscience, 16*(7), 1302–1318.

Hald, L. A., Bastiaansen, M. C., & Hagoort, P. (2006). EEG theta and gamma responses to semantic violations in online sentence processing. *Brain and Language, 96*(1), 90–105.

Kielar, A., Meltzer, J. A., Moreno, S., Alain, C., & Bialystok, E. (2014). Oscillatory responses to semantic and syntactic violations. *Journal of Cognitive Neuroscience, 26*(12), 2840–2862.

Kikuchi, M., Shitamichi, K., Yoshimura, Y., Ueno, S., Remijn, G. B., Hirosawa, T., ... Minabe, Y. (2011). Lateralized theta wave connectivity and language performance in 2-to 5-year-old children. *Journal of Neuroscience, 31*(42), 14984–14988.

Klimesch, W. (1999). EEG alpha and theta oscillations reflect cognitive and memory performance: A review and analysis. *Brain Research Reviews, 29*(2–3), 169–195.

Kutas, M., & Federmeier, K. D. (2011). Thirty years and counting: Finding meaning in the N400 component of the event-related brain potential (ERP). *Annual Review of Psychology, 62*, 621–647.

Lam, N. H., Schoffelen, J. M., Uddén, J., Hultén, A., & Hagoort, P. (2016). Neural activity during sentence processing as reflected in theta, alpha, beta, and gamma oscillations. *Neuroimage, 142*, 43–54.

Lewis, A. G., Schoffelen, J. M., Bastiaansen, M., & Schriefers, H. (2014). Discourse-level semantic unification: ERPs and oscillatory neuronal dynamics. *In Donders Discussions 2014.*

Lewis, A. G., Schoffelen, J. M., Schriefers, H., & Bastiaansen, M. (2016). A predictive coding perspective on beta oscillations during sentence-level language comprehension. *Frontiers in Human Neuroscience, 10*, 85.

Maguire, M. J., Brier, M. R., & Ferree, T. C. (2010). EEG theta and alpha responses reveal qualitative differences in processing taxonomic versus thematic semantic relationships. *Brain and Language, 114*(1), 16–25.

Maguire, M. J., Schneider, J. M., Melamed, T. C., Ralph, Y. K., Poudel, S., Raval, V. M., ... Abel, A. D. (2022). Temporal and topographical changes in theta power between middle childhood and adolescence during sentence comprehension. *Developmental Cognitive Neuroscience, 53*, 101056.

Mai, G., Minett, J. W., & Wang, W. S. Y. (2016). Delta, theta, beta, and gamma brain oscillations index levels of auditory sentence processing. *Neuroimage, 133*, 516–528.

Marslen-Wilson, W. (1973). Linguistic structure and speech shadowing at very short latencies. *Nature, 244*(5417), 522–523.

Meyer, L. (2018). The neural oscillations of speech processing and language comprehension: State of the art and emerging mechanisms. *European Journal of Neuroscience, 48*(7), 2609–2621.

Meyer, M., Endedijk, H. M., Van Ede, F., & Hunnius, S. (2019). Theta oscillations in 4-year-olds are sensitive to task engagement and task demands. *Scientific Reports, 9*(1), 6049.

Meyer, L., Obleser, J., & Friederici, A. D. (2013). Left parietal alpha enhancement during working memory-intensive sentence processing. *Cortex; A Journal Devoted to the Study of the Nervous System and Behavior, 49*(3), 711–721.

Momsen, J., Schneider, J. M., & Abel, A. D. (2022). Developmental differences in EEG oscillations supporting the identification of novel word meaning from context. *Developmental Cognitive Neuroscience, 58*, 101185.

Morgan, E. U., Van der Meer, A., Vulchanova, M., Blasi, D. E., & Baggio, G. (2020). Meaning before grammar: A review of ERP experiments on the neurodevelopmental origins of semantic processing. *Psychonomic Bulletin & Review, 27*, 441–464.

Peña, M., & Melloni, L. (2012). Brain oscillations during spoken sentence processing. *Journal of Cognitive Neuroscience, 24*(5), 1149–1164.

Pfurtscheller, G., & Da Silva, F. L. (1999). Event-related EEG/MEG synchronization and desynchronization: Basic principles. *Clinical Neurophysiology, 110*(11), 1842–1857.

Prystauka, Y., & Lewis, A. G. (2019). The power of neural oscillations to inform sentence comprehension: A linguistic perspective. *Language and Linguistics Compass, 13*(9), e12347.

Roehm, D., Bornkessel-Schlesewsky, I., & Schlesewsky, M. (2007). *The internal structure of the N400: Frequency characteristics of a language related ERP componentAdvanced Methods of Electrophysiological Signal Analysis and Symbol Grounding: Dynamical Systems Approaches to Language.* Nova Publishers, 227–257.

Schneider, J. M., & Maguire, M. J. (2018). Identifying the relationship between oscillatory dynamics and event-related responses. *International Journal of Psychophysiology, 133*, 182–192.

Schneider, J. M., & Maguire, M. J. (2019). Developmental differences in the neural correlates supporting semantics and syntax during sentence processing. *Developmental Science, 22*(4), e12782.

Schneider, J. M., Abel, A. D., Ogiela, D. A., McCord, C., & Maguire, M. J. (2018). Developmental differences in the neural oscillations underlying auditory sentence processing in children and adults. *Brain and Language, 186*, 17–25.

Schneider, J. M., Poudel, S., Abel, A. D., & Maguire, M. J. (2023). Age and vocabulary knowledge differentially influence the N400 and theta responses during semantic retrieval. *Developmental Cognitive Neuroscience, 61*, 101251.

Snedeker, J., & Huang, Y. T. (2009). *Sentence processing. The Cambridge handbook of child language*. Cambridge University Press. 321–337.

Trueswell, J. C., Sekerina, I., Hill, N. M., & Logrip, M. L. (1999). The kindergarten-path effect: Studying on-line sentence processing in young children. *Cognition, 73*(2), 89–134.

Wang, L., Hagoort, P., & Jensen, O. (2018). Gamma oscillatory activity related to language prediction. *Journal of Cognitive Neuroscience, 30*(8), 1075–1085.

Wang, L., Zhu, Z., & Bastiaansen, M. (2012). Integration or predictability? A further specification of the functional role of gamma oscillations in language comprehension. *Frontiers in Psychology, 3*, 20589.

Weiss, S., & Mueller, H. M. (2012). "Too many betas do not spoil the broth": The role of beta brain oscillations in language processing. *Frontiers in Psychology, 3*, 25102.

Wianda, E., & Ross, B. (2019). The roles of alpha oscillation in working memory retention. *Brain and Behavior, 9*(4), e01263.

Wiig, E. H., Semel, E., & Secord, W. A. (2013). *Clinical evaluation of language fundamentals–fifth edition (CELF-5)*. Bloomington: NCS Pearson.

Printed and bound by CPI Group (UK) Ltd, Croydon, CR0 4YY

31/08/2024

01030797-0006